The New American
LANDSCAPE
GARDENER

A Guide to Beautiful Backyards
& Sensational Surroundings

Phebe Leighton and Calvin Simonds

Rodale Press, Emmaus, Pennsylvania

To P. C. and A. L. with thanks

Printed in the United States of America on acid-free paper

Book Design by Karen A. Schell
Illustrations by Elayne Sears

Photographs (by photo number): Marilyn Stouffer, 4, 10, 14, 15, 17, 19, 21, 22, 27, 31, 33, 56, 69; T. L. Gettings, 2, 6, 30, 41, 43, 49, 51, 60, 67; Michael Kanouff, 1, 3, 12, 13, 34, 36, 40, 58, 70; Alison Miksch, 18, 25, 45, 53, 54, 57, 74; David Cavagnaro, 5, 20, 32, 47, 62; Gary Mottau, 26, 29, 38, 61, 73; Jerry Pavia, 28, 63, 64, 75; Joanne Pavia, 24, 46, 71; Carl Doney, 9, 65, 72; Patti Seip, 37, 42, 44; John Hamel, 16, 68; Mitch Mandell, 39, 59; Carl Reik, 7, 35; Candice Billman, 14; Margaret Skrovanek, 55; Rodale Press Photography Dept., 8, 11, 48, 50, 52, 66.

Grateful acknowledgment is made to Crocker Nurseries, Brewster, Massachusetts, where the cover photograph was taken.

The authors wish to emphasize that the profiles of individual gardens in this book are composites which have been fictionalized in order to better illustrate specific landscaping principles. All of the gardens portrayed in the profiles are entirely feasible designs, but they and the gardeners are fictional.

Library of Congress Cataloging-in-Publication Data

Leighton, Phebe.
    The new American landscape gardener.

    Bibliography: p.
    Includes index.
    1. Landscape gardening.   2. Landscape architecture.
3. Backyard gardens.   4. Landscape gardening—United
States.   5. Landscape architecture—United States.
6. Backyard gardens—United States.   I. Simonds,
Calvin.   II. Title.
SB473.L44   1987   712   86-27986
ISBN-0-87857-672-X   hardcover

Distributed in the book trade by St. Martin's Press

    6 8 10 9 7   hardcover

Contents

Introduction

This is a book about making yards into gardens. A yard is an open space around a group of buildings. It is often devoted to a practical public purpose—a shipyard, a lumberyard, a barnyard, or even a junkyard. A garden, on the other hand, is a piece of ground which is organized for growing and enjoying plants. It is a personal and private space designed to express the individuality of the people who live in it.

Traditionally, Americans have *kept* gardens and *lived in* yards. For us, the yard has been the space around our homes, and a garden has been a comparatively small space within the yard which we devote to flowers or vegetables. But in recent years, that perspective has been changing. Because the suburbs have burgeoned and property values have soared, most of us have had to settle for smaller spaces around our homes. As our yards have become smaller, we have begun to look at the entire yard as a place for living—for sitting in the sun or shade, for planting vegetables, for growing colorful and graceful trees, for enjoying the company of friends and family.

All over the country, people have started to view their entire yard as a place to cultivate and plan. Suddenly everybody is buying new planting stock. Garden stores and tree nurseries are booming. New plant and garden mail-order companies seem to spring up every day. Each time people arrange and put new plants into the ground, they extend the part of their property that is personal and expressive, and push aside the part of their property that is public and impersonal. They are transforming their yards into gardens.

Transforming a yard into a garden takes four steps, and each step is the subject of one of the sections of this book. The first is to gather information to help you decide what kind of garden will fit your site and your lifestyle. This is described in the first section, "Getting Ready." The next step is to decide what sorts of attractive features you want to have in your garden. Do you want a sunspot, a rock garden, or a water garden? Do you want a shady walk or a sunny meadow? Ideas for different sorts of gardens are offered in the second section, "Special Features." "Doing the Design" is the subject of the third section. Here you learn how to turn your knowledge and your dreams into garden plans. The fourth and final step is described in the section "From Plans to Plants." Here you learn how to plant and maintain the landscape with a maximum of pleasure and a minimum of fuss.

We hope that you are on the threshold of an entirely new way of looking at and using the space around your house. We don't want you to see your landscape as an irritating source of chores: grass to be mowed, trees to be pruned, driveways to be edged, and so forth. Rather, we want it to be the part of your home that gives you the most peace, the most pleasure, and the most pride.

Part One

Getting Ready

CHAPTER 1

Knowing Yourself

You want to make your yard a better and more enjoyable space, right? Perhaps you have seen some attractive features in the garden of a friend—gorgeous borders with dazzling red, blue, and yellow flowers; a sensuous water garden with the sound and sparkle of trickling water; a hedge of fleecy evergreens that screens a patio and makes it a serene and private place. You wonder if something similar could be incorporated into your garden.

Perhaps you have an eyesore in your yard. You want to screen a hydrant or a power pole so that you don't have to look at it every day. Perhaps you are weary of looking at a litter of cars and tricycles when you are trying to commune with your roses.

Or perhaps you are building a new house and you just have no idea where to begin placing lawns, driveways, shrubs, and trees

One way or another, you have the feeling that your life could be more pleasant, more harmonious, more aesthetic, or simply more *fun,* if the land around your house were laid out more thoughtfully.

Now, since you went to the trouble to buy this book, or borrow it, or take it from the library, you probably are interested in doing your own landscape design. We are going to help you do just that. But first we need to explore with you what landscape designing is all about. We need to say what it means to design a landscape. And what it doesn't mean.

Imagine for a moment that you are going to hire a professional landscape designer. In fact, imagine that you called Phebe Leighton, and she is about to visit. The appointment is for 10 A.M. It is now 9:30. You are having a cup of coffee and trying to get your thoughts together. What are you thinking about?

Chances are, if you are like most people, you are wondering what Phebe will advise. Inviting a landscape designer to examine your yard is a little like inviting a clothes designer to look over your laundry. Perhaps Phebe will insist that you remove that crabapple tree in the front yard. You suspect it's in the "wrong" place, but you are awfully fond of it.

You might even be a little apprehensive. After all, isn't a landscape designer a kind of artist? What if Phebe thinks your house is ugly? What if she notices the dandelions in your lawn? What will she think of you when she sees that your foundation plantings have overgrown your living room window ledges? The more you anticipate her arrival, the more the landscape around your house seems like an amateurish painting by a weekend dauber. What will a professional artist think of it?

But such apprehensions are based on a misunderstanding of what landscape designers do. There's no mystery to landscape design. True, a landscape designer is an artist, but with an important difference. An artist starts with a blank canvas. A landscape designer starts with most of the "canvas" already filled in. The house and the landforms are the foundations of the design. The people who live in and enjoy the landscape will be its most important features. A good landscape designer sees your site and your lifestyle clearly and makes a design that is harmonious with both.

So, as Phebe waits outside the door for you to answer her ring, nothing could be further from her thoughts than criticizing your yard. Dozens of questions rush through her mind about the people for whom she will be designing. How many people live in the house? How old are they? Do they have pets? Do they spend a lot of time in their yard? Are they formal or informal people? What do they want to do in their yard? Grow flowers or vegetables? Work on their motorcycles? Barbecue hamburgers or watch warblers? Coming to know the people for whom she is designing is Phebe's first and most important job.

Seeing Yourself as a Landscape Designer Would See You

If you are going to be your own landscape designer, then you must get to know yourself as Phebe would know you. You must take a careful look at the patterns of your life and see how you actually use the space around your house.

Even more difficult, you must try to predict how you would use your yard if its design were improved. You must try to figure out how much of the way you use space today is determined by your habits and preferences. Would you have more cookouts in the summer if you had a shady patio, or do you simply prefer your summer suppers in the kitchen? Sometimes a design change can result in a dramatic increase in the amount a space is used. For instance, many people don't like the feeling of being watched that they get when they sit in their front yard, so they sit in their backyard or indoors. Those same people would begin to use the front yard if a screening hedge and fence were put along the street line. Now, instead of an exposed public stage, the yard is a private, secluded enclosure.

Coming to know yourself in this way is hard work and requires honesty and perceptiveness. Wishful thinking is always a risk. I'm sure you know of hammocks that are never slept in, borders that are never planted, stone barbecues that are never cooked on, and front gates that are never opened. Phebe often discovers that homeowners don't know basic and important things about the way they themselves use the land around their house.

A homeowner will say, for instance, that nobody uses the front yard. But when Phebe inspects the front yard, she will find a track beaten across it from the front door to the street. Inquiring, she learns that once a day the homeowner walks through the front yard to the mailbox and returns, slowly reading the mail. It is an important ritual, a moment of peace, a reason to go outdoors in even the foulest weather. Phebe knows that she must not put a barrier to that daily perambulation into her landscape design.

Putting Yourself into the Design

Design mistakes are often made because when people are making plans for their own yard, they forget to put themselves in the plan. There are three vantage points from which to look at a yard.

The most obvious is from the street. You see your house and yard from this vantage point just before you turn into the driveway or turn up the front walk. It is the way strangers see your property. From this point of view, it is the setting of the house, a physical embodiment of your lifestyle by which strangers may know you as they pass.

The second vantage point is from inside the house. From this perspective, the yard is an interior decoration like a picture on the wall. A moment of staring out the windows into the yard can refresh your spirits during a harried day.

These vantage points are important. The view of the yard from the street is a source of pride; the view from the house, a source of enjoyment. But what of the view of the yard *from* the yard? It's a view you often neglect, because while you often pass through the yard on your way to and from the house, you don't very often stop in it. It is almost as if the yard were a kind of no-man's-land, a frontier between the intimate space of the home and the impersonal public space of the city street or country road. A place between places, not a place in itself.

If Phebe came to your house to advise you, the first thing she would do is try to get you to look at your yard *from* the yard. To view a yard in this way is to view it as an outdoor room, a living space that you will use and enjoy year-round. It's odd that people don't think of their yards in this way

more often. People who will spend $10,000 to add a 400-square-foot room to the interior of their house will hesitate to do a few weekends of work that will add hundreds of square feet of living space outside the house. But this unwillingness may change if they once get a vision of themselves as they use their yard, or as they might use it if it were better designed.

Doing an Inventory of Your Landscape Needs

To help you get a picture of yourself and your family *in* your yard, we have designed a simple inventory. We recommend that you sit down with the members of your family some evening and fill in the blanks. Assign each family member a column in the inventory and then, opposite each type of activity, fill in a number indicating how important that activity is to that person. Put zeros beside the things that you would never do in a yard, and put a 5 beside one thing that is most important to you. Rate activities of intermediate importance 1 through 4.

Importance of an activity to a person is difficult to define. Usually its importance can be measured by its frequency or by the amount of time expended on it. For Calvin, growing vegetables is the most important use for a garden. He spends at least a few minutes every day, seven months of the year, tending his vegetable garden. For Calvin's wife, outdoor reading is most important. For Phebe it's the care and feeding of flowers. Everybody cares about a yard in a different way.

Infrequent activities can be important, too. For some member of the family, a rare ceremonial occasion such as a wedding may be so significant that a garden's design must be consistent with it, even though such an event may occur only once or twice in a lifetime.

Landscape Use Inventory

How do you use your landscape?

Who lives in the landscape?

Person **A** _____

Person **B** _____

Person **C** _____

Person **D** _____

Person **E** _____

What will each person use it for?

	A	B	C	D	E		A	B	C	D	E
Grow vegetables	—	—	—	—	—	Take naps	—	—	—	—	—
Plant flowers	—	—	—	—	—	Hang out wash	—	—	—	—	—
Play rowdy games	—	—	—	—	—	Tinker with machines	—	—	—	—	—
Read or reflect	—	—	—	—	—	Exercise pets	—	—	—	—	—
Watch wildlife	—	—	—	—	—	Store trash	—	—	—	—	—
Park automobiles	—	—	—	—	—	Show off the garden	—	—	—	—	—
Swim	—	—	—	—	—	Other activities	A	B	C	D	E
Stroll	—	—	—	—	—	_____	—	—	—	—	—
Sunbathe	—	—	—	—	—	_____	—	—	—	—	—
Entertain	—	—	—	—	—	_____	—	—	—	—	—
Cook out	—	—	—	—	—	_____	—	—	—	—	—

Other people's activities may also be important. A father may think that having a space for his children to play is so important that he rates it a 5.

And don't forget the unromantic things like parking automobiles and storing trash and fuel oil. These functions must go on somewhere, and most of us end up doing them in or near our yards. To fail to recognize this reality when you are designing your landscape is to end up with a smelly trash can in the midst of your garden party.

Interpreting Your Inventory

The third part of this book, *Doing the Design*, describes how to get from what the Landscape Use Inventory reveals about you to the actual design of your yard. We will talk about these issues at length in that section. But as a background for reading the intervening chapters, you need to think about your inventory and the issues it raises.

Notice the variety of your responses. The more activities you anticipate doing in your yard, the more thoughtfully you have to design it. With every additional activity, the potential for conflict increases.

Pay attention also to the harmony among the responses. Notice the extent to which different members of the family agree on what will be done in the landscape. If everybody agrees that the purpose of the yard is to grow flowers and grass, then it will be easy to design. But if each member of the family wants to use the yard for a different activity, you may have to do some careful negotiation before you start to design.

If family members propose different activities, think about whether the activities are compatible. Some activities go well together; some do not. Boisterous games, like touch football and Frisbee, do not go well with delicate prize roses. Noisy jobs like tuning an engine do not go well with quiet pursuits such as reading.

Where conflicts arise, three basic strategies are helpful in reaching a solution: time-sharing, separation, and deciding among activities. Time-sharing involves allocating the conflicting uses to different times of the day or different days of the week. For instance, you could agree that engine-tuning will take place only on Saturdays, while on other days, quiet activities will prevail. Separation involves isolating the conflicting activities in different parts of the landscape where they won't interfere with one another. Obviously, your capacity to use this strategy will depend on the size of your property. Deciding among activities involves agreement among family members that one of the conflicting activities will be excluded from the design. Whichever of the three strategies you use, the resolution must ultimately depend on how strongly people feel about each item.

How Other People Use Their Yards

We asked several of our friends to fill out the inventory to see how it worked. Their responses are interesting, and we'll pass some of them along to you with comments. We'll call the friends Abercrombie, Barton, Devereaux, and Edison, and we'll change enough details to protect their anonymity.

The Abercrombies: Peace and Quiet

The Abercrombies are a middle-aged couple living on a 1-acre lot in the country. Their children have grown up and moved to neighboring states, and come home only for holidays. There are no grandchildren, yet. Mr. Abercrombie is an electrician for whom vegetable gardening is an avid hobby. Mrs. Abercrombie is a teacher. She enjoys reading outside, in the sunshine in the spring and fall, and in the shade at midsummer. She also loves wildlife and wildflowers. Both Abercrombies are out in the yard at all times of the year, he working in his vegetable garden, she reading, poking around, planting bulbs, and pruning.

The Abercrombies are a landscape designer's dream. Both enjoy low-key activities in the garden, and their pleasures don't encroach on each other. The only potential area of conflict is between Mr. Abercrombie's vegetables and Mrs. Abercrombie's wildlife and shady reading spot. But these are relatively minor difficulties. A prudent design might divide the Abercrombies' property into two different areas, the vegetable garden area, which is sunny and open, and which might have a fence around it to discourage the raccoons and rabbits, and the reading and nature-observation area, which might have a tiny wildflower meadow, a sheltered shady area, a quiet, meandering walkway, and a birdbath and feeder.

Another potential area of conflict looms on the Abercrombies' horizon. Children often produce grandchildren, and grandchildren inevitably come to visit. If the property were large enough, the meadow might be designed to permit some latitude for romping grandchildren. But considering the size of the Abercrombies' lot, the grandchildren might better be encouraged to do their romping at the park down the street.

The Bartons: Urban Common Sense

The Bartons are an urban family. They already had redesigned their backyard when they filled out the inventory. Theirs is a tiny, narrow lot. In the winter, the lot is shaded by surrounding buildings. In the summer, it gets strong sun at the far end and deep shade from a large sycamore tree growing near the back steps. Mrs. Barton likes to use the backyard for quiet morning coffee with the newspaper. Her husband will join her for coffee, but soon begins tinkering with the motorcycle he rides each weekday to the university. Mrs. Barton enjoys his companionship, but finds the motorcycle loathesome.

The three Barton children all have tried from time to time to use the backyard for active sports. The oldest has played a variation of handball against the garage doors. All three children have thrown Frisbees and baseballs in the yard, much to the distress of Mrs. Barton. She has tried to main-

The Bartons' yard.

tain a small vegetable garden against the fence at the far end of the yard. The tomatoes grow poorly in the impoverished urban soil, and a single blow from a Frisbee could reverse several weeks of hard-won growth.

To solve their myriad conflicts, the Bartons used a canny mixture of all three adaptation strategies. They kept the large sycamore tree and bricked in about a third of the yard under the tree and next to the back steps. Here they put a picnic table. During the summer, it is shady here, but in spring and fall, the lower rays of the morning sun often strike in under the tree, and it is sunny and warm. Along the property line, the Bartons put up a high stockade fence. They encouraged Dr. Barton to work on his motorcycle outside the fence, in the right-of-way between the tightly packed houses. There, the worst of its offensive sights and odors don't interfere with the civilized atmosphere of Mrs. Barton's Saturday morning coffee, but he is nearby and they often talk back and forth while he is tinkering.

Next to the picnic table the Bartons put a tetherball court. In a relatively small area of 120 square feet, the tetherball provides a place for the children to play vigorously. But the tetherball, unlike a baseball or Frisbee, never escapes to the coffee area near the house nor to the garden area beyond, so Mrs. Barton's tomatoes are now safe.

The outer third of the yard is devoted to a

tiny lawn and large raised bed for vegetables. Before he put up the stockade fence, Dr. Barton carted in a truckload of topsoil and two tiers of railroad ties. The tomatoes are now raised above the poor city soil and are growing fine. The lawn is used for sunbathing in the summer and an occasional mini-croquet or horseshoe game.

The Devereaux:
A "Danish Modern" Landscape

The Devereaux present quite a different sort of problem. Both are business people. They are often away from home and don't have much time to putter. On the other hand, they enjoy entertaining when they are at home. They want their yard to be a showcase, but they don't have a lot of time to work at it.

A good design for the Devereaux would be a formal affair, composed of extremely stable elements. The Devereaux live in New England, where stone walls are a familiar landscape feature. Their design will employ stone walls, stone walks, slow-growing evergreens, and simple rectangular lawns that can be easily maintained.

One of the Devereaux' landscape problems concerns the parking of cars. Most of the time, they only need a small parking space in front of the garage. But when they entertain they need more space, and cars end up strewn all over the lawn. Occasionally, drivers leaving a party late at night

The Devereaux' yard with parking area.

PARK
HERE

have backed into some of the shrubs and damaged them. Sometimes the parking overflows onto the street, and neighbors have complained because the country road gets narrowed to a single lane.

The Devereaux will solve their parking problem by an efficient use of their lawn for parking from time to time. By building a stone wall parallel to the driveway and about 15 feet from it, and by skillful arrangements of plantings behind the wall, the Devereaux will be able to create a well-defined spillover car park. Because of the arrangement of walls and plantings (and a sign the Devereaux will put out on a sawhorse whenever they have a party), drivers will be encouraged to park their cars in a neat row against the wall. The shrubs will be spared and the grass won't object to the occasional use it will get as a parking surface.

The Edisons: Good Fences Make Good Relatives

Mrs. Edison is a single parent, attempting to make a living while raising two small children. When she was separated from her husband a few years ago, she invited her parents to live with her. Since then, the parents have occupied a lower apartment in the split-level house, while Mrs. Edison and the children live in the upper apartment. Each apartment has its own entrance.

The arrangement has worked pretty well. The grandparents love the grandchildren and enjoy looking after them. Their help makes it possible for the children to be well cared for while their mother is getting on with her professional career.

But some conflicts have arisen, mainly concerning the uses of the yard. Mrs. Edison's father is fond of birds, and would like to have a quiet place where he can maintain a feeder and some birdhouses. Mrs. Edison's mother has tried to raise some roses. But the children—and their two setter pups, Smash and Grab—constantly race around outside the house, trampling down Grandmother's flowerbeds and scaring off Grandfather's birds. For her part, Mrs. Edison would like to be able to entertain friends every so often, out of the sight and hearing of her parents. Sometimes these problems become so intense that both daughter and parents fear that their extended family may have to break up.

These problems really arise from how the grounds around the house are landscaped. The house was landscaped by the developers to be attractive to potential buyers passing by in the street. The space around the house is neither sheltered from public view nor divided into functional areas.

When they realized the source of their difficulty, Mrs. Edison and her parents sat down and made a careful design plan for the house lot. First they screened off the street. Then they divided the lot into two yards, one outside the downstairs apartment, the other outside the upstairs apartment. These were separated by a wooden fence and a thick hedge. This barrier is broken only by a formal garden gate and arbor, over which Mrs. Edison's mother has started to train her roses.

Both households are amazed at how effectively the fence and hedge filter out noise and bustle. Grandmother's roses now grow in peace, and the variety of birds appearing at Grandfather's feeder has already increased noticeably. Each family member expects to have all the old benefits of proximity with the new benefits of privacy.

A Design for You

As we have been talking about the Abercrombies, the Bartons, the Devereaux, and the Edisons, no doubt you are thinking, "Hey, what about me? None of these people is exactly like me."

The Edisons' divided yard.

Of course. And that's just the point. You can get ideas from studying other people's design problems, but ultimately the design you make must suit you. You need to see yourself, without prejudice, without preconception, as if you had suddenly come upon yourself in your yard, doing the things you enjoy most.

Once you have an idea of who you are and how you would use a well-designed landscape, then you are ready to turn to the next chapters. There you will learn how to recognize the opportunities and limitations presented by your site and your locality. You will also learn enough of the principles of landscape design to get you started.

Wrap-up

The first step in designing a yard is to become thoroughly familiar with the people who are going to live in it. There is no such thing as a bad landscape design if its owners enjoy it to its fullest.

These words are obviously important guides for the professional landscaper. But they are equally significant for the person who would design his or her own landscape. Before you design for yourself, you must have a realistic appreciation of who you are and how you are likely to use the space.

Those who would design for themselves must understand themselves.

CHAPTER 2

Knowing Your Site

*O*nce you have a clear idea of your landscape needs, you must get to know those characteristics of your site and its surroundings that will affect your design choices. Some of these are obvious. The composition of the soil, the length of the growing season, the size of the property, the amount of shading and root competition from trees and hedges in your neighbors' yards, all are factors which will determine what you can and cannot do with your property.

Other influences are less obvious. Characteristics of your community will also affect your design. On the one hand, locally available materials and the skills of local carpenters, masons, and other craftspeople can provide unique opportunities for landscaping features. On the other hand, zoning regulations often limit design possibilities by dictating the sort of plantings or structures that can be made along property lines and frontages.

If you would know your site as a landscape designer would know it, you must first know what is *good* about it. It's easy to fall into the trap of feeling that the landscape features are always better in your friends' yards: Her view is better; his house is set farther back from the road; more sun comes into their yard. But envying your friends isn't going to get *your* yard designed. Instead, start by determining the advantages of your own site so that you can capitalize on them. The key to making a successful landscape design is to accentuate the positive.

So, as you cast your eye about your property, try to see the good side of everything. Do you have a wet, mucky place in a low corner of your yard? Stop thinking of it as a mosquito trap and start thinking of it as a potential garden pool. Is your site on a ledgy hillside? Don't immediately wish the ledge buried in 3 feet of level topsoil. With a little excavation, that ledge might become a sunny rock wall with niches full of colorful wildflowers.

The purpose of this chapter is to help you gather crucial information about your site and its surroundings. To assist in preserving and summarizing this information, we have provided a format for a site inventory questionnaire. Write your answers on a sheet of paper. If you are newly moved or are building and landscaping an entirely new house, this inventory will be particularly useful. But even if you have lived in your present home for years you will find that the inventory will guide you to see new possibilities in your familiar surroundings.

The Site

A good way to come to know your site is to give yourself a tour of it, just as if you were the landscape designer seeing it for the first time. Take a clipboard and a copy of the site inventory questionnaire so you can make notes as you go along. Make a rough map of the lot and the house. Nothing fancy! Just a few quick lines to outline the lot and a few more to show where the house, outbuildings, and driveways are. This sketch will provide you with a convenient key for locating the prominent features of your landscape.

Now you are ready to begin your tour. Your first task is to inventory the good things about your property. Write down the things you like about your place. Only when you have identified these good features should you let yourself focus on the eyesores. Write them down, too.

Tour One: The Approaches

Start at the street and approach your house as if you were a stranger coming up the walk or into the driveway. What pleases you about the view of the house from this perspective? What would you like to change? If you have a back entrance to your lot, approach the house from there as well. Make a note of your thoughts.

Tour Two: The Boundaries

Next, walk the boundaries of your property, looking out toward the street and neighboring properties. What do you see from this perspective? Are there pleasant scenes to look at? Or unpleasant scenes? Do you see large trees and smooth green lawns, or parking lots and convenience stores? What do you know about the neighboring properties? Can you count on them to stay the way they are, or are they likely to change?

Tour Three: The Views from the Windows

Go inside the house and look out each of the windows in turn, upstairs and down. What do you like about the view from each window? What do you dislike?

Tour Four: The "Yards"

Unless you live in a very densely settled neighborhood, you probably have four "yards" around your house, a front yard, a backyard, and two side yards. Take out a lawn chair and sit quietly for a few moments in each. Start with the front yard. Look around you. Do you see people passing in the street? Does that make you feel comfortable and a part of a community, or vulnerable and exposed to strangers? Pay attention to noises. Do you hear robins or lawn mowers or both? Do you smell honeysuckle, wet earth, and mown grass? Or diesel exhaust? Keep jotting down your impressions.

Repeat the process in the backyard. Don't skimp on time. Take a book or some handwork and stay there a bit. Sit in the sun if the air is cold; in the shade if it's warm. Try to make yourself comfortable so that you can relax and feel the space around you. What feels good about it? What doesn't feel so good?

Now, move on to the side yards. The way most American houses are set out, one of the

Site Inventory Questionnaire

Highlights and Eyesores

List all of the highlights and eyesores visible in each of these places:

    Approaches
    Boundaries
    Windows
    Front yard
    Side yard (both the garage side and the "other" side)
    Backyard

Vegetation

Write down the kind, location, and description of all the plants on your property, organized under these headings:

    Large trees
    Small trees
    Bushes, shrubs, and vines
    Small perennials and vigorous annuals

Climate

Use a diagram like the one below to draw in the principal features of your landscape as they relate to the path of the sun:

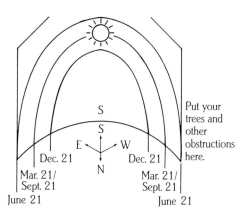

Using sun arc to plan your landscape.

Make notes about your average climate and growing season by recording the following:

	last day in spring	first day in fall	number of frost-free days
Frost	_____	_____	_____

Growing degree days _____

Hardiness zone _____

Hottest month _____   How hot? _____

Coldest month _____   How cold? _____

Average yearly rainfall (include melted

    snow) _____

Average yearly snowfall _____

Driest month _____   How dry? _____

Wettest month _____   How wet? _____

Soil

Note your soil test results here:

    Subsoil type: Clay   Sand   Gravel
        Loam   Other _____
    Where sampled? _____
    Nitrogen _____   Phosphorus _____

Potash _____   pH _____
Trace elements _____
Contaminants _____
Organic material _____

Resource People

List names, addresses, phone numbers, and what you use them for.

side yards is a public yard where guests, delivery people, and children selling cookies come to the door. The other is often a no-man's-land between your house and the public side of the neighbor's house. Take your chair and spend a few minutes in each of these yards, even though you may never have sat there before. If the yard is open, try turning your back to your neighbor's property so you can get some feel for what the side yard would be like if it were properly screened. If it already has a hedge, peer over the shrubs to see what the side yard would be like if it were opened up.

Vegetation

Once you have identified the principal good and bad features of your present landscape, you are ready to list and locate on your sketch map all the large plants and clumps of small plants. If you know the species name, fine, but a rough description is just as important. Notes like "tall, deep-shading tree (might be oak); holds its leaves late in fall" will be more useful to you than simply *"Quercus rubra,"* even though the Latin sounds more impressive.

Whether you are fond of a particular plant or not, be sure to note if it seems healthy and vigorous. Even if you are planning to remove a plant, the knowledge that a member of that species is growing well on your property is crucial information. Rhododendrons only grow in acid soils. Camellias only grow south of Hardiness Zone 6. Knowing that white pines are growing on your site suggests that such acid-loving plants as blueberries, mountain laurels, and rhododendrons might also grow well. Knowing that a southern tree like the crape is growing suggests that other southern species such as the southern magnolia might be suitable. So, before you cut down the camellia or tear out the rhododendron, be sure to let them teach you everything they can about your site.

Sun Arc

How much sun you get in your yard throughout the year depends on the path the sun traces through the sky and the location of obstacles such as buildings and tall trees. Every day, the sun moves in a slightly different arc. From December 21 to June 21, the sun cuts a slightly higher path through the sky each day, and from June 21 to December 21, it cuts a lower path.

The difference in the height of the noontime sun at the winter and summer solstices is dramatic. Annually, the sun dips and rises half the distance from the horizon to the zenith. These movements of the sun have an even more dramatic effect on the shade cast by objects. A 10-foot fence which casts a 5-foot shadow at midsummer will cast a shadow of 15 feet or more at the winter solstice. These relationships are fixed for any particular locality. Knowing them can save you a lot of disappointment. You could put in a flowerbed or a patio in late May, only to have the sun disappear behind a tree or building on August 1 and never reappear until the following April.

At any season of the year, you can figure out exactly which parts of your yard will be in the sun and which parts will be in the shade by tracing the sun arc. The first step is to find the position of the noontime sun (1 P.M. during daylight saving time). That direction is always south. If you want to know how high the sun is at different times of the year, start by checking an atlas to find out what your latitude is, that is, how many degrees you are north of the equator. For instance, Boston has a latitude of about 44 degrees; Washington, D.C., about 40 degrees; and Florida about 35 degrees. On September 21 and March 21, the sun will be about as many degrees below the zenith as you are north of the equator.

Once you have the September and March sun height, you can readily envision the height of

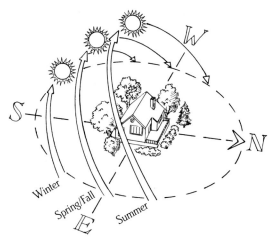

This diagram shows how the sun's angle changes through the year.

the noonday sun in midsummer and midwinter. Bear in mind that the sky, from horizon to zenith, is 90 degrees. Mentally divide that distance into halves and then quarters. Now, in midsummer, the noonday sun is one-quarter of that distance higher than it is in March and September. At midwinter, it is one-quarter lower.

The duration and direction of morning and afternoon sun also change enormously during the year. Go around to the "morning" side of the house and note down where east is on your sketch map. If you stand facing south, east will be on your left hand. East is roughly where the sun will rise on the first day of spring. All spring and summer it rises to the north of east; all fall and winter it rises to the south of east.

Around on the "afternoon" side of the house, note where west is. If you stand facing south, west is on your right hand. The sun sets in the west on the first day of autumn. All spring and summer it sets to the north of west, and all fall and winter it sets to the south of west.

Now that you have in mind the sunrise point, the sunset point, and high points of the sun at different times of the year, think about the arc that

the sun cuts in the sky. The first day of summer, it comes up behind you in the northeast and reaches a point more than two-thirds up in the southern sky at 1 P.M., daylight saving time, before it sets in the northwest. On the first day of spring and the first day of autumn, it rises in the east on your left hand, climbs a little more than halfway up the southern sky, and sets in the west. On the first day of winter, it rises in the southeast, climbs only a third of the way up in the southern sky, and sets in the southwest.

With these sun arcs firmly in your mind, look around to see what obstacles will prevent sunlight from getting into your yard. Mark these obstacles down on your sketch map. If you are putting in any permanent feature that relies on the sun—like a greenhouse or deck—you should probably do an "elevation" of the sun's path. Draw an arc on a piece of paper and go to the place where the feature will be. Using the technique described above, use your imagination to project the arc of the sun onto your surroundings, and then make a rough sketch to show which trees or buildings get between you and the arc.

Such an elevation of the sun over your property will be a great help when you are trying to decide where to place trees, shrubs, and vegetable and flower gardens. Make notes on your sketch map such as, "Tall apartment building next door shades backyard in winter." Note if the obstacle is beyond your control, like a neighbor's tree, or something that you can control, like a tall fence or hedge of your own. Better still, make a little map of your property and show which areas are sunny and which are shady at different times of day.

Climate and Microclimate

The climate of your region has two important effects on the landscape designs which might be desirable for your site. One effect is through you, the site user. To a large degree, the climate determines the uses to which you are likely to want to put your property. For instance, if you live in a climate with a long, hot summer, shade is going to be an important consideration. If, on the other hand, you live in a climate with a long winter and a short summer, the more important consideration is going to be shelter from winds and openness to the winter sun.

Climate also determines the kinds of plants that you can put in your landscape. Each combination of climatic variables, say, sunny, dry, and hot or cloudy, damp, and cool, favors a different collection of garden plants. Consequently, it makes sense at an early stage in your planning to gather and record crucial climatic information.

Not only must you consider the climate of your region, you must also consider the microclimate of your site. Every site has specific climatic characteristics which may render it unique within a region. City sites, for instance, have microclimates which are warmer, cloudier, and more moist than rural sites. South-facing slopes have longer growing seasons than the north-facing slopes of the same hills. Entire agricultural industries are based on microclimates. For instance, the grape-growing industry of New York and Southern Canada is based on the microclimate of the lake shores. Without the lake-moderated climates, there would be no New York grape industry.

Microclimates can be extremely important and are often overlooked by people choosing plants for a landscape. If you live on a particularly sheltered site, you may be able to have trees and shrubs which usually grow hundreds of miles to the south. On the other hand, if yours is a windy site or one where cold air puddles on still nights, you may not be able to have plants which your neighbors grow easily on more sheltered sites. You should even consider the *micro*-microclimate generated by your house. Heat escaping through the foundation of a house can advance the growth of bulbs like snowdrops and crocuses ahead of their fellows planted in beds away from the house. The same effect will prolong the fall beauty of chrysanthemums and marigolds. Remember, it's the climate around your plant—not the climate in your region or even in your neighborhood—that makes the difference.

Information about your climate is available at your local office of the Agricultural Extension Service or at the nearest office of the National Oceanic and Atmospheric Administration (NOAA). Surprisingly, NOAA is listed under the Commerce Department among the U.S. government listings in your telephone directory. If you visit the local NOAA office, they may have pamphlets on local climate, and forecasters who will be happy to discuss your particular microclimate as well.

Temperature

Next to sunshine, temperature is the most significant factor in plant growth. Both the daily average temperature and the nighttime minimum temperature are important. The daily average temperature is the average of each day's highest and lowest temperatures. Snowdrops and crocuses aside, most plants do not begin to grow until this average reaches around 43°F. Only at this temperature does the soil become warm enough to support substantial biological activity.

Nighttime minimum temperatures matter because, for a great many plants, the growing season is limited by the first frost in fall and the last frost in spring. The amount of chilling that is damaging to an actively growing plant differs among species. Just a cool night can stun a tomato or a coleus. But a frost that would murder a bean plant would be merely titillating to a Brussels sprout plant.

Because of the sensitivities of plants to temperature, a few temperature statistics about your site are enormously useful in making planting decisions. The first of these is the duration of the frost-free period, that is, the number of days between the last killing frost in the spring and the first killing frost in the fall. Another useful statistic is the number of growing degree days for your area. Growing degree days are analogous to heating degree days. Each day, the number of degrees the average temperature exceeds 65°F is calculated, and these numbers are accumulated over the whole season. Growing degree days are calculated by NOAA and by the Agricultural Extension Service because of their importance in selecting different corn varieties. But they are such an accurate measure of the heat available for growing plants that you can use this same information to determine the suitability of your region for growing heat-loving flowers and vegetables.

For a tree or shrub that has to stand out in the cold all winter long, a third temperature number is useful, its hardiness. Plants protect themselves against the extreme cold of winter in different ways, most often by diminishing the amount of water in their tissues. Like different concentrations of antifreeze in your car, these methods confer resistance to varying degrees of cold. For instance, the hardiest varieties of peach can only stand temperatures down to −20°F, whereas the hardiest apricots can take temperatures to −30°F and come back strong. Just as a single night too cold for your antifreeze can kill your car, a single night too cold for a plant can kill it. Consequently, the hardiness of a plant is defined in terms of the average coldest night it can withstand.

Information about hardiness is usually presented as numbered zones that stretch across a map of the United States and Canada from west to east. The lower the number, the lower the average annual minimum temperatures are in the zone, and the hardier the plants you put in the ground must be if you want them to survive. In general, the zones are farther north near the coasts and dip down near the center of the country where the influence of the oceans is less. For instance, Zone 6 extends southward from New York City to southern Missouri and New Mexico before it turns northward through western Nevada to western Washington State.

We have included on the opposite page a Hardiness Zone map based on the one prepared by the U.S. Department of Agriculture. While you can roughly determine your Hardiness Zone from a map, be sure to take microclimate into account, as suggested above.

Water

The two most important factors to keep in mind concerning rainfall at your site are annual total and seasonality. The total rainfall in the year varies enormously around the United States, from near zero in the deserts of the Southwest to hundreds of inches in the mountains of the Northwest. The Eastern Seaboard, the Gulf, and the Pacific Northwest states are in general wet, with more than an inch a week of rainfall averaged over the year. The Midwest is dry to moderately dry, and the Southwest is arid.

Within this general pattern, there is a tremendous difference in the seasonality of rainfall. The Pacific coast gets most of its rainfall in the winter, whereas the Appalachian Mountains get most of theirs in the summer. The timing of rainfall may be just as important to your plants as its total quantity. As temperatures rise, the water requirements of plants increase enormously. Consequently, places with warm, dry summers support a different kind of natural vegetation than places with cool, dry or warm, wet summers.

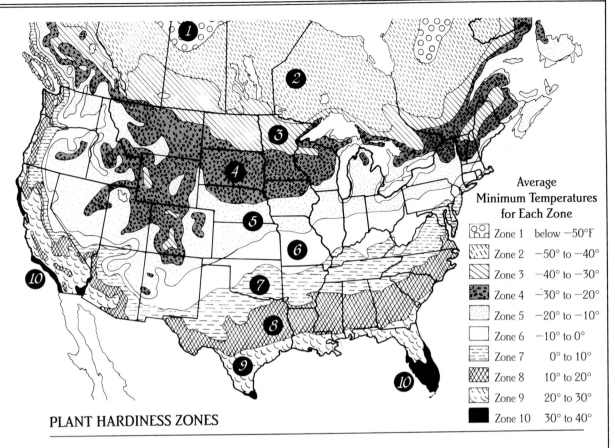

Average Minimum Temperatures for Each Zone

	Zone 1	below −50°F
	Zone 2	−50° to −40°
	Zone 3	−40° to −30°
	Zone 4	−30° to −20°
	Zone 5	−20° to −10°
	Zone 6	−10° to 0°
	Zone 7	0° to 10°
	Zone 8	10° to 20°
	Zone 9	20° to 30°
	Zone 10	30° to 40°

PLANT HARDINESS ZONES

In some regions, you may have to choose between plants which are "traditional" in the country as a whole and those which grow naturally in your region. As with sunlight and temperature, this decision is in part a practical one. The arid-country homeowner who plants a thirsty tree like a willow must be prepared for high water bills and constant vigilance.

Where water is concerned, the decision to choose naturalized plants can take on a moral dimension. More and more, as populations increase and aquifers become exhausted and contaminated, clean water becomes a precious resource. Watering bans are becoming a regular feature of summer life in many communities. We have every reason to believe that this trend will continue. If you live in a dry climate and put in temperate or tropical trees and shrubs, you may be committing yourself to a life of crime. While all your neighbors are virtuously skipping showers, stacking dishes, and not flushing toilets, you will be out in your garden, surreptitiously pouring water onto the roots of your thirsty willow tree.

Consequently, we urge you not to put in trees and shrubs that need more water than your climate naturally provides. When you are buying plants, check with your nursery owner to make sure that the plants you are buying can get all the water they need without your help. And if an adequate water supply is ever a problem in your area, consider some of the more drought-tolerant plants for your landscape.

Soil

After climate, soil is the most important characteristic of your site. The soil consists of a topsoil and a subsoil layer. While the topsoil can be amended, or even trucked away and replaced, your subsoil was laid down by glaciers, floods, or volcanoes tens of thousands of years ago, and you are probably stuck with it.

Subsoil

For landscaping purposes, the most important characteristic of subsoil is its ability to retain water, and this is determined by its particle size. The larger the particles in the soil, the less water it can hold. Sandy and gravelly soils consist of large particles. They drain quickly and thus hold water poorly. Clay soils consist of tiny particles. They hold water extremely well and drain very poorly. In conjunction with your rainfall, the kind of subsoil you have will determine the wetness or dryness of your topsoil. If you have lots of rainfall and a tight, clay subsoil, then you will have boggy conditions, almost no matter what your topsoil is like. If, on the other hand, you have light rainfall and a gravelly subsoil, you are likely to have droughty conditions, even if your topsoil consists of 2 feet of pulverized peat moss.

There are three ways to determine your subsoil's water-retention capacity. You can ask the contractor who built your house. Or, if your house sits on former farmland, you can consult soil maps at the Soil Conservation Service in your area. Or you can dig a hole. A posthole digger is a convenient tool for the purpose. Examine each core of soil as you pull it out. At first you will remove topsoil, which contains organic matter and is usually darker than subsoil. Unless your topsoil layer is exceptionally thick, you will break into a paler, coarser layer of soil within a few feet of the surface. You are now into the subsoil.

Usually, you can tell everything you need to know about the fineness of a soil just by looking at it. Sometimes with fine soils, however, it's useful to make a measure of just how fine the particles that make it up are. The finer a soil is, the more it behaves like putty when it's wet. If you press it across your palm with your thumb, it forms a smooth smear or sheet. The longer and smoother the smear, the smaller the particles in the soil. This same technique can be used to judge the particle size of your topsoil.

Topsoil

Your topsoil will be much more a matter of social history than of geology. If you are like most Americans, the place where your house sits was used for some other purpose as recently as 50 years ago, perhaps as a farm, or perhaps even as a dump, gravel pit, or industrial site. The characteristics of your soil will be determined by what was done at the site before it became a residence, by what was done during the conversion, and by what has been done to the soil by previous owners since the conversion. Unfortunately, many of our residential soils bear the chemical scars of these earlier uses.

Because you must understand your soil before you can successfully landscape it, we urge you to get a comprehensive soil test, particularly for parts of your yard where you plan to grow edibles. A comprehensive soil test will do more than tell you about the fertility and acidity of your soil and its critical nutrients. It will also warn you of some possible contaminants in your soil. Lead contamination is a particularly frequent problem around the foundations of older, wood-frame houses, in city lots, and along roadways.

Comprehensive soil tests can be obtained through your Agricultural Extension Service for under $10. If you are interested in organic gardening, some commercial labs specialize in doing soil tests for organic gardeners. These tests cost a bit more, but they are more complete and their recommendations will be tailored to organic methods. In particular, a test from an organic soil-testing service is more likely to give you information about the content of organic matter in your soil, a particularly useful measure for an organic gardener.

The soil-testing organization will usually send you a kit with instructions for how to collect and mail your sample. But you can also bag up some soil and send it directly. To collect a sample, take a bucket and a trowel out into your yard. Your goal is to collect a small sample that represents the top 6 inches of the soil. Scrape any litter off the surface. Drive the blade of the trowel into the ground, spread the ground to make a small hole, and then use the trowel to shave a bit of the dirt off the side of the hole, from the surface down as far as the trowel reaches. Put this bit of dirt in the bucket with obviously different soil types.

Repeat this procedure several times, moving systematically across the space you want to sample. The more holes you dig (within reason, of course—eight to twelve should do it), the better the sample will represent the space.

When you have dug as many holes as you want, mix the soil you have collected very thoroughly in the bucket. Then take about one measuring cup of soil and put it in a sturdy plastic bag. Label the bag clearly with something to identify the area where the sample was taken. Put the sample or samples in a book mailer along with your payment and a letter which gives your address, the source of the sample(s), and a request for a comprehensive soil test. Address the mailer to the soil test lab at your nearest Agricultural Extension Service office and drop it in the mailbox. You can expect your report within a few weeks.

A soil test report can be a bewildering docu-

Sources of Organic Soil Tests

Your state's land-grant university is the most convenient and inexpensive source of soil tests. Ask if the lab will provide organic recommendations if you request them. If they won't, and you don't want to convert the chemical recommendations to organic equivalents, a few labs specialize in organic soil tests. Write the one nearest you for costs and procedures.

Chemical Service Laboratory
3408 Industrial Parkway
Jeffersonville, IN 47130
(Say that you are an organic gardener and wish to add organic amendments only.)

The Maine Soil Testing Service
Deering Hall
University of Maine
Orono, ME 04469

The Necessary Trading Company
New Castle, VA 24127

Woods End Laboratory
P.O. Box 337
Temple, ME 04984

ment. To make the best use of it, focus on certain crucial pieces of information.

Organic Content of the Soil. If your sample was tested at an organic laboratory, this number will probably appear near the top of the test report. It is the percentage of the soil that is made up of organic matter. Organic matter facilitates the growth of your plants and makes your soil more resilient. A soil that is well provided with organic matter is less likely to have a fertility problem, an acidity problem, or a toxin or micronutrient problem than a soil that is not well provided. Three to 5 percent is a good quantity of organic matter—the higher the better.

Soil Acidity. The acidity or alkalinity of the soil is measured by its pH. On the pH scale, 7.0 is neutral. Numbers greater than 7.0 indicate an alkaline soil; numbers less than 7.0 indicate an acid soil. For most purposes a slightly acid soil is best, with a pH between 6.5 and 7.0. Some plants, like potatoes, rhododendrons, blueberries, and Japanese iris, do better with a more acid soil. If soil is too acid, it can be corrected by adding lime. Liming recommendations will usually accompany your soil test report.

Lime comes in high-magnesium (dolomite) and high-calcium (calcitic) forms. If you examine your soil test report closely, you will usually see information about the calcium and magnesium content of your soil. Whether you treat your soil with dolomite or calcitic lime will depend on whether your soil is magnesium-deficient or not.

Soil Fertility. Soil fertility is usually measured in terms of its content of nitrogen, phosphorus, and potassium. Soil test reports and fertilizer recommendations often refer to these elements using their chemical symbols, N, P, and K. (That chemists refer to potassium as "K" is one of those scientific obscurities we all have to live with.) The phosphorus and potassium content of soils is relatively stable and easy to measure and report. Not so, unfortunately, the nitrogen content of the soil. Thus, when you go looking for a report on the nitrogen content of your soil, you may not find it.

This omission doesn't present as many difficulties as you might expect. Even though your soil test report doesn't contain hard information about the nitrogen content of your soil, it will usually contain recommendations for nitrogen application.

Soil Toxins. A soil test report will usually contain information about the concentration of a few of the most important soil contaminants, notably aluminum, arsenic, cadmium, and lead. Of these, aluminum seems to be toxic to plants, the other three to humans. Your Extension Service agent can make recommendations about what to do if you find heavy metals in your soil. If the toxins are substances poisonous to humans, one obvious action you can take is not to grow fruits, vegetables, and herbs in the contaminated soil. This rule will protect your health against all but the most extreme cases of contamination, and it still leaves open to you all the pleasures of growing flowers, ornamental trees, and shrubs. Bear in mind, however, that the greatest risk from contaminated soil is that children will eat the soil itself or stick dirty fingers in their mouths while playing.

Micronutrients. Your soil may be reported as deficient in one or more substances that are required by plants in very small quantities. These are known as micronutrients. What to do about micronutrient deficiencies is a bit of a puzzle. Although these substances are necessary in small quantities, they can also be toxic to plants and humans in large quantities. Seaweed fertilizers may provide a source of micronutrients at safe levels. In general, we would urge you to make a thorough application of compost and/or manure. Add plenty of humus—grass clippings, leaves, and rotten straw. Then wait to see what happens. If, after a year or so, you suspect that micronutrient deficiencies are still a problem in your landscape, seek expert assistance from your nearest Agricultural Experiment Station.

A Word of Caution about Soil Tests. Many things can go wrong between the time you go out your door to collect your soil sample and the time your report comes back from the testing agency. Clots of lime or fertilizer can get into your bucket, technicians can mix up samples, or machines can go on the fritz. If your soil sample comes back with some extreme readings or radical recommendations, you would probably be wise to get a second test before taking any drastic action.

The Community Context

The community in which you live can sometimes impose restrictions on your landscaping project. In a legal sense, you simply don't have the right to do whatever you want to your own property. Hindrances usually take the form of zoning, building, and conservation regulations. In most communities, zoning laws regulate how close to a boundary you can build any kind of structure, such as a deck or porch. Some communities, in order to maintain an open and expansive look in their neighborhoods, also regulate the kind and height of fences that may be constructed along street frontage or between lots. Most communities jealously guard their wetlands against filling, draining, or flooding. The homeowner who makes changes in his landscape without asking about these laws may risk an unfriendly visit from a building inspector or conservation commissioner.

But even though you may feel some limits to your freedom from living in a neighborhood, you will also find that the community can be an enormous help to home landscapers. The chances are that right in your neighborhood are two or three people with hard-won expertise about the soils, trees, shrubs, bedding plants, building materials, and landscaping professionals of your area. The advice of such people can often be worth a hundred times the advice a book or a county agricultural agent can offer, because it is advice which is "naturalized" to your neighborhood. Don't be afraid to ask to see your neighbors' gardens and to seek their advice. Most gardeners love nothing better than to share experiences and garden lore, bumper crops, and bouquets of flowers.

Moreover, every community has craftspeople with unique talents. For instance, all over the eastern United States can be found stonemasons who have studied the craft of building dry stone walls and have become wondrously adept at it. A few inquiries around the neighborhood or at the garden store might lead you to such a craftsperson. Or you might learn of a carpenter who is particularly skilled at building decks and fences from locally plentiful kinds of wood. Such people are usually only discovered by asking around. You won't find their names in the Yellow Pages or newspapers, because they are so well regarded in the community that they have no need to advertise. You may have to wait a year to get the services of such craftspeople, but their work is worth the wait.

Perhaps the most important asset of a good community is a nursery run by an experienced staff. The local nursery must maintain a year-round operation, and its plants are often more expensive than those obtained from catalogs or cut-rate garden shops. You will be tempted to pass up your local nursery and buy bargain planting stock at these other places. But is such a purchase wise?

Think about the situation for a moment. Every May, the established nurseries in your town, the garden shops with seasonal specials, and the supermarkets with weekend shipments of fruit trees in their parking lots all sell thousands of trees and shrubs to you and your neighbors. Properly planted and cared for, each of these trees has a lifetime of at least half a century. If they all survived, there wouldn't be enough room in all the yards in the country to hold all of those trees and shrubs. So what is happening to them?

We suspect that most of the trees that people bring home during these spring buying frenzies are dying. If this hunch is accurate, then the buyer of a tree should think more about its care and less about its cost. A cheap tree, even if it only costs half the price of a tree from an established nursery, is no bargain if it dies from weakness or lack of water and has to be replaced. A reputable nursery will stand behind its stock and will scrupulously instruct you on how to plant it. In the long run, the tree you buy from the nursery may be cheaper than the "bargain."

But apart from the survival of your plants, another crucial reason directs you to your local nursery. Just like the person who runs your lumberyard or hardware store, the owner of your local nursery can be a source of valuable information. To do business in plants in a particular area for several decades is to become a repository of lore concerning soils, climate, and locally adaptable varieties of plants.

Wrap-up

Learning about your site and its surroundings is essential to making a good landscape design. The characteristics of your site and your area will determine which landscape features you can have easily and inexpensively, and which you can have only with the expenditure of much money and effort. Once you have evaluated your site, investigated your climate, tested your soil, and identified and consulted local resource people, and once you have all this information safely noted on your site inventory, then you are ready to begin thinking about the design possibilities for your landscape.

The Possibilities

25

Photo 2

A well-designed landscape extends the living space of the house. This small patio (Photo 1, preceding page) has everything—flowers, vegetables, shade, sunlight. All the features are compact and convenient to the house, but the patio and timber edges define the garden's areas and give it a sense of order.

Fences and walls can do so much to enhance and define space. The gate in Photo 2 sets a mood of elegance. Not only does it give you intimations of the space that lies beyond it, but it is a feature in itself, setting off the groupings of plants on either side. The screen in Photo 3 helps to focus your

Photo 3

26

Photo 4

Photo 5

attention on the house entry, leads your eye to the door and plant setting, and is carefully designed and placed so as not to seem intrusive. A stone wall gives a reassuring feeling of permanence. It also serves as an ideal frame for flowers beside, below, or above it, as in Photo 4.

With careful plant selection, wonderful scenes can be created, even in small spaces. Note how in Photo 5 the lightness of the blooming cherry tree is complemented and anchored by the red azaleas. The house and its reflecting glass are a perfect foil for this gay splash of color.

Photo 6

Photo 7

Photo 8

Whatever function a space is supposed to serve, plantings can help it to do its job effectively and gracefully. Plantings such as those in Photo 6 help to cut down the cold geometry and vacantness of a driveway. The plants in Photo 7 help the

Photo 9

different deck areas to flow together into an overall scheme: cozy for one person, plenty big enough for several. The shady arbor in Photo 8 has a lighter, airier feel than a solid overhang would, yet it provides an oasis from the scorching sun, where people can hide and view the world.

These scenes illustrate how inviting a skillfully designed landscape can be. The boardwalk in Photo 9 urges you onward and calls your attention in turn to the varieties of texture and color of the plants that lap up against it. Low-voltage lighting encourages nighttime strolls. A comfortable and stylish bench such as that displayed in Photo 10 invites you to pause a bit, take a load off your feet, and experience the life of the garden. Every garden needs a comfortable place to sit, set among sweet-smelling flowers in a sheltered part of the garden.

Photo 10

Would that all front entries were as welcoming as the rustic doorway in Photo 11! Plants for an entry should be chosen for their attractiveness year-round, and their blooms should blend with and enhance the architecture of the entry. Wax begonias and an assortment of coleus add the color to this scene.

Differences in texture can add enormously to the drama of a landscape. Photo 12 illustrates an ingenious use of architecture in relation to plant material. The fence echoes the fan-shaped foliage of the palms and the palms seem almost to satirize the symmetry of the fence. Both distract the eye from the rather humdrum facade of the house

Photo 11

Photo 12

behind. In Photo 13, notice how the fine detail of the bright marigolds and low-growing purple lobelia complements the stronger elements of the tree, shrub, walk, palings, and clapboards. This landscape demonstrates the importance of restraint. Think how much this scene would suffer from a busy arrangement of several different kinds of plants in the flowerbeds. In landscaping, less is often more!

How satisfying a design is when all its pieces come together. In Photo 14 (next page), all the elements work together to make a composition that is simple yet dynamic, understated yet effective. The door and the trellis with its garland of clematis: Each is complete, yet harmonizes with the other.

Photo 13

Photo 14

CHAPTER 3

Knowing the Possibilities

When Phebe comes to your door, she brings in her mind not only a list of questions concerning you and your community, but also a catalog of possibilities. These are what landscape designers call design elements. In nuts-and-bolts terms, they are whatever can be put in a landscape that contributes to its total effect. Design elements should not be confused with ornaments, such as plastic deer and silver balls. On the contrary, design elements are flowerbeds, trees, fences, walks, driveways, slopes, ponds, and decks—all the structures and features that make a landscape delightful and useful.

A designer's knowledge of design elements helps her see the ways in which your landscape can be wonderful. She selects from this knowledge design elements for your garden just as a painter selects colors from her palette to make a painting. She says to herself, "Perhaps I could have a terrace over there. What could I shelter it with? Hmm! How about a copper beech with its dramatic foliage? Oh, flagstones would go wonderfully with the gray stony tint of the tree's bark. And I'll put a flowering cherry just over here for accent and some kind of hedge here to hide the service entrance. Terrific!" This is the chapter where you learn about the basic elements that make up a useful and enjoyable landscape.

In selecting elements, it makes sense to start with the largest and most stable elements and move gradually to the smaller and more dynamic elements. In this way, you will be proceeding like a painter, who blocks out the gross forms and colors of the composition before painting in the details.

Landforms

Landforms consist of the slopes, flats, dips, bumps, and hollows that nature or the developer has left you. The surface of your property is like the stage on which the drama of your landscape will be played out. To think of the shape of the ground as a design element may seem odd—almost like thinking of the sky or the clouds as design elements. But unlike the sky and the clouds, the landforms of your property are to some degree under your control. Depending on your patience and your financial resources, you can decide to accept or alter any or all of them. Changing landforms is easier than you might suppose. In an hour, a bulldozer can move more soil than most homeowners would want moved in a lifetime.

Moving earth is a brutal craft, and it may take months to heal your landscape after the bulldozer has been carted off. But if you are willing to think on a smaller scale, you can often make small landforms that will give texture to your landscape without the expense and violence of major earthmoving. A truckload of topsoil, dumped in the right spot, carefully shaped with rakes and hoes, and planted over with soft, lush grass, can be a pleasing miniature knoll with which to frame a flowerbed. And if your family craves with all its heart a sunken sheltered patio for summer evening barbecues, you will be surprised what you all can accomplish together with the patient application of wheelbarrows and shovels.

To think about possible landforms for your yard, you have to look at it as if it were undressed, so to speak. Imagine what the surface of your land looks like without any trees: just the smooth contours of the earth. For all practical purposes, you can think of landforms as slopes, verticals, and flats.

Most developers do their best to turn a piece of ground into flats. Flat places are useful. They are restful to the eye, do not obstruct views of other things, are ideal for recreation, and usually don't have to be protected against erosion. And, of course, they're the best sites for houses and septic fields.

But they are not the only kind of landform, and they are certainly not the most interesting kind. Slopes and verticals provide definition, screening, and variety. Give a group of children access to a grassy slope or mound, and they will instantly claim it for a game of "king-of-the-mountain." Even for an adult, slopes have their benefits. Being at the top of a small slope or looking down from a higher to a lower level can give a subtle sense of being above it all, of being able to see things more in perspective. So if you have ups and downs in your landscape, don't be too hasty to have them leveled.

Natural slope in a lot offers a variety of design opportunities. You can, for instance, make use of a slope as it is. Gentle slopes surround a space with "soft" boundaries. When the space is not crowded, people will tend to be kept together by slopes surrounding them. But when the space becomes crowded, they can and will spread out and use the slope to good advantage. For instance, if you have a patio which is bordered on one side by a sunny slope, guests at a small party will use only the patio. Guests at a large party, on the other hand, can spill out onto the slope. The larger the party, the more the slope will be used.

Sloping ground can also be shaped into large steps or terraces. Terracing sharply defines spaces. Guests at a party on a terraced patio cannot readily use the nearby lawn. The terrace boundary, however, provides opportunities for low walls or benches which are ideal for sitting in a garden.

Because of the cost and clumsiness of earthmoving, the most practical approach is to capitalize on the landforms you already have and make only minimal changes. However, accepting your landforms the way they are doesn't mean giving up on landscaping dreams. The trick in elegant, economical, do-it-yourself landscaping is to look with an envious eye at the design elements you already have.

Trees and Shrubs

After the land itself, the most stable elements in a landscape are its trees and shrubs. Like landforms, trees can be changed. But if you start with small economical nursery stock, even fast-growing trees take a decade or two to begin to have an appreciable effect on your surroundings. So, as with landforms, it's best to try to work with what you have.

Trees and shrubs have four principal functions in a landscape: They provide shade, beauty, screening, and shelter and food for wildlife. The distinction between trees and shrubs has never been very clear, and with the introduction of many new varieties of dwarf trees, the distinction has become even muddier. For the present purposes, a tree can be thought of as any plant tall enough to cast substantial shade on a standing human being.

Trees

If the landforms are the stage of your landscaping drama, then the trees are the backdrop. They provide the basic forms, colors, and patterns of light and shadow against which the other elements of your landscape will appear. They also provide screening against large eyesores, such as distant water towers or apartment buildings.

Trees are either evergreen or deciduous. The distinction is particularly important to landscape design because evergreens are an unchanging element in a design, whereas deciduous trees are very dynamic. During the time that a spruce tree remains a dense, dark, massive green cone, a swamp maple is first a bare skeleton with reddish limbs and buds, then a brilliant reddish green frame, then a green blur, then a red flame, then a muted, grayish red skeleton again. Thus evergreens are particularly suitable where you want a reliable, all-season screen, and deciduous trees are appropriate where you want a dynamic backdrop or different patterns of light and shade in summer and winter.

Deciduous trees vary widely in their characteristics. They can have a weeping shape like a willow, a pyramidal shape like a pin oak, or a columnar shape like a Lombardy poplar. Some have an umbrella shape, like a silver maple or a zelkova. Others are wider at the crown, like a sugar maple, or form a spherical ball of foliage, like an apple tree. Some, like the red oak, have a particularly intricate pattern of branches, so that they are as delightful to look at in winter as they

Trees vary greatly in shape, as these crown silhouettes show.

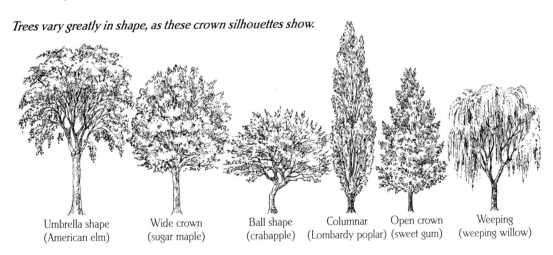

| Umbrella shape (American elm) | Wide crown (sugar maple) | Ball shape (crabapple) | Columnar (Lombardy poplar) | Open crown (sweet gum) | Weeping (weeping willow) |

are in summer. Others have striking trunks, like the beech, with bark that reminds Calvin of dinosaur skin.

Trees vary in the quantity and quality of shade they cast. Some, like locusts and birches, cast a light, thin shade; others, like the Norway maple, cast a shade so dense that grass cannot grow beneath them. Some, like the silver maple, cast shade over a long season, virtually from first to last frost, whereas others, like the ashes and oaks, are slow to put on their leaves in the spring.

A few large deciduous trees in a garden help to increase the variety of creatures that live there. Essentially, all plants, whether 50-foot trees or microscopic algae, survive by combining the materials in the soil with the energy from the sun. The difference between a cell of alga and a large oak tree is that in an alga, the two functions, gathering nutrients and absorbing energy, occur within a millimeter of each other, whereas in the oak, they may be separated by dozens of feet of trunk. Thus, large trees spread out the zone of biological activity. Every inch of the distance between the tips of their roots and the tips of their leaves offers opportunities for unique species of birds, little mammals, insects, and other plants.

Because many kinds of tree take so long to grow to significant height, your first strategy should be to try to make use of the trees you already have. But, if you want to buy large trees, you can do so. They are expensive, so make sure you buy them from a reputable dealer. Have them put in by a qualified professional and guaranteed for at least a full year by the person who puts them in.

Shrubs

If trees are the backdrops on a stage, shrubs are the large props. The most common function of shrubs is to define your garden into spaces, to decorate it, and to screen it. Shrubs fill in where trees leave off. Tall spreading trees like sweet gums, oaks, and tulip poplars often leave a clear park-like area beneath them. Shade-loving shrubs grown in this area can screen or define into areas an otherwise undefined shady spot. Shrubs can be evergreen or deciduous. Broadleaved evergreen shrubs, such as rhododendrons, are useful for screening. Even deciduous shrubs often have significant screening effects because many have very dense branches.

Shrubs and small trees are also excellent sources of food for both humans and wildlife. The dense cover provided by shrubbery makes suitable nesting sites for a great variety of birds. Plant a lilac bush and you are sure to have a catbird move in before very long. Plant a hedge of autumn olive or highbush cranberry and a grateful mockingbird will treat you to the delights of his song off and on all winter long.

Finally, many species of shrub have beautiful or fragrant flowers. Forsythia bears brilliant blooms in the early spring, when your spirits may need a boost. Later in the spring, lilac's intoxicating fragrance flavors the air. The deeply saturated colors of azalea flowers seem to glow from the shadows where these broadleaved evergreens prosper. Honeysuckle flowers literally hum with insect life throughout June.

Because of their size, variety, and the speed with which they grow, shrubs are a quick and comparatively inexpensive way to get started on a long-term planting program. A small sprig of lilac or forsythia that will grow to be a substantial bush in five or ten years costs just a few dollars and thrives with little assistance. Less familiar shrubs, which offer many creative opportunities for gardeners, can be found at your nursery.

Flower Borders and Vegetable Beds

The most flexible and easily controlled living landscaping elements are flower borders and veg-

Flowerbeds can serve many functions. They can soften the edges of a patio and provide close-up visual interest (top), or they can define a distant property line (second from top). Flowers are delightful borders for walks or paths, where they also aid in traffic control (third from top). Island beds of flowers can be designed in any size or shape you need to fill up empty space and add interest to the yard (bottom).

etable beds. Like shrubs, flower borders and vegetable beds provide a quick way to improve your landscape at a minimum of cost and effort.

Many of us put flowers and vegetables in an isolated place called "the garden." Like so many of our practices, this treats the outdoors as if it were merely a place from which to bring things inside: cut flowers from the flower garden, vegetables from the vegetable garden. Once you begin to see the garden as a place in which to spend time, you realize that flowers and vegetables not only supply bouquets and food, but can serve to decorate an outdoor living space as well.

Flowerbeds can be designed entirely of perennial flowers, of annuals, or of a mixture of perennials, biennials, and annuals. Perennial flowers are those that winter over year after year in your region; biennials live for two years, often blooming only in the second year; and annuals must be replanted each year. A carefully conceived perennial flowerbed can provide color from snowmelt to snowfall, year after year, while an annual flowerbed can be composed anew every year, like a painting.

Flowerbeds are the subtlest method of defining space in a garden. Flowers can be designed for close viewing. For instance, a bed can be planted alongside a patio, inviting guests to lean over and sniff or pick a blossom or two. A flowerbed can define a distant edge, as a row of scarlet salvia planted against a gray stone wall. Or bright flowers such as marigolds can be planted along the edges of walks or driveways as a subtle and ingratiating form of traffic control.

Groundcovers

When you have selected your trees and shrubs and designed your flower borders and vegetable beds, you will still have space left over. Obviously, you must plan for this space or nature will plan it for you. On your designer's palette you will find a variety of ways to cover ground which is not being specifically planted. These groundcovers cannot be chosen carelessly because they form part of the backdrop against which the features of your landscape will be seen.

You have two basic ground-covering strategies available to you. The first is to plant something. The most obvious plant to put in is grass. Lawns are the ideal groundcover if you have ample natural moisture and lots of sunlight. Lawns can be formal or informal, but, as we shall see, the more formal a lawn is, the more the lawn keeper is engaged in a battle with nature.

Where sunlight and/or moisture are inadequate to maintain a lawn, other sorts of groundcovers can be planted. Pachysandra is a common groundcovering plant. It stays green all winter long even in the harshest climate, and grows well—grows best, in fact—in shade. Numerous other groundcovers are available. Some tolerate more sunlight; some have decorative flowers, leaves, or berries. Some, such as ivy and wintercreeper, will not only cover the ground but clamber over walls and up tree trunks as well.

If you don't want to grow a living groundcover, you can cover the soil with a deep mulch. Bark, wood shavings, peat moss, even brick or stone can form a mulch which makes the ground look neat and well cared for even under trees or in the deep shade on the north side of a house. Mulches, of course, are not entirely carefree. They must be renewed regularly, and you must keep your eye peeled for weeds which will poke up whenever the mulch gets thin.

Barriers

When you design your landscape, you may want to erect one or more barriers. It seems paradoxical, but barriers often function as a kind of lubricant. They minimize friction. They make it possible for the different parts of your landscape to work well together, and for different activities to coexist peacefully in the same landscape.

When you are considering putting up a wall or a fence, you have to think about what it is that you hope to confine or exclude. The list is surprisingly long. Not only might you want to confine or exclude people or animals, but you might also want to exclude the wind, confine the heat from the winter sun, confine your own vision, exclude the vision of others, confine automobiles, channel foot traffic, exclude noise, and keep private conversations private, to cite only a few examples. The various landscaping barriers are more or less effective for each of these purposes, so you must be careful to choose the right kind.

Also, you must bear in mind that a barrier designed for excluding also confines, and vice versa. The wall you build to keep your neighbors from treating your barbecue as a spectator sport will also keep you from watching the robins feed on their lawn. In the construction of every barrier, something is always gained and something else lost, and you want to make sure before you start to build that the gains are going to outweigh the costs.

Basically, the three kinds of barriers are walls, fences, and hedges. High walls and fences are particularly effective all-purpose barriers. They exclude everything, from wind to people to the neighbor's dalmatian. But they also confine everything, and can sometimes give a space a shut-in feeling. Low walls and fences do not confine the wind, the view, or sounds, but they do usually keep most people and some animals in line. Some kinds of fences provide some of the benefits of exclusion without quite so much confinement. Latticework and paling fences are more difficult to see through from a distance than from up close. As

you sit by the fence, passersby on the street may not notice you, but you can see out well enough not to feel so shut in.

Wire fencing can be very effective in excluding and confining animal and human traffic. Installed carefully, vinyl-coated fencing can be neat, inconspicuous, and inexpensive, and it's surprisingly durable as long as its coating is not damaged. Calvin has used the same length of vinyl-coated fencing in his vegetable garden for 25 years. It's not very elegant by now, but it still does the job.

Hedges are different from nonliving barriers in several important ways. Unlike constructed barriers, they take several years to grow. Early in their lives, they barely serve the function of definition and traffic control. But when they are full grown, they are among the most effective of barriers. Hedges muffle sounds that come from your neighbor's yard and those that come from your own. Hedges can be an extremely important feature for wildlife. Some hedges provide food for wildlife, and all provide shelter for small birds and animals.

Hedges have many advantages, but they also have two drawbacks: higher maintenance needs than other barriers and lower "invasion-resistance." A hedge by itself is more permeable than a fence or wall. Given time and incentive, animals and children will make a path through a hedge, even a full-grown hedge. Consequently, hedges are often planted along a wire fence so that as the hedge grows, it encloses the fence within it. Such fence/hedge combinations are more impassable even than a wall. Not only can they not be penetrated, they cannot be climbed.

Barriers vary enormously in price and quickness of result. Because of the expert labor involved, masonry walls can be extremely expensive. Wooden fences are often specialty items which can be ordered at garden supply stores. Most are simple enough to install, but even so, given the materials involved, you will probably be surprised at how expensive they are. Wire fencing, on the other hand, is often mercifully inexpensive. Hedges vary in price depending on the size and number of hedge plants you start with. If you are willing to be patient, a hedge can also be inexpensive.

Outdoor Living Areas

The spaces close by the house are good choices for outdoor living areas. They are often partially sheltered from the wind and other elements, and close to the phone, refrigerator, and all the other conveniences of the house. Well-designed outdoor living areas can be particularly useful because they have the benefits both of the house and of the outdoors. Badly designed, they have the drawbacks of both. Depending on how well an outdoor living area is planned, it can mean either a lot of good food served outdoors or a lot of bad mud tracked into the kitchen.

Porches

The most "civilized" of these interior-exterior spaces is a porch. A porch is a roofed, framed living space which is open to the outdoors. The most "interior" of porches are provided with storm sashes in the winter and screens in the summer.

The advantages of a porch at first seem overwhelming. Properly oriented, a porch provides access to fresh air and sunshine and protection from rain and bugs. South-facing porches provide for shade in the summer and sun in the winter, since the high sun of summer is cut off by the porch roof, but the low sun of winter is let in.

The drawback of porches is their effect on the house. A south-facing porch excludes sunlight from the southern rooms of the house, and a north-facing porch turns its abutting rooms into dismal

tunnels. Where Calvin lives in New England, amateur architects seem often to have fallen prey to the porch trap. It seems to happen like this. Ma and Pa are sitting in front of the open windows of the living room some hot summer night, and Ma gets a bright idea. "Pa," she says, "if we had a sitting porch, we could be outside where the air is cool." So, the next day Pa goes and buys some lumber and some screens, and they build a sitting porch. Well, that's just fine and they spend their summer evenings happily lounging on the porch, watching the fireflies and listening to the frogs.

Summer days are another story. Then Ma and Pa don't spend much time on their porch because it gets too hot. But, come September, when the days are cooler and the sun strikes in on a slant, the porch begins to be a nice place to have a noon meal or a weekend breakfast, or to sit in of an afternoon and do the knitting.

Long about October, though, it's getting too cool to sit out on an open porch. But when Ma and Pa move back indoors, they make a sad discovery. The sun doesn't get into their living room anymore because the porch roof blocks it.

So Ma says to Pa, "Gee, we like our new porch so much, maybe we should winterize it." So they go to the lumberyard and pick up some windows and doors, and they put up insulation, and maybe they run the steam pipes out onto the porch so they can have a radiator there, and the porch becomes their living room for most of the year. Except on the coldest winter evenings, the living room of the house is never used. It becomes a dark and drafty corridor between the porch and the rest of the house.

Come next summer, Ma and Pa are sitting on their porch of a hot summer evening. They've opened all the windows, but it's still dreadfully hot and stuffy because the winterized porch just doesn't get rid of the day's heat so fast. So Pa gets a bright idea. "What we need," he says, "is a porch *outside* the porch!"

This account is a bit exaggerated. Calvin has never actually seen a porch built *onto* a porch. But he has seen several porches removed which were put on houses less than a generation before.

Summerhouses

One way to have the good effects of a porch without suffering all the disadvantages is to have a summerhouse. A summerhouse is essentially a porch which is detached from the house. As its name implies, it is used only in the warm months. Sometimes summerhouses are glazed or screened, sometimes not. Because they are open on all four sides and disconnected from the house, they cool quickly on hot summer nights. And, of course, best of all, they don't shade the windows of the house in winter.

Despite these advantages, summerhouses are an expensive way to provide transitional space, and a paradoxical one as well. Because they are separate structures away from the main house, they are not really transitional anymore. Either you must carry out food, reading materials, and lights every day, or you must outfit the summerhouse with these amenities permanently. Perhaps a television for summer baseball games? Perhaps a cooler for beer? Before long, the summerhouse may become as hot and cluttered as the house itself.

Patios

A patio is a surfaced, sheltered open space usually constructed next to a residence. A patio can be terraced so that it is more or less level with the doors of the house, or it can be at ground level, so that one walks down from the house to reach it. Patios are generally surfaced with flagstone, brick, or concrete. They are usually open to the sky, but sometimes are partially covered with arbors.

Patios look like casual, easy-to-maintain spaces, but looks can be deceiving. Unless they are very carefully designed, natural processes can quickly reverse the work put into a patio. If drainage is not carefully provided, rain can puddle on the patio or water can flow between the stones and undermine it. Tree roots can expand and rumple the patio surface. In winter, frost can get under the stones and heave or split them. Grass can gain a foothold between the bricks or stones of the patio and spread rapidly, until you can't distinguish the patio from the lawn.

But a well-conceived patio can be a wonderfully comfortable and convivial living space. Aesthetically, patios are ideal transition spaces because they blend so readily with lawns, flowerbeds, and walkways. By carefully placing trees, you can make a patio shady during the hottest part of the day, and yet warm and pleasant for a delightful outside breakfast. In wintertime, the stonework of patios can be a very effective heat sink, catching the sun's warmth and giving it back when the sun ducks behind a passing cloud.

Decks

One of the most practical forms of outside living area is a deck. A deck is a flat wood floor open to the sky. It is usually constructed of wood 2×4s or 2×6s spaced slightly apart to allow rainwater to drain through. The flooring is nailed to a frame, which is set on concrete or stone footings. Decks can be made of naturally weather-resistant woods like redwood or of pressure-treated wood. If you are concerned about chemical contamination, we recommend that you construct your deck out of redwood, red cedar, or black locust, rather than pressure-treated woods, since questions have been raised about the toxins with which pressure-treated wood is injected.

A deck on the sheltered side of the house is

an ideal kind of living space for fall and spring days. At this season bugs are not a problem, and you will be grateful for the heat of the sun. One disadvantage of decks is that they do weather and may need to be replaced every 20 to 30 years or so. Also, they aren't much use on hot summer evenings when the bugs are active. But even when these disadvantages are considered, a deck is one of the cheapest and most flexible ways to provide outdoor living space.

Walks, Driveways, and Paths

The purpose of these design elements is to channel and accommodate traffic of various sorts. The heavier the traffic, the more permanent and stable must be the pathway. Durable, stable paths can be made of asphalt, cement, stone, or brick. Asphalt must be resurfaced every few years or so, or it will crack. Cement is more durable, but it too will crack and eventually must be redone.

For walks and small driveways, cobblestones or bricks can form an attractive and effective surface for foot and auto traffic. The soil under such surfaces must be firm and even, and drainage must be provided, or they will heave from frost or subside from erosion. Loose crushed stone or gravel is another form of surfacing. Its advantage is that it has no drainage or frost problems. Its chief disadvantages are that it doesn't stay put and is difficult to plow or shovel in winter.

The classic country driveway consists of sand, crushed stone, and graded gravel, so that the driveway sits directly on undisturbed subsoil. As traffic passes over the driveway, the driveway packs down and forms a surface which is almost as resilient as asphalt. The disadvantage of such a driveway is that traffic casts stones out into the surrounding lawn and wears ruts in the roadway. A neat gravel driveway requires an annual raking and leveling.

Calvin's favorite driveway is essentially a track beaten in the grass by the passing of automobiles. As the track develops ruts and puddles, the homeowner adds loads of crushed stone which the tires of vehicles press into the soil. It makes a cheap and serviceable driveway surface, if you don't mind the way it looks. Calvin actually *likes* the way it looks, particularly when the grass grows up between the ruts and tickles the cars as they come in the drive.

The equivalent in footpaths to Calvin's driveway is the bare track in the grass. Away from areas of heavy traffic, informal footpaths can be very successful. If the path begins to be soggy, as it may where it winds through shady areas, you may want to add wood chips or bark mulch, both of which give your path a woodsy look.

Pools, Ponds, and Trickles

We think every garden ought to have some sort of water feature. Not only is water in a garden pleasing to look at and soothing to hear, it is also a convenience to wildlife. Birds and small animals make great profit of the opportunities to bathe, drink, and feed that are often provided by water sources in a garden. With a little ingenuity, in most climates you can create a pool where goldfish can live.

Water features come in every imaginable shape and cost. At the modest end of the scale, consider a birdbath set elegantly in the middle of your garden. Each day you bring a bucket of fresh water and fill it. The birds frolic gratefully. Or consider a container set in the ground to catch the water that streams out of your downspouts. Every week or so, rain tumbles down the spout and renews the water in your little wildlife pool.

Upward in scale and contrivance from these two examples, one can consider every imaginable kind of water feature. If you have any kind of natural wet spot on your property, a little digging or channeling may enhance it. Uncover an underground spring and a bog becomes a pond. Clear out a channel in some rocky ground and a damp ledge becomes a miniature waterfall. If you have no natural wet spots, then all manner of guileful contrivances are available which will simulate them. Plastic or metal pools can be dug into the ground and supplied with underground piping. Recirculating pumps can pump water from the bottom of a rock ledge to the top, creating the illusion of a spring. Of course it's more than an illusion, because while *you* may know that it's faked, the plants, animals, lichens, and mosses will take it for real, and you will end up with a water feature that is artificial only in its source.

Fixtures and Furniture

Save room in your landscaping budget for objects that will make the outdoors an easy, convenient, and pleasurable place to be. Sturdy, durable garden furniture makes your garden comfortable to sit in and encourages family members to get out in the yard and enjoy it. Hammocks and swings are wonderful garden fixtures. You have never truly napped until you have taken a summer nap in the shady embrace of a hammock, nor have you daydreamed till you've daydreamed swaying on a swing. And don't forget garden games. Save space and money for a croquet set, a tetherball court, a horseshoe pitch, or a volleyball or badminton net.

Wrap-up

As soon as you begin to think about your landscape as a place to live in and enjoy, you will begin to see the world around you, the garden shops, the hardware stores, the nurseries, even the gardens of your neighbors and friends, as a buffet

Design Elements

Landforms
___ Flats
___ Slopes
___ Verticals

Trees and shrubs
___ Evergreens
___ Deciduous trees
___ Large trees
___ Small trees
___ Shrubs
___ Flowering
___ Fruiting

Flower borders and vegetable beds
___ Flowerbeds
   ___ Perennial
   ___ Annual
___ Vegetable garden
___ Herb garden

Barriers
___ High walls
___ Low walls
___ High fences
___ Low fences
___ Solid barriers
___ Barriers you can see through
___ Hedges

Transition areas
___ Porches
___ Summerhouses
___ Patios
___ Decks

Trafficways
___ Asphalt
___ Cement
___ Brick, flagstone, or cobblestone
___ Crushed stone
___ Rural path or driveway

Fixtures and furniture
___ Hammock
___ Swing
___ Croquet set
___ Tetherball
___ Horseshoe court
___ Volleyball net
___ Badminton net
___ Benches
___ Outdoor tables
___ Table umbrellas
___ Outdoor chairs
___ Swimming pool
___ Ornamental pool
___ Fountain
___ Birdbath

of landscaping ideas for your own garden. Land-forms, trees of various sizes, different kinds of barriers, outdoor living areas, walks, beds, and fixtures of all kinds, all are available to you, depending on the effort and investment you want to put into your garden.

Now that we have discussed the possibilities, we suggest that you take some notes about the features we have mentioned that tempt you. To help you, we have included a checklist. Take a moment now, while the chapter is fresh in your mind, to mark off and comment on those design elements which appeal to you. These notes will be helpful when you are reading the next section of the book and are considering the many highlights we suggest for your garden.

Part Two

Special Features

CHAPTER 4

Lawns and Meadows

*T*o many people, a lawn *means* summer. The sounds and sights associated with lawns—the hissing of sprinklers and fat robins gratefully foraging on damp turf—bring back memories of pickup baseball games, Frisbee tosses, family cookouts, and fleet races barefoot over cool grass. A succulent lawn seems connected to everything that is homey and safe.

For others, a lawn means endless labor in the service of flatness. First they fertilize to get the lawn to grow, then mow to level it, then rake to take away the cut grass, and then water to keep it from turning brown. For these folks, a lawn is nothing but a lot of work and not much to show for it: no fruit or vegetables, no colorful flowers. Just a flat green surface.

Of course, both viewpoints are true. A lawn can be the most soothing and enjoyable part of your landscape, and it also can be a lot of work. Striking a balance between pleasure and pain in lawnmaking means overthrowing the tyranny of the straight line. Let's face it, the human eye can be greedy for uniformity. Imagine that you start out with an informal, rough-and-ready lawn. It's usable, it's comfortable, there are even a few wildflowers in it, but your eye is critical. Tufts of grass stand out. There is an unevenness of color and texture as well as of height. Your rough lawn looks fairly flat and uniform, especially from a distance, but your eye wishes it still flatter and more uniform. So you weed it and try to scratch in some seed where the weeds were, and then you roll it, and it looks pretty good for a while. "Now that's a good lawn!" you say.

But pretty soon, your eye starts nagging again. Look at that edge, it says, where the lawn meets the driveway. It's not clean, that edge. And look at those ugly grass clippings. Don't they just spoil the effect? So you go out and buy an edger and a bagger and you edge your driveway and you bag your clippings and for a while the lawn looks pretty good again. But then the weather turns dry for a week, and your grass begins to lose its luster, and some parts of it begin to look a bit yellow. So you go out and buy one of those sprinklers that trot across the lawn dragging the hose behind them and you turn it loose. Well, after a day or so, your lawn has pretty much recovered.

But now you begin to notice that the texture isn't quite right. The shady parts under the trees seem to sport a sparser, lighter, slow-growing grass, while the sunny areas display a lusher, softer grass. You think to yourself, "This lawn needs reseeding."

So you tear the whole thing up and reseed it, or perhaps you buy sod from one of those sod companies that come and lay a lawn like it's a wall-to-wall carpet. And once your new lawn is established, doesn't it look nice! But after a day or so, you notice that your rotary mower doesn't follow the contours of the ground precisely so that there are a few spots where it cuts the grass too close, scalps it, you say, cursing your bad fortune. So you go out and buy a new mower, one of those riding mowers that really cuts level and close. And for a while the lawn looks really good, particularly if you fertilize it several times a summer and water and mow it every other day. And so it goes. You're thousands of dollars poorer and still worrying about your lawn.

Before you get yourself caught up in this lawn-improvement trap, be realistic and know your limits. If what you want is Astroturf, for heaven's sake put in Astroturf and be done with it. But if what you want is *grass,* then recognize that grass is alive. It's more amenable to regimentation than most growing things, but even grass has its limits.

Whatever else you may say about a lawn, it's not natural. The natural equivalent of a lawn is a meadow. Meadows spring up because natural disasters like fires, floods, and earthquakes clear the land of trees. Meadows are maintained for a time by the grazing of animals, and then grow up to shrubs and small trees and, eventually, forests. To try to preserve a meadow is to try to resist the natural succession from bare ground to grass to forest. Given that you are resisting nature, you should expect that keeping a lawn should be work. And the more you try to resist nature, the more work your lawn will require.

Which Kind of Lawn for You?

To help you decide which sort of lawn you want, we are going to describe what's involved in having three kinds of lawns: a closely manicured, beautifully defined carpet of delicate grasses; an informal lawn of tough, hardy grasses; and a meadow of wildflowers and tall grasses. We will call these lawns "The Emerald Sward," "The Down-Home Lawn," and "The Mini-Meadow," respectively. We'll try to give you a sense of what it feels like to have each kind of lawn, its joys, its miseries, and how much work it involves.

The Emerald Sward

An emerald sward is supremely restful to the eye. It is a uniform swath of green that emphasizes the contours of the land and shows off the forms of tree shadows. It is cool and silky underfoot, and you can walk on it without fear of treading on a thistle or on the hard, cut stem of a dry weed.

An emerald sward is pure grass. In order to get an even and luxurious growth, its seed mix is composed of particularly lush, delicate grasses. No weeds mar its uniform texture. No leaves are allowed to collect on its surface.

The emerald sward is sharply defined. Whatever is not grass in the yard is masonry or decking or flowerbeds or mulch. Crisp boundaries are maintained between the sward and its surroundings.

This classic type of lawn is idyllic for occasional luxurious use. What a delight it is to be able to walk in your bare feet across a cool grass surface as soft and springy as a rug! What a pleasure to watch your dinner guests stroll across the sward in their party clothes! What fun to practice your putting or to play an exacting game of croquet on your front lawn!

Emerald swards are so commonplace that we tend to think that they are the natural state of the surface of the earth. We see them all the time around factories, banks, and in expensive housing developments. But normal as such lawns seem, they are actually very fragile and can only be maintained through a combination of high technology, expensive machinery, and/or hard labor. The fragility of a sward is due mostly to the fact that it does not form a natural community. Only varieties of bluegrass grow in this type of lawn, and constant watering, fertilizing, and mowing are required to keep them thick and beautiful.

To keep the grass growing rapidly and healthily it must be mowed to 1 or 2 inches so that the sun can reach the bottoms of its leaves. Clippings cannot be left to lie on the surface of the lawn because they will mat down the delicate grass blades beneath them. Because the clippings are being removed, the lawn must be fertilized three times a year. The soil should be tested each year, and its pH maintained with lime.

Swards are subject to insect attack, and most sward owners we know spray their lawns periodically with insecticides and/or fungicides. A sward must be watered. Closely cropped grasses are shallow-rooted, and the top few inches of the soil must be kept constantly moist. A sward must also be weeded vigilantly. Perennial weeds such as crabgrass compete vigorously and spread rapidly in the fertile, well-watered soil of the sward. Nowadays, with labor costs so high and time in the yard at such a premium, weeding lawns usually means the regular application of chemical weed-killers which linger for many years in the soil and groundwater.

Swards are also vulnerable to competition from tree roots. To maintain an even surface on the sward, it must be bounded several feet from the trunk of each large tree, a brick or wood barrier installed, and some sort of mulch, such as bark or coconut hulls, spread around the foot of the tree. To maintain the sharp definition of the sward, you'll have to use edging tools or clippers every week where the sward meets these barriers.

Think of this kind of lawn not as a place where you do your outdoor projects but as a project in itself. An emerald sward is a stern disciplinarian. Forget to feed it and it begins to yellow. Fail to mow and rake it one week, and it will look ragged and unkempt. Miss a watering, and it develops brown spots. Take a vacation from edging for a week and it begins to sprawl over walks and into flowerbeds. The maintenance of a sward is gardening of the most exacting kind. Nothing looks as untidy as a neglected sward.

A Down-Home Lawn

A down-home lawn is more informal. Before it is mowed, it is shaggy. After it is mowed, it is flawed by the grass clippings strewn on it. But for a few days in each mowing cycle, the lawn comes into its own. The freshly mowed tips of the grass push up through the clippings and form a wonderful flat surface of which any gardener could be proud.

A down-home lawn has a variety of plant species in it. It forms what ecologists call a community. The grasses in it are of many types which are constantly replacing each other as weather conditions and the seasons change. Moreover, a down-home lawn contains more than grass. Parts of it may be strewn with violets, which have spread out from a shady spot on the north side of the house; or with dandelions, which turn the lawn brilliant yellow in early spring; or with Indian paintbrush, which rewards the procrastinating late-spring mower with wonderful orange and yellow flowers; or with wild strawberry, which provides a little fruit in early summer. In the autumn, a down-home lawn may be strewn with yellow, red, and orange maple leaves.

The boundaries of a down-home lawn are not fixed. In the summer it encroaches on driveways and walks, only to retreat again in fall and winter. In spring, the grass grows vigorously between the large roots of tall trees, forming soft green pockets where a child can sit as if in an armchair. But in the summer, when the leaves shade the ground and the tree roots are greedily sucking all the water out of the topsoil, the grass turns brown and sparse near the tree trunks.

A down-home lawn may even have a path or two running across it where the children rush to the schoolbus every morning, or where the dog rounds the corner of the garage on his way to chase the mailman. This easy-going lawn is useful for a multitude of purposes. You can sunbathe or picnic or have a barbecue on it. You can play volleyball, horseshoes, badminton, or Frisbee on it, if you don't do these things every weekend in the same place. You can even park cars on it from time to time. But the down-home lawn is probably not much good for a serious game of croquet or bowls.

A down-home lawn is moderately easy to maintain. To be in its best condition, it will require an inch of rainfall a week or the equivalent from a sprinkler. But if it gets dried out, the consequences are not terrible. It will look brown and unhappy for a while, but when the rains begin again, it will come back green and strong. Most people mow a down-home lawn once a week or so, but if your lawn mower can handle longer intervals, so can

your lawn. By August, the grass starts growing much more slowly, and a biweekly or even monthly schedule is adequate. A down-home lawn is not raked after every mowing, and the clippings serve to fertilize the grass.

Apart from weekly mowing during the growing season, a down-home lawn may require two periods of maintenance. The first is in the spring, when you may want to test the soil every few years and perhaps apply an organic fertilizer and lime.

The second major maintenance time is in the autumn after leaf fall, when you may need to rake your down-home lawn. Heavy leaf falls and the accumulation of rotting grass clippings can smother the grass after a while, so a good vigorous raking in the fall will make a neater lawn in the spring.

That's the only care this kind of lawn requires. No intensive fertilizing campaigns. No weedkillers. No tight mowing and watering schedules. No aerators and rollers.

The Mini-Meadow

A mini-meadow is really a specialized form of perennial garden. Its leaves, flowers, and seedpods provide an ever-changing variety of textures and colors. It is an insect menagerie, with butterflies and bees visiting the flowers, and every manner of beetle and grasshopper scurrying around on the soil's surface. For sports or entertaining, a mini-meadow is usually a bust. But it's a wonderful place to relax. When you sit in a mini-meadow, your gaze wanders through a haze of tiny flowers dancing in the wind. When you lie down in a mini-meadow, suddenly you are enclosed in a warm world of buzzing insects and the gentle hiss of wind rustling the grass. In fall, a mini-meadow is a source of myriad dried grasses and pods for arrangements.

A mini-meadow is composed of wildflowers and ornamental grasses. Meadows require full sun

that are likely to occur in his meadow over the years. The owner of a mini-meadow can't be fussy about which grasses and flowers grow in his meadow. If he insists that his mini-meadow look exactly like the luxurious color photograph in the seed catalog, he is bound for disappointment or for the labor and expense of reseeding. Mini-meadows are for laid-back gardeners.

Wildflower mixes and wildflower landscaping are some of the most rapidly developing landscaping "technologies" of our day. In the last decade, highway administrators have become more and more leery of the huge sums of money they must spend on mowing the roadsides: money for labor, money for expensive machines, money for gasoline and oil. In the course of hunting for ways to save money on roadside maintenance, they ran across horticulturists trying to preserve and spread natural stands of wildflower. A rare meeting of minds occurred between the road-maintenance contractors and the flower conservationists. Experiments with seeding wildflowers on interstate roadsides are going on all over the country. Because of the huge scale of these operations, an industry in wildflower seed has started to grow up, and more information is being collected every day about how to seed and maintain wildflower stands.

The technology of meadows is so new that you should carefully investigate local sources of information. Call local garden clubs, horticultural societies, Agricultural Extension Service agents— even state highway engineering departments—to find out what has worked in your area.

Our Recommendation

Of the three types of lawn, we think the down-home lawn will suit most readers best. The emerald sward, we think, demands too much, from the gardener and from the environment. To main-

and a well-prepared seedbed. The fastest way to establish a mini-meadow is to buy a meadow mix which is suitable for your area. The grower has carefully chosen grasses and wildflowers that are hardy or will reseed readily in your climate. To create the meadow area, clear the ground, grade it, and make sure the topsoil is 6 inches deep before planting.

Once your meadow is planted, there is not much work to maintaining it. It must be mowed once a year with a cutter bar to keep trees and shrubs from growing up in it. But the low maintenance of a wildflower meadow presupposes that the gardener will accept the succession of changes

tain such a lawn by organic means requires you to cultivate the lawn as intensively as you would a flowerbed. To maintain it by any other means is to constantly douse your ground with chemicals dangerous to yourself and to the life of your soil.

The mini-meadow, on the other hand, is unsuitable for most of the purposes to which lawns are traditionally put. Moreover, meadows have an unkempt appearance which we suspect won't wear well with many gardeners or with their neighbors. (In fact, in some communities they are actually illegal!) Finally, we think mini-meadows are too chancy for most gardeners. Some gardeners may boast of effortless displays of wildflowers in their yards, year after year after year. But we suspect that most such plantings must be carefully watched and perhaps reseeded from time to time, if they are to maintain their variety.

So, for most readers, the lawn we recommend is probably the lawn you already have. It's not glamorous, but it's enjoyable, and serviceable, and not too much work. If it looks a little shabby, there are five things you can do which will improve its demeanor almost immediately. You can test it, lime it, fertilize it, water it, and mow it. These procedures will have the effect of favoring the grasses in your lawn at the expense of everything else. Lawn grasses like a sweet, rich, well-watered, well-drained soil. We won't say that grasses *like* being mowed, but they tolerate it a lot better than

Phebe's Favorites for Lawns and Meadows

As for lawns, much as I hate to admit it, there is nothing so beautiful as a perfect bluegrass lawn. Any cultivar will do. It sets off any house, garden, patio, or planting. No other grass has its wonderful texture, neither fine nor coarse, with a beautiful dark, really bluish color. It just can't be beat.

The plants that I like best for a sunny meadow are the ones that come at the end of the season when little else has much color in the landscape.

Asters are wonderful meadow plants, especially the blue ones, which combine so nicely with goldenrods and black-eyed susans in the late summer. I am thinking of the New York asters that are readily available. Michaelmas daisy *(Aster frikartii)* and hybrids are super, slightly earlier asters.

Black-eyed susans are great, especially 'Goldsturm.' These flowers go on and on and on. They are wonderful for cutting, grow in all sorts of places, and can't be beat for meadows. Even in winter, the leftover cones are pretty with snow on them. Not for close inspection, these plants are great in the distance.

Not far behind the black-eyed susan and cer-tainly a companion for it, the purple (or white) coneflower is just as sturdy, and it has all the same attributes.

Shasta daisies are a must. I also love the ox-eye daisy, looking like a brush of snow in the field in July—but Shasta daisies are the cultivated equivalent, and again are wonderful for flower arrangements. They provide showy white flowers to add harmony and coolness to a summer landscape.

No meadow should be without yarrow. Unlike the daisies, yarrow's foliage is ornamental, and this plant takes its place very easily in the summer perennial garden with its ferny, soft green, lasting foliage, nice as an accent in itself. But it is also sturdy, with bright yellow, white, or red flowers all summer. I love them all, but if I have to choose, 'Moonshine' is a winner, and 'Cerise Queen', if you have the right place for "hot pink" flowers.

Getting back to goldenrods, the *Solidago* hybrids are among my favorite meadow plants for summer. Their cheery yellow blooms are a perfect foil for a blue summer sky with white wispy clouds!

most growing things. Unlike many other plants, which add leaves to the top of a stem, grass grows by expanding at the bottom of the leaf and by putting out runners along or under the surface of the earth. Most mowed plants have to start all over again and make a new stem. Grass is barely inconvenienced at all. It just carries on with what it was doing. Consequently, if you encourage all the plants in the lawn with water and fertilizer, and then mow it scrupulously, the grass will eventually begin to crowd out most other plants.

You can find details on soil testing and lawn installation and maintenance described in chapter 2, "Knowing Your Site," 16, "Putting in Plants," and 12, "Maintaining Your Landscape." If you carry out these suggestions faithfully, your lawn will improve.

For those of you who don't already have a lawn and are contemplating putting one in, how elaborate a procedure you want to engage in depends on how formal you want your lawn to look and how long you are willing to wait. If you are patient and not particularly fussy, making a lawn can be as simple as seeding the lawn and then mowing it regularly. Eventually, the grasses will take over. If you are impatient and meticulous, then you will have to prepare the soil carefully following the guidelines in chapter 16, "Putting in Plants."

Some Successful Lawns

The No-Nuthin' Lawn

When the Thomases moved into their new house, it had a big U-shaped driveway with two entrances off the street and a big arc of gravel through the front yard. The Thomases quickly became fed up with the driveway. They had a potentially elegant front yard, but it looked like a highway or a parking lot.

They wanted badly to close off one side of the driveway and seed it over so that they could have a proper front yard. But money was tight and they didn't see how they could afford to have a contractor tear up the old driveway, put down topsoil, and seed it down.

One day, Ellen Thomas was out picking up the mail and was passed—well, almost run down, actually—by a town highway truck, loaded down with what looked like topsoil. The next day, when she was out in the front yard raking stones off the lawn into the driveway, she heard the truck toiling back up the hill. So she strolled out to the road, and when it finally reached her, she flagged it down, thinking perhaps that the town had some cheap source of topsoil.

The driver said he was carting a load of road scrapings to the town dump. He explained that all winter long, as road crews sanded the road, the sand built up and the grasses and weeds encroached, narrowing the road and cutting off its drainage. Every few years, they used the grader and the front-end loader to scrape off the road edges and load the scrapings in a truck for hauling to the dump. If she wanted a load, he would dump it wherever she wanted it.

Ellen hesitated for a few seconds, worrying about lead residues and other toxins in this material. Then she decided that, for a lawn, not a garden, she would run the risk. During the afternoon, the highway department brought three loads of scrapings and dumped them on the old driveway. By pulling ahead as the truck dumped, the driver was able to even the piles out some. Just before quitting time, on the way back to the town barn in the front-end loader, the supervisor stopped to thank Ellen for saving his men so much hauling time. He took a few moments with the loader to smooth out the scrapings some more. When Ron Thomas came home from work that evening, he

The Thomases' low-maintenance lawn.

found half of his driveway covered in what looked like a very rough seedbed.

The next weekend he worked at the scrapings, smoothing them and getting out the largest rocks. It was difficult stuff to work with because it was full of clods of grass. The more he moved it around, the worse it looked. So he quit. He went down to the farm store, bought a sack of grass seed—the kind the highway department spreads on banks to prevent erosion—went home, and sowed the seed by hand. It wasn't a very neat job, but he did the best he could.

The next two weekends it rained. Ron and Ellen were busy with other things and didn't pay the old driveway much attention. The third weekend was sunny, and they went out to inspect the

driveway. It was covered with a haze of spindly, weak-looking grass seedlings. It looked awful.

But neither of them had time to do anything about it. The established grass was almost out of control in the front yard, and Ron had to mow it. Mowing the new planting was easier than turning the mower around, so he mowed it, too. The mower snarled and balked as he hit the clods and lumps in the old driveway, but he persevered. The following weekend he mowed it again, and thereafter, he mowed it whenever he mowed the front lawn, even though the thinner grass of the driveway didn't seem to need mowing as often. By the end of summer, the old driveway was covered with a thin cover of grass, clover, and weeds. The next summer, the clover grew vigorously and excluded the weeds. Ron kept mowing faithfully, and by the end of the summer noticed that the grasses were gaining on the clover.

Three summers later, the driveway was completely indistinguishable from the rest of the front lawn. Satisfied that his program of neglect was the right strategy, Ron continued to do nothing but mow his lawn. He never has raked it, limed it, or fertilized it.

Still, almost ten years after the highway department dumped it in their yard, the Thomases' driveway lawn looks almost like any other lawn in their neighborhood. The only difference is that just before the end of each mowing cycle, their lawn is covered with little blue, red, white, and orange flowers. Recently Ron got a friend who was interested in wildflowers to walk over the old driveway with him and identify all the volunteer flowers in it. She found ten species—cinquefoil, sorrel, chickweed, butter-and-eggs, Indian paintbrush, clover, buttercup, violet, dandelion, and gill-over-the-ground—as well as four different kinds of grass.

A Precious Postage Stamp

When Mrs. Johnson was moving to be near her children, a real estate agent took her to see a cottage with a tiny backyard. The backyard was a sad sight. The entire south side of the yard was dominated by an arborvitae hedge which had not been trimmed for years and which now dominated the yard. On the other side of the yard, an ancient trellis sagged under the weight of some ivy vines which were trespassing from a neighbor's groundcover. In the corner stood a rusty jungle gym and swing set. At the center of the yard, where the one shaft of sunlight fell, was a sandbox where a child had left a miniature dumptruck, fully laden with sand. As Mrs. Johnson looked over the backyard with the real estate agent, she wondered if she could ever get it into shape.

She relayed her concern to her son-in-law, who relayed it in turn to his brother, who, as luck would have it, was a landscape designer and contractor. He offered to come over and advise her on whether the yard could be salvaged or not. The designer's first question, of course, was about her plans. What sort of a yard did she hope for? She said that through all the years of raising children in the suburbs, with dogs, cats, bicycles, and cars scattered all over her sprawling lawn, she had dreamed of a yard so tiny that she could have it exactly the way she wanted it. At the center of this jewel of a yard, she had always imagined an immaculate lawn maintained with military precision, a crack regiment of bluegrass tips—not a dandelion, not even a buttercup to mar its perfect patina.

Standing in the rundown yard, the designer described his vision of a garden that would meet her needs. He would tear out the old arborvitae hedge and trellis, cart away the sandbox and the swing set, and bring in two loads of topsoil. He would install a sprinkling system so that Mrs. Johnson could water the new garden from her back step with the twist of a valve. He would put up a prefabricated cedar stockade fence around the entire yard. Against the fence he would plant several small ornamental trees: a crabapple, a dogwood, and a flowering cherry. Inside this perimeter of trees he would plant flowering shrubs—azaleas, viburnums, and rhododendrons—as well as some hostas, all plants that could take the shade of the fence and of the trees. In front of the shrubs, he would leave space for Mrs. Johnson to plant perennial and annual flowers—peonies and daisies, with accents of bright red salvia. He would edge these flowerbeds with brick.

Within the edging strip would be the lawn. He would grade the topsoil to a precise, level surface. Then he would roll out a lawn of the finest bluegrass turf, one of the new varieties that could tolerate the bit of shade that the small garden got in the early morning and late afternoon.

The landscape designer did have one concern. He wondered who Mrs. Johnson could get to take care of a lawn like that. But for Mrs. Johnson, lawn maintenance was not a problem. In fact, the pleasure of caring for the lawn herself was part of her plan. She bought the cottage, hired the designer, and had the garden put in. The job took several days, and the tiny backyard looked like a battlefield while the work was going on. But finally, it was done. The last of the workmen had gone away and taken with them the last of the tools. Mrs. Johnson went out on her back step and looked down at the smooth rolled surface of her new lawn, glistening with water from the sprinkler. She felt like a parent who has just brought a new baby home from the hospital.

As the lawn grew, she watered it meticulously. The fine grass grew quickly and soon needed to be mowed. She purchased a hand-pushed mower and mowed the grass herself. In a few months she had a fine stand of grass, which she still cares for entirely by herself. She weeds it by hand, and if any little part of the lawn ever starts to look poor, she buys another sod or two, cuts out the damaged part of the lawn, and fits in new pieces of sod. Her son-in-law visits her monthly to sharpen and oil her mower, so that it purrs as it glides across the lawn. Mrs. Johnson sweeps the clippings off her lawn and puts them in a compost bin near the fence. Into this bin she puts a coffee-can full of dehydrated cow manure once a week. From it she removes compost three times a year and sprinkles it on the emerald surface of her postage-stamp lawn.

Mrs. Johnson's postage-stamp lawn.

A Wildflower Meadow

There were many features of the new housing development that the Rossinis liked, but the lawns were not one of them. On every hand, neighbors had diligently seeded down their lawns, and by now most of them were out on their riding mowers, harvesting the fruit of their labors. In the front yard, facing the street, the Rossinis knew they must follow suit, or possibly earn the disfavor of their neighbors. But what about their backyard? It was almost an acre of ground leading down to a forest and a small stream that were on conservation land. This piece of ground wasn't easily seen from the rest of the development. Couldn't they possibly do something different?

Michael was poring over a gardening magazine one day, when he noticed an advertisement for wildflower mixes. The ad said that the seed company could send him a mix adapted to his region that would turn a bare piece of ground into a wildflower meadow. Michael decided to find out more.

By writing and calling various companies, he located a mixture especially designed for the Midwest. It had more than twenty species of wildflowers, carefully planned to provide bloom throughout

The Rossinis' wildflower meadow.

the season. They included such familiar names as black-eyed susan and cornflower, but they also included such esoteric names as coreopsis and gayfeather.

The seeds were expensive—it would cost more than $200 to seed his acre. With such an investment, Michael decided to follow the instructions of the seed company to a T. He did his work early in the spring when soil moisture was most reliable in his region. Before seeding, he asked a farmer in the neighborhood to disk up the acre to a depth of 6 inches and rake it. He then borrowed a cyclone seeder from his local garden store and seeded the acre, first going up and down, then back and forth, each time setting the spreader for half the application rate. Included in the seeding with the wildflowers was a "nonaggressive" grass, a fescue, which would help hold the soil but which would not dominate the wildflowers. He did not fertilize, because the seed company warned him that fertilization encourages grass growth. He then set about raking the seed in lightly. For such a large area, this was a laborious and tedious job, and it took him the better part of a day.

At first he was lucky with the weather. Solid soaking rains fell during each of the first three weeks. But then the weather turned dry, and after ten days Michael realized that he was going to have to water. He bought extra lengths of hose and a new sprinkler that could reach an area 50 feet in diameter. To water the entire acre required him to move the sprinkler nearly 30 times. Fortunately, the following week the rains came again, and throughout the summer they were fairly reliable.

A year later, Michael is fairly well satisfied with his meadow. He is midway through the summer and has already identified at least half of the species in the mix, but he does have the impression that not as many of the showy annual flowers came up this year as in the first year. The flowers have taken better in some parts of the acre than in others, and Michael thinks the dry period may have had something to do with it. His neighbors have not complained, so on the whole, he considers the experiment a success. He is happy not to be a member of the mower brigade every Saturday morning, or at least, not a member for such a long time. Last fall he realized too late that he would need a special mower to cut the meadow. He prevailed on the farmer to bring over his old cutter bar and cut the field. This fall, Michael has decided, he will have to buy his own small cutter bar to do the job.

One thing is clear to Michael. Without the aid of the farmer to disk, rake, and cut his mini-meadow, it would have been a disaster. He tells anybody who asks that attempting a meadow of over a quarter-acre without the proper mechanized equipment is folly.

Wrap-up

To stroll on your own beautiful grass lawn of a summer's evening is a soothing and nostalgic experience. It recalls memories of hot summer evenings when the family gathered to talk, watch the fireflies, and wait for night to bring a breeze or a thunderstorm to cool things off. Although a lawn is a cherished American tradition, it is not natural. To keep a lawn healthy and vigorous over a generation is like defying gravity. The more meticulous the lawn, the more one defies the natural order of things in one's yard, and the greater is the labor that one must perform. We urge you to keep an informal lawn. Mow it regularly, water it in times of drought if you like, fertilize it from time to time if you must. But do not rake it regularly, and do not use harsh chemicals on it. We think you will have a lovely lawn which is more informal than your neighbors', but also a lot less work.

Plants for Meadows

Plant Name	Meadow Feature	Description	Culture
Bird's eyes (*Gilia tricolor*)	Small, fragrant, trumpet-shaped flowers, lavender and white with gold throats; spring	Ferny foliage and multiple flower clusters are borne on erect 2-foot stems	Full sun; drought tolerant; self-sows; annual; widely adaptable
Black-eyed susan (*Rudbeckia hirta*)	Yellow-gold daisy-like flowers with velvety dark brown centers; summer and fall	Low rosette of lance-shaped, hairy leaves; flowers are borne on 2-foot stems covered with barbs	Full sun to partial shade; moderate water needs; grows in sandy or clay soils; perennial; widely adaptable
Blanketflower (*Gaillardia aristata*)	Large, deep red, daisy-like flowers, tipped with gold; summer and fall	Mounds of gray-green, lance-shaped leaves; flowers are borne on 18- to 24-inch stems	Full sun to partial shade; drought tolerant; thrives in heat; average to poor well-drained soil; perennial; Zones 3-9
Blazing star (*Mentzelia lindleyi*)	Very showy, yellow, 2-inch-wide, saucer-shaped flowers; spring	Deeply toothed leaves; flowers are borne on 2-foot stems	Full sun; drought tolerant; well-drained clay or sandy soil; annual; West Coast and Rockies
Blue-eyed grass (*Sisyrinchium bellum*)	Violet-blue, inch-wide flowers with yellow centers; spring	Flowers are borne on foot-long strap-like stems; grass-like clumps, but this plant is actually in the lily family	Full sun to partial shade; drought tolerant; any soil; perennial; West Coast
Blue flax (*Linum lewisii*)	Lovely blue, 5-petaled flowers; spring and summer	Needle-like foliage; flowers are borne on 2-foot stems	Full sun; drought tolerant; well-drained soil; perennial; widely adaptable
Butter-and-eggs (*Linaria vulgaris*)	Lemon-yellow, snapdragon-like flowers in spikes; summer	Needle-like foliage; flowers are borne on 1- to 3-foot stems	Full sun to partial shade; drought tolerant; self-sows; annual; widely adaptable
Butterfly weed (*Asclepias tuberosa*)	Very showy, small, bright orange flowers in clusters; draws butterflies, especially monarchs; July and August	Shrubby, 2-foot-tall plants; foliage is large, lance-shaped, and coarse; flowers are followed by milkweed-like pods	Full sun; poor, well-drained soil; perennial; Zones 3-8
California poppy (*Eschscholzia californica*)	Glorious, bright orange, 2½-inch-wide flowers; summer and fall	Ferny foliage; flowers are borne on 18-inch, slender stems	Full sun; drought and heat tolerant; self-sows; annual; perennial in California; Western half of the U.S.
Chicory (*Cichorium intybus*)	Pale blue, single, rayed flowers, taller than most meadow plants; summer and fall	Green-gray foliage; basal leaves are large and deeply toothed; upper leaves are much smaller; flowers are borne along 3- to 5-foot stalk	Full sun; drought tolerant; clay soil; perennial; widely adaptable

Plant Name	Meadow Feature	Description	Culture
Cornflower, bachelor's buttons (*Centaurea cyanus*)	Intense true-blue flowers with many small petals that give them a pincushion look; spring and summer	Flowers are borne on 2- to 2½-foot stems; gray-green, slightly fuzzy, strap-like leaves	Full sun to partial shade; drought and salt tolerant; annual; widely adaptable, but prefers cool climates
Crimson clover (*Trifolium incarnatum*)	Very showy, scarlet clover-heads up to 4 inches long; summer	Small, slightly hairy, trifoliate clover leaves; flowers are borne on 2½-foot stems	Full sun to partial shade; drought tolerant; perennial, but easily winter-killed in North; widely adaptable
Daisy, ox-eye daisy (*Chrysanthemum leucanthemum*)	Wonderful, 2-inch heads of crisp white ray-petals surrounding a yellow center; early summer	Toothed, dark green leaves; flowers are borne on 1- to 2-foot stems	Full sun; any soil; perennial; widely adaptable
Evening primrose (*Oenothera lamarckiana*)	Clusters of brilliant yellow, 2- to 3-inch, glossy, single flowers; open in late afternoon; summer	Spear-shaped, dark green leaves; flowers are borne on 3½-foot stems	Full sun to partial shade; drought tolerant; annual; widely adaptable
Farewell-to-spring (*Clarkia amoena*)	Showy pink to red, cup-shaped flowers; summer	Spear-shaped leaves with crenellated edges; flowers are borne on erect stems, up to 2½ feet tall, with multiple flowers on each stem	Full sun; drought tolerant; self-sows; annual; West Coast
Globe gilia, blue thimbleflower (*Gilia capitata*)	Clear blue, globe-shaped flowers; spring	Bushy, 2-foot-tall plants covered with flowers	Full sun to shade; drought tolerant; annual; West Coast and Rockies
Gloriosa daisy (*Rudbeckia gloriosa*)	Daisy-like flowers 4 inches long, pumpkin-yellow with mahogany centers; summer and fall	Flowers are borne on 2- to 3-foot stems	Full sun; perennial; widely adaptable
Goldenrod (*Solidago* spp.)	Large, glorious, showy, golden-plumed flower-heads; August and September	Slender, usually toothed leaves; flowers are borne on erect, 2- to 7-foot stems	Full sun; average to poor, well-drained soil; perennial; Zones 4–10
Goldsturm black-eyed susan (*Rudbeckia fulgida* 'Goldsturm')	Daisy-like flowers, 3 to 4 inches tall; deep golden-yellow petals and blackish brown, conical centers; July through September	Large, coarse, spear-shaped leaves; flowers bloom profusely on 2-foot-tall, many-branched stems	Full sun; average, well-drained soil; perennial; Zones 3-9
Indian blanket (*Gaillardia pulcella*)	These daisy-like flowers have finely toothed bright red petals with a yellow fringe; summer	Low rosette of lance-shaped leaves; flowers are borne singly or in multiples on 1- to 2-foot stems	Full sun; drought and heat tolerant; self-sows; sandy soils; annual; widely adaptable

(continued)

Plants for Meadows—*continued*

Plant Name	Meadow Feature	Description	Culture
Lance-leaved coreopsis (*Coreopsis lanceolata*)	Gorgeous, pumpkin yellow, daisy-like blooms with toothed petals for a fringed effect; summer	Lance-shaped, basal evergreen leaves, 3 to 6 inches long; flowers are borne on 2- to 3-foot stems	Full sun to partial shade; moderate water needs; any soil; perennial; widely adaptable
Mexican hat, prairie coneflower (*Ratibida columnaris*)	Red, daisy-like flowers with cone-shaped brown centers; yellow variety is called prairie coneflower; summer and fall	Flowers are borne on 2-foot-tall, branching stems; airy, open growth habit	Full sun; drought tolerant; any soil; perennial; widely adaptable
Michaelmas daisy (*Aster ×frikartii*)	2½-inch, lavender-blue, daisy-like flowers with golden centers; June through September	Stiff stems with lance-shaped leaves; 2½ to 3 feet tall	Full sun; average, well-drained soil; perennial; Zones 5-9
New England Aster (*Aster novae-angliae*)	2-inch, deep purple flowers borne in loose clusters; August through October	Many-branched stem with lanceolate leaves; 3 to 5 feet tall	Full sun; average, well-drained soil; perennial; Zones 4–9
Plains coreopsis (*Coreopsis tinctoria*)	Bull's-eye, daisy-like flowers, with brown centers circled by maroon, then by yellow; summer and fall	Profusion of blooms from thread-like foliage; flowers are borne on 2- to 3-foot stems	Full sun to partial shade; drought tolerant; self-sows; annual; widely adaptable
Purple coneflower (*Echinacea purpurea*) 'White Luster'	Lavender-purple, daisy-like flowers curve down from orangish centers; 'White Luster' is a white variety; summer and fall	Low rosette of spear-shaped, dark green leaves, some leaves are borne on 2- to 3-foot flower stems	Full sun; drought tolerant in cooler areas; rich, sandy, well-drained soil; perennial; Zones 3-9
Rocky Mountain penstemon (*Penstemon strictus*)	Deep blue, snapdragon-like flowers in spikes; summer	Lance-shaped evergreen leaves are borne along 2-foot stems	Full sun to partial shade; drought tolerant; perennial; widely adaptable
Scarlet flax (*Linum grandiflorum* 'Rubrum')	Deep red, 5-petaled, single flowers; spring and summer	Needle-like foliage; flowers are borne singly or in multiples on 1- to 2-foot stems	Full sun to partial shade; drought and heat tolerant; self-sows; any soil; annual; widely adaptable
Scarlet larkspur (*Delphinium cardinale*)	Commanding red flowers in spikes; summer	Flowers are borne on 4-foot spikes; goes dormant in summer after blooming	Full sun to partial shade; moderate water needs; perennial; West Coast and Southwest
Scarlet sage (*Salvia coccinea*)	Showy, bright red flowers; summer	Roughly triangular, opposite leaves, with irregular margins; tubular flowers are borne on 2-foot stems	Full sun; drought tolerant; perennial; South

Plant Name	Meadow Feature	Description	Culture
Shasta daisy (*Chrysanthemum ×superbum*) 'Alaska' 'Cobham Gold'	Showy, 3- to 5-inch, daisy-like flowers, white with gold centers; some varieties are double, and 'Cobham Gold' is creamy yellow; June through August	Basal rosette of long, narrow, glossy, toothed, dark green leaves; flowers are borne on 2-foot stems	Full sun; rich, well-drained soil; perennial; Zones 4–9
Showy blue gilia (*Gilia leptantha*)	Deep blue, globe-shaped flowers; summer	Fine, thread-like foliage; plants are bushy, 1 to 2 feet tall; profuse flowering; neat growing habit	Full sun to partial shade; drought tolerant; self-sows; annual; West Coast, Rockies, and Southwest
Sunflower (*Helianthus annuus*)	Large, yellow, daisy-like flowers with prominent brown centers; summer and fall	Coarse, large leaves; plants are bushy, upright, 6 feet tall; profuse flowering; 3- to 6-inch flowers are borne singly or in multiples	Full sun; drought tolerant; any soil; annual; widely adaptable
Texas bluebonnet (*Lupinus subcarnosus*) (*L. texensis*)	Spikes of blue flowers with white or yellow spots on standards; wing petals are light blue and inflated; *L. texensis* has dark blue wing petals	Foliage compound, 5 or 6 obtuse or rounded leaflets; *L. texensis* leaflets are acute; flowers are borne on 1-foot spikes	Full sun; drought tolerant; annual; Southwest
Toadflax, spurred snapdragon (*Linaria maroccana*)	Bicolor, snapdragon-like flowers; spring and summer	Light green, needle-like foliage; flowers are borne on 2-foot stems	Full sun to partial shade; drought tolerant; annual; widely adaptable
White evening primrose (*Oenothera pallida*)	Large, fragrant white flowers open in late afternoon; summer	Spear-like leaves on 14-inch stems topped with flower clusters	Full sun; drought tolerant; self-sows; annual; West Coast, Rockies, and Southwest
Wild yarrow (*Achillea millefolium*) 'Cerise Queen'	Decorative, aromatic, ferny foliage; cream white, flat panicles of flowers; 'Cerise Queen' and other cultivars in pinks and reds; summer and fall	Feathery, evergreen foliage; flowers are borne on 2-foot stems	Full sun; drought tolerant; any soil; perennial; widely adaptable
Wind poppy (*Stylomecon heterophylla*)	Brilliant, tangerine flowers; early summer	Compact, 1- to 2-foot plants covered with blooms	Shade; moderate water needs; annual; California and Southwest
Yarrow (*Achillea filipendulina*) 'Coronation Gold' 'Gold Plate'	Mustard yellow, 3-inch, flat-topped panicles of flowers; June through August	Feathery, gray-green foliage; flowers are borne on 3- to 4-foot stems	Full sun; average to poor, dry soil; perennial; Zones 3–8

CHAPTER 5

Flower Gardens

*I*n your neighborhood, there's sure to be at least one beautiful flower garden that everybody envies. You crane your neck to see it as you drive by on your way to work. Walking down to the corner to get groceries, you detour by the garden to discover what new flowers are in bloom. When you take the dog out for his bedtime stroll, you arrange to pass the garden again, hoping to catch its fragrance on the night wind.

Every time you go by the garden, it seems, the proprietors are out working in it. Often the owners of such a garden are an elderly couple. She is picking off faded flowers, he is staking tall annuals. She is setting young bedding plants, he is spading soil. They work at a leisurely pace, enjoying themselves. They gladly come to the garden gate to answer your questions. They always urge you to come in to "take a tour," and when you do, they send you on your way with a gift: a spectacular peony blossom in spring, a half-dozen roses in summer, a great bunch of chrysanthemums in fall, or some dried strawflowers early in winter.

Often you have asked yourself how you could have a flower garden like theirs. Their secrets are experience and dedication. That people with spectacular flower gardens are often elderly is no coincidence. To have a large, varied, and ever-blooming flower garden requires a lot of knowledge, both of plants in general and of the particular garden's site. That sort of know-how accumulates gradually over the years. No book can give it to you. But we can help you get started. And once started, you will experiment and learn more until, in time, your flowerbeds will be as beautiful as any in your neighborhood.

Six Issues to Think About

Before you begin selecting and arranging your flowers, there are some basic questions that it will be helpful to ask yourself. Some of the questions will require definite answers before you can begin to plant. Others won't be answered soon, but thinking about them will help you settle the more specific issues.

Do You Want Your Flowerbeds to Be Formal, Informal, or Some Combination?

Broadly speaking, there are two types of flowerbeds: formal and informal. "Formal" flowerbeds call to mind the gardens at the grand chateaus of France: crisp linear beds of gorgeous annual flowers set out in disciplined geometric patterns, ranks of scarlet salvia or wax begonias flanked by borders of gray dusty miller. Every angle is a right angle; every curve is a piece of circle or classical ellipse. Every feature on the right is balanced by a feature on the left. And all around, you hear the urgent muffled consultations and the snip-snipping of expert gardeners at work.

"Informal" flowerbeds make you think of the gardens at some of the country houses of England: Here, the beds are arranged in gracious sweeping curves. As you survey the garden, everything seems to be in the right place, but you can't quite say why. The curves seem to wander at random, yet the effect is pleasing and harmonious. Within the beds, the flowers are arranged in flowing masses, flocks of sweet alyssum and pinks shepherded by delphiniums, hollyhocks, and lilies. The design seems natural, simple, and unaffected, but everywhere there is evidence of the subtle scheming of the designer. The arrangements seem always to bring out some feature of the plants: the color of their blooms, the texture of their leaves, their shape. And overall, the garden's bloom is an intricately orchestrated sequence which unfolds season after season.

These two extremes of formality and informality would not be worth mentioning except that we all seem to carry them in the back of our minds whenever we start to design anything, particularly a flower garden. Somewhere in between the two, we bet that you'll find most of the flowerbeds in your neighborhood. The neighbor on your right may not exactly have been thinking of Versailles when he put in his bedding plants, but the balanced, regimented ranks of begonias that line his straight brick walk each summer are definitely formal. The neighbor on your left may never have been to Anne Hathaway's cottage near Stratford-on-Avon, yet the flood of sweet william spilling out onto her lawn is informal.

Don't confuse informal with sloppy. An informal garden must be as scrupulously planned and maintained as a formal one. Its informality lies not in its ease of maintenance but in its subtlety of line. In a formal garden, it's easy to see that things are "right," the circles are perfect, the lines are straight. In an informal garden, the patterns are less evident. But an informal garden still must be designed, cultivated, weeded, and fertilized. In some ways, an informal flowerbed is harder to design than a formal one, because you can't make your decisions with a ruler and compass. The decision making is more intuitive.

The question of whether your garden is formal or informal probably won't ever be completely settled in your mind. Most people's gardens are a combination of formal and informal elements. The straight front walk of your house is a formal element, but the curves in the lawn that edge your foundation plants are an informal element. Although you need not decide between these styles of gardening, it helps to recognize them. Are you standing in your garden with four plants, asking yourself, "Shall I put two on one side and two on the other, or shall I put three on one side and one on the other?" Are you unable to decide between making the edge of the bed a right angle or a billowy curve? Do you wonder whether to set your flowers out in ranks like soldiers, or in flocks like sheep? Such choices may be confusing, but at least it's some comfort to think that you are not alone: Striking a balance between formal and informal elements has confounded gardeners for at least two centuries.

How Large Should Your
Flower Garden Be?

If you're just starting out in flower gardening, take it easy at first. Don't go hog-wild. More than any other form of gardening, flower gardening should be pure pleasure. Your flowerbeds should be enjoyable to work in as well as to see. Don't turn flower gardening into a chore through poor planning or an overly ambitious design. The elegant centerpiece of homegrown flowers on your dining room table won't look half so beautiful if you are sitting down to dinner with an aching back. Begin your flower-gardening career with a project that's going to be easy and fun. We say: start small, start simple, start *successful.*

For a freestanding flowerbed, a nice starting space is about 120 square feet. Of course, you can work with a smaller bed. You could put a few flowers along the front walk, around your number post or mailbox, or at the foot of a birdbath. But we think 120 square feet—a rectangle 8 by 15 feet or 6 by 20 feet, or a circle 12 feet in diameter—is about as small as a flower garden can get and still provide enough space for arranging plants in interesting ways. A flowerbed is most effective if you have room to mass the flowers. A bed 4 to 5 feet wide is ideal. If it's much narrower, there won't be room to group plants and include a pleasing variety. Wider than that, and you have to trample down some parts of the bed to reach others.

Where Should You Put Your Flowerbeds?

The most important consideration in deciding where to place your flowerbeds is sunlight.

Although some flowers tolerate shade, most grow best in full sun. Full sun means, at the very least, six hours of sunlight grouped around midday. If you want to grow a flowerbed in a place with less than full sun, choose shade-tolerant flowers such as impatiens, wax begonias, coleus, astilbes, lungwort, nicotiana, hostas, epimedium, or Bethlehem sage. (Look for other recommendations on shade gardening in chapter 11, "Woodswalks.")

Topsoil and subsoil will also determine the site of your flowerbed, but of the two, subsoil is the more important. Topsoils can be enriched with compost, peat moss, and other natural amendments. Moreover, many flowers can be grown on poorer soils as long as there is plenty of sunlight. The subsoil, however, often limits the success of a garden, because subsoil determines drainage. Correcting poor drainage requires major reconstruction: burying tiles, raising all the flowerbeds, or digging runoff channels. Consequently, choose a site for your new flowerbed that is well drained.

The larger your proposed flower garden and the more inexperienced you are at flower gardening, the more important it is to pick a site with good topsoil, subsoil, and sun exposure. The relationship between size and placement will be clearer if you compare the results of two flowerbeds. Imagine that one is a tiny bed in good soil in full sunlight, which you plant on the south side of the boundary fence with your north neighbor. The other is a large, shady bed, which your neighbor has unwisely planted in construction rubble on the north side of the fence. Both beds begin with perky bedding plants—petunias in red, white, and red-and-white stripes.

On your side of the fence, the small, bright bed will be the highlight of your yard. Because of the bed's manageable size, you will be able to maintain it with a minimum of time spent weeding and watering. The petunias will have healthy green leaves and robust blossoms. On the other side of the fence, the plants will be drab, anemic creatures covered with aphids, mildew, and whiteflies. The stems will grow too long and fall over. There will be very few blooms, and they'll be half the size of yours. Your neighbor will have to be constantly weeding and spraying if he wants to just keep his plants alive. Moreover, the large size of the bed will make these chores seem eternal.

After you've pinpointed the parts of your yard that are sunny and have decent soil and drainage, you can begin to think about design considerations. A flowerbed is not only a place where you put flowers, but also a part of the design of your yard. However big or small your flowerbed is, it should fit in its place. For more advice on how to site and shape your flowerbeds, look in the section on design principles in chapter 12, "Things to Keep in Mind." For a formal effect, plant flowerbeds as edgings for linear elements such as walks, driveways, and fences. For a less formal effect, lay out flowerbeds as interesting shapes of their own, burgeoning out from edges or standing free as "islands" within the lawn.

Remember to place the bed where you can see and enjoy it. Don't be unrealistic about what can and cannot be seen from a distance. We don't recommend putting a border with a background of shrubs 50 feet away from the terrace where you plan to sit and look at it, unless, of course, the effect you are seeking is of a distant haze of color. For its details to be enjoyed, a flowerbed should be within about 20 feet of the person viewing it. Flowerbeds arranged around an arbor or bench are best. They allow you to actually view the flower garden from its midst.

How the bed is framed makes a tremendous difference in how well it can be seen. Because gardeners naturally focus on the flowers within the bed, they often neglect to think about the back-

ground against which the flowerbed is seen. The frame can be as important to the success of the garden as the flowers themselves. Plant your bed against a dark gray stone wall, and its color will show from dozens of feet away. But plant it against a row of deciduous shrubs or a field of long grass, and your flowers may simply disappear into the background. Think of your flowerbeds as part of the total design of your yard, and place them where they will be seen and will enhance the beauty of the trees, shrubs, and lawn around them.

The basic criterion in framing is whether the bed "looks good" where it is. To be successful, the bed should not appear to be just placed at random but be connected in some way to the features around it. It can appear as part of a larger display, such as a grouping of perennial flowers backed by azaleas and a cedar fence. Or it can appear as part of a pattern, such as a flowerbed which marks the boundary between two different parts of a yard. Flowerbeds are often well framed by horizontal elements such as driveways and walks or vertical elements such as buildings, walls, fences, hedges, or arrangements of shrubs and trees. Vertical elements have the advantage of not only framing the bed when seen nearby from above, but also when seen at a distance from the side.

The best places to display flowers are, fortunately, the easiest places to grow them. Perennial gardens in open, sunny spots with lawn or paving to set them off are ideal. The border of a south-facing terrace is a wonderful place to edge with a flowerbed, and, of course, an exceptionally fine place to display one.

Another important consideration in deciding where to put your flowerbeds is the location of existing beds. The shape, size, and composition of a new bed should harmonize with established beds if you plan to keep the other plantings. Whether you choose to keep it or not, if you already have a perennial flowerbed in your yard, don't, for heaven's sake, till it up until you know what's in it. It's true that rejuvenating an old perennial flowerbed is a lot of work. Usually such beds are full of weeds, grass, even tree or shrub roots. But such a bed can be a priceless resource. Remember, everything growing in it will obviously live in your area and is naturalized to your particular garden. Even if you don't want to leave these perennials in their present locations, you may want to transplant them

later to a new bed. In any case, do not destroy them until you are sure you have no use for them. Some may be delightful heirloom varieties that are no longer available.

Do You Want Annuals, Perennials, Biennials, Bulbs, or a Combination?

Another crucial way in which flowers differ is in their pattern of cultivation. Annuals, perennials,

Phebe's Favorites for Flower Gardens

This is a hard selection to make because there are so many wonderful perennials and annuals. I tend to be biased toward perennials that can be used as cut flowers, as I like to keep flowers from my garden in the house, on the dining room table and in the kitchen.

My favorite perennial is not a perennial at all, but really a small shrub, the tree peony. These plants need some shade, but have the most beautiful plates of blooms—yellows, pinks, reds, whites, singles, doubles. I once knew someone who had many tree peonies, and always gave a spring garden party around these wonderful plants.

Besides tree peonies, herbaceous peonies are wonderful. It is hard to pick varieties because it really depends on color, but 'Festiva Maxima' is a backbone type, double white with red flecks; 'Mons. Jules Elie' and 'Sarah Bernhardt' are nice pinks. When choosing, it is worth the effort to select early and late bloomers to get a longer season.

Although some gardeners feel that mildew is such a problem with summer phlox that they refuse to grow it, I don't agree. I do agree that this plant is for the really sunny, well-drained perennial garden, and I try to surround it with more attractive foliage plants so the doggy base of the phlox doesn't show, but I think it's a stalwart flower for the July garden. Fragrance, and lots of pretty colors to choose from (but no

yellows), make this a worthwhile plant. 'Fairy's Petticoat', 'Sir John Falstaff', and the related white, 'Miss Lingard' *(Phlox carolina)* get my vote.

Every spring I am tempted to tuck a rose in somewhere. It is hard to beat roses for summer flowers, and I feel you don't have to have a rose garden to enjoy them. The small hybrid tea roses are probably best for a perennial garden, but some of the grandiflora and miniature roses will also fit (floribundas too!). It is hard to equal a rose for beauty of form and fragrance, and the potential color combinations are endless. As for sharing these plants with Japanese beetles, just put the roses in a sunny location and be prepared for a few holes, which won't detract at all from their beauty. Don't forget some lavender nearby to complement the roses with their bluish flower spikes and scented gray foliage.

No garden should be without iris. The blues and whites of Siberian iris are a nice foil for peonies and daylilies. Bearded iris are spectacular, and again offer endless color possibilities. I am not a devotee of the all-iris borders, but clumps of iris are a must in mixed borders, where their leaves give a nice vertical accent for the rest of the season. In July, Japanese iris are just as beautiful as beardeds, with their graceful, elongated stems and leaves, and open, flattish fleur-de-lis flowers in blues, whites, and pinks. These iris are also lovely beside water.

biennials, and bulbs all require mulch or cultivation to keep down weeds during the summer, but they differ otherwise in the rewards they give and in the pattern of care they require. Throughout the growing season, annuals give a showy display, often of bright, primary colors. They demand a lot of work in the spring, preparing and seeding the beds or caring for the young bedding plants. Once their growing season is over, however, the plants can be removed and the soil left tilled, mulched, and ready for the spring, or planted with a cover crop to increase fertility. Keeping annuals under control is rarely a problem, because the plants die down each year. Unwanted seeds that germinate the following year may be dealt with like any other weed.

Perennials and biennials characteristically give a more subtle display of color, usually over a shorter season, but the care they require can be distributed over the season pretty much to suit the

The artemisias and santolinas are a must for gray foliage accents in every perennial garden. They cool down hot reds and pinks, complement soft blues, pinks, and yellows, and give a cooling and welcome break to the dominant greens in the border. These plants can create order out of chaos in the flowerbed.

Every garden needs a blue flower or two, or related color such as lavender or purple, for contrast and accent. Some blue flowers are the campanulas (bellflowers), balloonflower, and veronicas. Some are spiky, some are low, but all species are dependable. Bellflowers, which are mostly June-flowering, and balloonflowers, summer performers, have bell-shaped flowers of blue and white. Carpathian bellflower, great bellflower, and peach-leaved bellflower are all attractive. Veronicas, like clump speedwell and spike speedwell, have spiky blooms pretty much throughout the summer. Spike speedwell also comes in pink, red, and white.

No garden can be without a lily or two. The August hybrids are beautiful, often fragrant, and can be tucked into any garden. I love the *Lilium auratum* derivatives, huge whites with recurved petals, beautiful markings, and wonderful fragrance. Lilies are useful for color in a tight spot, and also add height and nodding charm to the garden. There are so many nice ones.

To many gardeners, daylilies would certainly be a backbone plant. I find them a little overwhelming, and feel you need a really large border to accommodate many varieties. I consider daylilies strong enough, with the possibility of a very long blooming season (certainly June through August), to stand on their own: for instance, a stone wall along a driveway lined with daylilies. I guess I am a little prejudiced because they do not make good cut flowers, but certainly they are handsome in bloom, with strong foliage for a dominant position in any garden border. Try a large clump of daylilies at the base of a tree. They combine showy, erect flowers with wonderful, waterfall-like foliage that remains attractive throughout the season. I discovered the little yellow 'Stella d'Oro' still blooming on December 1!

I like to add these annuals for summer-long color and cut flowers: Snapdragon produces wonderful cut flowers of many colors. Dahlias are handsome too. You can grow them as bedding plants or save the roots from year to year. Like lilies, they can be worked into the garden for color as well as height, from 8 feet to 2 feet. Petunia hybrids add carefree flash in virtually every color and many combinations. Blue salvia hybrids are much better than perennial salvia, with blue blooms until frost. Nasturtium is my favorite edging flower.

convenience of the gardener. Maintaining the health of a perennial, keeping it well fed, and weeding it are complicated by the fact that the plant stands in place year after year, so that you don't start fresh each year with a fertilized, weeded bed. The beds must be mulched, or you'll have to weed perennials pretty much any time the ground isn't frozen. Other work, such as dividing the plants or pruning to contain them, can be carried on at various times when they are not in bloom. If you want to maintain a balance in your garden, perennials must be kept under control or the more aggressive of them will push out all the others and take over your garden. Biennials are treated as perennials during their two years of life, then pulled like annuals at the end of the second growing season.

Bulbs characteristically give a single bloom over a short period. However, many kinds of bulbs divide naturally, so that in time they may produce spectacular drifts of flowers. Apart from the usual growing-season cultivation, bulbs demand care in the early spring or fall when they are put in the ground and fertilized. Some tender varieties of bulb, such as dahlias, fancy-leaved caladiums, tuberous begonias, and gladioli, are dug in the fall (to protect them from the freezing of the soil), stored over winter, and replanted in the spring.

Most flower gardeners grow both perennials and annuals. They may have a flowerbed that is filled with perennials, then edge it with some particularly colorful, low-growing annuals such as petunias, impatiens, or marigolds. Or they may have a bed that is basically composed of annuals, anchored with a few hardy perennial favorites, such as daylilies or iris.

When Do You Want Your Flowers to Bloom?

It's useful to know when you want your garden to be in bloom. Well, you might say, I want my garden to bloom all the time. Why not? The reason is, of course, that each flower has its season and so, for each season, you will need different flowers. And unless you are going to have only one color and size of plant for every season, you will want a variety of flowers blooming at the same time. The longer you want your garden to bloom, the more varied and bigger your plant selection must be. A garden that appears to be in full bloom through the entire growing season is the hallmark of the master gardener.

Consequently, it makes sense, particularly at the beginning of your flower-gardening career, to concentrate on one season and get it right. For most people, all the seasons don't have the same importance for gardening purposes. You may be away during several weeks of the summer, or concentrate on your work in the fall, or be a late riser when it comes to spring gardening. Consider doing yourself a favor and eliminating the seasons that aren't important to you. Concentrate on plants that bloom in the seasons that are. To find out more about matching flowers to bloom season, consult our table, "Plants for Flower Gardens," at the end of this chapter. Good books on flower color and seasonal bloom include Penelope Hobhouse's *Color in Your Garden* (Boston: Little, Brown and Company, 1985) and Jeff and Marilyn Cox's *The Perennial Garden* (Emmaus, Pa.: Rodale Press, 1985).

What Colors, Fragrances, and Textures Do You Want in Your Flowerbeds?

Flowers are like a very complex "palette" from which you compose your flowerbed. Like the colors in an artist's palette, there are flowers in every imaginable shade. Colors can be vibrant or subtle, deep or pastel, solid or variegated. Different colors can enhance each other. Reds appear particularly intense against green foliage, yellows and blues more vibrant in each other's company than by themselves. Yellow tends to blend with green foliage, but remains distinct when paired with gray or burgundy; similarly, purple and blue become indistinct and confusing when planted together. Grays help modulate bright colors, whites and blues to define and organize them. All these relationships are as true of flower colors as they are of watercolors or oils.

But the flower gardener's palette is in many ways more complex than the painter's. Flowers vary not only in color but in fragrance, texture, shape, and size. Flowers can be odorless or fragrant, they can be coarse-leaved or fine, fat or skinny, tall or short. Flowers can be flat "singles," full "doubles," or anywhere between. The petals can be glossy like a tulip's, papery like an iris's, velvety like a rose's. Foliage can be powdery like a dusty miller's, ruffled like a coleus's, waxy like a begonia's. All these characteristics present different artistic opportunities for the flower gardener.

Selecting and Arranging Plants

Once you know where and how big your flowerbed is going to be, it is time to begin selecting plants. The first step in making your selections is to make up a wish list. On the wish list, note down all the flowers you ever wanted to have in a garden. You should include the plants that you have admired in your neighbors' gardens, the plants you remember fondly from your grandparents' gardens, striking plants from famous gardens you've visited, and anything else you have yearned for in catalogs and gardening magazines. Now is the time to let your imagination sail. Think not only about color, but also about the textures and forms of the plants. Some plants which don't have beautiful blossoms have wonderful foliage. Remember that the shape, color, and texture of the leaves—to say nothing of

the plants themselves—can be as important as the bloom, especially in the case of perennials. (Think about fans of sword-like iris foliage, gray-leaved santolina, or handsome dark green peony bushes that remain on display all season though the flowers last only a week or so.)

From the giddy heights of your wish list, you must somehow get down to reality. Look up each plant that you have wished for in a seed or nursery catalog and find out about its basic characteristics. Learn whether it's a perennial, biennial, annual, or bulb, what its color and bloom season are, what zones it's appropriate for, when you can plant it, what its soil, moisture, and sunlight requirements are, whether it's tall or low-growing, and whether it's bushy or spindly. Cross off your wish list the plants which are not appropriate for your climate, soil, or sunlight conditions, and any which don't correspond to your preference for bloom, seasonal maintenance requirements, and color. Be absolutely rigorous about eliminating unsuitable plants, particularly if you are planning your first flower garden. The list which remains might be called your feasible wish list. Now arrange this list in order of preference.

Just as we think it is worthwhile to make a scale drawing of your whole yard, we think it makes a lot of sense to make a scale model of your flowerbeds. You will need all the tools suggested in chapter 13, "Doing Your Own Design," and a big set of children's watercolor felt markers. Determine the scale so that the whole bed fits on a convenient sheet of paper. We find a scale of ½ inch to 1 foot often gives a good size.

The next step is to make scale-model "plants." Cut out lots of little circles to represent plants of different sizes: 1½-inch circles (equivalent to 3 feet in diameter) can represent large plants, 1-inch circles (equivalent to 2 feet in diameter) can represent medium-sized plants, and ½-inch circles (equiv-

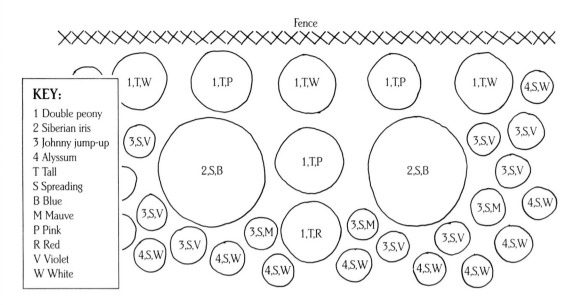

Fence

KEY:
1 Double peony
2 Siberian iris
3 Johnny jump-up
4 Alyssum
T Tall
S Spreading
B Blue
M Mauve
P Pink
R Red
V Violet
W White

As this sample layout shows, designing a flowerbed on paper with cut-out circles lets you easily add or subtract plants or move them around.

alent to 1 foot in diameter) can represent small plants. Look at the first plant on your wish list. How many plants of that variety do you want in your flowerbed? Phebe encourages you to arrange plants in groups rather than lines. She thinks that groups of three, five, and seven seem to work visually better than groups of two, four, and six. Don't stint on your favorite plants. If you limit yourself to one or two of everything, your flowerbed will look more like a Noah's ark than an enticing design.

Cut out some circles appropriate to the mature size of your favorite plant, write the number 1 on them, put some color on the circle to represent the flower color, and an abbreviation to help remind you of its characteristics. You might, for instance, write "F" to remind you that the plant blooms in the fall, or "T" to remind you that it is a tall plant. Jot down whatever you think will be important to you.

Set the circles down on your plan in a way that looks attractive. If you are working with a tall

plant, put its circles at the back of the bed, if the bed is to be viewed from the front only. If the bed is an island bed to be viewed from more than one side, put the tallest plants in the center. Surround them with plants of intermediate height, proceeding in descending order to the shortest (even prostrate) plants at the front or outside edges of the bed. Now is the time to put into effect all your decisions about formality and informality, height, color, and texture.

Place circles to represent your second-favorite plant, then your third, and so forth until the circles begin to touch. At this point, stop adding circles. "Oh!" you say in horror, "I haven't gotten very far down my list." Nevertheless, resist the temptation to fill up your bed with all the plants you ever wanted. Crowding the beds will not only make more work for you. A crowded bed *looks* crowded. Far from bursting with life and vitality, it will look busy and bewildering. The plants will suffer, too, struggling to survive and get their share of water and nutrients. Crowding may promote disease, weakening plants further. Give your flowers room to stretch. They'll fill out faster than you think.

Next, check the arrangement of plants to see if it makes sense. Are you going to get blooms at the seasons you want them? Are the color mixes going to be attractive? For the best effect, group plants of the same color together, and contrast them with groups of different colors. If you are planning an entire flower garden, then you might want to have a bed that is dominated by red, a bed that is dominated by blue, and so forth. But if you are starting out with one small bed, as we recommend, then you'll probably want to have patches of contrasting or complementary colors in different parts of the bed.

Once you have "planted" your flowers on graph paper, you are ready to buy and plant them outdoors. For advice on how to do this, turn to Part Four, "From Plans to Plants." It will give you the detailed instructions you need. For examples of some successful flower gardens, read on.

Some Successful Flower Gardens
The Semples' Simple Garden

Jane Semple wanted a flower garden that was easy and sure to succeed. Her spot was ideal. She had a straightforward modern house with sliding doors that opened to the east onto a brick terrace. The left end of the terrace was framed by a lawn and a low stone retaining wall. Behind the retaining wall, a sunny slope led up to some shrubs and trees along the property line. The spot she had picked for the flowerbed was a strip 5 feet deep and 15

The Semple flower garden.

feet long running the length of the retaining wall and just in front of it. With the wall and the slope behind the bed, it would be the perfect place to display her flowers.

In her planning, Jane concentrated on plants that were vigorous, easy to maintain, and with foliage that looked good even when the plants weren't in bloom. Since the family often took vacations in July and August, she featured flowers which bloom fairly early in the growing season. Along the back of the bed, she chose peonies for their spectacular showy blooms and lush, shiny foliage, one at each back corner of the bed, and a third at its center. Between and slightly in front of the peonies, Jane planted two groups of bearded iris and three campanulas. She bordered the front of the bed with pinks. On the slope above the retaining wall, she planted vinca as a groundcover and daffodils, narcissi, snowdrops, and crocuses to provide early spring color.

Jane's garden is as easy to take care of as she had hoped. She has to weed it regularly, but because she has left lots of space in the bed and made it narrow, she finds it easy to weed. The bed rarely needs watering because the slope and the wall behind it tend to collect water and supply it to the garden. She finds that the pinks begin to look skimpy every few years, and when this happens, she tears them out, redigs the border, and replants with new bedding plants. So far, she has only had to do this twice in the seven years she has had her flowerbed.

A Yellow and Blue Garden

Zeke Brown grew up on a farm in coastal Maine. For the most part, the farm was a practical place with every square inch devoted to pasture, forage, or vegetable garden. But Zeke remembers that against the zigzag split rail fence that separated

The Browns' blue and yellow flowers.

the small lawn from the huge west cow pasture, his mother kept a wonderful garden of yellow flowers.

One evening, more than twenty years after Zeke had moved away and his father had dispersed the herd and sold the farm, Zeke and his wife, Anne, were sitting on the tiny terrace of their New York apartment, discussing Anne's idea of putting flowers along the parapet of the terrace. Suddenly, for the first time in years, Zeke remembered his mother's garden. He remembered being a little child watching her weed the garden and asking her again and again the name of each of the flowers. He tried to reconstruct that garden in his mind and describe it to Anne, exactly as it had been.

He remembered that it was a summer- and fall-blooming garden that came into its prime during the second cutting of the hay and continued blooming long after tomatoes and beans were canned and the frosts had cut down the vines. In the front of the bed, he was almost certain, were daylilies. Behind were groups of sunflowers, New York asters, rudbeckias, and coneflowers. In the early fall, a blue flower—another aster, he supposed—bloomed and seemed to make the yellow flowers around it even yellower.

Talking about the garden brought back images of his childhood in a rush, images that stayed with him as he and Anne prepared and ate their dinner, did some family paperwork, and went to bed. The next day, when Zeke got home from work, Anne was already at home and was eagerly engaged in a project out on the terrace. "Don't look!" she called. "It's not ready!" So he poured himself some beer and waited in the kitchen, rereading the morning paper until Anne called out, "Ready!"

When he stepped out onto the terrace, he saw that the top of the parapet was covered with planters, and in the planters were dozens of yellow and blue flowers. "They're pansies," Anne said. "They aren't the family farm; but they'll have to do."

A Setting for a Birdbath

It all began with a birdbath that Edward Leger's son gave him for a Christmas present years ago. The birdbath was a large, ornate affair that Paul had rescued from the dusty back room of an antique shop. "What am I going to do with it?" Edward asked the assembled family on Christmas day, as they all admired the monstrosity beside the Christmas tree. "It's much too fancy for the garden." Paul replied, "You'll just have to redesign the garden for it!"

The next spring the Legers rolled the birdbath out into the backyard and pondered where to put it. The yard formed a narrow box, open on the side toward the house and framed by a 5-foot-tall yew hedge. Before his retirement, Edward had never had much time to putter in the backyard. He had kept the hedge trimmed, and tried some roses and a few annuals against the sunny backdrop of the hedge's south side, but little more than that. After some deliberation, they moved the birdbath into

the sheltered courtyard formed by the hedge and set it at the geometric center of the square. They agreed that it looked pretty smashing.

Over the summer, father and son chatted from time to time about designing a formal garden to go with the birdbath. Edward checked several books on classical gardens out of the library and studied the illustrations. He found one of a classical garden from the part of France where his grandparents had lived more than a century ago. He decided to put that garden around his birdbath.

The design he contrived had grass walks all the way around the inside of the hedge, as well as two walks, one down the center of the garden, the other across it, which intersected at the birdbath. The grass walks thus framed four beds arrayed around the birdbath. The beds were to be perfect rectangles, except where they met the circle of grass around the birdbath. On that side, each bed had a truncated curved edge instead of a corner.

Each bed was to be planted so that it formed precisely the same pattern when seen from the birdbath. The inner edges of the bed were bordered with lavender, a shrubby herb with needle-like, fragrant foliage, and beautiful, pungent, blue flower spikes. Beyond the lavender, Edward would plant white and pink turk's cap lillies, and in the back corner of each bed, a group of hybrid tea roses, which would grow to be about 3 feet tall. The back two sides of each bed were to be framed with a small boxwood hedge. Beyond the garden, against the yew hedge, the plan called for a cement bench on which Edward planned to sit, looking down the central path of his garden, across his beautiful new birdbath, to his home beyond.

Paul and his father spent their spare time for the better part of a year putting in that garden. First they had to measure out and cut the beds. They dug each bed up, broke the sod, and raked away the grass, roots, and other litter. Then, just to make

Mr. Leger's classical garden with birdbath.

sure that their soil was as fertile as could be, they brought in a load of topsoil and spread it 3 inches deep on each of the beds. Next they brought in the boxwood and lavender seedlings and planted them along the outer edges of each bed. By that time, the season was getting late, so they stopped for the winter.

The following spring, the Legers cultivated the bed again to loosen the surface, then put in the lilies and roses. As a final flourish, they dug a circular bed around the foot of the birdbath and planted blue lobelia.

It didn't take Edward long to learn how much work is required to maintain such a formal garden. In their new role as the frame for the garden, the yew hedge and lawn required scrupulous maintenance. The hedge had to be kept closely trimmed, and the lawn kept free of weeds. Edward spent many an hour that summer on his hands and knees in the grass pathways, pulling dandelions and plan-

tain with a forked weeding tool. He was also busy edging the grass to keep it from encroaching on the beds. Defending the curved edges of the beds where they skirted the birdbath was particularly difficult. His new garden required enough water so that his new plants would grow strongly, but not so much as to encourage mildew on his roses. Much time and effort were required to protect the roses against Japanese beetles. The following spring, he would try an organic control, milky spore disease, to kill the beetle grubs before they emerged. For this season, however, handpicking seemed the best control, and every morning he carefully examined his rosebushes and removed the day's beetle crop.

Winter also provided many chores. Although the yew hedge sheltered his garden, Edward wanted to play it safe and protect his young roses and boxwood plants from winter winds and snow. He cut and sewed burlap covers for them which could be stapled to frames and reused year after year.

The following spring, he gave his roses a good feeding of composted cow manure and began to shape his boxwood edgings, giving them their first pruning and trimming.

Now, three years later, the garden is beginning to look the way Edward envisioned it. The roses are framed by the boxwood, the lavender forms a beautiful low "hedge," and the lobelia huddles against the ornate pedestal of the birdbath. Recently, at a family party, Paul's wife suggested that perhaps it was time to put some water in the birdbath. Paul filled it, and within a few days the birds were using it regularly. Often Edward sits on his bench and watches them, just as Paul imagined he would.

Wrap-up

Growing flowers is a fine art. Because flowers vary in so many ways—color, fragrance, foliage texture, size, hour and season of bloom—a flowerbed is as much an artistic creation as the finest of oil paintings. If you have never tried your hand at flower gardening before, guarantee your success by starting small, in a sunny, well-fertilized spot, with perennials and annuals well suited to your climate. Concentrate on flowers with fragrances and colors you like, which bloom during parts of the year when you will be around to enjoy them. Keep your bed well watered and well cultivated, and soon you will wonder how you ever lived a season without the pleasures of flower gardening.

Plants for Flower Gardens

Plant Name	Bloom Feature	Description	Culture
Perennials for Flower Gardens			
Allwood pink (*Dianthus ×allwoodii*)	Small, single, fringed flowers; fragrant; white or salmon pink, sometimes with a deeper pink eye; May and June	Hummocks, 1 foot tall and wide, of evergreen, blue-gray, lance-shaped foliage; slender stems bear a profusion of graceful flowers	Full sun; well-drained, slightly alkaline soil; deadhead for continued bloom; Zones 4–8
Balloonflower (*Platycodon grandiflorus*)	Star-shaped, single or semidouble flowers; white, blue, violet blue, or pale pink; July and August	Graceful plants 2 to 3 feet tall; slender stems bear gray-green foliage; flower buds are balloon-shaped	Full sun to light shade; light, acidic, well-drained, moderately fertile soil; plants are slow to emerge in spring, so mark planting sites; Zones 3–8
Bearded iris, German iris (*Iris ×germanica*) many cultivars	Fulsome flowers with rounded, upright, graceful, trailing petals; every color except true red, and many combinations; May and June	Stout, 9-inch- to 4-foot-tall, fan-like clumps of sword-shaped, pale powder green leaves; flowers open successively on tall stalks	Full sun; fairly rich, well-drained, neutral to slightly alkaline soil; tall varieties may need staking; plant so rhizomes "sit" in the soil; susceptible to iris borer; Zones 4–8

(continued)

Plants for Flower Gardens—*continued*

Plant Name	Bloom Feature	Description	Culture
Chinese peony (*Paeonia lactiflora*) 'Festiva Maxima' 'Mons Jules Elie' 'Sarah Bernardt' many others	Baroque confections 4 to 10 inches across; single, semidouble, or double; luscious fragrance; white, pink red, burgundy, creamy yellow, or combinations; June	Handsome plants 2 to 4 feet tall and wide, with glossy, medium to dark green, divided foliage, often turning bronze or reddish in fall; sturdy stalks bear flowers in profusion at the top of the plant	Full sun; rich, deep, well-drained soil; plant with eyes (growing tips) 1 to 2 inches below the soil surface; tall, heavy blooms may need staking; susceptible to botrytis blight; Zones 3–8
Clump speedwell (*Veronica longifolia* var. *subsessilis*)	Spires of dense, small blooms; blue, white, or rose pink; July and August	Clumps, 2 feet tall, of handsome, grayish green, oval, toothed foliage	Full sun to light shade; well-drained, moderately fertile soil; plants do not need staking; Zones 4–8
Columbine (*Aquilegia ×hybrida*) 'Biedermeier' 'McKana Hybrids'	Striking flowers with long-spurred, rounded petals and longer, lance-shaped sepals, often in a contrasting color; bright colors to pastels; May and June	Graceful plants 1 to 3 feet tall, with green fern-like foliage; tall, very slender stems bear flowers	Partial shade to full sun; well-drained soil; plants tend to self-sow; Zones 3–8
Coral bells (*Heuchera sanguinea*) many cultivars	Sprays of airy, small, bell-shaped flowers; pink, red, rose, white, or chartreuse; May to July	Clumping plants 1 to 2½ feet tall, with glossy, evergreen, maple-like foliage; flowers are borne high on stiff, dark, needle-like stems; some varieties have darkly mottled foliage	Full sun to light shade; rich, moist, well-drained soil; deadhead for prolonged bloom; mulch; Zones 3–8
Daylily (*Hemerocallis* hybrids) 'Hyperion' 'Stella d'Oro' many others	Handsome, bell-shaped flowers of 3 recurved petals and 3 recurved sepals; last only a day each; every color except pure white and blue; May to September	Dwarf varieties as short as 1 foot, others up to 3½ feet tall; fountains of arching, strap-like, medium green leaves; long, slender stalks bear a profusion of blooms	Full sun to partial shade; moist, well-drained, moderately fertile loam, slightly acidic to neutral; Zones 3–8
Delphinium (*Delphinium elatum* hybrids) many cultivars	Majestic spikes of single or double flowers, many with a central spot of contrasting petals (bee); white, blue, or purple; June and July	Dwarf varieties up to 2½ feet tall; others are a stately 5 to 6 feet tall; deeply cut, light to medium green, maple-like foliage; tall, leafed spires bear flowers	Full sun to partial shade; rich, moist, alkaline to slightly acid soil; tall varieties must be staked; need protection from wind; Zones 3–7
Early phlox (*Phlox carolina*) 'Miss Lingard'	Cylindrical clusters of white flowers; June and July	Large flower clusters on 2- to 3-foot plants; glossy, bright green foliage; basal leaves narrow, those on stems spear-shaped	Full sun; rich, humusy, moist, well-drained soil; mildew resistant; Zones 3–8

Plant Name	Bloom Feature	Description	Culture
Floribunda rose (*Rosa floribunda*) many cultivars	3- to 4-inch flowers borne in clusters; often fragrant; generally double; many colors and combinations; June and July	Short, fairly handsome bushes 2 to 3 feet tall; foliage borne thickly, giving a full effect; thorny stems	Full sun; very well-drained, humusy soil; mulch in winter; prune dead canes in spring; give plants plenty of room to combat disease
Goldband lily (*Lilium auratum*)	10- to 12-inch, bowl-shaped white flowers; each petal has a central band of gold, yellow and brown freckling; mid-July to mid-August	Plants 5 to 7 feet tall; sweet-scented flowers borne in profusion above 6- to 8-inch-long, 2-inch-wide, lustrous green lanceolate leaves	Sun; humusy, well-drained soil; intolerant of alkaline soils; susceptible to mosaic virus; Zones 3–8
Grandiflora rose (*Rosa grandiflora*) many cultivars	4- to 5-inch, generally double flowers; often fragrant; many colors and combinations; June and July	Bushes 4 to 6 feet tall, bearing flowers intermediate in size and number between hybrid teas and floribundas	Full sun; very well-drained, humusy soil; mulch in winter; prune dead canes in spring; give plants plenty of room to combat disease
Great bellflower (*Campanula latifolia*)	Bell-shaped flowers on spiky stems; blue, violet-blue, or white; summer	Plants 3 to 4 feet tall; stiff stems	Light shade to sun; moist, well-drained, moderately fertile soil; self-seeding; Zones 3–8
Japanese iris (*Iris ensata*) often listed as *I. kaempferi* many others	Large, velvety, single or semidouble flowers; white, blue, purple, or red-violet; June and July	Striking plants up to 4 feet tall; flowers borne over ribbed, sword-shaped foliage	Full sun; rich, moist, acidic soil; alkaline intolerant; often grown beside water; Zones 3–8
Lavender (*Lavandula angustifolia*) 'Hidcote' 'Jean Davis' 'Munstead Dwarf'	Graceful wands of small, pungent flowers; blue, violet-blue, pale pink, or rosy purple; June to August	Bushy plants up to 18 inches tall; silver-gray, needle-like leaves are fragrant when crushed; beautiful silver-white color in winter	Full sun; light, sandy, alkaline soil; mulch over winter in colder climates; Zones 5–9
Lavender cotton, santolina (*Santolina chamaecyparissus*)	Solitary, ¾-inch-wide, button-like, yellow flowers; August and September	Shrubby, evergreen plant up to 12 inches tall; silver-gray, aromatic, woolly leaves	Full sun; average to poor, sandy, well-drained soil; Zones 6–8
Maiden pink (*Dianthus deltoides*)	Small, single flowers; brilliant pink, white, or crimson; May and June	Mats 4 to 6 inches tall, with tiny, bright green, grass-like leaves; semi-evergreen; covered with hundreds of flowers	Full sun; sandy, well-drained, alkaline soil; plant self-sows; Zones 4–8
Miniature rose (*Rosa roulettii*) many cultivars	Small, single to double flowers; many colors	Small, bushy roses up to 15 inches tall, with flowers and foliage perfectly in scale	Full sun; very well-drained, humusy soil; mulch in winter; prune dead canes in spring; ideal for pot culture; hardiest popular rose

(continued)

Plants for Flower Gardens–*continued*

Plant Name	Bloom Feature	Description	Culture
Oriental hybrid lily, August hybrid lily (*Lilium* Oriental Hybrids)	Large (6- to 12-inch), trumpet-shaped, flat, recurved, or bowl-shaped flowers; fragrant; white, pink, red, or purple; August	Huge flowers cluster at the top of dark green stalks, 2 to 7 feet tall, with glossy blade-like foliage	Full sun to partial shade; humusy, well-drained soil; Zones 3–8
Oriental poppy (*Papaver orientale*) many cultivars	Large, gaudy, crepe-paper-like, cup-shaped flowers; white, salmon pink, orange-red, or carmine, often with a purple center; June	Plants can grow 1 to 6 feet tall, but usual range is 3 to 4 feet, with a 3-foot spread; hairy stems and coarse, toothed foliage	Full sun; well-drained soil; foliage dies back in July, then reemerges in September; Zones 3–8
Peach-leaved bellflower (*Campanula persicifolia*)	Single or semi-double cup-shaped flowers in tall spires; blue, white, or violet; June to August	Slender flower spikes 2 to 3 feet tall, over spreading mats of bright green, peach-leaf-shaped foliage; evergreen in mild climates	Light shade to sun; moist, well-drained, moderately fertile soil; plant self-sows and spreads by roots; Zones 3–8
Shasta daisy (*Chrysanthemum ×superbum*) many cultivars	Large, striking, single, semi-double, or double, daisy-like flowers, up to 5 inches across; white or creamy yellow with a bright gold center; June to August	Bushy clumps up to 2 feet tall; long, narrow, glossy, dark green foliage; flowers borne in profusion	Full sun to light shade; rich, moist, well-drained soil; deadhead for extended bloom; Zones 4–9
Siberian iris (*Iris sibirica*) many cultivars	Dainty, graceful flowers; white, blue, purple, creamy yellow, or wine red, or combinations; June and July	Beautiful clumps of dark green, grass-like foliage, 1 to 4 feet tall; flowers borne profusely just above the foliage	Full sun: humusy, moist, slightly acidic soil; Zones 3–8
Silver Mound artemisia (*Artemisia schmidtiana* 'Silver Mound')	Nondescript flowers; plants are grown for silver accent in flowerbeds	Cloud of beautiful, finely cut silver-green foliage, in a mound 1 foot tall and 18 inches wide	Full sun; average to poor, well-drained soil; shear plants back before they flower to keep them compact; Zones 4–8
Spike speedwell (*Veronica spicata*)	Strong, compact spikes of small flowers; blue, lavender-blue, rose, or white; June to August	Mounds of matte green, lance-shaped leaves, 15 inches tall, support the flowers	Full sun to light shade; well-drained soil; Zones 3–8
Summer phlox, border phlox (*Phlox paniculata*) 'Fairy's Petticoat' 'Sir John Falstaff' many others	5-petaled flowers massed in pyramidal clusters; often mildly fragrant; white, pink, rose, magenta, salmon, lilac, or purple, some with contrasting eyes; July and August	Plants 18 inches to 3 feet tall, with coarse, dark green, lance-shaped foliage; some varieties have variegated leaves	Sun; deep, rich, moist, porous soil; protect from wind; susceptible to powdery mildew; deadhead for longer bloom; Zones 3–8

Plant Name	Bloom Feature	Description	Culture
Tea rose, hybrid tea (*Rosa* Hybrid Teas) many cultivars	Large, fully double flowers, up to 6 or 7 inches across, on straight stems; often highly fragrant; many colors and combinations; June	Small, often scrawny bushes, 4 to 6 feet tall, with thorny stems and dark green to bronze, semiglossy foliage	Full sun; very well-drained, humusy soil; give plants lots of room to combat foliar diseases; mulch in winter; prune dead canes in spring
Tree peony (*Paeonia suffruticosa*)	Large, single, semi-double, or double flowers 2 to 12 inches across; white, pink, yellow, red, crimson, maroon, or combinations; May and June	Woody shrubs up to 4 feet tall; soft green, large but gracefully dissected foliage; older bushes bear dozens of blooms	Full sun to partial shade; well-drained, deep, humusy, sandy loam; needs protected site, wide spacing; to Zone 3

Annuals for Flower Gardens

Plant Name	Bloom Feature	Description	Culture
Alyssum (*Lobularia maritima*)	Clusters of tiny, fragrant, white, pink, rose, or purple flowers; spring and summer	Mats 3 to 6 inches tall, with a 12-inch spread; bright green, slender, strap-like leaves	Direct-seed several weeks before last frost, or indoors 4 weeks before setting out; scatter seeds on soil surface; full sun; well-drained soil
Annual candytuft (*Iberis umbellata*) 'Dwarf Fairy Mixed Colors'	Dense masses of flower clusters; flat-headed flower umbels up to 1½ inches across; white, pink, rose, burgundy, or mauve; early summer and fall	Compact plants 12 inches tall and wide, covered with bloom; short, dark green, strap-like, slender foliage	Direct-seed when soil warms in spring, or sow indoors 6 to 8 weeks before setting out; cover seed with ¼ inch of soil; full sun; drought tolerant once established; plant self-sows
Blue salvia (*Salvia farinacea*) 'Victoria'	Slender, intense blue flower spikes; also a white variety; summer	Plants 2 feet tall and wide, with gray-green, spear-shaped foliage	Sow indoors 10 weeks before setting out; do not cover seed; sun to partial shade; well-drained, moist loam soil; heat and humidity tolerant
Cosmos (*Cosmos bipinnatus*) (*C. sulphureus*) 'Diablo' 'Sensation Mixed Colors'	*C. bipinnatus*: large daisy-like flowers, up to 4 inches across; white, pink, or red; *C. sulphureus*: perky flowers up to 2 inches across; yellow, orange, or red-orange; both species flower early summer to fall frost	Feathery plants up to 5 feet tall, with a 2- to 3-foot spread; dwarf varieties are 1 to 2 feet tall, with a 1-foot spread; *C. bipinnatus* has fern-like, airy foliage, while *C. sulphureus* is more marigold-like	Direct-seed after all danger of frost has passed, or sow indoors 5 to 6 weeks before last frost date; cover seed lightly with soil; full sun; heat and drought resistant
Dahlia, bedding dahlia (*Dahlia hybrida*) 'Redskin' 'Rigoletto'	Double flowers; white, pink, red, purple, yellow, orange, or bicolors; early summer to fall frost	Compact plants 12 to 15 inches tall; green or bronze oval, toothed leaves	Direct-seed after all danger of frost has passed, or sow indoors 8 weeks before last frost date; cover seed with ¼ inch of soil; full sun; moist, loose, humusy, loamy soil

(continued)

Plants for Flower Gardens—*continued*

Plant Name	Bloom Feature	Description	Culture
Marigold (*Tagetes* spp.) 'Lemon Drop' 'Marietta' series 'Sophia' series many others	Single or double, 1- to 5-inch-wide flowers; usually pungent; white, yellow, gold, orange, rust, or red; early summer to fall frost	Compact plants 8 inches to 3 feet tall, with a spread up to 2 feet; ferny, pungent, rich green foliage (some unscented varieties); profuse blooms	Direct-seed after all danger of frost has passed, or sow indoors 6 to 8 weeks before last frost date; cover seed lightly with soil; full sun; well-drained, light soil; deadhead flowers
Nasturtium (*Tropaeolum majus*) 'Double Dwarf Jewel' 'Whirlybird'	Single or double, somewhat cup-shaped flowers; spurred varieties face sideways with a long spur below the petals; 'Whirlybird' is spurless and faces up; white, gold, orange, pink, or red; summer to fall frost	Bushy varieties 1 foot tall with a 2-foot spread; vine types can reach 6 feet; fleshy plants with large, saucer-shaped, pungent, powder green leaves; bloom best in cool weather	Direct-seed as soon as soil warms in spring; cover seed with 1 inch of soil; full sun; moist, well-drained soil; tolerates poor soil; susceptible to aphids
Petunia (*Petunia hybrida*) many cultivars	*grandiflora* types: flowers up to 5 inches across, single or double, fringed, ruffled, or smooth-edged; summer *multiflora* types: a profusion of smaller single or double blooms. Virtually every color and many combinations; summer	Bushy, compact plants 12 to 15 inches tall with a 2-foot spread; medium green, fuzzy oval foliage; sticky buds	Sow seed indoors 8 to 10 weeks before last frost date; do not cover seed; full sun; fertile, well-drained, sandy soil; susceptible to mosaic virus; larger flowers suffer considerable rain damage
Snapdragon (*Antirrhinum majus*) 'Bright Butterflies' 'Floral Carpet' 'Rocket' series	Tubular, broad-lipped flowers are borne on stunning spikes; also double and open-flowered varieties; white, yellow, orange, pink, red, or bicolors; summer and fall	Plants from 6-inch mats to 3 feet tall with a 12-inch spread; bright green, narrow, lance-shaped foliage	Direct-seed several weeks before last frost, or sow indoors 8 weeks before setting out; do not cover seed; full sun; loose, fertile, moist loam or sandy soil; pinch tops to encourage branching; tall kinds may need staking; shear after bloom for fall flowers
Wax begonia (*Begonia semperflorens*) many cultivars	Bright, fleshy, shiny flowers, about an inch long, single and double forms; white, pink, rose, or red; early summer to frost	Bushy plants 6 to 12 inches tall and wide; waxy, rounded leaves, green or bronze; very fleshy stems; covered with a profusion of flowers	Set out bedding plants after soil warms; full sun to partial shade; moist, well-drained, rich, loam soil; can be propagated from stem cuttings
Zinnia (*Zinnia* spp.) many cultivars	Cactus-flowered or dahlia-flowered, single or double blooms up to 7 inches across; virtually every color, including green, except the blues; some bicolors; summer to fall frost	Bushy plants 6 inches to 3 feet tall, with a spread up to 2 feet; glossy, bright green, opposite, lance-shaped leaves	Direct-seed after all danger of frost has passed; cover seed lightly with soil; full sun; fertile loam or sandy soil; susceptible to powdery mildew and alternaria blight

CHAPTER 6

Sundecks and Other Sunspots

A "sunspot" is a place where you can be toasty warm in the fresh air and sun when most of your neighbors are shivering in their houses. Imagine that you have already read this chapter and have set up your sunspot, a beautiful redwood deck. Pretend that you wake up some February morning. You are greeted as you look out your bedroom window by a snowstorm so thick you can barely see out to the street. The sounds of people hurrying to work are muffled and indistinct. But by the time you get your coffee, the snow has stopped falling, and by the time your muffins are ready, the sun has come out.

So you put your muffins and coffee on the warm top of the stove, take a broom outside, and sweep off the wooden surface of your deck. As soon as the dark boards of the deck are uncovered, the February sun warms them and they begin to steam. By the time you have swept the snow off the entire deck, the part near the kitchen door is dry. You get out a lawn chair, put it against the wall of the house, and bring out your coffee and muffins.

At first the air seems chilly and you are grateful for the sweater you are wearing. But as the sun strikes you, you become hot, *hot in February*! So you take your sweater off. A moment later, you are rolling up your sleeves. The sun warms your skin, lulling you. In the distance, you can hear the cold north wind rushing through the needles of your cedar hedge. If you close your eyes you can make it the sound of waves on a warm Caribbean beach.

Is a Sunspot for You?

The advantages of a sunspot rely on your being the sort of person who enjoys the sun. To decide if you would use a winter sunspot, think about how often you're out in the sun during the warm months of the year. Are you one of those people who is out gardening, or reading, or doing handwork on every sunny day? When you are away on vacation, do you like to take meals outside on a hotel terrace, or enjoy fine-tuning your suntan on a beach? You probably would make good use of a sunspot.

Perhaps, on the other hand, the coming of summer doesn't make much of a change in your living pattern. You're the sort of person who likes eating in the dining room, reading in the den, and entertaining in the living room no matter what the weather. For you, a sunspot might not be worth the effort and expense necessary to create it.

The usefulness of a sunspot will depend not only on you but on your climate. Heating experts call the temperatures from 65 to 85°F the comfort range. At the bottom end of the comfort range, a person may add a light sweater if he is sitting very still. If the temperatures are near the top of the range and he is active, he may change to a short-sleeved shirt. But basically, the comfort range includes those temperatures at which people can pursue quiet activities with only minor adjustments of clothing. Remember, for the purposes of the comfort range, sun and wind translate to heating and cooling.

In planning your sunspot, you can't fudge the comfort range; human beings are a fussy lot. When the temperature hovers around 75°F, the guests on your shady patio will be happy. But if it creeps above 85° or below 65°, they will get restless. Overheated guests will remove clothing, fan themselves, or go looking for a breeze. Chilly guests will put on their jackets. Let a little bit of sun shine on the overheated guests or a little wind blow on the chilly ones, and your party will break up or move to a different location.

One measure of the usefulness of a sunspot in your climate is the number of days in a year when the day's temperature doesn't reach 75°F, the middle of the comfort range. We assume that on such days, most people would appreciate some

sunshine when they are outside. Boston has around 250 such days in a year; San Francisco has 365! In fact, for people who live along the West Coast, a sunny place to sit is desirable almost every day of the year.

So it's clear that in most parts of the United States, creating a spot where you can make use of the sun's heat to be comfortable is going to increase your outdoor time. But there may be exceptions. If you design a spot that is sunny in winter, you run the risk that it will be baking hot in summer. In San Antonio, where the temperature fails to reach 75° on only 120 days a year, gardeners can expect the daily high temperature to exceed 85° on 180 days of the year. Each of these is surely a day when San Antonians want an outdoor space where they can hide from the sun. In San Antonio, you might increase your outdoor time more by building a shady spot than by building a sunspot.

But few places in the United States are as warm as San Antonio. We may be biased, but we think that almost every house ought to have a sunspot. Even if it's only a third floor fire-escape landing with a few geraniums, everybody ought to have a spot where they can get out in the sunshine for a cup of tea in the morning, for lunch, or for a family dinner in the late afternoon sun. If these ideas tempt you, watch the sun as it wheels around your house. See which sheltered nook it illuminates, and begin to plan your sunspot today.

The Basics of a Sunspot

In an ideal world, a sunspot would be sunny and sheltered from the wind when the temperatures were cool, have a dappled shade and light breezes when the temperatures were warm, and deep shade and a steady breeze when the temperatures became hot. Unfortunately, no sunspot is ever going to have all these characteristics. You are going to have to make choices and have priorities which depend on where you live. The longer, colder, and sunnier your winters, the more the design of your sunspot will be determined by openness to the sun and protection from cold winds. The longer, hotter, and sunnier your summer, the more the design of your sunspot will have to be modified to provide for shade and cooling breezes.

We think it's important to begin by securing the basics, the things without which a sunspot would not *be* a sunspot. The basic elements of a sunspot are the sun in front of you, a barrier against the wind behind you, and a dry, warm surface beneath you. You will probably put your sunspot near your house, because the house is convenient for carrying food, answering the telephone, and other necessities, and because the house forms a natural barrier. You need only find a sunny spot downwind of the house, some sort of a surface to get you up off the cold ground, and your sunspot is ready to use.

Securing the Sun

Above all, you must make sure that your proposed sunspot is actually sunny during the times you hope to use it. The most prudent course is to try out potential sunspots in different seasons and at different times of day before you do any construction. Put stakes in the ground to mark the extent of shadows at particular times of year. Use copies of your site plan to make maps of the outline of shade patterns. Do your best to actually get out in your proposed sunspot and try it out. If you are considering a sunspot on the disused south wall of your garage, get out there in March and clear yourself a spot in the brambles. Improvise a tarpaulin between two trees as a windbreak. See what it's like before you commit yourself.

If you are too impatient to wait for a full year

before you start construction, then at least use the calculations suggested in chapter 2, "Knowing Your Site," to locate protected spots convenient to the house, where the sun shines during the cool days and during the cool hours of warm days. Remember, the June sun may not give a reliable indication of a good place for a cool-weather sunspot. Seen against a tall tree or building 60 feet away, the noonday sun descends approximately 85 feet from June to September and another 35 feet between September and December. Put another way, a tree which casts a 25-foot shadow at midday in June will cast a 60-foot shadow in September and March, and a 145-foot shadow in December!

If you are wondering whether the sun will clear an object at some crucial time of the year, be careful not to succumb to wishful thinking. The box, "Making a Sun-Angle Calculator," tells you how to manufacture a primitive device for figuring out how high the sun will be at different times of the year. Try it out. Be careful not to kid yourself, particularly if the obstacle is a tree. Remember: Trees grow. Young trees, in particular, often grow several feet a year. Be sure to put your sunspot somewhere where your growing trees and those of your neighbors won't shade it in a few years.

A Barrier against the Wind

If your sunspot is to be successful, shelter must be provided from the wind. Shelter usually takes the form of a barrier of some sort: commonly a wall of your house and often a fence, a wall, or a hedge as well.

Which winds is it most important to shelter against? Keep in mind what you want your sunspot to do—to provide you with a place to enjoy the sun when the weather is clear and cool. The trick to planning the orientation of a sunspot lies in knowing some facts about the weather. Not all winds are equally likely when the weather is clear and cool. Winds that accompany the sort of weather in which your sunspot would be most useful are usually west, north, or northwest winds. Winds that accompany inclement weather are usually east, south, or southeast winds. So chances are that you want your barrier to shelter you from the west, north, and northwest wind and not from the south, east, and southeast wind.

One very important exception to this rule occurs along coastlines. If you live near the ocean or another large body of water, the wind will tend to blow onshore during fair days when the air temperature over land is warmer than the water

Making a Primitive Sun-Angle Calculator

As an inexpensive antidote to wishful thinking, you might make yourself a simple device for seeing whether or not a given obstacle will shade a given spot at a given time of year. Get yourself a carpenter's level at least a foot long, a protractor, a pair of scissors, a pencil, some tape, and three rectangular pieces of cardboard. Best for the purpose are the backs of 8½-by-11-inch pads of paper, but any cardboard roughly that size and shape will do.

Look up your latitude in an atlas. It is the number attached to the horizontal line on the map nearest your location. For the northern tier of states and southern Canada, it is about 45 degrees, for the southern tier of states, about 35 degrees, and for the middle of the country, about 40 degrees. From your latitude, you can easily calculate the height of the noonday sun for the 21st of December, June, March, and September. December's noontime sun height will be 90 degrees, minus your latitude, minus 22.5 degrees; June's sun height will be 90 degrees, minus latitude, *plus* 22.5 degrees; and September and March's sun height will be 90 degrees minus the latitude.

Now you are ready to manufacture your sun-angle sighter. The idea is to cut a piece of cardboard for each of the seasonal sun angles. To cut the first one, take the level and align one edge with the lower edge of the cardboard. Now draw a line on the cardboard along the other side of the level, so that you end up with a line parallel to the edge and one width of the level away from it. Let's call this the first line. Place the protractor with its base on the first line so that the protractor's center point is exactly where

the first line meets the left-hand edge of the paper. Now draw a second line which makes an angle with the first line equal to the sun angle in December.

Proceed to cut the cardboard along the second line. You now have a piece of cardboard shaped like the silhouette of a saltbox, which will fit conveniently on your level and which you can use to direct your eye to the proper angle for the December sun angle. Make equivalent pieces of cardboard for the Septem-

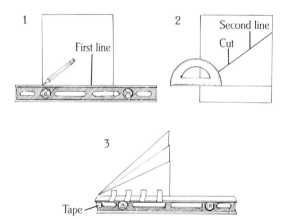

STEP 1: *To cut a piece of cardboard for your first seasonal sun angle, draw a line parallel to the edge of the cardboard.*
STEP 2: *Use a protractor to measure the angle to draw the second line. Cut the cardboard along that line. Repeat for the other two sun angles.*
STEP 3: *Tape all the cardboard pieces to the end of the level.*

temperature. If the body of water is a cold one, these "sea" breezes can be unpleasantly chilly, particularly in the spring. Gardeners who live in such locations may want to shelter their sunspots from the onshore direction, whichever that direction happens to be.

A great variety of barriers are suitable to shelter a sunspot. Buildings, walls, fences—even hedges—can provide the necessary barrier to the wind. The two most important things to consider in a barrier are its height and its "hardness."

The effects of height are obvious: The higher a barrier, the more shelter it provides. But high barriers have some disadvantages. A high barrier not only keeps out the wind, it closes in the space in every other way as well, and may give it a shut-in feeling. If being able to see out of your sunspot is important to you, you might consider having some of the perimeter enclosed by a lower barrier, say a low wall which you can see over when seated in a lawn chair but which keeps the draft off your body.

The effects of the hardness of a barrier are equally important but less obvious. Hard barriers are inflexible structures like walls and fences that don't move in the wind. You would think that "harder" barriers would provide more shelter than "softer" ones, but the reverse is true. Rigid barriers encourage the development of an eddy downwind of the barrier. A person hiding on the south side of a hard barrier from a north wind may actually be chilled by a persistent *south* wind. The wind swirls around the sides or over the top of the barrier and then blows back toward the barrier on its "sheltered" downwind side.

The obvious solution is to plant a soft barrier like a hedge or a windbreak. A thick evergreen hedge is an excellent barrier, breaking the force of the wind without deflecting it. But to function by itself as a barrier to the wind, a hedge must be thick and carefully maintained so that it doesn't develop any leaks.

Very often, gardeners do not have the patience or the space for such a solution. They want a wall or a fence because it provides a lot of security, is quick to put up, and is easy to maintain. There are several ways to modify a hard barrier to deal with

ber and March sun angle and for the June sun angle. Tape the three pieces of cardboard to the end of the level as shown.

Now you need an accomplice. Go sit in your lawn chair in the place you are considering for a sunspot. Let's start with the largest angle. Point the level south and ask your accomplice to level it. Hold the level so that the intersection of the two lines is against your eye like a gunsight and look up the top edge of the largest angle. This will give you the position of the sun at noon in June. Let your eye stray in an arc to the northeast horizon behind you, then back to the south, and then in an arc to the northwest horizon behind you. You are tracing with your eye the path of the sun in midsummer. Now do the same with the smaller angles, except that with the smallest angle, let your eye stray to the southeast and southwest horizons, and with the medium-sized angle, let your eye stray to the east and west horizons. You will be tracing the sun arc for December, and for March and September, respectively.

The sun will clear any obstacle lower than the smallest angle every day of the year. Any obstacle larger than the largest angle, the sun will never clear. Obstacles between those extremes will obscure the sun during some parts of the year and not others. Obstacles as high as the middle angle will obscure the sun in the winter and fall, but not in the spring and summer. Remember that the sun makes most of its upward motion between late January and early May. If the sun hasn't cleared an object by early May, it probably won't ever clear it.

the problem of eddies and backdrafts. One is to add a strip along the top of the barrier, 1 or 2 feet wide, which leans toward the prevailing wind. This strip creates turbulence along the top of the barrier and diminishes the backdraft. Oddly enough, putting holes in your barrier also makes it more effective. A fence with a toothed top like a stockade fence or a fence with louvers is a better shelter than a solid fence of the same height. A vertical slat fence with overlapping offset slats is even better.

The best solution of all is to combine a hard with a soft barrier. Shrub, vine, or tree plantings made on the upwind side of a solid barrier are an excellent way to soften the barrier and make it more effective. This solution means that you have to live with the eddies for a few years while the plants are growing, but once they clear the top of the barrier, your troubles are over. Your plants keep eddies from tumbling over the top of the barrier and make it a better shelter. Meanwhile, the barrier protects and stabilizes the plants.

You can soften the sides of a barrier in a similar way. An evergreen, carefully planted at the corner of a building or beside a fence, cushions the turbulence of winds that eddy around the corner and increases the effectiveness of the building as a barrier. A short section of louvered fence at the end of a barrier will have the same effect.

Surfacing a Sunspot

The third most important element in a sunspot is a surface material to keep you off the cold ground. The surface of a sunspot should dry quickly so that you can use it as soon after a rain as possible.

The surface materials of a sunspot also serve a heat-storage function. They absorb heat when the sun is out and release it later to keep your sunspot cozy even when the sun has slipped behind a cloud. The obvious storage materials are wood, masonry, and stone. Of these, wood has the least storage capacity and stone the greatest.

You would assume, therefore, that people would always use stone as a surface for a sunspot. But storage capacity is a double-edged sword. The greater the storage capacity, the slower the material heats. Consequently, wood heats up the fastest, but it also cools the fastest. Stones heat up slowly but also release heat for the greatest length of time afterwards. The most elaborate sunspots, therefore, have surface materials of both types: a bit of deck or a bench for a place to sit just after the sun comes out, and an area of flags or bricks, or a stone wall or parapet, to store heat during longer sunny periods.

Fine-Tuning Your Sunspot

Once you have assured yourself of the basics of your sunspot, you can employ various tricks to extend its season and mitigate any negative effects it may have on your house in warm weather.

Hot-Weather Shade

To keep your sunspot from overheating in the warmest parts of hot days, you may want to shade it. It seems paradoxical to worry about shade on a sunspot, but the reason that many people don't have sunspots is their concern about the space being too exposed during summer and contributing to the overheating of their house. Because of the way plants grow and the way the sun moves at different seasons of the year, you can, to a certain extent, have your sunspot in the spring and fall and have a shady spot in summer. This desirable state of affairs can be obtained by planting an arbor or building an overhang which shades out the high summer sun but lets the lower spring and fall sun come in.

The problem with overhangs is that the weather

is not the hottest when the sun is the highest. The sun is at the highest on June 21, lowest on December 21, and midway on September 21 and March 21. But the average temperature is hottest around August 1, lowest around February 1, and midway around May 1 and November 1. Most people who want shade would like it to be timed for the hottest time of the year, but shade from an overhang comes earlier. Consequently, if you want the sunlight in your sunspot during the chilly days of April, you will have to suffer the heat of the sun during the dog days of August.

Shade from plants comes at a more useful time than shade from overhangs. Plants, like people, center their activities around the heat cycle of the year, so a plant doesn't begin to provide shade until it's needed in the late spring and continues to provide it through the warm days of late summer and early fall. The disadvantage of plants, even deciduous ones, is that even their bare branches cast considerable shadow.

Growing a shade plant on an overhead arbor combines the advantages of both shading techniques while minimizing their drawbacks. The arbor extends partially over the sunspot. During the late fall and winter months the low sun comes in under the arbor and strikes the sunspot directly. During late spring, the sun begins to shine through the arbor, but the branches are bare and the shading effect is not too great. In summer, the arbor leafs out and provides a dense, cooling shade which lasts right through to early fall. By the time the weather has cooled, the sun has lowered and is once again coming in under the arbor.

Another useful technique is to plant for shade on the west and northwest sides of a sunspot. Because of the changes in the path of the sun, it only shines from the northwest in the hottest time of the day at the hottest times of the year. So if you shade a sunspot from the northwest, you will prevent much undesirable heating and lose very little that is desirable.

If neither permanent shade trees nor permanent overhangs appeal to you, you might consider some of the variety of awnings and similar devices that have been developed to provide temporary shade. These fabric or wooden structures can be put up to exclude the sun when the weather is hot, and taken down as soon as the sun's heat is needed.

Hot-Weather Breezes

If overheating of your sunspot is likely to be a problem, then you may want to become an expert on summer breezes. Hot days can be either breezy or still. On breezy, hot days, the wind blows from the southwest across most of the United States in a broad band that stretches from Texas to New England. On still, hot days, local winds take over. If you live near a body of water, you already know that the breeze tends to blow off the water on hot, still days. If you live in the mountains, you know about the odd shifts that occur in mountain breezes. Winds tend to blow toward the heated slopes of mountains during the day, toward west slopes in the morning and east slopes in the afternoon, and they tend to blow downslope in the evening.

These rules about summer breezes may give some clues for how to ease the effects of overheating in your sunspot. Once you know which way your summer breezes blow, you can arrange plantings and structures to enhance and direct them. You want an opening on the upwind side of your sunspot to let the summer breeze in, and an opening on the downwind side so that the wind will flow across the sunspot. A funnel-shaped pattern of plantings upwind of this opening will actually collect the breeze and focus it on your sunspot.

In some locations, sunspot designers may experience a conflict between providing a barrier against winter winds and leaving their sunspot open to cooling summer winds. Such conflicts can be resolved by putting up temporary barriers of canvas, lattice, or glass (or even plastic) panels for the winter and taking them down in the summer to let the air in.

Plants for a Sunspot

Plants have two important roles to play in a sunspot. The first is to provide midsummer shade. Ideally, we would want a plant to provide shade only when the temperature is above 75°F. Such

Phebe's Favorites for Sunspots

Nothing surpasses the sugar maple as a shade tree. It should be seen as a specimen alone, with its beautiful round shape, lovely crinkly bark, and, of course, its stunning fall color—the epitome of New England. Imagine winding old country roads, informal post-and-rail fences lined with sugar maples, and the fields beyond, on a rainy, misty fall day. Of course, it would be beautiful on a crisp, sunny, blue fall day, too. I don't believe this scene has an equal.

I suggest the monarch birch because it is supposedly more resistant to bronze birch borers and "urban conditions." But the fact remains that all birches are wonderful trees, and discounting the Japanese maple, there really isn't a more popular tree. They are beautiful alone or in clumps, the wonderful bark lightens up any dark corner, the foliage is soft and quivering. Birches seem to welcome other plants around their trunks. In fact, they seem like mother hens, protecting any plant that finds their welcoming shade. The bark just can't be equaled, but it is amazing how many people plant birches against a white house! Unforgettable scene: the yellow birch, only really at its height of beauty in the Northeast woods, seen as the winter sun dipped behind the horizon. Several clumps of birches were backlit by the sunset—they were golden against the rosy glow, casting cool blue shadows on the clear snow.

No one could think about tall trees without including an oak. Because I am a New Englander, I pick the white oak, mostly because of its wonderful branch structure and shape, and its furrowy bark. It richly deserves to be called "majestic." Unfortunately, this oak has a long taproot and does not respond to

transplanting when it gets larger, but we certainly should be planting more of these magnificent trees for future generations to realize how insignificant their lives really are!

Everyone should have a pine. They are sturdy and undemanding as a group. Pines are wonderful, thick, and fuzzy when young, and get more and more picturesque with age. Summer, winter, spring, fall—they are always there, always green, growing exposed to winds, with wet feet, whatever. I once transplanted a white pine we got from a friend who had it in sandy soil. We threw some plastic around the ball, popped it into the car, drove home with the pine dragging out the back, dropped it on the road somewhere, lost any soil that had remained around the roots, got it home, planted it a week later in our wet, clay Cambridge soil, and it is now at least 30 feet tall. Oh yes, this all occurred in November!

Magnolias are real aristocrats. Not only do they reward us after a long winter with flowers that are almost tropical, they have beautiful gray bark, picturesque branching, and leaves that never get munched by beasties. Some are fragrant, too. They are shown off to advantage as a formal entrance plant against a brick building. I have to admit that, in a cold climate, the blossoms can sometimes get nipped by a late frost, but if planted with some shelter they reward you most springs. The lovely autumn yellow of the deciduous species is an added plus, and the red fruits are often quite visible. I love the fuzzy flower buds before they open; they remind me of pussy willows. Although the sweet bay magnolia (Magnolia virginiana) is not the most handsome, the blossoms in July are unbelievably

design criteria are obviously unreasonable, but we can approach this ideal by having a plant that leafs out very late. Several trees meet the requirements of being good sunspot shaders. The ash and the honey locust both leaf out only after all danger of frost has passed. Of the two, the ash provides the denser shade, the honey locust a light, airy shade which is wonderful for patios in regions where the summer sun doesn't get extremely hot.

A gardener who wants to shade his sunspot

fragrant, and this small tree should be squeezed in somewhere just for that reason.

No garden should be without a cherry. Of course, the most popular are the weeping varieties, and these with a pond or water are very, very pretty indeed. The sturdy Sargent cherry has soft, misty pink flowers in April, good foliage, and lovely, almost mahogany-red foliage in fall. I think it is the misty fuzz of pink flowers on a damp spring day that is so appealing. This tree epitomizes the soft pink feel of spring. Many cherries have stunning shiny, satiny bark that is a prominent feature, especially when the leaves drop. However, cherries do have some drawbacks. All cherries are fairly short-lived trees, and many weeping varieties have rather ugly grafts. Although weeping cherries are always popular, I am not inclined to think them all that spectacular when they are not in bloom, especially if water is not present.

The witch hazels have weird ribbony flowers, but they are the first sign of spring, and their welcome fragrance and bright yellow blooms renew your faith that the earth is shedding her winter mantle and spring will really come.

Forsythia is spring. Its cheery yellow blossoms are so ubiquitous in the landscape that the sun seems to have returned everywhere. Any variety is nice. The *ovatas* are paler yellow in general but tougher, the *intermedias* gaudier. This is a shrub for the distance. After it has bloomed, the foliage and really messy weeping habit do not put this plant in the forefront. I like to tuck one in a corner, not only for spring but also so I can bring in branches to force in the house about February. Don't forget that the yellow blossoms

are not always that compatible with the spring pinks of the cherries and magnolias.

No early spring list is complete without the P.J.M. rhododendron. Its foliage is great, bronzy in winter, nice and green and perky in summer, but the flower color is another matter. Either you love its bright magenta bloom, or you consider it gauche. Too many are planted against brick buildings, where the flower color looks nothing less than awful, but a single specimen against a white house in the sun is very cheery indeed.

Shy spring bloomers bring the early bulbs to mind. Snowdrops, with their drooping white bells, are adorable in the snow. And who can forget the sight of a carpet of little blue squill in bloom under a gigantic beech tree, the gray of the enormous trunk complemented by the large carpet of blue?

Vinca, or myrtle, with its pretty blue blossoms, combines well with yellow spring daffodils and is a good groundcover with bulbs. Because it is not an invasive creeper, the myrtle graciously allows clumps of daffodils and narcissi to thrive in its midst, and its leaves still look ornamental when the bulbs fade. Planting ferns or epimediums in the groundcover lets them take over when the bulbs are done, adding interest with their new green growth.

Bethlehem sage 'Mrs. Moon' is my favorite, with dainty pinkish blue flowers in April. It's a good massed groundcover, for accent rather than cover. Bethlehem sage is really grown for its foliage, which remains all summer, a pretty speckled green and silvery white (almost blue). The flowers offer a nice misty cover in spring. Bethlehem sage is also shade tolerant.

with an arbor has a variety of vines from which to choose. Wisteria and grape are widely used. In addition to shade, wisteria provides fragrant blossoms and grapes provide fruit. Honeysuckle, trumpet vine, silver fleece vine, climbing roses, summer jasmine, and clematis are other flowering vines that can be successfully grown on arbors. Bitter-sweet vines are loaded in fall with attractive yellow-orange and red berries, but they grow so rampantly that horticulturists regard them as pests. With such a wide selection, a gardener may have his choice of a great variety of decorative plants to shade his sunspot.

Another function of plants in a sunspot is to reduce summer glare. Almost any plant will reduce glare from masonry and asphalt surfaces, but in a sunspot you want to choose plants that do so only during the warmest summer months. At other seasons of the year, these surfaces provide welcome reflected heat. Climbing hydrangea, woodbine, and Boston ivy will cover a wall with their foliage in the summer, leaving only a network of stems in the cool months. Boston ivy turns a beautiful red color in the fall and is covered with showy blue berries. If your glare problem is not severe, it can sometimes be solved by growing striking annual vines, such as morning glories or scarlet runner beans, on a trellis.

Some Successful Sunspots
Sunbathing in the Snowbelt

The Thompsons now live in a part of the country where winters are long and very cold, and summers are short and warm. Having lived for many years in California, the Thompsons were reluctant when they first moved East to give up sunshine for most of the year the way their neighbors seemed to. They noticed that despite all the snow, long periods of clear weather occurred during the winter when the sun was surprisingly hot. They

decided to convert a covered porch on the southeast side of their house into a sundeck.

The location the Thompsons chose for their sunspot was just about ideal for their climate. It was sheltered from the north by the bulk of their two-story house and from the west by the one-story garage and kitchen wing. Because their winter sun rises barely 30 degrees above the horizon, the Thompsons had been careful about letting trees grow on the south side of the house. They planted forsythia, flowering quince, and P.J.M. rhododendron for some bright, early color in the yard, but no large tree had been allowed to grow within 100 feet of the house on the south or east, so that the sun could have unimpeded access to the porch. Under the shrubs, they planted daffodils, crocuses, and snowdrops.

To save money on reconstruction, the Thompsons used much of the old covered porch. They removed the roof and the side walls down to the bottom of the window frames. Then they nailed flat boards along the top of the truncated wall, which transformed the wall into a plausible para-pet. The floor of the former porch had been constructed of subflooring and tongue-and-groove. This was not the most durable outdoor surface, but the Thompsons kept it, because it was already there and because it excluded air coming up from under the porch.

Wood seemed an ideal surface for the Thompsons because, unlike masonry, it heats and dries very rapidly. Architect friends assured them that the water would puddle and rot the floor in a few years. But they cut several drain holes, and it drains within minutes after a rain. If the sun comes out, the deck dries off within ten minutes. The smooth surface of the deck is easy to shovel, and the winter sun quickly melts and dries any snow that cannot be swept or shoveled, no matter how cold the temperature.

The Thompsons' sunspot on a converted porch.

Drafts are a problem in a winter sunspot, and the Thompsons have worked hard to minimize them. The parapet left over from the wall of the former porch helps to cut down on drafts and eddies. In addition, planted just beyond the northeast corner of the porch is a Norway spruce whose branches baffle the north wind, which tended to sweep down the east face of the house and around the corner into the sunspot.

The Thompsons have found their sunspot enormously useful throughout the cold months. Their use of it is limited more by the availability of sunlight than by the outside temperature. Even when the temperature is in the twenties, they take to their sunspot anytime the sun is shining brightly. But the sky has to be absolutely clear at these temperatures; even the slightest veil of high cloud or a passing puffy white cloud can diminish the intensity of the sun enough to send them inside. As long as the sun is strong, the wind is rarely a problem. In fact, they report one day in which they were driven from their sunspot not by the wind, but by the snow blowing off the garage roof behind them onto their heads.

They didn't bother to shade their winter sunspot against summer sun because in their climate, the sun never resulted in an unacceptable heat gain to the house, and because they had an alternative sunspot on the west side of the house which they used in summer. The Thompsons found that when temperatures reached around 75° or more, they would move to the breezier west side of the house. The west sunspot was a redwood deck with 2×8s spaced ½ inch apart. This not only provided for drainage of the water on the deck, but also allowed some air to move through it, supplying an additional source of cooling.

When the temperature got above 90° or the breeze fell off to nothing, the Thompsons found that even the west deck could become too hot. Consequently, they have encouraged the growth of three birch trees and a cherry northwest of the deck, so that the hot sun is excluded on late summer afternoons. In addition, they have temporary awnings, like tent flies, that they deploy on hot days to keep the sun from shining on the deck. This may seem like a lot of trouble, but to former Californians, almost any trouble is worth the pleasure of getting outdoors.

A Sunspot for a Hot Climate

Where the Carters live, the summer is long and hot. Temperatures climb into the nineties almost every day. Winters are cool and short. The Carters thought they would like to have a sunny spot to sit in during nice winter days, but they were concerned about opening up their house to hot midday and afternoon summer sun. Consequently, they put their sunspot on the southeast corner of their house, next to the kitchen, where it was particularly convenient for weekend breakfasts but shielded from the summer afternoon sun. The back of the garage shelters the area from north winds, and a 5-foot wall shelters the sunspot from the east. The surface of the sunspot is brick, with raised flowerbeds

The Carter sunspot.

along the back of the garage and the wall. The winter morning sun slants into the kitchen. On cool sunny mornings, the Carters can either eat breakfast inside with the sliding glass door open or eat outside in their sunspot. At lunchtime, when the sun is in the south, they will move the picnic table out near the wall, where they can bask in its reflected heat.

Because of the hot summer climate, the Carters took care to provide shading for their sunspot. Along the entire south and east walls of the house is an overhanging arbor festooned with a wisteria vine. A magnolia tree overhangs the sunspot, providing spring flowers and summer shade. By noontime, the arbor, the magnolia, and the bulk of the house itself begin to shade the sunspot, and by 6:00 in the evening, when the Carters are cooking their evening meal, the sunspot is completely shaded.

The Carters were also worried about glare in their summer sunspot. Without something to cut down reflected light, their sunspot could become an oven, with heat and light bouncing back and forth from its reflecting surfaces. Consequently, they planted climbing roses along the west-facing wall of the sunspot. The south-facing wall of the garage they reserve for flowering and fruiting climbers which they grow on a permanent trellis. By April, this wall has a lush growth of pole beans, cherry tomatoes, and morning glories which fruit and flower several weeks early in the protected environment of the sunspot.

Sunspot in a Cellar Hole

When the Wallachs bought their stone house 25 years ago, it wasn't much to look at. It was the rundown home of an unlucky farmer who had survived for a decade on the milk from a few cows, and who deferred maintenance. The property's most undesirable feature was a ramshackle barn so rickety it supported itself by leaning against the south side of the house. The Wallachs decided to tear the old barn down to make room for a sunken garden within the stone walls of the barn's foundation.

Nowadays, when you stand in the midst of the Wallach's garden, you would never know that it once was a barn cellar. The garden is a sunken grassy court entirely surrounded by a 2-foot-high dry wall composed of neatly arranged flat square stones. Access to the garden from the house is provided by stone steps, and on the other three sides by grassy ramps that lead down from the shady lawn that surrounds the walled garden.

The Wallachs have been lucky with trees. By selecting and encouraging two of the young trees that had grown up near the dilapidated barn during the farm's decline, they now have two tall oaks on the west side of their walled garden. The lower branches of these trees have been repeatedly pruned over the years so that the trees shade the garden from the west when the sun is high in summer but let the sun in under them from late August to early April. On the northwest corner of the garden they planted a crabapple years ago which shades the garden and part of the house from the hot summer sun.

To the south of the garden, the lawn is shaded by woods, and against this background the Wallachs have planted witch hazel for its early bloom. On the east side, the walled garden is screened from the road by a lilac hedge. The lilacs not only provide a gorgeous display of white and purple flowers in spring, but also catch most of the snow that comes on easterly gales in winter, before it finds its way into the garden. Between the hedge and the front of the house, the Wallachs were careful to leave a wide gap to encourage airflow through their garden on hot sunny days. The prevailing summer wind in their region is southwesterly. When this breeze blows, air flows in under the oaks on the southwest, across the gar-

The Wallachs' sunken garden sunspot.

den, and out through the gap left for it between the house and the hedge.

Over the years, the Wallachs have made their barn cellar a luxuriant perennial garden. Almost everything they plant thrives, because the soil is composed of generations of cow, horse, and chicken manure that sifted through the rickety boards of the old barn floor. Early and late flowers, tall and short flowers, flowers of every conceivable shade bloom in a cascade of color from early spring to late fall.

The Wallachs had once thought that they might put a brick surface over some of their sunken garden to provide a quick-drying and durable surface. But they found that this extra work was really unnecessary. In the bright sunlight and excellent

soil of the barn cellar, the grass sod is sturdy and resilient. Their favorite use of the sunken garden is for noontime or afternoon parties, so that the dew that collects on the grass overnight is rarely a problem for them.

Wrap-up

Of all the features you can put in your garden, a sunspot will transform your life most. For much of the year, a well-conceived sundeck or patio can greatly increase the effective living area of the house at a fraction of the cost of an addition of comparable size. Your sunspot should be open to the sun, protected from cool-weather winds, and surfaced with an all-weather material with good heat-storage capacity. If overheating will be a problem, it should also be provided with shade and be open to cooling breezes. Sunspots are not only great places for people, they are good for plants as well. In the warm, protected environment of your sunspot, you can expect to have flowers and vegetables several weeks—perhaps months—longer than in surrounding areas.

Plants for Sundecks and Sunspots

Plant Name	Sundeck/Sunspot Feature	Description	Culture
Trees to Shade Sunspots			
Monarch birch (*Betula maximowicziana*)	Large, showy catkins up to 2¾ inches; cordate leaves give this tree the appearance of some lindens; decorative peeling bark	45 to 50 feet tall; bark is gray or orange-gray and flaking; leaves are broad-ovate, up to 6 inches long, dark green; yellow fall color	Sun or partial shade; moist, well-drained, sandy soil; tolerates urban conditions; resistant to bronze birch borer; to Zone 5
River birch (*Betula nigra*)	Trunk divided into several arching limbs, forming irregular crown; foliage is dark green, yellow in fall	40 to 70 feet tall; leaves are simple and alternate, irregularly oval, 1½ to 3 inches long, coarse, with doubly toothed margins; bark is thin and pinkish to reddish on young trees, dark reddish on older	Sun or partial shade; will tolerate almost any soil, but needs adequate moisture; to Zone 2
Sargent cherry (*Prunus sargentii*)	Single pink flowers, 1½ inches across, appear before leaves; fruits are ⅜ inch long and dark purple	Up to 50 feet tall; leaves are 2 to 5 inches long, elliptic to oval, long, pointed, sharply serrate, shiny dark green; bronze to red fall color	Full sun, sheltered from wind; average, well-drained soil; Zones 4–7
Saucer magnolia (*Magnolia soulangeana*)	Large, goblet-shaped, pink or white flowers, 4 inches across; blooms fall as leaves appear	Broad, spreading small tree 20 to 25 feet tall, 20 to 30 feet wide; leaves are glossy, oval, thick, and soft, with smooth margin and pointed tip, light to medium green	Sun to partial shade; rich, moist, well-drained soil; to Zone 5
Star magnolia (*Magnolia stellata*)	White to pink flowers, with many more petals than *Magnolia soulangeana*; flowers appear before leaves	Shrubby tree, 6 to 12 feet tall; compact and rounded in habit; leaves are oval to oblong, and pointed	Sun to partial shade; fertile, moist, well-drained, loamy soil; Zones 5–9
Sugar maple (*Acer saccharum*)	Dense foliage, medium to dark green in summer; spectacular, brilliant yellow, orange, and red in fall	Dense, rounded tree 60 to 75 feet tall; leaves have 3 main lobes, dozens of smaller lobes ending in points; bark is firm and ridged; greenish yellow flowers in April; winged fruit	Sun or partial shade; rich, well-drained soils; Zones 3–8

(continued)

Plants for Sundecks and Sunspots—*continued*

Plant Name	Sundeck/Sunspot Feature	Description	Culture
Sweet bay magnolia (*Magnolia virginiana*)	Fragrant, cup-shaped flowers, 2 to 3 inches in diameter, with 9 to 12 creamy white petals; dark red fruit	Usually 10 to 30 feet tall; deciduous in North; leaves are 4 to 6 inches long and 1 to 3 inches wide, blunt-pointed apex, shiny green above, whitish below; bark is light brown, scaly	Partial shade; fertile, well-drained, loamy soil that holds moisture; tolerates lime; Zones 5–9
Weeping Higan cherry (*Prunus subhirtella* var. *pendula*)	Pink to nearly white flowers appear before leaves; fruits are nearly black; early flowering ornamental with branches weeping to ground; flowers appear before leaves	Up to 25 feet tall; slender twigs, pendulous and crooked; leaves are oval to elongated, pointed, doubly serrate, 1 to 3 inches long.	Full sun; average, well-drained soil; to Zone 6
White oak (*Quercus alba*)	Imposing rounded form; oblong acorn, about 1 inch long, bowl-like cup shape with warty scales, shallow cap; attractive, deep green, fingered leaves; gorgeous red to burgundy fall color	80 to 100 feet tall; deciduous; leaves are 5 to 9 inches long, 2 to 4 inches wide, with 7 to 9 rounded lobes; gray bark, with narrow vertical blocks of scaly plates; wide spreading crown	Full sun; fair to good soil; plenty of moisture; to Zone 3
White pine (*Pinus strobus*)	Stalked, curved cones are 4 to 8 inches long; foliage is medium green to blue-green; handsome pyramidal to plume-like form	75 to 100 feet tall; needles in bundles of 5 are 3 to 5 inches long, soft, and flexible; bark is smooth and gray on young trees; broken into small rectangular blocks on mature trees; pyramidal crown of whorled, horizontal branches	Sun; prefers moist, sandy loam soils; Zones 3–8

Shrubs for Sunspots

Plant Name	Sundeck/Sunspot Feature	Description	Culture
Arnold Promise witch hazel (*Hamamelis ×intermedia* 'Arnold Promise')	Extra large 1½-inch primrose yellow, fragrant flowers last up to 3 weeks; blooms in February; brilliant orange fall foliage	Vigorous, vase-shaped shrub up to 20 feet tall; foliage is downy gray-green	Full sun to partial shade; needs some shelter; rich, moist, well-drained soil; Zones 5–8
Chinese witch hazel (*Hamamelis mollis* var. *brevipetala*)	Deep yellow, fragrant flowers appear in winter and early spring; foliage turns yellow in autumn	Shrub or small tree up to 30 feet tall; broad, rounded shape; trunk is short; bark is thin, smooth to slightly scaly, light brown; leaves are alternate and toothed; deciduous	Full sun to partial shade; needs some shelter; rich, moist, well-drained soil; Zones 5–8

Plant Name	Sundeck/Sunspot Feature	Description	Culture
Forsythia (*Forsythia ×intermedia*)	1½-inch, 4-lobed, pale sulfur yellow blossoms, twice the number of common forsythia; great for forcing in January and February	Up to 6 feet tall; robust with simple or 3-lobed leaves which are simple, opposite, and toothed	Full sun to partial shade; rich, well-drained soil; Zones 5–9
Forsythia (*Forsythia ovata*)	Small, solitary, greenish yellow flowers, less than ½ inch wide; earliest-flowering forsythia	Spreading shrub up to 5 feet tall; leaves are ovate to broad ovate; up to 2½ inches long, not lobed, serrate	Full sun to partial shade; rich, well-drained soil; Zones 5–9
P.J.M. rhododendron (*Rhododendron* 'P.J.M.')	Profuse lavender-pink flowers in early spring; leaves turn to bronze and purple in fall, remain so all winter; old leaves turn red in summer	Rounded shrub 3 to 6 feet tall; evergreen, dark green foliage; vivid flower color	Filtered sun; well-drained soil, distinctly acid, of good organic content; to Zone 4
Winged burningbush (*Euonymus alata*), Dwarf winged burningbush (*E. alata* 'Compacta')	Excellent scarlet autumn color; *compacta* makes fine hedge; needs only to be clipped once a year	Valued for its vase-shaped, sometimes horizontal growth habit; *compacta* has rounded outline, corky ridges on twigs	Full sun; well-drained soil; Zones 3–9

Vines to Shade Sunspots

Plant Name	Sundeck/Sunspot Feature	Description	Culture
Autumn clematis (*Clematis paniculata*)	White, 1-inch, scented flowers; September and October.	Vigorous climber, up to 30 feet; semievergreen foliage is dark green, with 3 to 5 leaflets	Sun; some vigorous growers may need some shade; alkaline soil; to Zone 5
Chinese wisteria (*Wisteria sinensis*)	Fragrant, lilac blue flowers in racemes up to 7 to 12 inches long; May and sometimes again in August	Climbs by twining; leaves are alternate, pinnately compound; vigorous ornamental vine	Full sun; may need sheltered area; light, sandy to rich soil; to Zone 5
Clematis (*Clematis* spp.) many cultivars	Diameter of flowers ranges from 1 inch to 10 inches; brilliant colored sepals, not true petals, range from bell shapes to saucer-like shapes; variety of colors	Climbs by attaching leaf stalks about the means of support; leaves are opposite, compound, with solitary flowers or flowers in clusters	Vines in sun, roots in partial shade; rich, well-drained soil; Zones 4–9
Climbing roses (*Rosa* spp.) and hybrids 'Blaze' 'Golden Showers' 'Paul's Scarlet' many others	'Blaze' has 2- to 3-inch, cupped, scarlet flowers 'Golden Showers' has 4-inch, double yellow blooms	Leaves are alternate, pinnately compound; produces long shoots or canes which can be trained over trellis or other support	Sun; fertile, well-drained soil

(continued)

Plants for Sundecks and Sunspots—*continued*

Plant Name	Sundeck/Sunspot Feature	Description	Culture
Japanese wisteria (*Wisteria floribunda*)	Flowers borne in clusters 8 to 20 inches long, opening progressively from base to tip; whitish flowers with cobalt violet keel and wings; flowers draped on long racemes	Leaves are alternate, compound, with 13 to 19 leaflets in each leaf; ovate and dark green; velvety seedpods	Sun; drought tolerant; well-drained soil; Zones 4–9
Silky wisteria (*Wisteria venusta*)	Flowers, largest in genus, are white; slightly fragrant; borne on racemes 3 inches long	Leaves have 9 to 13 oval to ovate, downy leaflets; velvety seedpods	Sun; average, well-drained soil, not too rich; Zones 4–9
Trumpet vine (*Campsis radicans*)	Orange to scarlet, trumpet-shaped flowers; 2 inches wide; midsummer	Climbs to 30 feet; leaves are compound, opposite, with 9 to 11 leaflets; small, root-like holdfasts are not strong enough, so plant needs assistance for support	Full sun; average soil, not too rich; Zones 4–9

Flowers for Sunspots

Plant Name	Sundeck/Sunspot Feature	Description	Culture
Anemone, windflower (*Anemone blanda*)	2-inch, star-shaped flowers; pale to deep blue, mauve, pink, or white with yellow centers; April and May	Flowers are borne on 4- to 6-inch stems; divided leaflets	Full sun; likes chalky soil; perennial; Zones 5–8
Bethlehem sage, Mrs. Moon (*Pulmonaria saccharata* 'Mrs. Moon')	Large, pink flower buds turn blue when fully open; trumpet-shaped; April and May	Leaves are white-spotted, alternate, oval, pointed; 12 inches tall	Partial to full shade; rich, moist, humusy soil; perennial; Zones 3–8
Blue squill (*Scilla siberica*)	Deep blue, wheel-shaped flowers, ½ inch across; each spike about 3 inches long and nodding; April	Flowers are born on 8-inch stems; leaves are strap-shaped, appearing with blooms	Sun or shade; humusy, moist, well-drained soil; perennial; Zones 4–8
Christmas fern (*Polystichum acrostichoides*)	Dark, glossy foliage	Leathery fronds are once divided, up to 5 inches wide and 2 feet long	Partial shade; moist soil; perennial; to Zone 4
Crested iris (*Iris cristata*)	Large, lilac blue, 4-inch blossoms; falls 1½ inches long	Short, spiky, 5-inch plants; leaves are evergreen and sword-shaped	Partial shade; rich, moist, acid soil; perennial; Zones 3–8
Crocus (*Crocus* spp.)	Tube-shaped, flaring, or funnel-shaped flowers; white, yellow, or purple; solitary on 3- to 4-inch stems; spring	Leaves are grassy, usually erect, medium to dark green with white lines running down centers; 5 inches tall	Full sun; well-drained, sandy, peat soil; perennial; Zones 3–7

Plant Name	Sundeck/Sunspot Feature	Description	Culture
Daffodil (*Narcissus* spp.)	Flowers yellow and white; usually have 6 outer petals and inner cup or trumpet of varying lengths in shades of yellow, white, pink, and orange	Leaves are long, narrow, and flat (sometimes rush-like); 12 to 18 inches tall	Full sun or light shade; moist, well-drained soil; perennial; Zones 3–8
Dwarf iris (*Iris pumila*)	Yellow or lilac flowers; outer segments 2 to 3 inches long; beard dense on lower part of the falls; spring	Practically stemless, 4 to 8 inches tall; leaves grow longer after flowering	Full sun; well-drained soil; perennial; to Zone 4
Epimedium (*Epimedium ×youngianum* 'Niveum')	White flowers held well above foliage; foliage bronze-red in spring	Foliage is heart-shaped, compound, light green; leathery, on stiff, wiry stems to 1 foot tall	Partial to full shade; moist soil, rich in organic matter; perennial; Zones 5–8
Garland flower (*Daphne cneorum*)	Pink, 1½-inch candytuft-like flowers completely cover plant in spring	Leaves are 1 inch, narrow, and vivid, glossy green; 9 to 12 inches tall	Light shade; well-drained, sandy soil of low fertility; perennial; Zones 4–7
Moss pink (*Phlox subulata*)	Bright purple, lilac, pink, rose, or white flowers; ¾ inch across; in dense clusters	Foliage moss-like, evergreen; creeper, up to 6 inches tall	Full sun; rich, sandy, alkaline soil; perennial; Zones 3–8
Primrose (*Primula ×polyantha*)	1½-inch flowers in various colors with golden eyes; in clusters; May	Thick, light green, tongue-shaped foliage; plants 10 inches tall in flower	Partial shade; rich, moist soil; perennial; Zones 3–8
Rock cress (*Arabis procurrens*)	Showy, tiny white flowers on racemes; April and May	Up to 1 foot tall; creeper; foliage is shiny, dark green; spreads quickly	Full sun; gravelly, well-drained soil; perennial; Zones 3–7
Snowdrop (*Galanthus nivalis*)	Small, solitary, white flowers up to 1 inch long; globular or bell-shaped and drooping; flowers from midwinter	Leaves are 9 inches long and ¼ inch wide	Sun to partial shade; slightly moist, sandy soil; perennial; to Zone 3
Spring heath (*Erica carnea*)	Small, rose red or white flowers borne in 1- to 2-inch-long racemes; January to May (January in warmer climates)	Leaves are evergreen, needle-like; plants form ground-covering masses	Full sun to partial shade; acid to slightly alkaline soil; perennial; to Zone 6
Vinca, myrtle (*Vinca minor*)	Blue-purple, saucer-shaped flowers, with 5 lobes, 1 inch across	Leaves are elliptic to ovate, 1 to 1½ inches long, smooth, opposite, and somewhat shiny; trailing runners; makes a good groundcover	Partial shade to full sun; moist, humusy, well-drained soil; perennial; Zones 4–9

CHAPTER 7

Rock Gardens

Calvin is a vegetable gardener at heart. Until recently, he could never understand what anybody saw in a rock garden. Having spent the better part of his adult life taking rocks *out* of a garden, he wondered why anybody would want to put rocks *in* one. Many of the rock gardens Calvin had seen looked exactly as if the owners thought rocks were a crop: flat, barren expanses with rampant foliage, and the odd boulder plumped here and there like so many unharvested pumpkins. This phenomenon puzzled Calvin. Was rock gardening some kind of silly fad, like keeping pet rocks or Cabbage Patch Dolls? Or was there some good practical or aesthetic reason to plant a garden among rocks?

Rock gardens make more sense when you understand their history. We have rock gardens now because of a time-honored English tradition of capturing little bits of nature and bringing them into the garden. The most ambitious of these gardens attempted to capture whole natural features, such as trickling brooks, deep limpid pools, dappled shady woods, sparkling sunny meadows, and even craggy mountaintops. The rock gardens of today are descendents of these gentrified mountaintops of the eighteenth century.

The basic idea behind a classic rock garden is to bring a little of the spirit of a mountaintop into the yard. Not only does a rock garden reproduce the ledges and outcroppings of a mountain, it also features mountain plants. In among the rocks of his or her ersatz mountain, the avid rock gardener carefully installs as many miniature trees, shrubs, and flowers as can be made to survive below the tree line. Thus, a classic rock garden is not just a garden among rocks. It is a microenvironment for alpine plants—the same plants aristocratic English travelers saw in the Alps when they took "The Grand Tour."

Once Calvin learned about the theory of

rock gardens, he began to take an interest. He had climbed a few mountains in his younger days, and he remembered delighting in the ledges and outcroppings, and in the plants he found growing there. What is it about such places, he now wondered, that makes them so special?

Partly, it must be all the work that you invest in getting there. Moss can never be so soft to lie on, nor running water so sweet to drink, as when you have clambered up a few thousand feet of steep slope to get to them. And perhaps where fear of falling is a factor, you come to be particularly attached to the rocks and plants of such places because you so desire to stay close to them. Views from high places may be spectacular, but they can only be enjoyed if you have a good foothold on a solid ledge and a good grip on the nearest tree.

But mountaintops are also attractive because of what you find when you get there. There is something dramatic, dire, fundamental about ledges thrusting through the surface of the soil. Perhaps it reminds us of the primordial barrenness of our planet. To see some miniature shrub lodged in a crevice in the cliff, slowly forcing apart the sides of its niche, making a tiny pocket of soil by collecting debris in its roots, is to become acutely aware of the debt we owe all growing things in making the planet habitable.

Therefore, one very good reason to have a rock garden is that you, like your eighteenth-century predecessors, have an attachment to mountaintops. If you want to recreate an Alpine meadow or Alaskan tundra, you'll probably be drawn to the classic rock garden. A classic rock garden contains plants called alpines, which originate in high mountain meadows. These plants have very special requirements and do not grow easily in areas where the frost-free period is greater than 140 days and the summers are warm. Outside of the mountainous regions to which they are naturally acclimated, alpine plants are best maintained along cool coasts (such as those in Maine and the Northwest) and in the northernmost portions of the United States.

Because the plants traditionally grown in a classic rock garden are so hard to please, you shouldn't enter into this sort of gardening lightly. We recommend that you do more reading on rock gardening before you get started. Phebe thinks that the best book on the subject is H. Lincoln Foster's *Rock Gardening* (Portland, Oreg.: Timber Press, 1982). You will also find good sections on rock gardening in James and Louise Bush-Brown's *America's Garden Book* and Donald Wyman's *Wyman's Gardening Encyclopedia*. Look for a local rock garden society, a prime source of information and plants. If you can't find one, you can join the American Rock Garden Society (membership includes the Society's bulletin). For information, write Norman Singer, Secretary, American Rock Garden Society, Norfolk Road, Sandisfield, MA 01255.

If you don't feel ready to invest the time and effort necessary to maintain the classic rock garden, there's an easier but equally striking alternative. Consider the other places in the world where rocks and plants exist in a harmonious and romantic association. You may have seen flowers growing among the crags of the rocky New England coast. Or you may have seen herbs growing in the walls of ancient abbeys in France, or heroic little trees clinging to the cliffs of Devon, and said to yourself, "I want a little bit of that in *my* garden." If this is the sort of environment you admire, you can experiment with more ordinary plants in your rock garden, and perhaps with some of the more tolerant of the traditional rock-garden plants.

You may, of course, have a completely practical, unromantic, and unaesthetic reason to have a rock garden of sorts: You may have no other choice. When the bulldozer comes to terrace your slope, it may strike ledge, or the soil around your house may be full of large boulders. In either case, you may be rock gardening whether you like it or not. Unless your rocky location is also in one of the places where alpines grow well, you may want to avoid the classic rock garden altogether and put among your rocks only plants that thrive in your local conditions.

Whether you are a rock gardener by choice or by convenience, this chapter should help you make the best of your situation.

The Elements of a Rock Garden

The essential elements of a rock garden are the rocks, alpine or other small plants, and soil. We shall consider each of these in turn.

All authorities on rock gardens agree that there is a terrible risk in getting the wrong kind of rocks for a rock garden and arranging them in the wrong way. The one thing you want to be sure to avoid is a garden that looks like a child's boulder collection. The rocks in a good rock garden look as if a piece of the earth's bedrock just happens to protrude through garden soil. To achieve this effect, the rocks must be carefully chosen and arranged.

Before you go very far in planning a rock garden, take a look at the rock formations in your neighborhood. From an aesthetic point of view, you usually will find them to be of two kinds—horizontal and vertical rock faces. The stone of a horizontal rock face presents a more or less continuous surface approximately level with the surface of the earth. Horizontal rock faces give a tremendous sense of stability and safety. A vertical rock face presents a rough, cliff-like edge. Rain and wind have often eroded the rock so that it is constantly crumbling. Vertical rock faces suggest instability and the danger of falling.

The question you have to consider is which of these natural formations you are trying to emulate in your rock garden. If it is the horizontal rock face, then you should look for smooth, flat rocks that can simulate the upper surface of an outcropping showing through the soil. If you want to imitate a vertical rock face, look for sharp rectangular rocks that can be stacked and aligned as if they were the outward face of the massive layers of stone that make up a hidden cliff.

Once you know what kind of rocks to look for, the next question is where to get them. Believe it or not, you can simply buy them, if you care to spend the money. Limestone is often used in rock gardens. It is porous, is easy to work, weathers beautifully, and is a good environment for lime-loving plants. Rocks with obvious layers are excellent for vertical rock faces, because by aligning the strata in the rocks, you can create a very convincing simulation of an underlying outcropping emerging at the surface.

Some kinds of rock aren't very suitable for rock gardens. A type of rock called tufa has been recommended for rock gardens because it is porous and water-absorbent, and is therefore a particularly good environment for plants. Unfortunately, tufa doesn't look like the sort of rock you would find in a natural outcropping. Also, small rounded boulders have little use in a rock garden, since landscapes made with them usually end up looking like a used-rock lot. Rocks for a rock garden should be large. In fact, if you can pick the rock up by yourself, it's probably too small.

Even the most handsome rocks aren't going to be much use if they look out of place. You want the rocks of your rock garden to look as if they had lain for a million years exactly where you put them yesterday. If you can find suitable rocks in your neighborhood, they will probably look best.

You may want to model your garden on local rock formations. One way to approach such a project is to find some local rocky spot that you think is attractive and try to recreate it. Obviously, in most cases you are not going to transport the actual rocks to your home. Nor should you remove wildflowers from their native site. You will, however, want to imitate the way in which the rocks are arranged in the natural formation, try to create soils that are similar, and try to find plants in nurseries or catalogs that capture its spirit.

Choosing local rocks will be essential if any natural rock formations, stone walls, or stone foundations can be seen from your rock garden. A rock garden must be in keeping with other rocks within sight.

Plants for a Rock Garden

The traditional plants for a rock garden are, as we have said, called alpines. Alpines, as their name suggests, are plants which originated on the high slopes and crags of mountaintops. They are accustomed to a short growing season, cool summers (and particularly cool summer nights), well-drained soil, and a constant supply of moisture. Some like an alkaline soil, and most prefer a situation in which they are not exposed to the full effects of the midday sun. If these requirements seem stringent to you, you've gotten the idea: The traditional rock garden is not a low-maintenance proposition.

You can, of course, plant anything in your rock garden, including plants which have nothing to do with rocks in nature. One of the nicest rock gardens Calvin has ever seen was composed of the smooth tops of three truck-sized submerged boulders planted 'round with orange California poppies. That was it. That was the garden. No fussy alpines, no carefully contrived artificial ledge, no ingenious trickles of water: just the boulders and the poppies. The garden didn't require much work. The boulders were already there, and the gardener just had to dig around them to make a bed for the poppies. The effect was wonderful. The poppies lapped against the gray, lichen-covered boulders like an apricot ocean.

Bulbs are useful in rock gardens because they bloom early in the season, often providing the first spring color, which contrasts wonderfully with the gray tones of the rocks and the white flecks of late winter snow. Members of the lily family, the chionodoxas, which originate from the Mediterranean climates of Crete and Turkey, provide blue flowers in small sprays at the end of a stalk. As their name implies (chionodoxa means "glory of the snow" in Greek), these are hardy, early bulbs which often flower when snow is still on the ground. They aren't fussy and can be grown in any good, somewhat coarse soil.

Crocuses of various sorts do extremely well in a rock garden because its light, granular soil warms up quickly. Crocus colors vary from palest lavenders and creams to the most vibrant deep purples and bold yellows, and careful grouping of colors can produce spectacular effects. Fall-blooming crocuses, including the saffron crocus, are also available, as are miniature varieties of iris, narcissus, and tulip.

Various groundcover plants are useful in rock gardens. They flow around the rocks, eagerly filling up the crevices between them. Some, such as moss pinks, provide dazzling displays of color. Good groundcovers for rock gardens include rock cress, carpet bugle, bellflower, bearberry, snow-in-summer, and dianthus. Ornamental thyme, with its myriad lavender flowers, makes a good cover. Fleshy plants such as sedum and hen-and-chickens provide flowers, cover, and interesting texture as well.

Alyssum is often planted among rocks to good effect. Its white and purple blooms are like a foam that spills over the rocks and collects in their crevices. Thrifts, brooms, and evening primroses form bright mats of color that beautifully offset the gray colors of ledges. Many perennials and shrubs go well with rocks. Columbine, basket-of-gold, bleeding heart, daisies, yarrow, baby's breath, primroses, heathers, and heaths all can be planted in groups to form dense floods of foliage.

Every rock garden should also include a few focus plants, usually a larger shrub or small tree whose shape or hue complements or contrasts with the color or form of the rocks. Azaleas or rhododendrons do well in the shade of rock outcroppings or where larger trees crowd around a rock garden. Dwarf conifers, such as juniper, blue spruce, and mugo pines, drape and trail over the rock, their green foliage setting off the gray texture of the rock surface.

Plan carefully if you want to mix traditional rock-garden plants and ordinary garden plants in the same rock garden. The slow-growing alpines of the traditional rock garden simply cannot and

Phebe's Favorites for Rock Gardens

Shrubs and Perennials for the Sunny Rock Garden

Ledges and barberry seem to be made for each other. These tough plants can take the exposure, and reward us with bright yellow flowers in early spring and pretty red fruits in fall. I particularly like the 'Crimson Pygmy' dwarf Japanese red barberry which has pretty mahogany-red leaves for accent.

Two small falsecypresses for the rock garden are *Chamaecyparis plumosa* var. *compressa,* generally rounded with gold-tipped foliage, and the miniature silver falsecypress, with soft blue foliage. Both foliage colors augment any color scheme, to either blend or accent. Some falsecypresses need winter protection in exposed places. There are many other good dwarf conifers suitable for the rock garden.

Cotoneaster is also a made-to-order rock garden plant. The rock is a pretty foil for the small, glistening foliage and bright red berries that characterize the species. Some of the low cotoneasters mimic the soft undulations of the ledge in their patterns of growth. Early cotoneaster and cranberry cotoneaster are two varieties. The slightly taller rock spray cotoneaster will rise out of a rock crevice.

For a soft gray touch, the artemisias are welcome in every garden. 'Silver Mound', which stays low, is especially suitable for ledges.

No sunny wall or rock garden can be without basket-of-gold, with its soft gray-green foliage tumbling along the ledge or over the wall. It's a bright cheery note to start the spring.

A companion for basket-of-gold for walls and ledges is arabis or rock cress. The wall rock cress is covered with dainty white flowers in early spring and has a mat of gray-green foliage. There is also a pink-flowered variety.

I am always looking for ways to include some ornamental grasses in plantings, and blue fescue is an ornamental definitely worth featuring. The variety 'Sea Urchin' is more compact and quite blue, a nice accent.

The yarrows are another sturdy group of plants with feathery foliage and perky flowers. Whether you want hot pink flowers ('Cerise Queen') or sulfur-yellow ('Moonshine'), they are a dainty delight.

Many gardeners want to grow heather and achieve a gorgeous patterned carpet of gold, red, and green, as well as a showy display of late-summer bloom in pinks, lavenders, whites, and purples. Oddly enough, it probably is too much attention that does heather in, rather than too little. Sandy, organic, not too fertile, moist but well-drained soil, out of the wind but in the sun, suits this plant. Although plants are hardy, covering heather in winter helps protect the foliage, but if you don't cover it, early spring pruning will renew the plant. A wonderful opportunity for the designer!

will not compete with rampant garden-variety plants, and will be overcome almost immediately. Care must be taken when introducing any rampant plant into a rock garden. The rocks make it difficult to grub out an undesirable or undisciplined plant once it is established. You must think about where a plant is likely to wander before you put it in the ground. If you want to put an invasive plant in the ground and don't want to worry about its taking over the entire garden, put it in a pocket in a boulder, or in a group of stones with a metal root barrier to keep your vagabond from slipping out through the crevices.

Putting in Your Rock Garden

If you are determined to have a classic rock garden with traditional alpines, then at every stage of construction you must keep in mind the preferred habitat of many of these plants. Think of a high

One of the very best groundcovers for the sunny ledge is bearberry. It's evergreen, with small, pretty apple-blossom pink flowers in May and bright red berries. It can literally carpet a ledge and move out in fingers over the rock. This plant is also a good groundcover for sunny, well-drained banks.

No sunny wall can be without snow-in-summer. It has nice silvery foliage and "snowfall" flowers, and it's another tumbler.

I love the dainty, nodding heads of columbine with their pretty fern-like foliage, even though you never know where they are going to come up from year to year. (I have more growing in my driveway than in my garden!) They come in many colors—yellows, blues, reds—a nice foil for ledges.

For summer-long bright yellow, St. John's wort is the ticket, with nice dark green foliage and stiffly upright flowers. A golden touch against the gray tones of the rock.

Sedums and stonecrop are easy and colorful groundcovers for sunbaked rocks and walls, as the name stonecrop implies. Sedum foliage is succulent. Some have gray-green foliage like *Sedum reflexum*, or showy pink to red flowers, like 'Autumn Joy', a current favorite with many designers and gardeners. Some sedums are fairly rampant growers, like the goldmoss stonecrop.

Little patches of thyme at the base of a rock wall, where they hug the wall and creep onto stepping stones nearby, are attractive, sweet-smelling when touched or walked on, and colorful in their foliage variations. Plant some woolly thyme for gray foliage, the common mother-of-thyme for green foliage with white or lavender flowers, or variations of common thyme *(Thymus vulgaris)* for yellow-green or white-edged foliage and lemon scent. A few varieties of mother-of-thyme have reddish or pink flowers in summer. All make very colorful mats. In my experience, this is not a plant to count on to cover large areas, as it can die back in winter, leaving empty spots in an otherwise tight mat.

Annuals for the Sunny Rock Garden

Wallflower likes cool summers but is a traditional rock garden and wall plant, hardy for some. Known for its cheery yellow and orange flowers.

Try California poppy with bright yellow, apricot, and orange colors for a more naturalized effect.

Annual baby's breath is always a favorite for billowy shape and dainty blooms.

Color combinations with geraniums are endless. No summer garden can omit these sturdy, easy, colorful garden favorites.

Sweet alyssum blooms in dainty drifts of white, lavender, or rose flowers.

(continued)

Phebe's Favorites for Rock Gardens–continued

Plants for Shady Rock Gardens

Many low azaleas fit very nicely into a ledge pocket. There are so many varieties that color is the prime consideration in selecting plants, but I like 'Delaware Valley White', 'Blaauw's Pink' (a lovely salmon pink), and many others. 'Delaware Valley White' has light green foliage so that it shows up against a ledge.

Some of the smaller rhododendrons also fit nicely into a rock garden. 'Purple Gem' has wonderful, almost smoky green new foliage, and turns bronze in winter. Its flower is perhaps the main drawback, being a bluish lavender, but it comes early in April when not too many other plants are in bloom. The foliage is just superb, but it does need some sun.

Astilbes and rocks also fit well together. The finely cut leaves of the astilbe and saucy, colorful flower plumes in July give this plant a very welcome spot in the shady rock garden. Again, choice is based on color preference. I like a nice large drift of one color for the most dramatic effect, with perhaps one or two plants lighter or darker for accent. Choose a drift of 'Red Sentinel' along with a plant or two of 'Bridal Veil' or 'William Buchanan' (white) for a dramatic red splash, brighter for the white accent. All three are so-called late bloomers, and with planning, the blooming season can be extended by taking note of exact bloom times.

Ferns fit beautifully in the shady rock garden, large ones for a dramatic touch, small ones for softening a jagged bit of ledge.

Hostas seem to always come up for the shade.

There is nothing more dramatic in a rock garden than a drift of *Hosta sieboldiana* varieties with their large blue leaves, or some of the silver-leaved varieties, 'Silver Crown', *H. undulata* var. *albo-marginata,* or *H. crispula,* some with fragrant flowers of either lavender or white.

The climbing hydrangea is an indispensable vine for any garden, but lovely clinging to ledges or walls in sun or shade. The showy flat white flowers can bloom for two weeks or more in June to July, and the foliage is a handsome green throughout the season and well into the fall.

Primroses are not easy, as they demand moisture throughout the growing season as well as a fertile, humusy soil, but if you have ever been in an English garden in spring and seen the beautiful carpets of yellow primroses, you will be hooked on them for life. The polyanthus primroses are commonly grown here and come in lots of color combinations, which are showy in groupings in the shady rock garden. Again, I feel that for the most pleasing display you shouldn't try to display every color available, but should be harmoniously selective. It's not easy—there are lots of pretty ones.

Annuals for the Shady Rock Garden

Wax and tuberous begonias all have good colors and colorful foliage for the shade.

Impatiens is a standard for shade. I don't believe there are many people who have not planted impatiens somewhere in their garden.

mountain crag, where the stones radiate their heat to the thin air by night and are basted with cloud mists by day. The soil, where there is soil, consists of glaciated grit with ever so little organic matter from the few plants that have managed to get a purchase on the slopes. Alpine soils drain quickly, but their moisture is constantly refreshed by mists and underground seepage. Here, the summers are short and winters long. Deep snows cloak the crags from late fall to early spring. To the extent that you don't have these conditions in your garden, you are going to have to emulate them if you want to have a classic rock garden.

Preparing the Site

The first step in installing your rock garden is, painful to say, to remove the topsoil down to the subsoil. (Depending on which kind of rock garden you are building, you may want to amend the topsoil and put it back later, or you may keep it to use in your other gardens.) Once the topsoil has been set aside, give the subsoil roughly the contours you want for your finished rock garden.

Rock gardens, true to their mountain origins, are generally set out on a sloping site. Natural, rock-strewn mountainsides are rarely like the terraces of stately homes. If your site is flat, build it up in areas for a more realistic effect. One attractive contour is a small, shallow "valley" with a bit of meander in it. This landform gives you two slopes in which to put your rock garden, and a good place for a path down the middle. Beware of a rock garden set out on an artificial mound. Artificial mounds often end up looking just like—well, artificial mounds.

Before going on to the next step, examine your subsoil closely. If it is a coarse, droughty material such as you might find in a mountain streambed or the terminal moraine of a glacier, then you are ready to continue. If, on the other hand, the subsoil is clay, you must provide a drainage medium. In such cases you want to cover the subsoil with a deep layer of some coarse material such as gravel or stone chips.

Once the foundation of your rock garden is in place, you should begin to think about where to place the rocks. Why worry about the rocks before the soil is in place? The reason is that the rocks in a rock garden are set *in* the topsoil, not *on* it. An excellent choice for size and shape is a flat rock, narrower than it is long and much thinner than it is wide. Such rocks can be stacked like poker chips to give a convincing imitation of a ledge, or scattered on a flat surface to give the impression of an outcropping lurking just below the surface of the grass.

The careful placement of the rocks is important for both practical and aesthetic reasons. First of all, the rock should be placed on the subsoil so that its wider, heavier part is down. Such a placement is particularly important if the rock is to serve as a step. A rock planted heavy-side-up will in time begin to wobble and become a hazard. The second rule of placement is that most of the rock should be under the final soil line. A rock that is well dug in not only looks more natural, it is more stable: less likely to tip if it is walked on, less likely to wash out if it is on a slope. Third, the rock should be dug in so that it is tilted toward the slope. Rocks that are properly set in this way tend to drain water back into the slope toward the roots of the plants and discourage the formation of rivulets

There is an art to laying rocks so they look natural and hold a slope. Notice that these rocks are irregularly shaped, with lots of nooks and crannies; that they are of varying sizes, and tend to be flat; and that they are set vertically and deeply, with the heaviest side downward.

that trickle down the slope and erode soil and plants alike.

Once the rocks are in place, you are ready to put down the topsoil. Which kind of soil you put down will depend on the kind of rock garden you are making. The classical rock garden requires a very coarse sandy soil mixed with a moderate amount of coarse organic material, such as granulated peat moss. If you are not trying for a classic rock garden, any good garden loam will do. If you return your own topsoil to the site, be sure that you have carefully screened it for grass roots, or you may inadvertently plant your rock garden to grass.

Once the soil is ready, the plants can be put in place. Putting in rock-garden plants requires all the care of putting in any bedding plant, and more. In a classic rock garden, the plants will require constant watering until their roots become long enough to reach down under the rocks to the water supply that you have arranged for them. For any rock garden, weed control is a continuing problem. Because established weeds are difficult to dig out of the rocks, new rock gardeners are well advised to be in their gardens every day, picking out the

tiniest of weeds. Erosion control is another challenge. Carefully observe the flow of water down your rock garden in rainy weather. If plants or rocks begin to erode, try to channel the water into safer paths.

Some Successful Rock Gardens
A Cabin on a Boulder

Al Jones's retirement dream was a cabin on a mountain lake. So when he retired from his city job, Al and his wife Flora purchased a little lakeside cabin about an hour from their city home. Since Al didn't have to work any more, they planned to spend most of the warm months at the cabin.

When Flora surveyed the yard of their cabin for flower-growing possibilities, she was discouraged. Here and there the barren surface of the boulder emerged from the soil. Elsewhere the ground was covered with lowbush blueberries, grasses, and poison ivy.

The Jones rock garden on a boulder.

But Flora was determined. Together she and Al scrabbled the blueberry bushes out of two of the pockets where they were growing. Beneath the bushes, they found a shallow basin of soil, 1 to 2 feet deep at most, and a deeper crevice leading into the depths of the boulder. In each of the pockets, they loosened and dug up the soil, limed and fertilized it, added compost, and then planted nasturtiums, geraniums, and low junipers to scramble over the rocks.

Flora and Al would never call their composition a rock garden, but the flowers and the rocks together are a source of great pleasure to them. Planting the natural basins with flowers each spring symbolizes the coming of summer for the Joneses. Every Memorial Day, they bring the bedding plants up to the cabin. By the Fourth of July, the plants have nearly filled the basin and are starting to clamber around on the surface of the boulder. As long as Flora keeps them well watered and fertilized, they will spread extensively each season, their bright yellow, red, and orange blossoms picking up subtle orange tints in the granite and in the lichens that encrust it.

Flowerfall

The Gauchiers, Jeb and Julie, built their house in a wooded lot up in the Appalachians. The house site is cut into a heavily wooded, south-facing hillside. Their original plan was to bulldoze deeply into the hillside and draw out the soil onto the down slope to make a large terrace on which to build their house. This plan worked well for creating the house site itself and the front lawn, but when they cut farther into the hillside to make the backyard, they hit ledge, a limestone monstrosity receding backward into the hillside in a succession of little pockets and terraces.

Jeb called off the bulldozer and the Gauchiers forgot about their backyard for a while. They set about doing the basics, building the house and landscaping the front lawn and driveway. All this time, they put from their minds any thoughts about the great rock rampart in their backyard. But one evening, during their third summer, they were sitting in the shade of the trees that overhung their backyard and they got to talking about the ledge. Jeb suggested as a joke that Julie take up rock gardening. She accepted the challenge.

First, Julie went to the town library and took out a couple of gardening books that had sections on rock gardens. She learned that she lived too far south for classical rock gardening with alpines, but she also learned that her particular site had some advantages for maintaining more ordinary plants among rocks. Her southern mountain climate was cloudy and moist compared with the climate of the lowlands only a few hundred miles away. The overhanging trees on the top of the ledge and the shadows cast on the ledge by the house in deep winter were also advantages for rock gardening, the tree shade because it reduced the heat of the cliff during the hottest parts of the summer days, and the house shade because it kept the ledge from thawing during sunny winter days. Even the outcropping itself seemed particularly appropriate. Limestone is a soft, porous rock that holds water well, and the ledge had numerous trickles and seeps running from it.

The first step in the Gauchiers' rock-gardening program was to edit the ledge the bulldozers had left them. Having been raised with the granite of New England, Jeb was surprised at how easily he could work the limestone with a chisel and sledge. Being sure to always wear protective goggles, he enlarged and deepened several of the plateaus on the cliff and cut some channels to prevent erosion. He even cut a system of inconspicuous steps so that he and Julie could reach all the parts of their rock garden easily.

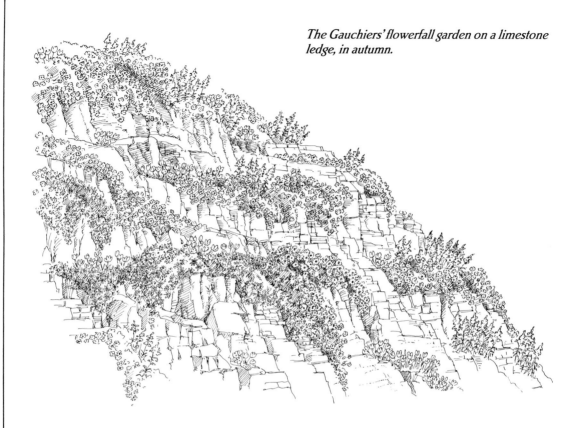

The Gauchiers' flowerfall garden on a limestone ledge, in autumn.

When it came to planting, Julie picked out several low, spreading plants. Her idea was to plant them on the plateaus of the ledge and allow them to spread and drape themselves down the rocks like a cascade. To heighten the cascade effect, she chose plants with yellow, blue, and white flowers to give the impression of sunlight and blue water.

Once it was established, her garden bloomed from snowmelt to snowfall. First to bloom were flocks of yellow winter aconite, followed by crocuses and pale blue dwarf iris. By April, the rocks were lit up by rock cress and basket-of-gold billowing down the rocks in festoons of white and gold. Next to bloom was the bugleweed, with spikey blue flowers poking up among the flowers of golden stonecrop. The snow-in-summer and low, blue-flowered veronicas of June gave way to creeping gypsophila and misty gray tones of santolina sparkling with tiny yellow blossoms. This, in turn, was followed by the dainty native goldenrod and low asters. And all through the season, the ledge sported, here and there, the nodding blue and white blossoms of bellflowers and columbine.

Now, a few years later, Julie and Jeb are absurdly proud of their rock garden. It is the part of their home that guests comment on most when they come to visit. They step immediately to the back terrace to look up at the ledge and its beautiful cascade of flowers. In fact, as a joke, Julie's sister, who has visited often, gave Julie some notepaper for Christmas last year with the simple address "Flowerfall" at the top.

A Stone Wall Garden

In the counties that border the Great Lakes in New York State, the rocks were laid down millions of years ago as thin layers of sediment. Everywhere you travel here, wherever the structure of the earth is laid bare, along the interstates, along the railroad cuts, along the sides of the canals, you see the layers of stone rising and falling as the rolling land rises and falls.

Anne Corbet lives in this part of New York. Anne is just starting out on her own as an interior designer, and she decided to use her new house as a showplace. Her house was on gently sloping ground, amidst a grove of Scotch pine. Instead of accepting the slope, Anne decided to terrace the area around the house into two levels bounded by retaining walls and reached by stone steps.

By terracing, she wanted to achieve the effect of a natural outcropping. She prevailed on a local contractor to excavate several layers of the natural stone from a disused quarry a few miles from her house. The contractor kept the different strata separate in piles so that the mason could reproduce the natural strata when he built the walls. In the particular deposit the contractor excavated, there were four layers. Two were a blackish stone that fractured into neat blocks. Between these two was a layer of slate-like rock that broke into flat plates, and a very thin layer of a white, quartz-like material.

Once her retaining wall was in place, Anne gave careful thought to her plantings. She wanted plants to complement the strict linear mood of the walls, and she wanted the overall effect to be somber and restrained, and to pick up the tone of the existing grove of conifers. Anne decided to feature conifers and heaths in her plantings around her new wall.

Atop the wall, Anne planted low trailing blue rug juniper, whose branches sprawled over the severe layers of the wall. At the foot of the wall, she

The Corbet terraced evergreen garden.

planted more junipers and miniature falsecypress with foliage of muted gold, silver, and dark green, accented here and there with miniature Scotch pine and spires of a tall blue juniper. Beside the steps between the levels, she put a dwarf blue spruce, its vibrant blue foliage framed by the stern lines of the rock staircase.

Wrap-up

In the classic rock garden, exotic alpine plants associate with carefully placed rocks in a poor, moist, cool, well-drained soil. These requirements are specific and difficult to meet in most gardens. But gardeners who are not fussy about history can find great enjoyment in maintaining a garden which captures some of the spirit of a classic rock garden, but uses more familiar plants and less extreme soil conditions. The challenge for any rock gardener is to make a composition of rocks and flowers that looks as if it had been in place for millennia, just waiting for you or your guests to come upon it in your garden.

Plants for Rock Gardens

Plant Name	Rock Garden Feature	Description	Culture
Shrubs and Vines for Rock Gardens			
Blaauw's Pink azalea (*Rhododendron* 'Blaauw's Pink')	Salmon pink flowers; April and May	Low, spreading, evergreen shrub	Partial shade; open, moist, well-drained, acidic soil; mulch; to Zone 5
Climbing hydrangea (*Hydrangea anomala* var. *petiolaris*)	Fragrant white flowers in several branched corymbs; large flat clusters 6 to 8 inches across; June and July	Can climb to 75 feet; small, root-like holdfasts all along stems; leaf margin is regularly serrated	Partial shade or full sun; highly tolerant of shade; rich, porous, somewhat moist soil; Zones 5–8
Cranberry cotoneaster (*Cotoneaster apiculatus*)	Pink, mostly solitary flowers; May and June; fruit forms in fall, ¼ to ⅓ inch in diameter	18 to 24 inches high; nearly ovate leaves, pointed; foliage shiny green; evergreen in mild climates	Sunny location, well-drained soil; Zones 4–7
Crimson Pygmy barberry (*Berberis thunbergi* var. *atropurpurea* 'Crimson Pygmy')	Dark red, grooved leaves throughout the growing season; bright red berries, ⅓ inch long; October, persisting into winter	Dwarf, compact growth; thorny; yellow flowers, ⅓ to ½ inch long; April and May	Full sun; can be grown in poor soils; withstands drought; Zones 4–8
Delaware Valley White azalea (*Rhododendron* 'Delaware Valley White')	Large, abundant, pure white flowers; spring; light green foliage	Low, dense form; fine foliage; evergreen	Partial shade; open, moist, well-drained, acidic soil; mulch; to Zone 5

Plant Name	Rock Garden Feature	Description	Culture
Early cotoneaster (*Cotoneaster adpressus* var. *praecox*)	Small, pinkish flowers; leaves turn red in autumn; small red fruits, ⅜ inch in diameter, appear in fall	Deciduous; broadly ovate leaves, wavy at margins; vigorous and prostrate	Full sun; well-drained soil; thrives in poor soil; to Zone 4
Falsecypress (*Chamaecyparis plumosa* var. *compressa*)	Branchlets are feathery, with related cultivars of various leaf colors	Extremely dwarf evergreen; very slow growing; dense and conical	Sun or shade; good, rich, moist soil; Zones 4-8
Miniature silver falsecypress (*Chamaecyparis pisifera* var. *squarrosa pygmaea*)	Soft, bluish green, needle-like foliage; several related cultivars of different habits and leaf colors	Coniferous, evergreen; narrowly pyramidal with horizontal branches; dense shrub; branches feathery; leaves smooth, blue-green	Sun or shade; rich, moist, well-drained, lime-free soil; Zones 3–8
Purple Gem rhododendron (*Rhododendron* 'Purple Gem')	Light purple flowers; mid-April	Rounded, dwarf evergreen shrub	Partial shade; open, moist, well-drained, acidic soil; mulch; to Zone 4
Rock spray cotoneaster (*Cotoneaster horizontalis*)	Pinkish flowers appear in mid-June; followed in fall by bright red berries, ³/₁₆ inch in diameter	3-foot-long, horizontal branches with rich, glossy, roundish leaves	Full sun; well-drained soil; Zones 5–9

Herbaceous Plants for Rock Gardens

Plant Name	Rock Garden Feature	Description	Culture
Annual baby's breath (*Gypsophila elegans*)	Small, ¼-inch, dainty white sprays of flowers on thread-like stems	Upright growth habit to 1½ feet; lance-shaped leaves	Full sun; well-drained soil; do well in soil with high lime content; annual; Zones 3–8
Astilbe (*Astilbe ×arendsii*) 'Bridal Veil' 'Red Sentinel' 'William Buchanan'	Rose pink, crimson, rosy lilac, or white plumes; June and July	Flowers on 2-foot spikes; semiglossy, bronze foliage	Sun to partial shade; moist, humusy soil; perennial; Zones 4–8
Autumn Joy stonecrop (*Sedum spectabile* 'Autumn Joy')	Slightly rounded flower heads; flowers pink, turning mahogany in fall; August to frost	Tall stalks with fleshy leaves; bushy plants reach 2 feet tall	Full sun; average, well-drained soil; perennial; Zones 3–9
Basket-of-gold (*Alyssum saxatile*)	Large clouds of small, bright yellow flowers; April and May	Gray-green leaves	Full sun; average, well-drained soil; perennial; Zones 3–9
Bearberry (*Arctostaphylos uva-ursi*)	White blossoms blushed with pink, followed by red berries	Tiny, glossy green, 1½-inch leaves form dense mat	Sandy, acid soils; good for oceanside plantings; perennial; Zones 3–8

(continued)

Plants for Rock Gardens—*continued*

Plant Name	Rock Garden Feature	Description	Culture
Blue fescue (*Festuca glauca*) and hybrids 'Sea Urchin'	Sapphire-blue foliage	About 10 inches tall; fountain-like tuft of wiry grass	Full sun; dry soil with good drainage; perennial; Zones 4–9
California poppy (*Eschscholzia californica*)	Apricot-orange flowers; 3 inches wide	Gray-green, finely divided, filigree-like leaves; flowers are borne on slender, 18-inch stems	Full sun; light, sandy, dryish soil; good near the coast; annual; perennial in California
Cerise Queen yarrow (*Achillea millefolium* 'Cerise Queen')	Flat, 3-inch panicles of flowers in summer and fall; bright cerise color; decorative, aromatic, ferny foliage	Feathery, evergreen, deeply cut leaves; plant is 2½ to 3 feet tall	Full sun; average soil; drought tolerant; perennial; Zones 2–8
Columbine (*Aquilegia ×hybrida*) (*A. canadensis*)	*A. canadensis* has graceful, nodding flowers with red spurs around bright yellow centers; hybrids in various colors; April and May	Long-spurred hybrids 1 to 3 feet tall; green to gray-green, fern-like foliage; flowers are borne on tall, very slender stems	Partial shade to full sun; average, well-drained soil; perennial; Zones 2–8
Geranium, cranesbill (*Geranium endressi*)	Masses of clear pink flowers, June to September	Plants to 15 inches with deeply lobed, 5-part leaves	Full sun; average, well-drained soil; perennial; Zones 4–9
Goldmoss stonecrop (*Sedum acre*)	Bright yellow, ½-inch flowers; May and June	Small, pointed, light green, succulent, alternate, evergreen leaves	Full sun; average, well-drained soil; perennial; Zones 3–9
Heather (*Calluna vulgaris*)	Diminutive white, pink, or red flower spikes	About 18 inches tall; evergreen foliage	Full sun, but tolerates shade; acid soil of poor quality; perennial; Zones 4–6
Hosta (*Hosta crispula*)	Lilac, funnel-shaped flowers on long spikes; decorative, variegated foliage	Dark green, waxy leaves up to 8 inches long, edged white	Partial to full shade; average, humusy, well-drained soil; perennial; Zones 3–8
Impatiens (*Impatiens wallerana*)	Bright scarlet 1½-inch flowers with thin, curving spurs; can also be pink, salmon, purple, or white	Succulent stems with alternate leaves; upper leaves sometimes whorled	Sun or shade; rich, sandy loam; annual; perennial in deep South
Moonshine yarrow (*Achillea taygetea* 'Moonshine')	Bright, canary yellow flowers; June to September	18 to 24 inches tall; feathery gray-green foliage	Full sun; average to poor soil; perennial; Zones 2–8
Mother-of-thyme (*Thymus serpyllum*)	Small, 2-lipped, lavender flowers; June; excellent groundcover	Low, aromatic creeper; mostly evergreen	Full sun; average to poor, well-drained soil; perennial; Zones 3–9

Plant Name	Rock Garden Feature	Description	Culture
Polyanthus primrose (*Primula ×polyantha*)	1½-inch flowers with golden eyes; variety of colors; May	Light green leaves in basal clumps	Partial shade; rich, moist soil; perennial; Zones 3–8
Rock cress, arabis (*Arabis procurrens*)	Very fine white flowers on elongated racemes; April to May	Compact growth of creeping, dark green foliage	Full sun or partial shade; gravelly, well-drained soil; perennial; Zones 3–7
St. John's wort (*Hypericum hidcote*)	Bowl-shaped, golden flowers; 3 inches wide	3-inch-long, light green ovate to lanceolate leaves with silvery undersides	Sun or partial shade; average soil; perennial; Zones 5–8
Sedum (*Sedum reflexum*)	Cup-shaped, yellow flowers; 2 to 3 inches and drooping in bud; summer	Evergreen; forms mat of gray-green narrow leaves and reddish stems	Full sun; well-drained, gritty soil; perennial; ultra-hardy
Seersucker hosta (*Hosta sieboldiana*) and hybrids	Soft lilac, bell-shaped flowers on tall spikes; late spring, early summer; decorative blue-green, seersucker-like foliage	Heart-shaped, 12-inch puckered leaves; blue-green with broad golden-yellow margins that deepen in color as season progresses	Partial to full shade; average, humusy, well-drained soil; perennial; Zones 3–8
Silver Crown hosta (*Hosta undulata* var. *albo-marginata*)	Lavender flowers on tall spikes; July and August; handsome variegated foliage	8-inch, twisting, undulating, broad, oval leaves with green margins and white centers	Partial to full shade; average, humusy, well-drained soil; perennial; Zones 3–8
Silver King artemisia (*Artemisia ludoviciana* var. *albula* 'Silver King')	Silvery foliage; aromatic	Leaves of various shapes; silver-gray with pungent scent	Full sun; average to poor, well-drained soil; perennial; Zones 4–8
Silver Mound artemisia (*Artemisia schmidtiana* 'Silver Mound')	Silvery foliage in handsome mounds	About 12 inches tall and 18 inches across; mounds of fine, silvery foliage	Full sun; average to poor, well-drained soil; perennial; Zones 4–8
Snow-in-summer (*Cerastium tomentosum*)	Masses of pure white, star-shaped flowers; ½ inch across; five petals	Silver-gray foliage forms dense mat; leaves ¾ inch long	Full sun; average to poor, well-drained soil; perennial; Zones 2–8
Sweet alyssum (*Lobularia maritima*)	Small, saucer-shaped white, pink, or violet flowers; profuse	Small, lanceolate to linear leaves; alternate with unbroken margins	Sun to partial shade; average soil; annual
Thyme (*Thymus vulgaris*)	Lilac to purplish, tiny flowers borne on small, upright spikes; whorled bunches; delightfully pungent foliage	Leaves are small, entire, linear, or elliptical; deep green; bushy habit, 1 foot tall	Full sun; average to poor, well-drained soil; perennial; Zones 3–9
Wallflower (*Cheiranthus* spp.)	Yellow, gold, red, or mahogany flowers; 4-clawed; fragrant	Leaves are narrow with few marginal teeth	Sun to partial shade; needs cool, moist air to do best; average soil; annual

(continued)

Plants for Rock Gardens—*continued*

Plant Name	Rock Garden Feature	Description	Culture
Wall rock cress (*Arabis caucasica*)	Small, fragrant white or purple flowers, often in ample spikes or racemes; loose clusters	Basal or stem leaves, usually hairy, gray-green	Full sun; dry soil; perennial; to Zone 4
Woolly thyme (*Thymus pseudolanuginosus*)	Tiny, rose pink flowers; handsome mats of foliage	Minute, silver-gray carpet of leaves	Full sun, average to poor, well-drained soil; perennial; Zones 4–9

CHAPTER 8

Winter Gardens

*T*he gardens of most readers of this book will grow only six months a year. But, except for a few scant weeks of vacation, you live in your yard twelve months a year. In fact, many of you spend more time in your yard when it is dormant than when it is growing. Yet how many people think about how their gardens look during the dormant season?

Calvin does his landscaping at the edge of Zone 5, where the land is dormant seven months of the year and where the frost-free period can be as short as 90 days! He does his writing at home, often searching through the windows of his study for inspiration in the surrounding landscape. Calvin spends a lot of time looking at a dormant landscape.

Such habits lead to strange tastes in plants, and new ways of looking at familiar plants. A well-kept lawn has little to offer in winter, but a weedy pasture is full of tufts, stalks, and seed clusters of wonderfully different colors and textures. Birds flutter among the seed tufts. Small animals scurry around the grass stems. When the snow falls, these little creatures cover the snow with webs of tracks and make intricate burrows under it.

During ice storms, the fine twigs of Calvin's lilac bushes capture the freezing rain and make the bushes into delicate ice palaces. After a blizzard, the cedars, the spruces, and the pines hold the snow in their branches in characteristic ways. The cedars are blotched with snow, as if an oil painter had dabbed at them with a white brush. The spruces and pines channel the snow in glaciers that spiral up each tree from base to top. In this sort of weather, Calvin is most grateful for colorful plants, the Virginia creeper with its blue berries, and the crabapple and hawthorn with their bright red fruit.

This is the chapter where we talk about your garden in the "other" time of year, the time when your plants are dormant. That a garden can be designed to give you pleasure at this time of year is perhaps one of the best-kept landscaping secrets.

The Dormant Season

For most plants, the dormant season extends from the first killing frost in fall to the last killing frost in spring. In regions where snow falls, the landscape is a dynamic place during the dormant season, visually speaking. The rapid changes that occur during this season are governed by two crucial events, the falling of the snow and the freezing of the ground. Snow totally transforms a landscape, drastically simplifying its aesthetic qualities. A landscape which is one day a fantastic study in browns and creams, with blotches of green lawn and evergreen, becomes overnight a white canvas on which only the gray-black lines of tree trunks, fences, and telephone poles and wires are sketched.

The freezing of the ground also makes a dramatic difference in the appearance of the landscape, although the effect takes longer to develop than the effect of snow. Many plants (common lawn grasses, for instance) are not killed by frost, no matter how deep it is. Such plants may brown or wilt in winter, but it is not because of the freezing of water in their tissues. On the contrary, it is because of the *lack* of water in their tissues. Once the water in the soil has frozen, the plant is unable to extract water from the soil and it withers from drought and turns brown. Consequently, the freezing of the ground is the time when the lawn grass turns brown, and it marks a crucial turning point in the visual character of the landscape. From this time on, any green color in the landscape comes solely from the broadleaved evergreens and the conifers.

Because of the importance of snow and ground-freeze, the dormant period divides itself into three periods, each with its particular visual character: late autumn, midwinter, and late winter.

Late Autumn

For the present purposes, late autumn can be thought of as the period between the time that killing frosts occur and the onset of snow and/or the freezing of the ground. In the North, it is a well-defined period that varies widely in length from year to year. In the South, "late autumn" often lasts for most of the dormant period, sliding imperceptibly into late winter. The bright foliage colors of summer and autumn are mostly gone. Lawns are often a brilliant green at this time of year, but the color of meadows is dominated by the dried topgrowth of summer grasses and displays a fascinating variety of browns and yellows.

Midwinter

With midwinter comes ground-freeze and snowfall. The freezing of the ground deprives even the hardiest plants of a moisture supply. Any grasses which have stayed green so far quickly turn brown. Except for evergreen trees, shrubs, and ground-covers, the landscape becomes a somber blend of browns, blacks, and grays. With the greens of the grass and deciduous trees removed, the evergreens suddenly emerge as strong, dramatic shapes in the landscape. Cold does not, for the most part, affect the color of evergreens, but it does affect the shape of some. Broadleaved evergreens such as rhododendrons curl their leaves and contract with the deepening cold.

When the snow falls, the landscape becomes for a time more monotonous still. A wet snow blankets everything, even evergreens and the branches of deciduous trees. Any trace of gray or green leaps out at your eye. But as the snow settles and melts, lines and forms emerge. A gray ledge of rock, the limbs of a tree, the green boughs of a balsam, the gray boards of a weathered fence suddenly become prominent.

In a midwinter landscape, form is the dominant aesthetic value. There is beauty of form in the stark skeletons of leafless trees. There is beauty of form in a dark stone wall seen against the white of snow. The snow itself forms sculptures downwind of tree trunks and shrubs. Even power lines can be transformed into elements of great beauty by the natural artistry of falling snow.

In such a landscape, a little color goes a long way. A shrub with red berries can be seen 100 yards away, so profoundly does the eye yearn for color. Trunks and limbs of trees, which at other seasons of the year would seem a uniform gray, now are revealed to have subtle differences of hue. Sugar maples seem a stark blue-gray, swamp maples a vibrant purple-red, willows and forsythia a golden yellow. Even the dead fronds of last year's asparagus lend a buffy warmth to the garden.

Late Winter

Late winter is like late fall, only duller. Many of the berries and other fruits which give color to the late fall landscape have been eaten by birds or simply worn off the trees by winter gales. Where no snow has fallen, the winter sun has bleached the browns in the landscape to khaki. Where snow has fallen, it now comes off the land in ragged patches, like the winter coat of a shaggy dog.

It's difficult to design an endearing landscape for late winter, surely the ugly duckling of seasons. It is a time to cut forsythia, pussy willow, quince, apple, and cherry branches, and bring them inside for forcing. Outside, where the land is sheltered and south-facing and the sun is warm, the ground thaws quickly, and here early spring flowers such as snowdrops, crocuses, and winter aconite will bloom and give promise of the cornucopia of life and color to come.

Plants for a Winter Landscape

Because the colors of a winter landscape are so simplified, the form of a tree becomes its most essential feature. Both evergreens and deciduous trees provide pleasing forms in a winter landscape, but the forms are dramatically different, so we shall consider them separately.

Evergreens

Against the dull browns of an autumn landscape or the white of a winter landscape, evergreens provide a dramatic contrast. Winter is the season of evergreens. Evergreens come in all sizes, from the giant spruces that can be a primary feature in a winter landscape to tiny groundcover plants such as wintergreen, which can offer a charming detail. Most of the larger evergreen plants are conifers: spruces, firs, cedars, hemlocks, and pines. Spruces and firs have a spare triangularity that gives a yard a crisp, formal look in winter. Cedars are cylindrical in form, and their growth is more formal and compact. Hemlocks have delicate fleecy foliage that displays snow and rime in a particularly pleasing way. Pines, especially mature trees, have an open, irregular form that makes them stand out as specimens in the landscape.

Smaller evergreen plants can be either needle-bearing conifers or broadleaved evergreens. In the first category are yews and junipers. Yews and junipers are the piney sort of plants that one so often sees in foundation plantings. Both yews and junipers have berries, the yew a red berry, the juniper a grayish blue berry with a fragrance of gin. Both are informal plants, inclined by nature to sprawl. But the yew can be trained so that it is as severe and formal a landscaping element as the most regimental blue spruce.

Two broad categories of broadleaved evergreen shrubs are commonly used in the garden.

Phebe's Favorites for Winter Gardens

Winter is the time you most appreciate conifers, big and little, with snow weighing down their branches, or wind sighing through their limbs, or outlined against a gray, foreboding sky. The stiff, majestic pyramids of the firs and spruces, and the more picturesque silhouettes of the pines, really come into their own in the winter garden.

The Nikko fir is a handsome representative of the fir group, dark green, vigorous, and large.

No list would be complete without the Colorado blue spruce, which has come to represent the spruce group. Another, the Serbian spruce, has good dark green foliage and a narrow habit.

Top pines include the Himalayan pine, a graceful tree with soft, long, drooping needles; Japanese white pine with blue-green needles; and Scotch pine with bluish needles and orange upper branches, a very striking combination. The Japanese red pine and its varieties have beautiful forms for specimen use.

Many dwarf conifers are excellent accent plants year-round. There are many cultivars of Hinoki cypress, with nice, dark green, scale-like foliage and pyramidal form. Fernspray falsecypress is representative of the fine-textured dwarfs with feathery foliage.

Junipers are another important feature in the landscape, and especially in the winter landscape. Easy to grow, there are many varieties, both upright and spreading, for accent and groundcover. Many upright varieties are in the "small tree" category and are useful for vertical accents in sunny, tight spots.

Chinese juniper (*Juniperus chinensis*) and its varieties—'Mountbatten' and 'Obelisk'—all have grayish foliage and are nice accent plants.

Red cedar's upright varieties include 'Canaert', which is pyramidal, and 'Skyrocket', which is narrow and columnar. Red cedar is also useful for narrow hedges.

No list of junipers is complete without the Pfitzer group, if for no reason other than that they are so dependable, adding a bulky 3- to 5-foot shrub with bluish and even gold foliage to the garden. 'Seagreen'

and the compact variety are nice. They're overused, but still have a place in the landscape.

Low junipers are indispensable for groundcover in a sunny area. Some nice varieties include Sargent juniper, with whip-like branches. It stays very nice and green. There is some discussion as to exactly how big it gets, but I feel it tends to be higher than 12 inches. Blue rug juniper looks just like a rug, a popular true groundcover with nice blue foliage. *Juniperus procumbens* var. *nana* is an aristocrat among junipers with bluish foliage and a mounded shape, very oriental-looking and a beautiful plant.

There are numerous other dwarf conifers, forms of pine, spruce, and fir, as well as falsecypress and arborvitae, that make beautiful specimen plants at any time of the year. Dwarf Arizona fir and low balsam fir are very fine low-growing firs. Both can be said to have glossy green needles. Bird's nest spruce, a very common dwarf plant, has a low form with a flat top that is supposed to look like a bird's nest.

No list is complete without mentioning the mugo (mugho) pine. It's thought of as a dwarf, but some cultivars can get surprisingly large. However, they can be kept pruned. Try for *Pinus mugo* var. *mugo* (up to 8 feet tall) or *P. mugo* var. *pumilio*, a prostrate form. Scale can be a problem, among other ills, so be sure to give this plant a deep, moist loam in the sun (though it can take partial shade) to keep it healthy.

There are many white pine cultivars, but the dwarf white pine is a nice round plant for the right place. It isn't that small. Hemlocks and yews also have their place in the winter garden, or indeed in any garden.

Being evergreen isn't the only thing that gives plants winter interest. Some deciduous trees have bark that is colorful or interesting, and is usually overlooked until the leaves fall off the tree in the autumn.

The bark of beech trees has the wonderful, smooth texture to which all others are compared. The habit and branching patterns of beeches also make them handsome without their leaves.

Birches are unique and wonderful for their smooth

or peeling white bark. All varieties have this characteristic and are quite distinct in the landscape.

The hornbeams or "blue beeches" are native or European small trees with beech-like bark. Magnolias all have nice gray bark, as does the yellowwood, a handsome tree not unlike the beech in form, with white, fragrant flowers in June.

The red- and yellow-stem dogwoods are important features in the winter landscape. Who can forget the bright red stems of the red-stem dogwood glowing in the sunlight, against the soft green background of white pines on a carpet of snow under a clear blue sky?

Red berries show up wonderfully well in winter. Many crabapples have small red fruit, but I often find that the birds eat it quickly and there are no berries left for winter viewing. I have a pair of Zumi crabapples which are supposed to have small red fruit remaining into the winter. Thanks to the birds, I find there is no fruit left by October.

Hollies are the number-one plant for red berries, and both the American and Meserve hollies are usually covered with fruit. The Meserve hollies are particularly handsome, with very dark blue-green foliage and a reputation for being very tough and winter-hardy.

Some trees and shrubs when "undressed" of leaves have particularly nice shapes. Outstanding are the dogwoods, especially the native dogwood, with its simple, clean branch structure, and of course the Japanese maples, from the delicate threadleaf maple to the larger forms. Crabapples, cherries, and magnolias all have pleasing silhouettes, including some weeping forms of cherry and some cherries with marvelous, shiny, mahogany-colored bark.

No list for the winter landscape would be complete without the willows. Long after the leaves have dropped, the golden stems of the willow appear in the landscape and sound a cheerful note throughout the winter. You know spring is right around the corner when the stems begin to look vibrant yellow and ready to burst.

The heath family contains plants such as rhododendrons, azaleas, and mountain laurels, which prefer partial shade and moist, cool, acid soils. Because of these requirements, rhododendrons and other heath family members are difficult to grow in some parts of the country. In general, if you don't have good growing conditions for these plants, it's best not to exhaust your enthusiasm and money on them.

The other important category of broadleaved evergreen shrub is the hollies. Hollies are particularly attractive as winter plants because of their berries. The hardiest hollies are the American hollies and the new Meserve hollies. Both are tough and pretty. They have brilliant red berries in winter and make excellent hedge plants. Japanese holly is handsome and has a blue berry. Best of all is the English holly with its shiny, thorny leaves and deep red berries, familiar from wreaths and other Christmas decorations. Unfortunately, the English and the Japanese hollies are less hardy, and often suffer winter damage if grown above Zone 6.

Another important group of evergreen plant is the evergreen groundcovers. Such plants may not provide much color when the snow is on the ground, but during open winters and in sunny, sheltered spots where the snow clears off quickly, they can provide a delightful microcosmic garden that can give enormous pleasure throughout the winter. Myrtle, wintercreeper, ajuga, galax, some ferns, ivy, and pachysandra have green foliage throughout the year. Many perennials, while not properly evergreens, hold their foliage all winter. Some sedums, dianthus, thyme, lavender, candytuft, heather, and thrifts all fall in this category. Some of these, such as dianthus and lavender, are gray and provide a pleasing contrast to green groundcovers.

Smallest of all the evergreen groundcovers are the mosses. Calvin thinks that there is nothing that soothes winter's woes quite as much as a snooze on a sunny, mossy bank in late winter. Even though moss looks uniformly green from a distance, up close it bears wonderful microscopic yellow "blossoms."

Deciduous Plants

While evergreens provide the most dramatic design elements in a winter landscape, deciduous trees are also important. Where evergreens provide blocks of foliage and color, the bare branches, trunks, and twigs of deciduous trees provide line and texture, and often just a touch of color.

Winter is the season to appreciate the architecture of trees. And some trees have particularly handsome skeletons. Sycamores have extraordinary, mottled, peeling bark in shades of white, gray, green, buff, and brown. Mature oaks have a marvelously scraggly structure that looks especially intriguing in the fogs that often gather over melting snow on warm winter days. Ashes have strong, dramatic frames that are visually pleasing. Swamp maples, sugar maples, and willows have tinted limbs that become immediately noticeable when the other colors of fall have been washed out or obscured. Some species of crabapple, as well as mountain ashes and hawthorns, carry colorful red, orange, or yellow fruit right through the winter, a boon to the eye and to wildlife as well.

Deciduous shrubs can also provide winter pleasures. Barberries, cotoneasters, bayberries, and roses all bear fruit into the winter. The complex, fine twigs of lilacs, blackhaw, and spiraea trap snow in delightful ways. Many shrubs provide late-winter forcing materials as well as spring flowers.

Even grasses can provide pleasure in winter. Some species of ornamental grass, like little bluestem, little blue fescue, switchgrass, maiden grass, and plume grass have dramatic spikes and spears that hold frost in beautiful ways. After an icestorm, the sunlight illuminates and transforms them into delicate glass sculptures. To encourage the growth of such plants, every garden needs at least a small wild area, perhaps a thicket, where the juncos can scratch and where you never quite know what sculptures the wind and ice will form.

Fixtures for a Winter Garden

If color in your winter landscape is important, consider setting up a bird feeder. Among the colorful birds that come to feeders are blue jays, cardinals, evening grosbeaks, and redwing blackbirds. Even plain birds like mockingbirds and titmice lend life to a landscape as they go about their business.

But more important than their plumage is the birds' songs. The winter landscape is often distressingly quiet. Gone is the clash and clatter of wind through fat, bright leaves. All we have left is the sibilant rush of air through the twigs of trees, the hum of the wind over the telephone wires, and the moaning of the drafts at our windows and doors. In such a hushed world, the rollicking late-winter song of a tufted titmouse can be heard over several acres.

A birdbath, trickle, or fountain can also be an enticing winter feature, both for people and for birds. Some avid bird-watchers even heat their birdbaths to provide a source of water to birds all winter long.

Walls and fences are attractive winter features. A familiar fence accentuates the forms of snowdrifts because it gives an accurate visual gauge of the actual depth of the snow. The blue-gray and green-gray tones of a stone wall can beautifully delineate a field of snow. Walls and fences—even a simple post or two—can form gracious swirls and scallops in wind-driven snow.

Birds bring lots of color and activity to the winter garden.

Some Successful Winter Gardens
Conifer Garden

When both Dick Berry and his wife Aida landed jobs as top administrators in the government, they built a house in a well-manicured development across the Potomac in Virginia. Theirs was a large lot, the squared-off top of a small hill, with a driveway which wound up the side of the hill. The house was built just south of a rocky outcropping that marked the top of the hill. The development had been tastefully done, and the developer had left the Berrys a stone wall which came up the hill from the street, and then took a sharp right bend to cross behind the house, where it separated the Berrys' yard from the tall oaks and maples in the next lot. The architect who built their house echoed the natural stone in the stonework of the foundation.

The Berrys' work required them to travel a great deal, and neither had a lot of time to maintain a garden. They wanted a garden that would be stable and elegant year-round, even in the winter, but not require much care on their part. Dick asked

a landscape designer to draw up a plan that would meet these requirements.

The Berrys' large lot provided the designer with numerous opportunities for the planting of conifers. Along the street, as sort of a loose hedge, he suggested a staggered line of spruces, red cedars, and pines. Planted together in this manner, the differences of colors and texture in the foliage of the trees would be emphasized when they grew together. On either side of the sinuous driveway, he planted two large deodar cedars, whose distinctive weeping form would make a nice accent in winter. These would eventually grow very tall and would not only make the entry to the house dramatic, but would also screen the house from the road.

In the backyard, between the house and the stone wall, the designer proposed two or three Scotch pines for a windbreak and a small group of Japanese black pines for accent. He also suggested a few reliable, strong-growing deciduous trees whose bark or skeletons made them an elegant contribu-

The Berrys' low-maintenance winter garden.

tion to a landscape, even when they were not in leaf. These included a Japanese maple, with its smooth gray bark and open branching habit, and two species of flowering dogwood—the native spring-flowering dogwood and the Kousa dogwood, valued for its later blooms and for its handsome, mottled, gray-and-cinnamon bark. Across the yard and along the inside of the wall, in the shade and shelter of the tall deciduous trees in the next lot, the designer suggested a collection of rhododendrons and azaleas, which would show dark green against the gray wall in winter and provide a distant blaze of color in spring.

Although such a garden might seem too static to many people, to the Berrys, with their harried, peripatetic life, it proved suitable. When they come up the driveway after a trip, they find reassurance in the soothing, harmonious stability of their garden. As they hoped, the landscape has been very easy to maintain. A landscaping service mows the lawn once a week. The evergreens have grown well, and have required no shaping during the five years since the garden was put in.

The Berrys are particularly happy with their yard as a winter garden. When the rest of the world is brown, their garden is still a setting of serene greens intermixed with the restful gray tones of stone features. Snow is not so common in their part of Virginia, and when it comes, it rarely stays for more than a few weeks at a time. The Berrys are always grateful for these interludes, however, because the white shroud accents the forms of the evergreens and makes their garden look even more graceful than it does in summer.

A Winter-Hater's Winter Garden

Melanie Anne Hiber doesn't remember a time when she liked winter. When she was 18, she left her native Pennsylvania and fled to Oregon. There she went to college and landed herself a good job with a western environmental organization. It was therefore a terrible shock when, one day, she received an offer to come work as associate director of a national environmental lobby whose head offices were just outside Boston.

Full of excitement about her new job and foreboding about the New England winter, she came East. The organization had its headquarters on an old estate in the countryside outside Boston. One of the perks of her new job was a residence, a Cape Cod cottage which had been lived in by the

Christmas roses bloom in Melanie Hiber's winter garden.

former associate director and which was now available to her. It seemed a pleasant little house. The feature Melanie liked best was a south-facing room which served as both a study and a living room. It had a bow window which looked out on the side yard, and through which the sun streamed almost twelve hours a day.

The garden of Melanie's cottage had the air of being well cared for. There was a small, neatly trimmed hedge by the front step, and a larger lush green hedge screened the south side of the property from one of the service buildings. The backyard was enclosed by the hedge on the south and by a fence on the east and north. It had a brick terrace near the house and a well-kept lawn which dipped down toward the northeast corner of the fence. Behind the fence were several large conifers and maples at the end of her neighbor's garden, and on her side of the fence, in a low, moist area where the two sections of fence met, was a grouping of trees and shrubs. Eager to get on with her work, Melanie concluded her brief examination of the cottage, pronounced it suitable, and moved in.

During her first summer, she had little time for the cottage or the garden. Melanie walked across the grounds of the old estate to her office each morning and back to her cottage each evening, exhausted. But as summer passed into fall and fall into winter, she had more time to herself, and she began gradually to appreciate her good fortune in having the cottage.

Whoever had planted the shrubs and trees around the cottage seemed to have planted them with fall and winter in mind. The hedge planted near the front door, she learned, was boxwood. Its small, rounded leaves were green throughout the winter. The hedge along the south side of the garden was holly. From the window seat in the bow window, Melanie liked to look at its glossy, prickly foliage and bright red berries, particularly when they were partially covered with snow.

The backyard also had numerous plantings which seemed to be contrived for the dormant season. The trees in the low northwest corner of the garden were paper birches. When early autumn passed into late autumn, and the scarlet, red, and orange leaves of the maples behind the fence had fallen, the white columns of the birch trunks contrasted starkly with the dark masses of the evergreens behind. At the foot of the birches she found a variety of groundcovers and shrubs in the moist ground. She identified partridgeberry by its green leaves and red berries, mahonia by its blue berries and shiny leaves, and evergreen ginger by its glossy, round, heart-shaped leaves. At the back of the garden, she found some mountain laurels and Christmas ferns planted along the east fence.

With all these delightful plants to entertain her, and her job to keep her busy, Melanie found that the winter passed quickly. One Sunday in February, the weather "broke," as New Englanders say. The air suddenly became mild and moist, and she could see that the snow was melting quickly in her backyard. Melanie stepped out on her terrace to breathe the soft air, and noticed the afternoon sun slanting across the yard and illuminating something bright and colorful along the east fence. She crossed the yard to the fence, her feet crunching in the patches of granular snow that littered the yard. There, scattered among the laurels and ferns, she found a Christmas rose, with its lovely white bloom, pushing up through the ground. She had survived her first New England winter!

Wrap-up

The dormant seasons are the unsung seasons of the garden. Gone are the bright colors of leaves and blossoms. But in a well-planned winter garden, these are replaced by shrubs and trees whose attractive form or evergreen foliage is displayed to good effect by snow, ice, and the dun background provided by other plants. Since the dormant season takes up half the year, it makes sense to plant some of these winter plants to assure you year-round enjoyment of your garden.

Plants for Winter Gardens

Plant Name	Winter Feature	Description	Culture
Trees for Winter Gardens			
American beech (*Fagus grandifolia*)	Outstanding smooth, silvery bark; commanding form; tan leaves often persist into winter; prominent glossy brown buds	Sturdy, short-trunked tree with wide-spreading crown; 50 to 70 feet tall; spread may equal height; leaves are coarsely serrated, oblong-ovate, dull, dark bluish green above, lustrous light yellow-green below; fall color bright clear yellow	Full sun to partial shade; moist, well-drained soil; tolerates alkaline soils; must be given lots of room; to Zone 3
American holly (*Ilex opaca*) many cultivars	Evergreen foliage and red, yellow, or orange fruit	Pyramidal trees 40 to 50 feet tall, with 15- to 30-foot spread; leaves are usually spiny-toothed, 2 to 4 inches long, dull to glossy depending on the variety, and medium to dark green; mature bark is smooth, light gray	Sun to shade; well-drained soil with a pH of 6.5 or lower; mulch; to Zone 6
American hornbeam (*Carpinus caroliniana*)	Steel-gray bark with muscle-like ridges on the trunk; wide-branching form	Crooked-stemmed tree with umbrella-shaped crown, 25 to 35 feet tall, with 20- to 25-foot spread; leaves are doubly toothed, 2 to 3½ inches long, oval to egg-shaped, dark green; pale yellow-orange fall color; flowers are catkins	Sun to partial shade; moist, fertile soil; to Zone 3
Canadian hemlock (*Tsuga canadensis*) 'Bennet' 'Coplen' 'Pendula' ('Sargentii')	Graceful pyramidal form; delicate evergreen foliage; small but plentiful brown cones	Pyramidal tree 40 to 70 feet tall, with 25- to 35-foot spread; some forms weeping or mounded; bark is brown, deeply furrowed; needles are green, with 2 whitish bands on the underside; cones are oval, brown, ½ to 1 inch long	Full sun to partial shade; cool, well-drained, acidic soil; mulch; will not tolerate wind, drought, or pollution; can be pruned to hedge form; to Zone 3

(continued)

Plants for Winter Gardens—*continued*

Plant Name	Winter Feature	Description	Culture
Carolina hemlock (*Tsuga caroliniana*) 'Arnold Pyramid' 'Compacta'	Dark, glossy evergreen foliage; handsome, compact pyramidal form; attractive inch-long cones	Spiring pyramidal tree 45 to 60 feet tall, with 20- to 25-foot spread; often slightly pendulous; bark is reddish brown, deeply fissured; foliage radiates around the trunk like a bottle-brush	Partial shade; moist, well-drained soil; mulch; will not tolerate wind or drought, but tolerates air pollution better than *T. canadensis*; to Zone 4
Colorado blue spruce (*Picea pungens*)	Striking blue evergreen foliage; very formal appearance; horizontal branches in whorls to the ground	Stiffly pyramidal trees 80 to 100 feet tall, often much shorter in a lawn setting (25 to 30 feet, with 10- to 20-foot spread); needles are 3- to 4-sided, stiff, sharp-pointed, 1 to 1½ inches long; drooping light brown cones, 2 to 4 inches long, in tops of old trees	Sun to partial shade; cool, moist soil; mulch deeply; to Zone 2
European birch (*Betula pendula*) 'Dalecarlica'	Smooth, white bark, marked with dark patches or rings; 'Dalecarlica' has weeping form	Umbrella-crowned, multi-stemmed tree 20 to 60 feet tall; occasionally oval-crowned, with a single trunk; leaves are triangular, shiny green above, pale green below, toothed; bright yellow fall color; 'Dalecarlica' has deeply cut leaves; brown catkins are 1 inch long	Sun to partial shade; moist loam soil; not drought resistant; mulch; to Zone 2
European hornbeam (*Carpinus betulus*) many cultivars	Gray bark with prominent lenticels; fluted wood; extremely handsome form, with slender, symmetrical branches	Egg-shaped trees 40 to 60 feet tall, with 30- to 40-foot spread; leaves are oval, doubly serrate; 2½ to 5 inches long, dark green; yellow or yellowish green fall color; prominent female catkins are up to 3 inches long	Full sun to light shade; well-drained soil; excellent specimen plants, but can also be pruned to a hedge; to Zone 4
Flowering crabapple (*Malus* spp.) many cultivars	Glossy, smooth, gray to gray-brown bark; low-branched, even horizontally branched shape; yellow, orange, or red fruits	Small, round-headed to cup-crowned trees 15 to 30 feet tall with a 15- to 35-foot spread; leaves are saw-toothed, green, red, or purple, oval, 2 to 4 inches long; flowers are white, pink, or red, 1 to 2 inches wide, in showy clusters in spring; fruit is small, tart	Full sun; prefers deep, moist, fertile soil; choose disease-resistant varieties, as crabs are susceptible to fireblight, cedar apple rust, apple scrab, and powdery mildew; to Zone 3

Plant Name	Winter Feature	Description	Culture
Himalayan pine (*Pinus wallichiana*) 'Oculis-draconis' ('Zebrina')	Wide-spreading form with branches to the ground; feathery; evergreen foliage; 'Oculis-draconis' has green-and-gold foliage with a cream-colored band	Broadly pyramidal trees 50 to 80 feet tall, with 25- to 64-foot spread; needles are in clusters of 5, grayish green, 5 to 8 inches long; light brown cones are 6 to 10 inches long and 2 inches wide	Full sun; sandy, well-drained, acid loam soil; severe winter winds can cause needle browning; tolerant of air pollution; needs sheltered position; good where it has room; to Zone 5
Japanese maple (*Acer palmatum*) 'Bloodgood' 'Burgundy Lace' 'Dissectum' (threadleaf) many others	Smooth, green, light brown, or gray-brown bark, slender and lacy in winter silhouette	Broad, round-headed trees up to 20 feet tall with 20-foot spread; pulmate leaves are doubly toothed, often deeply lobed, green to metallic purple-red; red to red-orange fall color; 1-inch winged seed through fall	Sun to partial shade (sun gives best red foliage color); moist soil; mulch; needs protected site; to Zone 5
Japanese red pine (*Pinus desiflora*)	Orange-red bark; tufted evergreen foliage; irregular, horizontally branching profile	Open, irregular trees 40 to 60 feet tall and wide; bark is orange to orange-red, maturing to gray oblong plates; needles are in clusters of 2, bright green, 3 to 5 inches long, borne somewhat upright along the stems; yellowish cones are up to 2 inches long	Sun; well-drained, slightly acid soil; to Zone 4
Japanese white pine (*Pinus parviflora*)	Fine-textured evergreen foliage; graceful form, pyramidal when young, flat-topped in age	Conical to wide-spreading trees 25 to 50 feet tall and wide; bark is smooth gray, becoming darker and plated; needles are in clusters of 5, bluish green to grass green, crowded and brushy, $4/5$ to $1\,3/5$ inches long; persistent, brownish red, $1\,3/5$- to 3-inch-long cones	Full sun; well-drained soil; somewhat salt tolerant; to Zone 5
Meserve holly (*Ilex ×meserveae*) 'Blue Angel' 'Blue Maid' 'Blue Prince' 'Blue Princess' 'Blue Stallion'	Lustrous evergreen foliage; purplish blue bark; large, shiny, deep red fruit	Compact, pyramidal to broad, shrubby trees 8 to 15 feet tall and wide; leaves are sharply toothed, crinkled, dark green to bluish green	Partial shade to full sun; moist, acidic, well-drained soil; protected site; must plant both male and female for fruit production; to Zone 4

(continued)

Plants for Winter Gardens—*continued*

Plant Name	Winter Feature	Description	Culture
Nikko fir *(Abies homolepis)*	White to buff or light brown bark on young stems; evergreen foliage; handsome form; 3- to 4-inch cones, purple when young	Conical tree over 60 feet tall; bark is deeply grooved; branches are horizontal and whorled from the trunk; green needles are ½ to 1 inch long, crowded on upper sides of branches	Full sun to light shade; moist, well-drained, acidic soil; tolerates air pollution better than most firs; to Zone 3
Paper birch *(Betula papyrifera)*	Chalky white, peeling bark on trunk and older branches, reddish brown bark on younger branches; reddish orange inner bark	Broad, round-crowned trees 50 to 70 feet tall with a 25- to 56-foot spread; branches are usually retained close to the ground; leaves are oval, coarsely serrated, 2 to 4 inches long, dull dark green; yellow fall color; catkins are 2 to 4 inches long	Full sun; well-drained, moist, acidic, sandy, or silty loam soils; not pollution tolerant; best for cold climates; striking in clumps or as a specimen; Zones 2–6
River birch *(Betula nigra)* 'Heritage'	Cinnamon to reddish brown bark; vase shape; young trees have peeling bark	Multistemmed or oval-crowned trees 50 to 60 feet tall (30 to 40 feet when multistemmed, with a 20- to 30-foot spread); leaves are egg-shaped, doubly toothed, sharply pointed, up to 3½ inches long, shiny, dark green, and leathery; bright yellow fall color	Sun to partial shade; moist, acidic soils; mulch; best birch for the South; Zones 4-9
Saucer magnolia *(Magnolia soulangeana)* many varieties	Striking bark, glossy brown on young branches, smooth silver-gray on trunk and main branches; graceful spreading form with numerous low branches; prominent fuzzy buds	Broad, small tree 20 to 25 feet tall, with a 20- to 30-foot spread; leaves are roughly egg-shaped, 4 to 7 inches long, 2 to 4 inches wide, light to medium bright green; pale yellow fall color; flowers are 4 to 6 inches long, purplish pink outside, creamy white inside; blooms profusely before trees leaf out	Sun to partial shade; rich, moist, well-drained soil; mulch; to Zone 5
Scotch pine, Scots pine *(Pinus sylvestris)* 'Argentea' 'Watereri'	Evergreen; picturesque umbrella shape; 'Argentea' has silvery needles, 'Watereri' steel blue	Irregularly pyramidal tree, becoming open and spreading, 30 to 60 feet tall with a 30- to 40-foot spread; blue-green needles are in pairs, 1 to 4 inches long; cones are 1½ to 3 inches long, gray or dull brown, single or in clusters	Full sun; well-drained, acidic soil; often used for Christmas trees; Zones 2–8

Plant Name	Winter Feature	Description	Culture
Serbian spruce (*Picea omorika*)	Glossy, dark green evergreen foliage; graceful pyramidal form	Narrow, pyramidal trees 50 to 60 feet tall with a 20- to 25-foot spread; flat needles are ½ to 1 inch long; bark is coffee-brown; drooping branches; cones are 1¼ to 2 inches long, blue-black aging to cinnamon-brown	Partial shade; rich, moist, well-drained soil; mulch; needs protected site; Zones 4–7
Southern magnolia (*Magnolia grandiflora*) 'Majestic Beauty' 'Glenn St. Mary'	Grand, large evergreen with large, shiny, dark green leaves that are fuzzy and coppery on the lower surfaces	Pyramidal to rounded trees 60 to 100 feet tall with a 30- to 50-foot spread; leaves are thick, leathery, 4 to 9 inches long, 2 to 3 inches wide, oval; flowers are white, cup-shaped, 6 to 9 inches wide, heavily fragrant; pineapple-like cones are hairy, 4 inches long and bear brilliant red seeds	Sun to partial shade; rich, moist soils; mulch; sensitive to magnesium deficiency; to Zone 7
Yellow-stem weeping willow (*Salix alba*) many cultivars	Very long, weeping, polished yellow branches	Round-headed trees 30 to 50 feet tall, with a 30- to 40-foot spread; leaves are narrow, lance-shaped, 3 to 7 inches long, medium to olive green; yellow fall color	Sun; moist soil; grows fast, but takes considerable space and is short-lived (15 to 30 years); roots can invade drains and septic tanks; to Zone 3

Shrubs for Winter Gardens

Plant Name	Winter Feature	Description	Culture
Bird's nest spruce (*Picea abies* var. *nidiformis*)	Evergreen foliage; spreading, dense, broad form, with characteristic depression in the center of the plant	Small, slow-growing shrub, eventually 3 to 6 feet tall; branches are reddish to orange-brown; stiff needles are ½ to 1 inch long, light or dark, often shining green	Sun to partial shade; sandy, acidic, moist, well-drained soils; best in cold climates; Zones 2–7
Blue rug juniper (*Juniperus horizontalis* var. *wiltonii*)	Intense silver-blue foliage has light purplish tinge in winter; flat-growing evergreen groundcover with trailing branches	Plants 4 to 6 inches tall and 6 to 8 feet wide; needles are ¹⁄₆ inch long	Full sun; tolerant of heat, drought, sandy, rocky, heavy, and alkaline soils; good groundcover for the South; Zones 3–9

(continued)

Plants for Winter Gardens—*continued*

Plant Name	Winter Feature	Description	Culture
Chinese juniper (*Juniperus chinensis*) 'Columnaris' 'Mountbatten' 'Pfitzerana' 'Sargent' many others	Green, blue-green, or grayish green foliage; slender, columnar small evergreen tree, bushy shrub, or groundcover depending on the variety	Columnar form 8 to 10 feet tall; 'Sargent' is 18 inches to 2 feet tall and up to 9 feet wide; leaves are $1/3$ inch long in whorls of 3 or opposite pairs; cones are blue to brown, fleshy, small	Full sun; moist, well-drained soil; tolerant of alkaline soils; Zones 3–9
Dwarf alpine fir (*Abies lasiocarpa* var. *compacta*)	Conspicuous blue-gray evergreen foliage; compact, conical habit	Slow-growing conical shrub; bark is grayish or buff-colored, thick, corky; blue-gray needles are 1 inch long; small cones are purple when young	Full sun to light shade; moist, well-drained soil; can tolerate some alkalinity; intolerant of air pollution; to Zone 3
Dwarf white pine (*Pinus strobus* var. *nana*)	Evergreen foliage; rounded or conical shape	Bushy, irregular, pyramidal shrub, more open with age, up to 16 feet tall; bark is deeply furrowed, dark grayish brown; needles are 3 to 5 inches long, in clusters of 5, slender, bluish green	Sun to partial shade; moist, well-drained, fertile soil; needs sheltered site; intolerant of air pollution, salt, and alkaline soil; susceptible to white pine blister rust and white pine weevil; Zones 3–8
Fernspray falsecypress (*Chamaecyparis obtusa* var. *filicoides*)	Ferny evergreen foliage; open, irregular habit	Bushy, often gaunt-looking shrub, up to 7½ feet tall and wide; branches are long and straggly, with dense, pendulous clusters of deep green, shiny, ferny foliage	Full sun; rich, moist, well-drained soil; prefers cool, humid conditions; needs sheltered site; Zones 4–8
Golden dogwood (*Cornus alba* var. *spaethii*)	Vivid yellow stem color	Sparsely branched shrub, 8 to 10 feet tall, erect to arching, with 5- to 10-foot spread; stems are slender, green in summer; leaves are oval, 2 to 4½ inches long, with bright yellow margins; flowers are yellowish white	Sun to partial shade; prefers moist, well-drained soil; prune out a third of old wood yearly or mow to ground in spring to maintain brilliant red winter color; Zones 2–8
Hicks yew (*Taxus* ×*media* 'Hicksii')	Lustrous dark evergreen foliage; columnar habit	Male and female clones, often with a central leader, up to 20 feet tall; slightly leathery needles are ½ to 1 inch long, lighter green beneath; females have fleshy red fruits, small but showy	Shade to sun; prefers moist, acidic loam soil; must be well-drained; Zones 4–7

Plant Name	Winter Feature	Description	Culture
Hinoki falsecypress (*Chamaecyparis obtusa* var. *gracilis*)	Shining, dark green foliage; compact, pyramidal form with slightly pendulous branches	Graceful weeping shrub 9 to 15 feet tall; branches are frond-like; bark is reddish brown, shed in long strips; foliage is dark green above with white X-shaped markings below; cones are small, orange-brown	Sun; moist, well-drained soil; high humidity; needs protection from wind; Zones 4–8
Japanese garden juniper (*Juniperus procumbens* var. *nana*)	Compact mat of purplish foliage; handsome winter evergreen groundcover	Spreading shrub 8 to 24 inches tall and 10 to 12 feet wide; overlapping branches form sprays of bluish green foliage, purplish in winter; needles in clusters of 3, $\frac{1}{3}$ inch long	Full sun; widely adaptable; tolerates alkaline soils; needs open site; Zones 4–9
Low balsam fir (*Abies fraseri* var. *prostrata*)	Shining, dark evergreen foliage; reddish brown to gray or pale yellow-brown bark	Broad-spreading shrub, up to 4½ feet tall and 12 feet wide; branches are wide, horizontal; needles are ½ to $\frac{7}{8}$ inch long, crowded on upper sides of branches; oval cones are 1½ to 2½ inches long, purple when young, becoming tan-brown	Sun to partial shade; prefers moist, well-drained loam, but can tolerate drier soil; suffers in hot, dry weather; Zones 4–7
Pfitzer juniper (*Juniperus chinensis* var. *pfitzeriana*) many cultivars	Wide-spreading shrub with slightly weeping branches; some cultivars have gold-tinged, yellow, gray-green, silver-blue, or purplish blue foliage	Variable shrubs, 5 feet tall and 10 feet wide; needles are bright green, awl-shaped; main branches are at 45-degree angle to trunk	Full sun; moist, well-drained soil; tolerant of alkaline soil; Zones 3–9
Prostrate mugo pine (*Pinus mugo* var. *pumilio*)	Excellent prostrate evergreen with attractive foliage	Low-growing shrub, up to 10 feet wide, usually prostrate; bark is brownish gray, plated; needles are medium to dark green, in pairs, 1 to 2 inches long; cones are small, oval, grayish black	Sun to partial shade; deep, moist loam; tolerates alkaline soils; good for mass plantings; Zones 2–7
Red cedar (*Juniperus virginiana*) 'Canaertii' 'Keteleeri' 'Skyrocket' many others	Handsome reddish brown peeling bark; densely pyramidal form	Pyramidal to pendulous shrubby tree with many shrub cultivars, 4 to 25 feet tall; strong cedar scent; needles are medium green, have sharp, spiny points	Sun; deep, moist, well-drained loam; pH tolerant; needs open location; susceptible to cedar apple rust and bagworms; Zones 2–9

(continued)

133

Plants for Winter Gardens—*continued*

Plant Name	Winter Feature	Description	Culture
Red-stem dogwood, red-osier dogwood (*Cornus sericea*) 'Flaviramea'	Red stems; 'Flaviramea' has yellow twigs	Fast-spreading shrub 4 to 8 feet tall; stems are upright with few branches, turning gray-brown at maturity; leaves are oblong or lanceolate, 2 to 5 inches long and 1 to 2½ inches wide, medium green; white flowers are in flat clusters	Sun to partial shade; moist soil; tolerates poor soils; to Zone 2
Sea Green juniper (*Juniperus chinensis* 'Sea Green')	Fountain-like, arching evergreen branches	Compact, spreading shrub 4 to 6 feet tall; needles are dark green, ⅓ inch long	Full sun; moist, well-drained soil; Zones 3–9
Siberian dogwood (*Cornus alba* var. *sibirica*)	Bright coral-red stems	Erect to arching shrub, sparsely branched, 8 to 10 feet tall, with a 5- to 10-foot spread; leaves are oval, 2 to 4½ inches long; flowers are in 1½- to 2-inch flat-topped cymes; bluish fruit is ⅜ inch across	Sun to partial shade; moist, well-drained soil; prune ⅓ of old wood each year or cut to ground in spring to maintain winter stem color; Zones 2–8
Silveredge dogwood (*Cornus alba* var. *argenteo marginata*)	Red winter stems	Shrub distinctly erect in youth, more open, loose, or arching at maturity; leaves are oval, 2 to 4½ inches long, subdued grayish green with an irregular creamy white margin	Sun to partial shade; moist, well-drained soil; prune ⅓ of old wood each year or cut to ground in spring to maintain winter stem color; Zones 2–8

CHAPTER 9

Water Gardens

*E*very landscape should have a pool, trickle, or fountain. Water features provide the sparkle of reflected sunlight, the beauty and variety of aquatic plants. They also provide refuge and sustenance to water creatures and other wildlife. And on still days, a pool mirrors its surroundings and lets you see their beauty twice.

Contrary to everybody's expectations, water gardens don't have to be difficult to construct or maintain. You can have a water garden which consists of a sunken barrel with a lily in it. Or a little damp spot with a thick growth of marsh marigolds. A pool 4-by-6-by-3 feet is large enough to provide not only for lilies, hyacinths, or other water plants, but for fish as well. The secret of success in water gardening is just a little careful planning.

How a Water Garden Works

When Calvin thinks of a garden pool, he thinks of a pool he once saw cut in the heavy clay soil of Suffolk, in England. This pool had been formed when the clay had been mined to build the fifteenth-century house that stood beside it. The pool had remained unchanged since that time. Grass grew up to its shallow edges, and breezes made little ripples on its glassy surface. Ducks, coots, and even the occasional swan paraded on its surface.

Suffolk clay pits notwithstanding, unless you have a high water table or are extraordinarily lucky in your soil type, the core of your water garden will be a pool with a cement or plastic lining to keep the water from escaping. But don't despair. Just because a pool is made of an artificial material like cement does not mean that it needs to look like a missile silo. In fact, many of the serene, natural-looking pools you see in other people's yards are probably cement pools. There are many effective ways to disguise a cement pool. If you simply paint the bottom of the pool black and let the grass grow over the edges, noboby will know the cement is there in a few months. If you are fussy, you can put pebbles in the top surface of the cement before it dries or cover the edges with sand to simulate a shoreline. With a disguise like this, your cement-lined pool will look natural to the most discriminating eye.

Plastic-lined pools are also easily disguised. Plastic can actually be put under the turf of your pond's banks so that its edges are completely invisible. If you use black plastic as your liner, it may make your pond look profound, but it won't look artificial. So there's no need to be put off by the artificiality of a cement- or plastic-lined pool. What you lose in naturalness, you gain back in control over the water in the pool. Nobody who has an artificially lined pool and a garden hose has ever lost a water plant to a drought.

The secret of constructing a healthy water garden is understanding the habitat of water plants. Each water plant is designed to thrive in a specific arrangement of water and soil. To get a variety of water plants in your garden, you must shape the walls of the pool to provide the mix of habitats that makes plant variety possible. Some plants like to sit in dry soil and have their feet wet, others to grow in soil that is wet right up to their stems, a third group to grow in soil that is several inches below the surface of the water, and still others to just float in the water and grow with little or no soil at all.

For each of these predilections, different provisions must be made in your pool. A simple tub or a rectangular box of a pool will grow waterlilies very nicely if its depth is right. To grow more than lilies, you must provide a pool with gently sloping sides and/or with pockets to hold soil at different depths.

What Kind of Pool for You?

Like almost every other landscape feature, there are two basic kinds of pool, formal and informal. A formal pool is geometric in shape, and its boundaries are rigidly formed. The shape of an informal pool is more flowing, with "natural," irregular curves.

Pools Made of Cement

Formal pools are usually made of reinforced concrete, and are edged with concrete, stones, bricks, or tiles. Since the bottom of the pool is usually rectilinear (like a box), a formal pool is

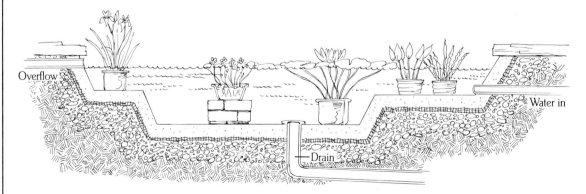

Cross-section of a formal, rectangular pool, with built-in ledges and pedestals for plants.

provided with various sorts of "furniture" to make it possible to grow plants that like different water depths. If it is a shallow pool, it may have pits in its bottom to hold pots for lilies. If it's deep, it may have underwater plant stands on which to put lily barrels so the plants will grow at their preferred depth. A deep pool may also have shelves—the aquatic equivalent of planter boxes—built into its sides, so that shallow-water plants can be grown.

The steps for building a formal pool are the same as those for building a swimming pool. A rectangular hole is dug, usually with a backhoe, unless the pool is to be very small. The hole is dug larger than the final pool to make room for the cement and for the sand or gravel that will help cushion the cement from the winter-heaving of the surrounding earth. The floor and walls of the hole are vigorously tamped to firm and stabilize the soil. At this point, the plumbing is laid: a drain at the bottom of the pool, an overflow drain at the water line in one of the sides, and an inlet pipe. Sand is poured on the floor of the excavation and tamped into place.

Then forms are built, the reinforcing mesh put in place, and the cement poured, sides and bottom at the same time so that there will be no seams at the corners. When the cement has dried adequately, the forms are removed, sand backfilled around the walls of the pool, and the topsoil or paving material put in place. When the cement has cured, the pool can be filled with water. This first water must be drained off and the pool rinsed and refilled two or three times before plants or fish can be put in the pool. Otherwise, toxic chemicals may leach out of the fresh cement into the water and kill your fish and plants.

Even a simple formal pool requires considerable technical skill and is probably not a do-it-yourself project for most gardeners. A complicated pool with a sloping bottom and/or niches and pedestals for various kinds of plants would certainly require the expertise of a professional. So if being able to do the work yourself is important, you probably don't want to install a formal pool.

An informal pool simulates the shape of a natural pool you might find along a wooded stream or in a marsh. Such a pool has rounded, irregular sides. It cannot be made with cement forms. But an informal pool can be lined with cement, all the same. The trick for doing this is to actually use the earth itself as the "form" in which your cement is poured. You mark the outline of your pool on the ground and then excavate a hole that will be the shape of the final pond bottom, only a bit larger. The extra size leaves room for the cement and for the sand or gravel that will cushion it. The pool should have shallowly graded sides so that the cement will not flow away when you try to cover them.

Thoroughly tamp the soil to compact it. Next, line the hole with several inches of sand or gravel, tamp it well, and then pour in a single layer of cement, about 3 inches deep. When the first layer of cement has hardened—but before it has set—line it with reinforcing mesh, conforming it to the shape of the pool bottom. Finally, pour in a second 3 inches of cement, which will enclose the mesh and give you 6 inches of reinforced concrete to hold the water.

Before the top layer of cement dries, give some thought to providing for shallow-water and wet-soil plants that will grow along the edges of your pool. One way to give them a foothold is to embed rocks in the cement a few inches down the slope of the pool so that the rocks stick up above the final waterline. After the cement is completely cured, place soil behind the rocks up to or slightly above the level of the pool's waterline, and put water-edge plants in these little niches of soil.

Surprising as it may seem, cement pools often

develop leaks. They can be sealed with tar or with epoxy. These materials don't seem to harm water plants, but their effect on fish is unknown to us.

Pools Lined with Plastic

Cement gives a sturdy and long-lived pool, but the cheapest and simplest way to line an informal pool is with plastic sheeting. Butyl plastics designed specifically for pool lining are surprisingly expensive, about ten times as expensive as the good-quality plastic sheeting available at hardware stores for household use. One possibility is to experiment for a few years with the cheaper materials. Once you are sure of the location and configuration of your pool, you can easily remove your plants, install the more expensive lining, and reset the plants.

The method of preparing the excavation is the same as with an informal cement pool, except provision has to be made just above the future waterline of the pool for holding the edges of the plastic. This can be done by digging a trench around the perimeter of the pool, putting the edge of the plastic in the trench, and backfilling the trench so that the earth pins the plastic in place. If you want to go to a little more trouble, you can remove the grass sod before you dig the trench. Once the topsoil has been put on the plastic, simply replace the sod, and your plastic pool will have grass banks from its first day.

Plastic-lined pools are easy to design because the form of the pool and the pool's bottom is completely under your control. Providing niches for shallow-water plants is simple with a plastic-lined pool. All you have to do is to contour the dirt which forms the bottom of the pool so that it has valleys whose rims are just the right depth below the future water level of your pool for the plants' crowns. When you put the plastic down, press it into the valleys before you cover its edges, forming

MAKING AN INFORMAL POOL

First, outline the shape on the ground with a garden hose.

After the pool is dug and lined with plastic, fill it with water to make the liner fit snugly before you cut off the extra plastic around the edges.

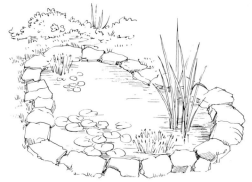

Here's the finished pool, edged with stone and planted.

depressions in the lining. Fill the valleys with top-soil, cover the soil with gravel to hold it in place, and you have the perfect place to grow cattails, pond lilies, lotuses, and yellow flag.

Obviously, the plastic lining of a pool is easily punctured, and children and animals must be instructed or trained to stay out of it.

Prefabricated Pools

In recent years, landscaping supply stores have begun to sell prefabricated garden pools made of fiberglass. The size of these pools varies from small to moderately large. We found one as large as 13 by 6 by 2 feet at a local supplier's. They come in a variety of styles, both formal and informal, and with and without accommodations for plants of different growing habits. Some are simple rectangles, some are round, and some have "natural" kidney-bean shapes.

Putting in a prefabricated pool involves some of the same difficulties as installing a cement pool. Because the prefabricated pools are of fairly light construction, they need the support of the earth around them to resist the weight of the water they contain. But unlike plastic liners, they do not have the flexibility to conform to the surrounding ground. Consequently, the hole in which they are installed must be carefully fitted to their shape and the earth well packed before the pool is put in place. The fitting is often accomplished by digging a hole that is larger than the prefabricated pool, lining the hole with sand, and then carefully pressing the pool into the sand. Once the pool is in place, sand must be firmly packed around the sides to support it. Care must also be taken with the drainage of surface water into the ground around a prefabricated pool. If the ground becomes saturated with water and subsequently freezes, heaving of the earth can pop a prefabricated pool right out of the ground.

Sources for Water Plants and Water Garden Supplies

Lilypons Water Gardens
3300 Organic Road
P.O. Box 10
Lilypons, MD 21717-0010
-or-
3300 Lilypons Road
P.O. Box 188
Brookshire, TX 77423-0188
catalog $3.50

Paradise Gardens
14 May Street
Whitman, MA 02382
catalog $2

S. Scherer and Sons
104 Waterside Avenue
Northport, L.I., NY 11768

Van Ness Water Gardens
2460 North Euclid
Upland, CA 91786
catalog $2

Wicklein's Aquatic Farm & Nursery, Inc.
1820 Cromwell Bridge Road
Baltimore, MD 21234
catalog $1

Plants for a Water Garden

One of the most important reasons to have a pool in your landscape is to grow water plants. The leaves and flowers of showy water plants like waterlilies and lotuses are a delight to see, and nothing quite like them grows on land. But be sure to leave space in your water garden for the sight of water. In fact, most water gardeners advise that you leave at least half the water surface clear to reflect trees, sky, and clouds, and to frame the

Trees and Shrubs

A few trees are real indicators of wet conditions:

There are very few people who are not aware of the first sign of fall when the red maples turn their gorgeous red, or indeed the first sign of spring when these maples produce their bright red blooms in March. A swamp tree, the red maple can also tolerate more normal garden conditions.

The larch looks like a conifer, feels like a conifer in summer, but loses its "leaves" in winter. This is a tree for groups in wet areas, with its soft, almost ferny foliage. It is rather open in habit. It's a graceful tree, and in fall turns a lovely soft yellow, looking like a golden haze.

Hemlocks are backbone evergreens, especially valued for holding their branches down low on the trunk. They are useful for hedges or specimens, and are beautiful all year long. Although not swamp trees, they are never very far away, demanding a constantly moist but well-drained soil. This tree doesn't make a good windbreak, but in a sheltered, shady location it is king. Most nurseries are constantly out of hemlocks in large sizes.

No water garden should be without its willows. A natural pond is wonderful for these ferocious rooters and spreaders. Everyone needs a pussy willow in early spring to cut for the house, and the French pussy willow fills the bill, but these are not handsome shrubs and definitely belong in a "natural" setting. The dwarf purple osier willow is much prettier. This water-lover has pretty blue-green foliage and makes a good hedge or grouping in the landscape. And, of course, one does not think of water without a weeping willow.

Any tree with a weeping habit seems to complement a waterside location. Cherry trees come most quickly to mind, whether weeping or not. All are beautiful, the water a mirror for reflecting form and blossom. The Higan cherry, with its weeping form, is a dainty, early, pink-blooming tree. Of course, all the oriental varieties, doubles and whites, are beautiful, an unforgettable sight when in full bloom, massed along the banks of a pond or stream.

There are a few species of native azalea that are pretty beside a pond. The sweet azalea is very fragrant, with mostly white flowers, while the pinkshell is spectacular in bloom, particularly in groupings, with soft, lovely pink flowers, splendid reflected in water. The swamp white azalea not only has a delicious fragrance, but also blooms late in the season (June). There are also pinkish hybrids.

Summersweet is another native plant to grow around a pond. Its flowers, very sweet-smelling and blooming in July, are a nice feature, in both white and pink. This shrub might be used more in a formal border. It can take shade, has nice yellow fall color, and can be thought of as an ornamental shrub. Blueberries are definite swamp-lovers, and although not often used for ornamental purposes, the white flowers are pretty, much like andromeda blossoms, and the fall color is a good red.

Perennials

There are some pretty spectacular perennials for use at the water's edge or in moist locations:

Goatsbeard is not unlike the astilbes in form, with a similar white flower, but it's bigger and can take shade. It is a nice, old-fashioned shrubby perennial, lately rediscovered because of its dependability and stately habit.

Many grasses, sedges, and cattails are at home in constantly wet areas. Lately there has been a new interest in some of the more ornamental grasses, and the waterside is very suitable for these fountain-like plants with gently swaying plumes, often showy into winter. Maiden grass fits this description. Another grass with conspicuous variegated foliage is the variegated manna grass, at home in the flower border or in wetlands. The flowers of this plant are not ornamental. Tussock grass, a smallish tufted grass with large delicate panicles of bloom, needs partial shade. A discussion of grass shouldn't leave out pampas grass (*Phragmites*), a plant that certainly doesn't need to be planted, and in fact could be considered a noxious weed.

The red cardinal flower and big blue lobelia are two very showy flowering plants with spiky flowers for summer bloom in wet areas.

Purple loosestrife is another plant that has escaped in some areas and become a noxious pest, but it is beautiful to observe the cloud of purple blooms in a low, moist area in August. Morden's Pink is a pretty pink variety, and there are others. The brown seed-pods are distinctive in winter.

Water and Japanese iris are another inseparable combination. Words seem inadequate to describe these stately plants with their large and beautiful blooms. Although they don't like to sit directly in water, they, like swans, seem to know where they are shown off best. And, of course, the common flags add color earlier in the season.

Plants *for* Water

No pond can be without a waterlily or two. Growing waterlilies is specialized, in that to get good blooms they should be just slightly below water level, while in order to insure that they winter over, they need to be moved to lower depths. All this can be accomplished by planting them in pots. Although they may seem extravagant, tropical waterlilies contribute greatly to the beauty of the pond. Fragrance, size, and length of bloom (including evening flowering) add to their list of attributes. Lotuses, both hardy and tender, also add tremendous blooms, fragrance, and variety to the water garden. There are other plants, including the "oxygenating" plants, for use in ponds. All of these plants are available only through specialized suppliers, and usually need to be mail-ordered.

green foliage of the water plants with the blue of the water.

Plants for a water garden are classified by where they like to put their roots and where they hold their leaves and flowers. The classical pond plant, the waterlily, grows best in about 8 inches of water. Its roots attach the plant to the soil of the pond bottom, and its leaves and blossoms float on the surface of the water.

There is an enormous variety of waterlilies available in catalogs. Their flowers are of many shades, not only white, but pink, red, orange, yellow, bronze, and even blue. The flowers of some lilies are held stiffly above the water, while some appear to float on it. Lilies are divided into two general types, hardy and tropical. Hardy lilies will overwinter in ponds. Even though the pond freezes over, the plants' tubers survive in the pond bottom and new shoots and flowers emerge the following spring. Tropical lilies, on the other hand, will die if left in the pond after frost, and so must be lifted and stored or replaced each spring. Since tropical lilies are so readily available, and so much favored for their large size, spectacular blooms, and fragrance, many gardeners simply replace them each spring, like annual bedding plants.

Waterlilies are usually grown in tubs set in the water, not in the soil of the pond itself. Water gardeners have traditionally gone to great lengths to provide the ideal 8-inch depth that lilies require. Sometimes pools are built precisely to the lilies' specification. In a shallower pool, waterlilies are often given a recess in the bottom; in a deeper pool, lilies are grown in tubs on stands set on the floor of the pool. In a sloping pool, a niche is made for waterlilies at the 8-inch depth in the side of the pool.

Waterlilies are somewhat fussy about growing conditions. They demand lots of sunlight, and they need quiet, warm water which, in turn, means

A tropical waterlily can be potted and set in a barrel of water to bloom happily all summer.

that any fountains or trickles in your pond must be well isolated from the lilies, and that your pond must be sheltered from brisk summer breezes. Lilies need a rich soil. The recommended mix is two-thirds aged manure and one-third good loam, covered over with sand or pebbles to prevent its diffusing into the water. Growing lilies in tubs facilitates their care. At the end of the season, the entire tub can be lifted, the old soil exchanged for fresh fertile soil, and the lily stored or discarded as the gardener prefers.

Floating plants are not attached to the pond bottom at all, but float free on the pond surface. Water hyacinth has lavender flowers and floats on the balloon-like bases of its leafstalks. Species grown mostly for their floating foliage include water lettuce, floating ferns, and duckweed. All floating plants have the potential of becoming messy pests, since they float in response to the wind and the currents of the water, not in response to your aesthetic requirements.

Some aquatics grow in very shallow water. These include pickerel weed and arrowhead, grown for their lush foliage and bright flowers. Water iris are available in blue and yellow. The cardinal flower, with bright red flowers, provides brilliant summer color and is a favorite of hummingbirds. It grows at the water's edge, along with the great blue lobelia. Among the largest of these edge plants are the reeds, some of which reach 6 feet in height, and the lotus, a plant with large nasturtium-like leaves that stand as much as 5 feet above the water surface.

Another very large group of plants are available for the margins of ponds and pools. Many familiar plants are in this group, including loosestrife, cattails, sedges, and rushes. Marsh marigolds, mallows, turk's cap lily, and turtlehead all thrive in the damp soil near the water's edge. For dramatic effect, consider senecio or ligularia, with large bold leaves and yellow blossoms in summer. No water garden is complete without Japanese iris, with its spiky leaves and white, pink, and blue flowers. Pussy willows are messy, but for gardens in northern parts, they provide one of the first signs of spring. Sweet-smelling shrubs such as the sweet pepperbush and the swamp white azalea add fragrance as well as color to your water garden. Trees with a flowing or "weeping" form are particularly suitable for planting near pools. These include the weeping cherry and weeping birch beside small pools, and the familiar weeping willow beside large pools.

Fish

Can you have fish in your pond? The answer is almost certainly yes. Calvin used to believe that you could not have fish in your pond unless you had 20 feet of water, sparklingly clean and constantly aerated. Although Calvin didn't know it, he was thinking of trout. It is true that you cannot have trout in your pool unless you maintain the water quality of a fast-moving mountain stream. But there are many fish that aren't trout, and many of them will beautify a pond and keep it free of insect larvae. Goldfish are the easiest to maintain and are available in different colors and forms. Consult your landscape supply store or pet store for other possibilities.

What are the minimum specifications of a fish pond? Fish can be maintained in a surprisingly small and simple pool. The secret to understanding fish culture is to recognize that fish, unlike mammals, have no need to eat to keep warm. A fish simply adopts the temperature of the water in which it swims. When the water gets very cold, the fish becomes more sluggish and needs less food. Many species of fish can burrow in the pond bottom or freeze in the ice and remain dormant throughout the winter months without harm. Goldfish will winter happily in any pond with at least 2 feet of water. When fish are active in the summer months, of course they must be fed. But because fish are not trying to maintain body heat like mammals, a day or two without food only means that the fish grows more slowly, not that it dies. In fact, overfeeding is by far the more serious problem in maintaining fish, because uneaten food fouls the water and encourages fish diseases.

Depending on the species of fish, the water must be kept more or less aerated, warm, and free of wastes. Species like goldfish and catfish can withstand a relatively low degree of aeration and a relatively high concentration of wastes. Stocking your lily pond with water plants goes a long way toward keeping the water quality up. But still, in every garden pool which is going to have fish, provision should be made for getting fresh water in and stale water out of the pool. That provision can be as simple as a garden hose which is used first as a siphon and then to refill the pool.

To use a hose as a siphon, fill the hose from the tap, holding the other end of the hose up at the same level as the tap so that the water won't spill out of either end when you detach the hose from the tap. Holding both ends of the hose at the same level, carry or drag the hose gently to the side of your pool. Simultaneously plunge one end of the hose into the pool while lowering the other end to a point outside the pool that is lower than the deepest part of the pool. Making sure that the pool end of the hose stays put, stretch the hose out so that more of its length is below the level of the bottom of the pool than is above it. The moment you get this balance right, the water will start to flow out of the pool and will drain until the air reaches the end of the hose where it lies at the bottom of the pool.

Draining and filling a pool are more easily done if plumbing is permanently in place. Providing proper intakes and drains for your pool may be somewhat difficult when you are building the pool, but their convenience may be worth the effort and expense.

Running Water for Your Garden

A small trickle of water or a fountain adds the sight and sound of moving water to the other delights of a water garden. Installing these need not be difficult. Tasteful (and tasteless!) fountains are available at garden supply stores specializing in water features, along with the pumps and plumbing supplies necessary to install them. You can even purchase ersatz waterfalls and rivulets. Or by laying a small concrete watercourse, disguised with pebbles pressed into the wet cement and closely planted with mosses, you can contrive your own miniature brook. Water can be supplied with a recycling pump, a downspout, or, for occasional use, a hose. Pumps can be placed in the pool and hidden under water plants or hidden in the foliage of plants growing around the pool. If you do put in a recycling pump and you are wiring it, be sure you know exactly what you are doing or get expert assistance. Electricity and wet earth are a lethal combination.

Once your miniature watercourse is in, you can plant around it some of the delightful flowers, such as forget-me-nots, primroses, and astilbes, that are happiest near water. And shallow running water will always attract birds who will come to drink and bathe.

Lighting

If you are already wiring for pumps, you might consider lighting your water feature. Lighting water turns it from a pleasant daytime feature into a nighttime fantasy. Seen through wide sliding glass doors giving onto a terrace, an illuminated water garden can be a dramatic and delightful attraction. Lighting can be used to highlight fountains and focus on the structure of such plants as willows and weeping cherries. Underwater lighting can reveal fish and the foliage of sub-aquatics, all but invisible during the day.

When you use lighting, be sure to illuminate features of the garden, not the people who are looking at the garden. Hide the light sources carefully. Keep your pool especially clean if you light it, or it will look messy with the lights on. As with everything else in landscaping, try out your lighting system before you invest time and effort in it. Electric lamps, gas lanterns, and flashlights can all simulate a lighting system and give you a chance to evaluate it before you commit yourself.

Safety

Water features are universally attractive, alluring to children and pets as well as to adults. Any gardener who puts in a water feature must consider the safety of children or animals that are likely to be drawn to it. The best insurance is a fence or other barrier that will prevent unsupervised pets and children from reaching the water.

Some Successful Water Gardens

Roof Pool

Jane Barnett and her husband Sam Turner bought the top floor of a Boston row house last year and converted it to a modern apartment. Both are dedicated urbanites, and except for a month's vacation each year, which they often take in the winter, they may be found in their Beacon Hill eyrie.

Part of their reason for buying the top floor is that Jane is an avid indoor gardener. Because the building is high up on the hill and the apartment is high up in the building, nothing intrudes between the couple's windows and the sun. The apartment is flooded with sunlight all day long.

The other reason they bought the top floor is so that they could have a roof garden. In the spring and summer, Jane makes quite a show of rooftop gardening. She grows lettuce, tomatoes, and peppers in planter boxes, and has a few beans climbing on the south wall of the chimney.

Unsatisfied with her other successes, Jane has always wanted to grow a waterlily. Last Christmas, Sam brought her a barrel which he found stored away in the loft of his father's barn. When spring came, they sawed the barrel in half and caulked the inside of each half. Thus, they made two large, bowl-shaped planters from the barrel. Near the top edge of each bowl, they mounted two sturdy handles to make it easier to move around. Near the bottom they drilled a hole, about the size of a wine cork, to serve for drainage.

Because of the warm summer climate of Boston and the comparatively long growing season of a roof garden which is warmed by heat escaping from the living space below, Jane decided to try tropical waterlilies. She ordered one white and one yellow lily from a catalog. When the lilies came, she potted each in a clay pot, covered the

The Barnett-Turner roof garden with waterlilies in tubs.

pot with pebbles to hold the planting mix, set one pot in each of the barrels, and filled the barrel until the water level was just 8 inches over the top of the pots.

The waterlilies have become the stars of Jane's roof garden. Each May, when the weather warms up, Jane and Sam reinstall the barrels and renew the soil in the pots. Then they position the lilies and fill the barrels with water. By the Fourth of July, the lilies are in bloom, and they continue to flower until mid-September. The only care the lilies need over the summer is an occasional change of water.

When the weather begins to cool down in late summer, Jane and Sam move the barrels downstairs to a spot in front of the south windows of their apartment.

A Magical Childhood Pool
A close friend of Calvin's remembers a pool from her grandmother's garden that had a magical quality for her. It was at the center of a small formal garden with meticulously maintained ivy-covered walls, precisely edged flowerbeds, and a lawn as closely cut, smooth, and lush as the fur of a mole.

The pool itself was a rectangle, about 4 by 6 feet, she remembers, although sizes are always deceptive in childhood memories. The pool was bordered with large square flagstones that slightly overhung the surface of the water. At one end was a little stone fountain—a statue of a naked little boy and a dolphin. Little sprays of water cascaded from the fountain down a channel in the flagstones and trickled into the pool. Tall ferns and large leafy plants, which she thinks were probably hostas, framed the fountain.

Calvin's friend doesn't know how deep the pool was. She remembers that it must have been fairly deep because she was never allowed to go near the pool alone. As a child, she didn't trust the motive behind these instructions. She knew that only a very silly and careless person could ever fall in a pool. So she assumed that there must have been some other hazard about the pool that her parents weren't telling her. Perhaps there was a troll that lived in the pool and snatched little girls that came too close to the edge.

Even so, she could never resist sneaking away to have a look at the pool, whenever the adults got to talking. She would say, "Gramma, may I go play in the garden?" And her grandmother would say, "Of course, dear, but don't go near the pool." And she would run outside and leave the adults talking in the sunporch.

Calvin's friend would always run directly to the little formal garden. First she would peer at the pool from around the corner of a hedge. Then she would sidle along the hedge until she was abreast of the pool. Here she would often sit for several

Grandmother's magical pool.

minutes, listening to the water trickle out of the fountain into the pool.

But soon even being that close wasn't enough. The pond seemed so peaceful. The voices of her parents and grandparents echoing from the sunroom seemed so close. How could she come to any harm? So she would creep across the grass to the pool's edge. Crawling the last few feet to give the troll the least possible chance to snatch her, she would put her tummy on the warm flagstones of the pool's border and look over the edge into its depths.

She never saw the troll. But she often saw huge dragonflies dart off their perches on the lily pads to snatch other insects, and the goldfish, flashes of white and amber in the depths of the murky pool. Sometimes they came to the surface to catch a fallen insect, with a sudden splash and a swirl of water. It always startled her and made her pull back from the edge of the pool.

And she saw many birds. If she lay quiet, the swallows would swoop over the water of the pool and the robins would come to bathe in the shallow channel of water that descended from the fountain. Once she saw a thrush drinking at the channel, with his big, dark, glossy eyes and his creamy breast flecked with fat black spots.

Every Christmas, Calvin's friend would go with her family to her grandmother's house for Christmas dinner. As soon as they arrived, Calvin's friend would rush out in the yard to see the pool while the adults prepared the meal. In the winter, she didn't worry about trolls.

But she did wonder about the goldfish. The little pool was a still place. No water bubbled out of the fountain or trickled across the flagstones into the pool. A heavy layer of pine boughs covered the surface of the pond. In a snowy winter, these would trap the snow and the pool would be entirely covered over. But Calvin's friend remembers one open winter when she could see through the boughs

to the surface of the pool. She cupped her hand around her eyes so that she could look down into the clear ice. There she saw two of the goldfish, frozen fast in the ice.

Her grandmother's house has since been sold. The pool was torn up years ago to make room for a tennis court. Calvin's friend mourns the passing of that pool. Calvin tells her that there's a lot more work in such a pool than meets the eye. There's a pump that recirculates the water through the fountain. And the lilies were probably in planters that had to be lifted each fall and put in a cool, dark place. But Calvin's friend still dreams of making a pool like it for her own grandchildren, some day.

A "Natural" Plastic Pool

The Tanners' neighbors had a natural spring-fed pool on their property, and the Tanners always envied them. Ann Tanner had always liked the idea of having water flowers such as waterlilies and rose mallows. John Tanner looked forward to watching the wildlife a pool would attract, and Freddy, their 9-year-old son, liked the idea of having his own lifetime supply of frogs. Unfortunately, soil cores showed that the Tanners' yard was on a huge underground sand dome, and no amount of excavating would ever turn up a natural spring on their property.

But the Tanners' property did have one advantage for pond-making. Just down the hill from the house was a natural bowl, about 20 feet across, which had been left by a huge chunk of ice when the glaciers were retreating from the Tanners' neighborhood hundreds of thousands of years ago. The Tanners had used this bowl as a drainage sump for their gutter and terrace drains. In winter, when the ground was frozen, the water sometimes collected in the bowl after a sudden warm spell. So Ann Tanner reasoned that if they were able to line the bowl in some way and supplement the drainage

The Tanners' natural-looking plastic pool.

water with a little water from their well, they might have a presentable little pond.

Their first problem was shaping the pool. A friend who was a contractor offered a few hours of his time with a small backhoe. He scoured the topsoil out of the bowl and piled it up on the lawn for future use. Then he lowered the downhill side of the bowl and pushed the sandy subsoil farther down to make a slight terrace, so that he made the bowl into a "gravy boat," with the "handle end" uphill and the "spout end" downhill.

Now the Tanners set about with hoes and spades to do the final shaping of the pond. All around the perimeter of the pond, they dug a trench just above the future waterline. Then, parallel to the sides of their gravy boat, they dug a second trench below the waterline.

The next step was to line their pool. John carefully examined the soil that lined the inside of the gravy boat. Even though the soil was sandy, it contained several large rocks which made the surface of the future pond bottom rough. Fearing for the integrity of the plastic, John had a load of fine clay trucked in and the family carefully spread it over the walls and bottom of their pond. Then they laid in the liner. The clay, John reasoned, would act not only as a cushion for the liner, but also as a backstop in case the liner developed a leak.

Once the liner was in place, nobody, not even the dog, was allowed to walk on it. Working from outside the pond, they tucked the liner into the lower of the two trenches and filled the trench with topsoil. This they then covered over with gravel, so that when they filled the pool, the topsoil wouldn't wash out of the trench. Then they tucked the liner into the higher trench, and filled this with topsoil. Some of this higher trench they covered with gravel, some they covered with sods, so that in some places the grass came right down to the water, and in others, the pond formed a miniature gravel beach.

In the trench below the waterline along the sides, they planted hardy waterlilies, lotuses, and red and blue lobelia. Where they had left exposed gravel along the waterline, they planted reeds. In the spout of the gravy boat they planted watercress, and in the wetlands formed below by the pond's runoff they grew some cattails and two huge hummocks of interrupted ferns with graceful arching fronds. To the side of the watercourse they put in three blueberry bushes and, a little higher, a red-stem dogwood.

A year later, their pool looks completely natural. Natural rainfall and the runoff from the terrace and downspouts keep it full most of the year. In dry periods, the Tanners add water. Filling the pool is very simple. John just runs water from a hose into the drain on the terrace and it trickles down the drainpipe into the pond. The mallows and waterlilies are doing well. Frogs have taken up residence, and the Tanners even thought they saw a prospecting muskrat: *Something* made a V-shaped wake as it slid across the surface of the pool in the last light of a recent summer evening.

Wrap-up

A water garden is one of the most delightful and attractive features a garden can have. A great variety of aquatic and waterside plants are available for the gardener who can contrive even a small pool of water or trickle in his garden. The pool itself, the centerpiece of your water garden, can be as simple as a pocket in the earth lined with plastic or a tub of lilies on your patio, or as elaborate as a formal, lined cement pool installed by a professional. Pools can be outfitted with trickles, fountains, and lights to increase their attractiveness. No matter what kind of pool you have, you will probably want to plant a lily, the queen of the water garden, with its delightful star-like flowers and its lush foliage.

Plants for Water Gardens

Plant Name	Water Feature	Description	Culture
Trees and Shrubs for Water Gardens			
Bald cypress (*Taxodium distichum*)	Pyramidal form with exotic, buttressed trunk; attractive, reddish brown, fibrous bark	Slender, deciduous conifer, 50 to 70 feet tall with a 20- to 30-foot spread; needles are yellow-green in spring, seagreen in summer, red-brown in fall; trees develop "knees" around base of trunk in wet areas	Full sun; deep, acidic, sandy loam; excellent for swampy areas; excellent wind resistance; to Zone 4

(continued)

Plants for Water Gardens—*continued*

Plant Name	Water Feature	Description	Culture
Canadian hemlock (*Tsuga canadensis*)	Graceful pyramidal form; delicate, evergreen foliage; small but plentiful brown cones	Pyramidal tree 40 to 50 feet tall with a 25- to 35-foot spread; some forms are weeping or mounded; bark is brown, deeply furrowed; needles are green, with 2 whitish bands on the underside; cones are oval, brown, ½ to 1 inch long	Full sun to partial shade; cool, well-drained, acidic soils; mulch; will not tolerate wind, drought, or pollution; to Zone 3
Carolina hemlock (*Tsuga caroliniana*)	Handsome, compact pyramidal form; dark, glossy, evergreen foliage; attractive, inch-long cones	Spiring pyramidal tree 45 to 60 feet tall with a 20- to 25-foot spread; often slightly pendulous; bark is reddish brown, deeply fissured; foliage radiates around the trunk like a bottle-brush	Partial shade; moist, well-drained soil; mulch; will not tolerate wind or drought, but tolerates air pollution better than Canadian hemlock; to Zone 4
Dwarf purple osier willow (*Salix purpurea* var. *nana*)	Purplish young branches; silver-gray leaves	Compact, finely branched shrub up to 5 feet tall and wide; lance-shaped leaves are 2 to 4 inches long, $\frac{1}{8}$ to $\frac{1}{3}$ inch wide; slender branches become light to olive gray at maturity	Full sun; moist soil; good for wet areas and to stabilize stream and pond banks; to Zone 3
Goat willow, pussy willow (*Salix caprea*)	Large, silky, inch-long male catkins; March and early April	Erect small tree 15 to 25 feet tall with a 12- to 15-foot spread; trunk is yellowish brown to dark brown; oblong leaves are 2 to 4 inches long, 1 to $2\frac{1}{4}$ inches wide, dark green above, gray below	Full sun; moist soil; to Zone 3
Golden weeping willow (*Salix alba* var. *vitellina*)	Golden-yellow, weeping branches; may have striking yellow fall color	Broad, round-topped, open tree with long, pendulous branches; bark is yellow-green; leaves are $1\frac{1}{2}$ to 4 inches long, $\frac{1}{4}$ to $\frac{5}{8}$ inch wide, bright green above, silvery beneath; may have golden fall color; catkins	Full sun; moist soil; spreading root system; susceptible to wind and storm damage; fast-growing; to Zone 2

Plant Name	Water Feature	Description	Culture
Highbush blueberry (*Vaccinium corymbosum*) many cultivars	Profusion of white, urn-shaped, 1/3-inch-long flowers in May; dense form with dark blue-green foliage; excellent yellow, orange, and red fall color; blueberries	Upright, multistemmed, rounded shrub, 6 to 12 feet tall with an 8- to 12-foot spread; dark green leaves are oval, 1 to 3½ inches long; bark is yellow-green, turning reddish in winter; berries appear in late July and August	Full sun or partial shade; moist, humusy, well-drained, acidic (pH 4.5 to 5.5) soil; does well on swampy sites; mulch; to Zone 3
Japanese flowering cherry, oriental cherry (*Prunus serrulata* 'Kwanzan')	Gorgeous, double, pink, 2½-inch flowers borne profusely along stems, April to early May; leaves may turn orange-bronze in fall	Upright tree up to 40 feet tall and wide; dark green, glossy, serrated leaves are 2 to 5 inches long and 1¼ to 2½ inches wide; new leaves are bronzed	Full sun; deep, moist, fertile soil; to Zone 5
Larch, European larch (*Larix decidua*)	Pyramidal, columnar, or weeping form; striking ochre-yellow fall foliage	Deciduous conifer 70 to 75 feet tall by 25 to 30 feet wide; needles grow to 1½ inches long, are clustered, bright green in spring, deep green in summer	Full sun; moist, well-drained soil; tolerates boggy conditions; intolerant of shade, drought, alkaline soils, and pollution; Zones 2–6
Pinkshell azalea (*Rhododendron vaseyi*) var. *album*	Spectacular, bell-shaped, clear rose or white, 1½-inch-wide flowers, in clusters of 5 to 8; May	Irregular upright shrub 5 to 10 feet tall; deciduous foliage is medium green; light red fall color	Partial shade; open, moist, well-drained, acidic soil; mulch; to Zone 4
Red maple, swamp maple (*Acer rubrum*) many cultivars	Smooth gray bark; reddish flowers, March and April; winged, often red fruit; can have stunning red fall color	Trees 40 to 60 feet tall and wide, with irregular ovoid or rounded crown; leaves are 3-lobed to 5-lobed, 2 to 4 inches wide, medium to dark green above, grayish below	Sun; slightly acidic, moist soil; intolerant of alkaline soils; to Zone 3
Summersweet (*Clethra alnifolia*) 'Paniculata' 'Pink Spires' 'Rosea'	Delightfully scented, 2- to 6-inch-long, upright, terminal panicles of white or pink flowers; July and August; pale yellow to rich gold fall color	Oval, dense shrub 3 to 8 feet tall, with a 4- to 6-foot spread; deep green, oblong leaves are up to 4 inches long; brown stems are upright; plants often clump; persistent capsule fruits	Shade to full sun; moist, humusy, acidic soil; tolerates swampy soils and salt; to Zone 3
Swamp azalea (*Rhododendron viscosum*)	White or pink, clove-scented flowers borne in clusters of 4 to 9; May and June	Loose, open shrub, 1 to 8 feet tall with a 3- to 8-foot spread	Partial shade; open, moist, well-drained, acidic soil; mulch; to Zone 3

(continued)

Plants for Water Gardens—*continued*

Plant Name	Water Feature	Description	Culture
Sweet azalea (*Rhododendron arborescens*)	Striking, white, 1½- to 2-inch-wide flowers; very fragrant; May to July; can have red fall color	Deciduous, loosely branched shrub, 8 to 20 feet tall and wide; stems are upright; oval foliage is lustrous dark green	Partial shade; light, constantly moist, acidic soil; to Zone 4
Weeping Higan cherry (*Prunus subhirtella* var. *pendula*)	Graceful, weeping form; single, pink, ½-inch-wide flowers, borne in clusters of 2 to 5; March and April	Weeping tree, 20 to 40 feet tall with a 15- to 30-foot spread; lustrous, dark green leaves are toothed, 1 to 4 inches long; round, shiny black fruit is ¹/₃ inch in diameter	Full sun; deep, moist, fertile soil; to Zone 4

Herbaceous Plants for Water Gardens

Plant Name	Water Feature	Description	Culture
Arrow arum, water arum (*Peltandra virginica*)	Yellow-green aroid flower spathe; summer	Plants are 2 feet tall, upright; leaves are glossy, arrowhead shaped	Full sun to partial shade; wet or boggy soil; plants can be submerged in up to 6 inches of water; perennial; Zones 5–9
Astilbe (*Astilbe chinensis* 'Pumila')	Lavender-pink flowers; August and September	Dwarf astilbe, 15 inches tall, with a creeping habit	Partial shade; moist, humusy soil; perennial; Zones 4–8
Big blue lobelia, great blue lobelia (*Lobelia syphilitica*)	Bright blue, tubular flowers; August and September	Flowers bloom in leaf axils on stiff, leafy, 2- to 3-foot-tall stalks	Partial shade to full sun; rich, moist, humusy soil; self-sows; perennial; Zones 4–8
Blue flag (*Iris versicolor*)	Graceful, medium blue flowers; spring	Flowers are borne on upright stalks 2 feet tall; foliage is grass green, strap-like	Full sun to partial shade; wet or boggy soil; plants can be submerged in up to 6 inches of water; perennial; Zones 4–9
Floating heart (*Nymphoides peltata*)	Yellow, 5-petaled flowers held slightly above the water surface; spring to fall	Like a small waterlily; leaves are 3 inches wide, rounded, variegated, green and maroon	Full sun to partial shade; floating water plant; perennial; Zones 6–10
Giant reed grass (*Arundo donax*)	Tall, imposing plants; bloom stalks bear panicles up to 2 feet long, erect or slightly drooping; red, turning white; September	Seed heads and foliage, which can reach 14 feet tall, last into early winter; glaucous green leaf blades are up to 4 feet long, alternate on the stems, arching	Full sun; moist, well-drained soil; perennial; to Zone 7
Goatsbeard (*Aruncus dioicus*)	Showy plumes of creamy white flowers; June and July	Impressive spires up to 6 feet tall; leaves are broad-toothed	Partial shade to full sun; rich, moist soil; perennial; Zones 5–9

Plant Name	Water Feature	Description	Culture
Golden club *(Orontium aquaticum)*	White spikes tipped with brilliant yellow; spring and early summer	Upright, 12-inch clumps of handsome, deep green, spear-shaped foliage	Partial shade; boggy or wet soil; plants can be submerged in up to 6 inches of water; perennial; Zones 6–10
Helmet flower, turk's cap, garden monkshood *(Aconitum napellus)* 'Album' 'Bicolor'	Spikes of blue, white, or blue and white, helmet-shaped flowers; July and August	Handsome, 3- to 4-foot plants; foliage is finely divided	Partial shade to full sun; rich, moist, deep soil; poisonous; perennial; Zones 2–7
Japanese iris *(Iris ensata)* sold as *I. kaempferi*	Flat, showy flowers up to 1 foot wide; in white, blues, purple, and red-violet; single, double, or peony-like; late spring and summer	Tall, striking plants up to 4 feet tall; foliage is deep green, strap-like	Full sun to partial shade; moist, humusy soil; intolerant of alkaline soils; perennial; to Zone 5
Maiden grass *(Miscanthus sinensis* 'Gracillimus')	Fine-textured grass; bloom stalks bear fan-shaped panicles up to 1 foot long; whitish, tinged red; September	Seed heads and foliage, up to 7 feet tall, last into early and late winter; curling, slender, long leaves are blue-green with a white midvein	Full sun; rich, well-drained, alkaline soil; perennial; to Zone 5
Marsh marigold *(Caltha palustris)* 'Flore Pleno'	Abundant, yellow flowers; 'Flore Pleno' has double flowers; spring	Clumping plants 1 to 2 feet tall; foliage is glossy, deep green, ivy-like	Full sun to partial shade; moist soil; can sit in shallow water; to Zone 3
Monkshood *(Aconitum carmichaelii)*	Spikes of helmet-shaped, dark blue flowers; September and October	Striking, 3-foot-tall plants; leaves are glossy, deep-fingered	Partial shade to full sun; rich, moist, deep soil; poisonous; perennial; Zones 2–7
Morden Pink *(Lythrum virgatum* 'Morden Pink') many other cultivars	Tall spires of clear pink, dark pink, rose red, carmine, or purple flowers; July to August	Well-branched, bushy plants, 18 inches to 3 feet tall	Partial shade to full sun; moist, well-drained soil; perennial; Zones 3–8
Ostrich fern *(Matteuccia struthiopteris)*	Imposing plants with fronds that resemble ostrich feathers	Large fern, up to 5 feet tall; fronds are toothed	Light shade; humusy, well-drained, moist, acidic soil; can be used to hold stream or pond banks; to Zone 3
Pampas grass *(Cortadera selloana)* many cultivars	Pyramidal female panicles up to 3 feet long and 1 foot wide; hairy, silvery white to rose-tinted inflorescence; male panicle is 3 feet long and narrow; late summer to fall	Tussock-forming, 9-foot-tall, densely tufted, evergreen grass; leaves are tapering, medium green to glaucous green, slightly arching	Full sun; fertile, well-drained soil; best color in sandy soils; intolerant of cold clay soils and wet feet; perennial; Zones 9–10

(continued)

Plants for Water Gardens—*continued*

Plant Name	Water Feature	Description	Culture
Purple loosestrife (*Lythrum salicaria*)	Tall, extremely striking spires of magenta-purple flowers; summer and early fall	Dark, strap-like foliage on clumps of wiry stems are up to 5 feet tall	Full sun to light shade; moderately fertile, moist soil; tolerates boggy soils; very aggressive; perennial; Zone 3
Pygmy waterlily (*Nymphaea colorata*)	Abundant wisteria-blue flowers; fragrant; May or June to frost	Waterlily spreads 1 to 6 feet wide; lily pads are green; flowers open in the morning and close at night; tropical	Full sun to partial sun; can be planted as shallowly as 6 inches deep in the water; ideal for tub culture; perennial; must be lifted and stored over winter except in Zone 10
Red cardinal flower (*Lobelia cardinalis*)	Tall spikes of scarlet-red, tubular flowers; July to September	Spikes rise 3 to 4 feet above a basal rosette of foliage	Partial shade to full sun; rich, moist, humusy soil; tolerates boggy conditions; perennial; Zones 4–8
Sweet waterlily (*Nymphaea odorata*) 'Sulphurea Grandiflora'	Lovely, lemon white, sweetly scented flowers, 3 to 6 inches across; spring to fall	Waterlily spreads 1 to 12 feet wide; lily pads are lightly mottled; flowers are held slightly above the water surface; hardy	Full sun to partial sun; plants need still water, 6 to 18 inches deep; Zones 3–10
Tussock grass (*Deschampsia caespitosa*)	Huge, extremely graceful, loose flower panicles, up to 20 inches long and 8 inches across; erect or slightly nodding; color variable; June to August	Densely tufted, evergreen perennial grass, 1½ to 3 feet tall; shiny, deep green, spiky leaves are up to 2 feet long and ¹/₈ inch wide; holds flower heads into winter	Partial shade; moist soil; self-sows; perennial; to Zone 5
Variegated Japanese sedge (*Carex morrowii* var. *expallida*) 'Aurea Variegata'	Graceful, arched foliage, striped cream and green; 'Aurea Variegata' has yellow stripes; into late winter	Eye-catching clumps 18 inches tall and 8 inches wide, with powdery yellow, brush-shaped flower heads in spring	Partial shade; mulch in winter; can be used massed or as a groundcover; perennial; to Zone 5
White waterlily (*Nymphaea alba*)	Cup-shaped, 4- to 5-inch-wide flowers; lightly scented the first day they are open; spring to fall	Large waterlily with pads 4 to 12 inches in diameter; young lily pads are red, mature pads are dark green; hardy	Full sun to partial sun; plants need still water, 6 inches or deeper; Zones 3–10
Yellow flag (*Iris pseudacorus*)	Rich yellow fleur-de-lis blossoms; June and July	Flowers rise 3 feet tall on stalks clasped by bright green leaves	Full sun; rich, wet soil; boggy conditions; perennial; Zones 5–8
Yellow lotus (*Nelumbo lotea*)	Native lotus with lovely lemon yellow flowers held above the leaves; heavenly scent; striking seedpods; summer	Large, dark green, saucer-shaped leaves are held above the water; flowers open in the morning and close in midafternoon	Full sun; pots or planted at 3- to 4-foot depth in pool or pond; perennial; Zones 4–9

CHAPTER 10

Wildlife Gardens

*I*magine that the season is early fall and you are taking a walk in your garden. As you step out your door, you startle a crowd of blue jays and a squirrel who have been foraging at your bird feeder. You step to the feeder to see if it is well stocked. Grateful for the relief from the noisy jostling of the jays, a chickadee flutters to the deck of the feeder. He perches inches from your face, so close that you can see his glossy eye within his black cap as he regards you judiciously. Then he snatches a seed and flies off, his wings whirring like the blades of a tiny fan.

The feeder stands at the edge of a small lawn, part of your own private quarter-acre wildlife refuge. At the center of the lawn is a birdbath which sports at this moment a cardinal, flinging water about as he nestles in the shallow water of the bath. The low morning light illuminates the droplets of water, making them glitter like jewels on his scarlet plumage.

The lawn is edged by flowerbeds. You have struggled all year to maintain the order in these beds, low annuals near the lawn, high perennials near the annuals, and shrubs at the back. But the rabbits have been busy at their own gardening program. Your flowerbed plan called for nasturtiums and snapdragons at the front, backed by asters, lilies, phlox, daylilies, tulips, monarda, and tall delphiniums. The rabbits didn't think you needed the nasturtiums or the tulips, so they ate them. Still, at this time of year, your flowerbeds make a showy display. A ruby-throated hummingbird darts among the blooms. You make a mental note to check your wildlife diary. Is this the latest that you've ever seen a hummingbird in the fall?

Behind the flowerbeds, the rest of the garden would have to be described as a brushy tangle. At this time of year, the red and orange berries of the bittersweet are beginning to show. Highbush cranberry viburnum, elder, autumn olive, and honeysuckle abound, each providing a different sort of wildlife food at a different time of year. It's not the sort of shrubbery collection you can show off to a garden club, but it's a veritable larder of wild foods, and the birds and animals love it.

Is a Wildlife Garden for You?

How you react to the image we have described will go a long way to helping you decide whether you are the type of person who wants a wildlife garden. If the garden I have described seems disheveled, if a squirrel at your feeder and a rabbit in your flowerbeds are going to seem like intruders rather than guests, then a wildlife garden is probably not for you. If, on the other hand, the garden we have described sounds romantic and full of fun, then read on.

Readers who have ever been on a nature walk with an experienced naturalist know that not all kinds of wildlife are found in the same place, no matter how verdant and undisturbed that place may be. Every plant, every animal has its own ecological niche. If it is an animal, its niche consists of the things it eats, the places it hides, the materials it uses for its nest, the water it drinks and bathes in—all the things it needs to make its living. To see many different kinds of plants and animals, you must go to different sorts of places—to salt marshes and seashores and rocky headlands, to the banks of freshwater ponds and streams, to pine woods and deciduous woods, brushy borders, meadows, fields, and pastures. Each kind of place has its own familiar plants and animals.

Gardeners who successfully attract wildlife to their own gardens exploit this principle on a small scale. Within the confines of a small space, they provide as many ways for wildlife to make a living as possible.

What Can You Hope to See in Your Wildlife Garden?

What sorts of wildlife might you attract to a wildlife garden? The list of possible creatures is almost endless and depends, of course, on what region you live in, whether you live in the city or country, and how many concessions you are willing to make to wildlife in your own lifestyle. To help you decide if you want a wildlife garden, here are 54 creatures that many of you can expect to find in your garden if you offer an inviting environment with a variety of natural features. As we list them, we'll try to tell you a little bit about what attracts them and why you might find them interesting.

Mammals

Of all the creatures in nature, our fellow mammals are most persecuted by us. But still several species of mammal come readily to gardens, some whether you invite them or not. Squirrels and their clan are ubiquitous, of course, ranging from the black squirrels of Canada to the tiny, mysterious flying squirrels of the middle and southern United States. Chipmunks will happily take up residence in your garden, particularly if you have a dry stone wall or a loose foundation. You can tame them so that they will come for handouts, if you are patient and provide bits of seed or grain. If you live next to a cow pasture or hayfield, you can expect to be visited by the large ground squirrel we know as a groundhog or woodchuck.

In some parts of the country, both coyotes and deer are making a comeback, and will pay a visit at locations surprisingly close to major cities. When the coyotes howl at night, they sound like a kennel full of demented puppies.

If you maintain some brushy areas in your garden or some parts with tall grass, you can expect to see rabbits and field mice, not to mention

Ecology and the Home Landscape

The important battle to save rare and endangered species of animals has had one unfortunate side effect. It has put a lot of people off ecology by making wildlife seem unreasonably delicate and fussy. Young people these days seem to have particularly elaborate notions of what wildlife is and where you find it. Calvin teaches a course in wildlife at his home. When the students first arrive, he shows them the lawn and fields and shrubbery right around the house, and points out the many birds, insects, and other animals that live there. Pretty soon, however, some students are getting restless. These are usually the ones wearing hiking boots with Vibram soles and carrying binoculars. They point to the deep evergreen and deciduous forests in the distance: "Why aren't we going there? Isn't all the wildlife there?"

"All right," says Calvin, "let's go see." So together students and professor trudge across the fields, up through the overgrown pastures, through a stand of softwoods and brush, over a stone wall, and finally into a mature stand of evergreens, oaks, and maples.

All along the path, birds of various species flutter up and signs of animals abound. But as soon as they enter the deep woods, silence closes around the group. Together, students and professor rest on the soft, needle-covered floor of the forest and listen. They can hear the wind flowing through the tops of the pine trees. In the distance they can hear the cry of a single jay. Still farther away is the equivocal song of a hermit thrush. And ever so faintly, just overhead, the thin wheezy whistle of a warbler. They strain their eyes to see it, but it's so high among the dense foliage that it is not to be seen. "Is this all?" the Vibram-soled students ask, and before long, they are restless to go back to the open land and secondary growth around the house.

There is a moral to this story, even though we may get into trouble with our ecologist colleagues for telling it. Unless the land has been contaminated by insecticides or pollutants, the disturbed ground around human habitations is often a very good place to see a variety of wildlife. You won't see any rare and endangered species, but few gardeners long to see a snail darter or an obscure warbler anyway. Most of us would take more pleasure in seeing the great variety of creatures that will come to a garden, if only a reasonable effort is made to welcome them.

the house mouse. Cute as house mice are, field mice are much cuter, and seem to have eyes big as ebony saucers. If you have a stream running by your garden, you may see muskrats. Raccoons may pay a visit to your corn patch or your garbage cans, even in the depths of the city. Give them a way in, and they'll set up residence in your attic.

Reptiles, Amphibians, and Fish

Maintain moist places in your garden, and you will see and hear amphibians. The common toad is a loyal friend of the vegetable garden. Leave a bright light on during hot summer nights and the toads will come and sit under it to take advantage of the attracted insects. Provide a small pond and you will have frogs: frogs that peep and frogs that boom and frogs that saw away at a bass viol all night. Newts and salamanders also thrive near moist areas. Some are brilliant shades of red or green.

If you have sunny rocks in your garden, you may see tiny lizards scurrying in and out of the crevices, and a garter snake or blacksnake may come to sunbathe on cool, sunny days. Despite their fearsomeness, most snakes are harmless, all are useful, and some are extraordinarily beautiful.

If you are lucky, you may host a corn snake, its skin an exquisitely modulated pattern of russets and mauves that would do credit to an oriental rug.

You can even have fish in a backyard wildlife preserve, if you plan carefully, pick your species well, and provide supplementary feeding. Although not (strictly speaking) wildlife, goldfish and koi—brilliantly colored Japanese carp—will survive in a garden pool for many years, hibernating in the muck at the bottom of the pool during the winter.

Insects

You may have doubts about how many kinds of insects you want to attract to your garden, but it's nice to have some of the most beautiful and interesting species around. Butterflies come to a garden which has open space and a variety of flowering plants. One of the most beautiful of butterflies, the monarch, is particularly fond of milkweed. The showy colors of butterflies are an interesting natural phenomenon. Most insects hide from their predators by adopting camouflages. When insects are brilliantly colored, their coloration usually gives warning that the insect is loaded with substances toxic to birds or other predators. Monarch butterflies feed on the poisonous foliage of milkweed, and jays quickly learn not to feed on them. Insects with "warning coloration" are often mimicked by other insects which do not feed on poisonous plants. One such faker is the viceroy butterfly, which is every bit as beautiful as a monarch, but would be much more tasty to a blue jay, if only a blue jay dared eat it.

Many bees and wasps are too aggressive to be good neighbors. But on a largish lot, a well-managed beehive can work well and even provide honey. There's a smug pleasure in knowing that while you are resting in your lawn chair, your bees are out foraging among your neighbors' flowers for nectar. Hornets (the wasps that are shaped and often colored like bees) are a contentious lot, and we don't recommend them as garden companions. But other wasps, such as the delicate mud daubers and polistes, rarely go looking for trouble. You can tell them by their graceful build and by the delicate fiber that connects the abdomen to the rest of the body. These wasps build flat, open cellular nests or mud "huts" in old sheds and under windowledges and overhangs. They are voracious worm-eaters, and can often be seen in gardens foraging for cabbageworms. They have a remarkable social life and can be approached safely, if you aren't allergic and don't do anything silly. Never, for instance, slap a wasp that lights on you. Brush it or flick it away.

Gardens with water may attract dragonflies, those iridescent "birds of prey" of the insect world that perch on the tips of marsh grass, waiting for passing insects to snatch or passing dragonflies to court.

Birds

Of all forms of wildlife, birds provide the most pleasure for the least effort. Many bird species are extraordinarily beautiful, sing glorious songs, and have fascinating habits. Unlike most mammals, birds are usually out and about in the daytime, and they readily become used to having people around. The only catch about attracting birds to the garden is the family cat. You should be careful not to feed and water birds near a place where the cat can hide in waiting.

The number and variety of bird species that can be attracted to a garden are enormous. Everybody has starlings, house sparrows, and pigeons. These European imports are not the most glamorous of birds, but they do have interesting habits. Starlings have an extraordinary song which sounds like a factory of elves working away with files and hammers on pieces of sheet metal, and house sparrows have a complex social life with communal nests and communal courtship. Pigeons are, well, pigeons.

Every bit of complexity you add to your garden will increase the number of different birds that visit. If you have an open lawn, you will have robins and flickers. Robins make wonderful garden companions. They will raise their young in a bush right next to a patio or in the eaves of a porch, close at hand for observation and comment. Flickers are the ground-feeding woodpeckers with black moustaches and red pates that come to your lawn in spring to search for grubs.

Plant flowerbeds and you may see hummingbirds. Barely larger than insects, these birds dart among your blooms like tiny helicopters, pausing in mid-flight to insert their long bills into the throats of red flowers and drink their nectar.

Protect a marsh on your property and you will see redwing blackbirds. The males of this species, jet black birds with fiery red epaulets, will compete vigorously for space in your garden. Each male is a devoted polygamist and will do his best to have several wives in his territory. Preserve a meadow, and meadowlarks and bobolinks will move in. Both are wonderfully entertaining. Meadowlarks wear yellow V-neck tennis sweaters with black necklines. Their song is a haunting, plaintive whistle. The bobolink's joyous bubbling song is accompanied by a dramatic aerial dance.

Let the grass and brush grow up in some portion of your property, and you are sure to see a song sparrow. They are mousy brown birds but have interesting singing habits. Each male song sparrow sings several different ditties, many of which seem like fragments from old familiar songs. He'll sing one ditty for a while, and then change to another, until eventually he works his way through his entire repertoire.

Protect an old bit of orchard in your yard and you might attract a bluebird. Bluebirds are proba-bly beyond the reach of most urban and suburban gardeners, but if you are determined to try, check with your local bird club or the Audubon Society for a pamphlet on how to provide suitable housing and habitat for these beautiful birds.

Frame your lawn with flowering and fruiting shrubs and you will have mimic thrushes: the catbird, the brown thrasher, and the mockingbird. The catbird is fond of singing from the depths of your lilac bush, the thrasher from the brush along the road, the mockingbird from the top of your television antenna. The mimic thrushes have the most complicated songs of any American bird, perhaps of any bird in the world.

If tall trees grow around your property, you will probably have orioles. These black and orange birds build woven nests that hang from the tops of trees like old knitted socks. Each male oriole has a distinctive whistled tune that he repeats all summer long. Learn the tune and whistle it back to him, and you may get him to sing for you on command. From tall trees, tanagers will sing their wistful whistle which always sounds far away to Calvin, no matter how close the singer really is. The effervescent songs of the purple finch and the house finch bubble forth from the tops of large ornamentals. From among the high foliage, vireos will render their lazy song as they search among the leaves for caterpillars. Even the wary crows will nest in your high trees and feed on your lawn soon after dawn, before the members of your family are stirring.

Keep a feeder in winter, and you will see dozens of different birds. You will be visited by the bossy blue jays with their harsh "jay" calls and their haunting bell songs. Each jay seems to have a unique pattern in the markings that frame the face and cross between the beak and the eyes like a moustache. With patient observation, you can learn to recognize some jays as individuals. The cardinal's brilliant plumage brightens a gray winter day, and his song is one of the earliest and most enthusiastic to grace the late winter woods. The evening grosbeak is a dramatic winter-feeder bird whose comic greediness and dramatic white, yellow, and black plumage make him fun to watch.

The most charming feeder birds are the titmice, such as the tufted titmouse and the chickadee. Titmice are the most companionable of birds. They are easily tamed and will learn without much prompting to come rap on your windows when the feeder is empty. They will take seed from your feeder even when they are not hungry and store it away in the crevices of rough-barked trees. During most of the year, titmice make companionable little noises which sound almost conversational. But in late winter, even when the snow is still on the ground, they sing simple whistled songs which echo through the leafless trees and give promise of early spring. Similar are the nuthatches, tiny winter seedeaters that distinguish themselves by walking upside down on the trunks of trees, poking into crevices looking for the seeds that other birds have hidden.

So, there you have them: 54 creatures you can plant for, design for, and be on the lookout for in your garden. We're sure you can think of 54 others that are peculiar to your region. If you can't, contact your local bird club or conservation organization. They are sure to have information on local wildlife.

Planning Your Wildlife Refuge

Three elements are essential in any garden meant to foster wildlife: sunlight, cover, and water.

Sunlight. For your soil to be productive, the sunlight must get to it. That means that the surface of the ground must not be completely covered with tall dense trees, but with grass, reeds, or brush, low plants which let the sun through.

Cover. Few animals like to be exposed to the open sky. Even if hawks are rare in your neighborhood, your animals are always instinctively on the lookout for them, and always prefer to have a few branches overhead. The best cover is a dense brushy tangle with some evergreens mixed in. By day, the birds will feed in the tangle, and roost by night in the evergreens.

Water. When people think of water in a garden, they usually think of neat water: a pool scrupulously edged in white stones, a pond with crisp green grass around its edges, a little brook cascading down a well-defined rocky bed. While water of any sort fosters wildlife, these forms of water are not the most attractive to animals. The most productive kind of water in a wildlife refuge is a marsh, a mucky bit of ground where the water is in the soil, not necessarily on view.

The land, water, and air in a wildlife garden must be as free as possible of contaminants. Apart from choosing a site for your garden that has never been contaminated by industrial wastes, you will be hard pressed to do anything about pollution that arises from sources outside your control. But you can make an absolute resolution never to permit chemical insecticides, herbicides, or defoliants to be used on your property, and never to spill or dump solvents or fuels on any part of your soil. These measures will go a long way toward protecting your animal visitors from pollution.

Plants for a Wildlife Garden

Where do you get your plant materials for a wildlife garden? Some, of course, will come to you naturally, once you make the right conditions available to them. Seeds are borne by the wind, as well as by birds and animals. You will find that any new piece of rich soil is quickly colonized by wild

Phebe's Favorites for Wildlife Gardens

Birds aren't the only ones who love dogwoods. I suspect that dogwoods are one of the most popular flowering trees. The native flowering dogwood certainly is the most spectacular of the dogwoods in bloom in the East, and their pretty, ornamental red fruits rarely escape the birds to become a feature. The Kousa dogwood is not far behind in beauty. Squirrels and other animals relish the raspberry-like fruits.

Not only do hawthorns offer animals protection with their thickly branching habit and (for the most part) dense and wicked thorns, but they also have colorful fruits which are, in my opinion, often more spectacular than the bloom. Many have very pretty, often glossy foliage and spectacular autumn coloration. The Washington hawthorn ranks high on my list, as do the cockspur hawthorn, with horizontal branching, and a thornless variety, 'Winter King', to name a few. All have white flowers, for only the English hawthorn derivatives produce pink blooms, but the English varieties have had foliage problems and so, in my opinion, do not measure up as well. Consideration should be made of the numbers of small children who might be playing in the vicinity before planting thorny hawthorns.

No wildlife garden is complete without a crabapple for beauty of flower, form, fruit, and foliage color. Due to successful hybridizing, it is possible to get crabapples that bloom every year, have foliage that remains robust and green (or red) throughout the summer, and wind up with small, showy fruits in shades of red, yellow, or combinations, which will disappear with the birds. A lot for one plant! Some varieties I like are the Zumi crabapple, with apple-blossom pink flowers and red fruit; Japanese crabapple, with apple-blossom pink flowers and yellow-red fruit; 'Bob White', with white flowers and yellow fruit; and 'Royalty', with red flowers, red foliage, and red fruit. There are many more.

There is one mountain ash that I particularly want to mention. It is totally outstanding and not so often planted. It is the Korean mountain ash, a tree with beautiful foliage, unlike other ashes—a nice, simple, dark green leaf, colorful in fall. Perhaps not quite as showy in bloom as other mountain ashes, but the red fruit is showy, and the bark of the tree is a smooth gray. It should be planted more.

The olives are sturdy, handsome shrubs that are drought tolerant and fast-spreading. They are excellent for birds, for hedges, along roadsides, and even for specimen use. The gray-leaved Russian olive can be grown as a small tree, very Mediterranean in feeling. The autumn olive is very vigorous and not for the small garden.

Although many would not think of bayberry as an ornamental plant, it is very serviceable, especially at the seashore and in poor soils. It will even adapt to light shade. The fragrant gray berries on the female plants are attractive, and groupings of this plant, with its narrow gray-green foliage, form pleasing clouds among rocks or along banks.

The shrub roses form nice thickets for birds and food for wildlife, as they have rather large rose hips. For us, it is a chance to include more of these beautiful and fragrant flowers in our garden. Tops is the rugosa rose, the parent flower, a controversial shade of rich purple-pink that's disliked by many gardeners and sometimes hard to integrate into a color scheme. Luckily, there are several good hybrids with white flowers. 'Blanc Double de Coubert' and 'Sir Thomas Lipton' have large, showy rose hips. 'Father Hugo' (*Rosa hugonis*) has pretty, single yellow flowers. The Japanese (multiflora) rose should not be planted in the small garden, but does make a good thicket. Other varieties include the Scotch rose and varieties, with flowers of many colors; the Virginia rose, with single pink flowers, good green foliage, fall color, and persistent red fruits; and the memorial rose, which is more like a groundcover, with white flowers, red fruits, and glossy green foliage. There are numerous varieties of shrub roses, many of them thought of as "old-fashioned."

plants, although perhaps not the plants you hoped for. Those of you who are unwilling to take pot luck should ask your nursery staff, a local naturalist, or a botany teacher for advice on wild plants or plants that naturalize well in your garden. Your local nursery will probably have a few species for sale. You may be able to locate a nursery in your area that specializes in cultivating wild plants, and there are a number of mail-order companies that specialize in seeds of wild plants.

Resist the temptation to dig up plants from the wild. You probably won't be able to duplicate in your own garden the soil conditions necessary for a wild plant's survival, and most wild plants transplant poorly under the best of circumstances. Many species are struggling to hold their own in nature. The best way to guarantee yourself and others the pleasure of seeing these beautiful plants in the future is to leave them right where they are.

How you introduce the crucial three elements—sunlight, cover, and moisture—to your wildlife garden will vary depending on the size of the garden, the natural features already existing there, and the degree to which you are willing to relinquish your garden to wildlife. You may want to start from scratch and put in a wildlife garden with running water, marshy land, and shrubbery all carefully balanced. Or you may simply want to make a few concessions to wildlife in your present garden—put in a birdbath and feeder and plant shrubs, such as highbush cranberry viburnum or honeysuckle, that provide good cover and a food supply. Between these extremes are a whole range of possibilities which the following examples will illustrate.

Some Successful Wildlife Gardens
Wildlife Refuge in a Postage Stamp

When Mr. Gerald Mason's wife died, he had to sell his house in the country and move to a condominium unit in a retirement community. The unit had a tiny, 20-by-15-foot fenced garden. A birch had been planted in one corner of the yard several years ago, and the tree now dominated the garden, casting a pleasant, filtered shade. Pleasing as the little garden was, Gerry had always enjoyed wildlife and open spaces. To think of himself living in an apartment with a shoebox of a yard depressed him terribly.

Gerry's daughter urged him to see how he might improve even this tiny garden as a place for wildlife. The first thing they did was dangle a bird feeder from a limb of the birch that reached out toward the room which Gerry would use as a sitting room and library. Next, in the corner of the garden near the tree's trunk, they put a small raised pool. By running a hose beneath the hedge that ran along the side of the garden, they rigged an inexpensive, inconspicuous water supply. From a faucet near the house, Gerry could maintain a constant drip of water into the pool. The overflow from the pool poured down through a brick channel to a drain. It wasn't long before a miniature water garden of mosses and algae formed in this channel. Next to the channel, his daughter planted a few Japanese iris, ferns, and forget-me-nots, which crowded around the pool. In front of the hedge, she planted creeping juniper for groundcover, daylilies for summer color, and cotoneaster for red berries in the fall and winter. Where the shade was deeper, she put in a couple of hostas for accent.

To supplement the feeder, Gerry wanted to have some plants for forage. On the far wall of the garden they planted a linden viburnum, a dogwood, and a dwarf winged euonymus, all plants with fruit that is attractive to birds. On an impulse, Gerry's daughter bought a firethorn with orange berries. She thought it would look particularly good on the protected south side of the fence.

Some of Gerry's bird forage came from "volunteers." All winter long the blue jays took sun-

Gerald Mason's tiny wildlife garden.

flower seeds away from the feeder, and what they couldn't eat at the moment, they hid away in little nooks and crannies in the ground. Most of these seeds the jays or other birds later found, but several always sprouted each spring, and Gerry would always let a few of them grow. He delighted in the bright, outsized blossoms, and he liked to watch the birds feeding on the enormous seedheads in the fall.

Cover was the hardest part of the miniature wildlife garden to provide. Along the front sidewalk, the previous owners had planted an evergreen holly hedge which they had kept trimmed to about 4 feet. Gerry and his daughter decided to let the hedge grow. Over the last four years, it has grown to 6 feet and thickened, and they have now begun to prune it again. At this size, it forms a bit of dense cover for birds to nest in during the summer and perch on in winter between trips to the feeder.

Big life changes like those Mr. Mason has gone through are never easy. But by helping him transfer fragments of the environment of his former life to his new home, Gerry's daughter has gone a long way toward maintaining her father's happiness and interest in life. From his chair in the study, he can watch the birds come and go to the feeder in winter and the little pool in summer. He keeps a list of the different species he sees, and he always calls to tell her of a new sighting. On his daughter's last visit, he proudly showed her where a yellow warbler had made its nest on one of the branches of the birch that overhung his miniature wildlife refuge.

A Wildlife Highway across Their Backyard

When the Joneses and their neighbors moved into a new housing development, they discovered to their dismay that the contractor had not fulfilled the landscaping specifications. A gully which ran down the backyards of all the houses had not been culverted and landscaped, and in fact had begun to grow up to large reeds, cattails, loosestrife, and redstemmed dogwood. Al Jones's neighbors were talking about how, perhaps, they should band together and sue the contractor to get him to clean out the gully and put in a culvert.

Al suggested an alternative. He had noticed that birds of many different kinds had begun to use the brush in the gully as a place to nest during the summer and a place to feed and rest during the spring and fall migrations. He suggested that the neighbors band together and approach the conservation board in their town with a proposal. Al and his neighbors would deed to the board a conservation easement on the gully. This would require them to maintain the gully in an essentially natural condition—no buildings, no roadways, no fences or other structures. Since they were donating something of value, they would be able to take a tax deduction for their gift. The board accepted the proposal. The neighbors built a fence which runs along the boundary of the easement and separates it from their backyards. Several of the landowners went to the extra trouble of putting gates in the fence to give themselves and their children access to the gully.

The neighbors then approached a local nursery and arranged a bulk purchase of native plants. Now the gully is a handsome thicket of willow, black alder, and summersweet. The birds and animals in the area use the gully as a sort of highway. Foxes, muskrats, and all manner of little mammals

A wildlife garden in a gully shared by the Joneses and their neighbors.

like mice and voles live in and travel through the tangle. The gully is a major attraction to children in the area, who use it to great advantage for games of hide-and-seek. The stream, which before was a silt-laden, dead, scummy trickle, runs cleaner now and is full of pollywogs and dragonfly nymphs. Its water life has been the subject of many a school science project for the Jones children.

But the Joneses' biggest pleasure is the birdlife. All year round, the tangle is alive with birds. In the spring, the lilting song of song sparrows and the wheezy chatter of goldfinches can be heard from the tangle, as well as the ubiquitous cries of redwing blackbirds and grackles.

An Ecologist's Garden of Eden

Rich Dobbs is an ecologist, making his living as a surveyor for the Forestry Department. When he and his family bought their place in the mountains, he thought about how he could have the most variety in animal life, and also a garden. He chose his spot carefully. After months of trucking around with real estate agents, he found a 5-acre lot next to some conservation land which, in turn, bounded on a national forest. He figured that if he made his land attractive to wildlife, he would get a lot of animal traffic coming out of the conservation land to visit his refuge.

The land had several features that lent themselves to Rich's purposes. Just up the hill, on the conservation land, was a spring, and all year long a trickle of water came down the hill and into a boggy place at the back of the Dobbses' land. The bog was filled with half-grown red maples, hummocks of sedge, and cattails. Redwing blackbirds were already visiting the bog on the raw March day when Rich and the real estate agent struck their bargain.

Rich was extremely ambitious for his wildlife preserve. Not only did he want a bog, he wanted some deep water and some shallow water as well. So after a lot of careful thought, and after seeking the proper permits from the local conservation commission, Rich called in a backhoe which excavated the lower side of the bog, mounding up the earth to form a low earth dam. Between the height of the dam and excavation of the bog, the maximum depth of the pond would be about 12 feet just above the dam.

While the backhoe was visiting, Rich also had the operator clear out the underbrush on the uphill side of the bog, about 20 feet all around. During the ensuing months, as the water filled in behind the dam, it formed a ⅛-acre pond, which flooded upstream toward the cleared area. Most of the old bog was flooded, but a new, larger bog was created in the area cleared by the bulldozer.

After the pond was dug, the Dobbses pretty much let nature take its course. Pussy willow, swamp azalea, purple loosestrife, and skunk cabbage quickly established themselves along the shallow margins of the pond. Beyond, some swamp maples and hemlocks took hold, and above that, the beech woodlands of the conservation area and national forest. The only concession the Dobbs family made to their nurseryman's suggestions was to plant a weeping willow at the water's edge on the far side of the pond.

The Dobbses' house is on a knoll overlooking the pond. Here, they took a more civilized approach to landscaping. To prevent the growth of reeds in this area, the pond banks were shelved off steeply and the slopes of the banks planted in grass. This was leveled off to provide a place for lawn chairs. The family planted a large vegetable garden on this side of the pond, and nearby they put in a perennial flowerbed with daisies, black-eyed susans, orange butterfly weed, and several varieties of yarrow for golden summer bloom.

To discourage the movement of wildlife from

The "wild" side of the Dobbs family's wildlife garden, as seen from the "civilized" side of the pond.

the wildlife-refuge side of the pond to the family side, the Dobbses installed two sections of hog fence running from the pond's edge. This provision, and the activities of their boisterous black Labrador puppy, have kept their garden relatively safe from the depredations of rabbits, raccoons, and deer.

The Dobbses are blissfully happy with their new wildlife refuge. Almost every evening during the summer, they sit on the slope overlooking their pond and look across the water at the wildlife area beyond. A muskrat has taken up residence in the pond, and often in the evening they see him sculling from one side to the other in search of food. Every so often, a small herd of deer comes down to drink at the water's edge. One night, the Dobbses saw a coyote hunting mice among the tussocks of sedge.

The pond is delightful in other seasons as

well. Spring brings the din of frogs. The Dobbses have identified three distinct types: one which makes a sound like a bass guitar string being plucked harshly with one hand while being held firmly against the fingerboard by the other; a second whose members collectively make a sound like the bass continuum in an antique string orchestra: "rum-hrum-hrum-hrum..."; and finally, of course, the tree frogs or peepers. The Dobbses had often heard peepers before, passing ponds in their car at night. But living next to a frog-filled wetland is a whole new experience. Some evenings, the chorus can rise to an amazing din that no longer seems to come from a single direction, but reverberates from every side.

In autumn, the swamp maple turns a brilliant red, the weeping willow, a pale yellow. The color contrast is stunning. Every so often, ducks will stop and pay the pond a visit. One late fall morning, the family awoke to see a pair of Canada geese resting in the last unfrozen bit of water at the deep end of the pond. Steam from the open water rose around the geese as they paddled sedately.

Even winter has its pleasures. In the deep New Hampshire winter, of course, the pond freezes over. This liberates the wildlife from the confinement of the hog fence, and every morning after a fresh snowfall the Dobbses can see signs of traffic across the pond. Rabbits, perhaps a hare, and foxes are all frequent visitors. One late winter a bear, who should have known better, crossed the pond, overturned the Dobbses' beehive, and devoured the combs.

From this experience they learned that bears, in their part of the country, are wards of the State. The Dobbses sought and received compensation for the damage to their hive.

Wrap-up

Sunlight, cover, and water are the essential features of a wildlife garden. With these features in place, your garden will attract and feed wildlife. But if a landscape that attracts wildlife is your dream, you can't be too fastidious. The land most attractive to wildlife is neither romantically natural nor pristine and well organized. It has a great variety of conditions. Some homeowners may want to go in for wildlife gardening in a big way and reorganize their landscapes to provide the maximum variety and resources for animal visitors. However, we suspect that most would settle for increasing the numbers and kinds of animals they see in their gardens. These gardeners should know that every small step they take to increase the variety of food and shelter around their garden will usually be followed within a few months by an increase in animal life.

Plants for Wildlife Gardens

Plant Name	Wildlife Feature	Description	Culture
Woody Plants for Wildlife Gardens			
Allegheny shadbush, Allegheny serviceberry *(Amelanchier laevis)*	Sweet, black fruit enjoyed by many birds and animals	Multistemmed, shrubby tree 15 to 25 feet tall; slender, reddish brown stems turn grayish brown; leaves are elliptic, serrated, 1½ to 3 inches long, bronze on opening, then purplish, finally green; flower racemes are white	Full sun to partial shade; moist, well-drained, acidic soil; to Zone 4
American elder *(Sambucus canadensis)*	Purple-black berries, ¼ inch in diameter, attract birds; August and September	Multistemmed shrub 5 to 12 feet tall; stems are thick, yellowish gray; foliage is dense; serrated leaves are compound, bright green; white flowers are borne in 6- to 10-inch flat clusters, covering the plant	Sun to partial shade; moist soils; good for wet sites or natural areas; suckers profusely; Zones 3–9

(continued)

Plants for Wildlife Gardens—*continued*

Plant Name	Wildlife Feature	Description	Culture
American holly *(Ilex opaca)* many cultivars	Red berries, $2/5$ inch in diameter, mature in October and persist into winter; evergreen foliage provides shelter	Pyramidal trees, usually 15 to 30 feet tall in cultivation, with branches to the ground; leaves are dull to dark green, spiny, elliptic, 2 to 4 inches long, with yellowish green undersides; flowers are dull white, not showy	Best in full sun, but can tolerate partial shade; loose, moist, acidic, well-drained, fairly rich soil; tolerates air pollution; does not tolerate dry, windy sites or poor drainage; must have 1 male for every 2 to 3 females; Zones 5–9
Autumn olive *(Eleagnus umbellata)* 'Cardinal'	Profusion of red berries, ¼ to $1/3$ inch long; ripen in September and October; attractive to birds	Large, spreading shrub, up to 18 feet tall and 30 feet wide; smooth leaves are 2 to 4 inches long, elliptic, bright green above with silvery undersides; funnel-shaped, fragrant white flowers, ½ inch long, in May and June	Full sun to partial shade; tolerates low-fertility, acidic loam or sandy soil; very drought tolerant; can be spread by birds and become a weed; best for naturalizing; Zones 3–8
Bayberry *(Myrica pensylvanica)*	Heavy crop of grayish white, waxy berries, $1/6$ inch across, on female plants; September through April	Deciduous to semievergreen, dense shrub, 5 to 12 feet tall and wide; stems are green; leaves are lustrous, dark green, oblong, $1^3/5$ to 4 inches long, aromatic when bruised; flowers not showy	Full sun to partial shade; poor, sandy soil to heavy clay soil; extremely adaptable; fixes atmospheric nitrogen; salt tolerant; does not tolerate alkaline soils; Zones 2–6
Blackhaw *(Viburnum prunifolium)*	Berries, ½ inch long, change from pinkish to rose to bluish black; September through fall	Stiffly branched, rounded shrub up to 15 feet tall and 12 feet wide; bark is gray-brown; lustrous, dark green leaves are 1½ to 3½ inches long and 1 to 2 inches wide; red, bronze, or purplish fall color; creamy white flowers are borne in 2- to 4-inch flat clusters in May	Sun or shade; adaptable to many soils; drought tolerant; Zones 3–9
Bob White Crabapple *(Malus 'Bob White')*	Persistent yellow to brownish yellow crabapples, $5/8$ inch in diameter	Rounded, densely branching, shrubby tree up to 20 feet tall; leaves are oval, serrated; fragrant, 5-petaled flowers open white from cherry-colored buds; blooms are 1 inch in diameter	Full sun; prefers heavy loam, but is adaptable; well-drained, moist, acidic soil (pH 5 to 6.5); moderately susceptible to fire blight; Zones 2–8

Plant Name	Wildlife Feature	Description	Culture
Boston ivy, Japanese creeper (*Parthenocissus tricuspidata*)	Bluish-black berries, ¼ inch in diameter; September and October	Vine 30 to 50 feet long; stems are squarish; bark is brownish; deciduous, 3-lobed, maple-like leaves are toothed, glossy dark green; some have brilliant red and scarlet fall color; greenish white flowers are not showy	Full sun to full shade; tolerates virtually any soil, wind, exposed sites, pollution; attaches itself to walls; Zones 3–9
Cockspur hawthorn (*Crataegus crusgalli* var. *inermis*)	Deep red berries, ⅜ to ½ inch in diameter; September through fall	Broad, low-branched tree, 20 to 30 feet tall and 20 to 35 feet wide; branches bear 1½- to 3-inch-long thorns (*inermis* is thornless); egg-shaped, lustrous, dark green foliage; foul-smelling white flowers borne in 2- to 3-inch flat clusters in May	Full sun; any well-drained soil; pH tolerant; pollution tolerant; susceptible to cedar hawthorn rust and leaf blotch miner; Zones 3–7
Father Hugo rose (*Rosa hugonis*)	Scarlet rose hips, blackish red when mature, ½ inch in diameter; August	Rounded shrub 6 to 8 feet tall, often wider; canes are upright, arching, often reddish; thorns are straight, scattered, often red; compound leaves have 5 to 13 oval leaflets; canary yellow flowers, 2 to 2½ inches wide, in May and June	Full sun; well-drained, humusy soil; to Zone 5
Flowering dogwood (*Cornus florida*) many cultivars	Glossy red, prominent fruit in clusters of 3 to 4; ⅖ inch long; ripen in September and last into December; favored by birds	Small, low-branched tree, usually up to 20 feet tall; can be considerably wider; branches have layered effect; grayish brown bark forms rectangular plates; dark green, smooth elliptic leaves are 3 to 6 inches long; red to reddish purple fall color; white, pink, or rose flowers, 2 inches wide, appear before trees leaf out	Partial shade; acidic, well-drained, humusy soil; mulch; not pollution tolerant; Zones 5–9

(continued)

Plants for Wildlife Gardens—*continued*

Plant Name	Wildlife Feature	Description	Culture
Hackberry *(Celtis occidentalis)*	Round berries, ¹/₃ inch in diameter; dark green, ripening orange-red to dark purple in September and October; favored by birds and wildlife	Broad, rounded tree 40 to 60 feet tall and wide; bark has corky projecting ridges; leaves are bright green, paler below, 2 to 5 inches long, oval, and serrated; yellow or yellow-green fall color; flowers not showy	Full sun; prefers rich, moist soil, but is widely adaptable; wind and pollution tolerant; susceptible to witches' broom and hackberry nipple gall; Zones 2–9
Highbush cranberry, American cranberrybush viburnum *(Viburnum trilobum)*	Bright red berries, ¹/₃ inch long; early September through February	Round-topped, fairly dense shrub 8 to 12 feet tall and wide; 3-lobed, maple-like leaves are 2 to 5 inches long, dark green; yellow to red-purple fall color; bark is gray-brown; 3- to 4½-inch-wide flat clusters of white flowers; showy	Sun to partial shade; good, well-drained, moist soil; Zones 2–7
Japanese crabapple *(Malus floribunda)*	Yellow and red fruits, ³/₈ inch in diameter	Rounded, densely branched tree 15 to 25 feet tall; leaves are oval, serrated; fragrant, 5-petaled, white flowers, 1 to 1½ inches in diameter, emerge from deep pink to red buds	Full sun; prefers heavy loam, but is adaptable; well-drained, moist, acidic soil (pH 5 to 6.5); slightly susceptible to scab and powdery mildew, moderately susceptible to fire blight; Zones 2–8
Japanese rose, multiflora rose *(Rosa multiflora)*	Brushy tangle provides shelter for birds and animals; ¼-inch, red, globular rose hips; August to winter	Fountain-like bush 3 to 10 feet tall and 10 to 15 feet wide; compound leaves have 9 oblong, serrated, lustrous, bright green leaflets; thorns are short, recurved; fragrant white flowers are 1 inch wide	Full sun; tolerates dry, heavy soils; very invasive; Zones 5–8
Korean mountain ash *(Sorbus alnifolia)*	Spectacular clusters of roundish, pinkish red to scarlet berries; ³/₈ to ⁵/₈ inch long; ripen in September and October and persist into winter	Pyramidal to almost rounded specimen trees 40 to 50 feet tall and 20 to 30 feet wide; beech-like stems are gray; lustrous, dark green, oval leaves are serrated, 2 to 4 inches long; beautiful 2- to 3-inch flat clusters of ¾-inch white flowers in May	Sun; any well-drained soil; not pollution tolerant; susceptible to fire blight and borers; Zones 3–7

Plant Name	Wildlife Feature	Description	Culture
Kousa dogwood (*Cornus kousa*)	Pinkish red to red, raspberry-like fruit, ³/₅ to 1 inch in diameter; late August through October	Vase-shaped tree, becoming layered at maturity, with horizontal branches; 20 to 30 feet tall and wide; leaves are smooth, oval, dark green; exfoliating bark is beautifully mottled in gray, tan, and brown; beautiful, white, 1- to 2-inch-wide flowers top the branches in June	Sun; needs acidic, well-drained soil; prefers sandy, humusy soil; Zones 4–8
Lodense privet (*Ligustrum vulgare* 'Lodense')	Shelter for wildlife; clusters of lustrous, black berries, ¹/₃ inch long; ripen in September and persist through spring	Low, dense, compact shrub up to 4½ feet tall; oblong to lance-shaped, dark green leaves, 1 to 2½ inches long, are held late into fall; young branches are green; dense, 1- to 3-inch-long panicles of white, smelly flowers in June	Full sun to partial shade; highly adaptable; susceptible to blight; Zones 4–7
Memorial rose (*Rosa wichuriana*)	Red, egg-shaped hips, ½ inch long; September to October	Prostrate, semievergreen canes 8 to 16 feet long; thorns are sparse, recurved; lustrous, dark green, compound leaves have 7 to 9 serrated leaflets; white, fragrant, 2-inch-wide flowers are in pyramidal clusters in June and July	Full sun; well-drained, humusy soil; good groundcover; prevents erosion; good pest and disease resistance; to Zone 5
Nannyberry, sheepberry (*Viburnum lentago*)	Bluish black, odiferous fruit, ½ inch long; September to December	Open, large shrub up to 18 feet tall and 10 or more feet wide; stems are slender, brownish, finely arching; oval, toothed, medium green leaves are 2 to 4 inches long; can have red fall color; creamy white flowers are borne in 3- to 8-inch-wide flat clusters in May	Sun or shade; tolerates moist or dry soils; adaptable; often suckers to form thickets; Zones 2–8
Red mulberry (*Morus rubra*)	Juicy red fruits ripen to dark purple; favored by birds	Broad, open, irregular tree 40 to 70 feet tall by 40 to 50 feet wide; thin, serrated leaves may be spear-shaped or mitten-shaped, pale to dark green; flowers are inconspicuous catkins	Full sun to light shade; rich, moist soil; Zones 5–8

(continued)

Plants for Wildlife Gardens—*continued*

Plant Name	Wildlife Feature	Description	Culture
Regal privet (*Ligustrum obtusifolium* var. *regelianum*)	Shelter for wildlife; clusters of black to blue-black berries, ¼ inch long; ripen in September and persist into winter	Shrub, 4 to 5 feet tall, with horizontal branching and leaves held out flat from the branches; oblong, smooth, medium to dark green leaves are ⁴/₅ to 2 inches long; can have russet to purplish fall color; nodding panicles of smelly white flowers in June	Full sun to partial shade; highly adaptable; excellent for preventing erosion on banks; Zones 3–7
Royalty crabapple (*Malus* 'Royalty')	Dark red fruit, ⁵/₈ inch in diameter	Upright tree, 15 feet tall; leaves are glossy purple in spring, purple-green in summer, brilliant purple in fall; crimson-purple, 5-petaled flowers	Full sun; prefers heavy loam but is adaptable; well-drained, moist, acidic soil (pH 5 to 6.5); severely susceptible to scab and fire blight; Zones 2–8
Rugosa rose (*Rosa rugosa*)	Large, brick red, urn-shaped hips, 1 inch wide; August through fall	Sturdy, upright shrub, 4 to 6 feet tall and wide; lustrous, deep green, compound leaves have 5 to 9 serrated leaflets; canes are densely bristled; fragrant, 2½- to 3½-inch-wide, single or double flowers are white, rose, or fuchsia-purple; June through August	Full sun; prefers well-drained, humusy soil; pH adaptable, but prefers slightly acid soil; salt tolerant; can be used in hedges; pest and disease resistant; Zones 2–7
Russian olive (*Eleagnus angustifolia*)	Yellow berry, ²/₅ inch long; sweet; August and September	Small tree or large shrub 15 to 20 feet high and wide, with a graceful open look; narrow, lance-shaped leaves are 1 to 3 inches long, silvery green; branches are silvery to glistening brown; flowers are fragrant, ³/₈ inch long	Full sun; prefers light, sandy loam, but fixes nitrogen and does well in any soil; open location; tolerant of drought and alkaline soils; very salt tolerant; Zones 2–7
Sassafras (*Sassafras albidum*)	Dark blue fruit, ½ inch long, on scarlet stalks; ripens in September; relished by birds	Irregularly shaped, shrubby tree 30 to 60 feet tall and 25 to 40 feet wide; bright green leaves are 3 to 7 inches long, entire, mitten-shaped, or 3-lobed; gorgeous yellow, deep orange, scarlet, and purple fall color; fragrant yellow flowers in April	Full sun to light shade; moist, loamy, acidic, well-drained soil; suckers to form thickets; Zones 4–8

Plant Name	Wildlife Feature	Description	Culture
Scotch rose (*Rosa spinosissima*)	Cover for wildlife; black or dark brown rose hips, ½ to ¾ inch in diameter	Dense, mound-like shrub 3 to 4 feet tall; covered with straight, needle-like bristles; compound leaves have 5 to 11 leaflets; many 1- to 2-inch-wide pink, white, or yellow single flowers in May and June	Full sun; well-drained, humusy soil; suckering can form thickets; to Zone 4
Shadblow, juneberry, downy serviceberry (*Amelanchier arborea*)	Rounded berries, ¼ to ⅓ inch in diameter, ripen from green through red to purplish black in June; enjoyed by birds; plants well suited to naturalistic plantings	Many-trunked, large, rounded shrub, 15 to 25 feet tall; bark is smooth, grayish, streaked; obovate, serrated leaves are 1 to 3 inches long, medium to dark green in summer; yellow, apricot, or red fall color; ornamental white flowers	Full sun or partial shade; moist, well-drained, acidic soil; not pollution tolerant; Zones 4–9
Tallhedge buckthorn, glossy buckthorn (*Rhamnus frangula*) 'Columnaris'	Red to purple-black berries, ¼ inch across; July through September; creamy green flowers draw bees in May	Upright, large shrub 10 to 12 feet tall by 8 to 12 feet wide; 'Columnaris' is narrow; lustrous, dark green leaves are smooth, oval, 1 to 3 inches long; greenish yellow fall color	Sun to partial shade; well-drained soil; spread by birds; Zones 2–7
Tatarian honeysuckle (*Lonicera tatarica*) many cultivars	Red berries, ¼ inch in diameter, borne profusely; ripen June to August	Upright, multistemmed shrub, 10 to 12 feet tall by 10 feet wide; smooth, bluish green, oval leaves are 1½ to 2½ inches long; profuse pink to white ⅗- to ⅘-inch-long flowers in May	Full sun to partial shade; good, loamy, moist, well-drained soil; intolerant of wet sites; to Zone 3
Tupelo, black gum, sour gum (*Nyssa sylvatica*)	Bluish black fruit ½ inch long, ripens September and October; eaten by many birds and animals	Pyramidal to irregularly rounded, densely branched tree, 30 to 50 feet tall by 20 to 30 feet wide; dark gray bark is in block-like sections; lustrous, dark green, elliptic leaves are 3 to 6 inches long; gorgeous yellow, orange, scarlet, and purple fall color; flowers are small, greenish white	Full sun to partial shade; moist, well-drained, acidic soil (pH 5.5 to 6.5); intolerant of alkaline soil; needs shelter from wind; Zones 3–9

(continued)

Plants for Wildlife Gardens—*continued*

Plant Name	Wildlife Feature	Description	Culture
Virginia rose (*Rosa virginiana*)	Red rose hips, ½ inch in diameter, persist through winter	Dense shrub up to 6 feet tall; reddish, upright canes have flattened thorns; glossy, dark green, compound leaves have 7 to 9 serrated leaflets; foliage turns purple, orange-red, crimson, and yellow in fall; single pink flowers 2 to 2½ inches wide appear in June	Full sun; tolerates sandy soil; salt tolerant; to Zone 3
Washington hawthorn (*Crataegus phaenopyrum*) 'Clark'	Bright, glossy red berries, ¼ inch in diameter, borne in clusters from September through winter; 'Clark' has especially heavy fruiting	Broadly oval, dense tree, 25 to 30 feet tall and 20 to 25 feet wide; 3- to 5-lobed, sharply toothed, lustrous, dark green leaves are 1 to 3 inches long; orange, scarlet, or purplish fall color; thorns are 1 to 3 inches long; clusters of white, mildly smelly flowers	Full sun; any well-drained soil; tolerates air pollution; susceptible to fire blight, leaf blight, and rusts; Zones 3–8
Winterberry (*Ilex verticillata*)	Shelter for wildlife; bright red berries, ¼ inch wide, borne in profusion; ripen in August and September, persist into January; relished by birds	Dense, oval to rounded shrub, 6 to 10 feet tall and wide; deciduous leaves are 1½ to 3 inches long, elliptic, serrated, rich green; flowers not showy	Full sun to partial shade; prefers moist, acidic, humusy soils (pH 4.5 to 5.5); Zones 3–9
Winter King hawthorn (*Crataegus viridis* 'Winter King')	Bright red, persistent berries; September through winter	Rounded tree, 25 to 35 feet tall, with vase-shaped branching; stems are gray-green; lustrous, medium green leaves are irregularly lobed, serrated; scarlet to purple fall color; thorny; white flowers in 2-inch clusters	Full sun; any well-drained soil; pollution and pH tolerant; less susceptible to rust than other hawthorns; to Zone 4

Herbaceous Plants for Wildlife Gardens

Plant Name	Wildlife Feature	Description	Culture
Bee balm (*Monarda didyma*) 'Cambridge Scarlet' many others	Red flowers attract hummingbirds, bees; July and August	Rugged, bushy plants, 3 feet tall; leaves are aromatic; stems are square; ragged flower heads have whorls of tubular blossoms	Partial shade to full sun; rich, moist, humusy soil; spreading; perennial; Zones 4–9
Butterfly weed (*Asclepias tuberosa*)	Clusters of small, bright orange flowers; very showy; draws butterflies, especially monarchs; July and August	Shrubby plants 2 feet tall; stems are hairy; foliage is large, lance-shaped, and coarse; flowers are followed by milkweed-like pods	Full sun; poor, well-drained soil; slow to appear in spring, so mark site; perennial; Zones 3–8

Plant Name	Wildlife Feature	Description	Culture
Rose campion *(Lychnis coronaria)*	Intense magenta-pink flowers attract butterflies; June and July	Flowers are borne on 2-foot-tall, wide-branching silver stems; spear-shaped leaves are woolly, gray-green; inch-wide flowers are 5-petaled	Full sun; average, moist, well-drained soil; short-lived; prefers alkaline soil; perennial; Zones 3–8
Summer phlox, border phlox *(Phlox paniculata)* many cultivars	5-petaled flowers, massed in pyramidal clusters, attract butterflies; often mildly fragrant; in white, pink, rose, magenta, salmon, lilac, or purple, some with contrasting eyes; July and August	Plants are 18 inches to 3 feet tall; foliage is coarse, dark green, lance shaped; some varieties have variegated leaves	Sun to light shade; deep, rich, moist, porous soil; protect from wind; susceptible to powdery mildew; deadhead for longer bloom; perennial; Zones 3–8
Sunflower *(Helianthus spp.)*	Black or black-and-white striped seeds form in tightly packed heads up to 1 foot across; relished by birds	Rather coarse plants, 3 to 10 feet tall; stems are strong; toothed leaves are large, green; single or double daisy-like flowers are up to 1 foot across, usually yellow with dark centers	Full sun; prefers fertile loam but is widely adaptable; direct-seed after all danger of frost has passed; cover seed with 1 inch of soil; annual

CHAPTER 11

Woodswalks

A woodswalk is a shady trail through a garden. It has places of special beauty or interest along the way which entice you to pause and contemplate. Because it is wooded, a woodswalk is sheltered from the sounds of the street and the inquisitive eyes of your neighbors. Because it is shaded, it is always cool. In the summer, you can hear the sound of wind in the leaves above your woodswalk. In the winter, you can see the intricate pattern of shadow made on the snow where the sun filters through the branches of the bare trees above.

A woodswalk is a place to experience the seasons of the year in special ways. In spring, the sun penetrates the canopy of the forest and warms the ground. For several weeks between the time that the snow is off the ground and the time that the trees leaf out, the smaller plants of the forest floor have a chance to compete with the leafless trees for light and nutrients. It is an opportunity for any plant that can get started quickly in cool soil.

Many kinds of woods plants have techniques to exploit this opportunity. Broadleaved evergreens like azaleas, rhododendrons, and mountain laurels grow happily in the shade of larger trees. Their thick, fleshy leaves harvest the thin light that filters down to them. Bulbs store nutrients from the previous summer to be ready to grab the light before their larger, slower-growing neighbors begin leafing out. The "clouds of golden daffodils" of the English woodlands, and our own dogtooth violets, primroses, dutchman's breeches, wood anemones, and bloodroot all hurry to get their growing and flowering in before the tall trees can hoard the resources of the forest floor.

In the summer, when the big trees are in full leaf, the forest floor may be carpeted in green or brown, depending on whether it's moist or dry. In a moist forest, ferns, mosses, and evergreen groundcovers like partridgeberry and goldthread will thrive among the tree trunks. The tiny woodsorrel, bunchberry, and Jack-in-the-pulpit will help give your forest the restful atmosphere so welcome on a hot summer's day. On the floor of a drier and darker forest, a carpet of brown needles or leaf duff will cushion your step. By autumn, when the deciduous trees shed their leaves, your woodswalk path is covered with red, brown, and gold. Shafts of light suddenly penetrate the forest again, giving the woods an airy, open feel it has not had for months.

In winter, the evergreens have their day. The contrast of their dark green foliage against the white snow creates stark compositions of line and form. Wet snow and freezing rain trace the outlines of evergreen needles and make fantastic patterns. The trunks of tall deciduous trees seem very stark and detailed at this time of year and their branches, highlighted with snow, make a dense network of converging and diverging lines. Forest floors, still green with wintergreen and partridgeberry, look as if they had been decorated for the Christmas season.

A Special Kind of Shade

A woodswalk is special because it has the feel—and a bit of the ecology—of a mature forest. Ecologists speak of mature forests almost as if they were a kind of building or tent. To an ecologist, a forest has a "canopy," one or more "understories," and a "floor." The canopy is composed of the branches of the tallest trees which tower over the forest. Only the trees in the canopy have the benefit of full sunlight. The middle and lower stories consist of the foliage of trees that can grow well in the filtered sunlight that penetrates the canopy. Finally, at the bottom of the forest, growing without the benefit of any direct sunlight, are the plants of the forest floor.

There's more to the ecologists' story. Mature forests not only have canopies, levels, and floors, they also have edges. Where flood or fire disturbs a forest, a boundary is formed between the deforested and forested areas, and here special varieties of plants thrive. The plants that grow well on forest edges must make do with full sunlight for only part of the day. Or they may get sunlight just after sunrise or just before sunset, when the rays of the sun strike in among the trunks of the canopy trees and briefly provide a little light to the forest floor.

Of course, a mature forest doesn't get that way overnight. Forests are born, grow up, and get old, like people. In an immature forest, the young trees grow very rapidly and compete among themselves to see which can grow the fastest. They have not had a chance to form a closed canopy yet, and much sunlight reaches the ground. Immature "forest" is frequently found in new suburban housing where the houses have recently been built. In a mature forest, the race to see who is to be the tallest is over. A few large trees have established themselves and the canopy is closed. Mature "forest" is frequently seen in older suburbs, where the ornamental oaks and maples of previous generations have become great shade-casting monsters, their tops sewn together in a seamless green canopy.

We tell you all this about forests because we want to stress that shade is not just the absence of sun. A shady place is special, with sights, sounds, and qualities all its own. To be a successful shade gardener, you must provide for the soil and moisture requirements of the plants you are asking to grow on the floor of your bit of forest. Tall trees not only hog the sunshine, they are inordinately greedy for soil nutrients and water as well. Moreover, their decaying leaves and needles often severely acidify the soil. Chances are that if you have a shade problem in your garden, you also have a water problem, a fertility problem, and an acidity problem. The secret of gardening in a shady place is to capitalize on the virtues of the kind of shade you have in your garden while minimizing the vices.

Degrees of Shade

From a landscaping point of view, the various kinds of forest translate into different kinds of shade, each with special qualities.

Deep Shade

Mature stands of evergreens such as hemlock, spruce, or pine, or of densely foliaged deciduous trees such as beeches or some species of maple and oak, make a shade so dense that practically no sunlight reaches the ground around their trunks. On the floor of an evergreen forest, the deep shade and acid soil prevent the growth of most shrubs. You can walk silently and effortlessly on the soft leafmold that covers the floor of such a forest. Some of the most beautiful and peaceful places in the world are deeply shaded. One thinks immediately of serene lakeside camps in the mountains, or of the redwood galleries of northern California which have such an aura of peace and safety. Deep shade gives a hushed, church-like atmosphere of the floor of a mature forest.

Moderate Shade

Moderate shade is the dappled or filtered shade characteristic of young deciduous forests. This sort of shade is visually exciting. As you let your eye travel across the forest floor, you see that every few inches or so, a shaft of light penetrates to the ground. As the leaves of the canopy blow in the wind, light dances on the forest floor, illuminating first one, then another patch of ground. Moderate shade is gentle, permitting many sorts of under-story plants to grow. For a woodswalk, it is ideal because it provides the peace and quiet of a forest, yet allows flowers and shrubs to grow.

Partial Shade

Partial shade in a landscape mimics the conditions at the edge of a mature forest, where plants get sunlight for several hours a day and moderate or deep shade for the rest. Partial shade is often found on the east or west side of houses. It is a dynamic growing condition, in which morning and afternoon are as different as night and day.

Because temperature and wind conditions are different in the morning and in the afternoon, the qualities of partial shade are dramatically different depending on which part of the day is shady and which is sunny. Morning sun and afternoon shade are the kinder pairing of the two, because the contrasts between the shade condition and the sunny condition are less. Mornings are more likely to be cool, moist, cloudy, and calm than afternoons. The sun gets things warmed up nicely in the morning, but then goes away before it gets too hot and makes things unpleasant.

Morning shade and afternoon sun are much more abrupt. Plants and people alike are kept cool and shaded all morning, and then suddenly exposed to sunlight just when the wind is strongest, the temperature is highest, and the air is driest. A house or a patio in morning shade remains clammy and cool all morning, only to be baked by afternoon sun.

If your partial shade is centered on midday, then you have light shade. For instance, a flowerbed under an arbor may get sunlight in the morning until 10:00 or so, then be shaded until 2:00 or 3:00, and get afternoon sun thereafter. Such a flowerbed is in light shade. Many plants will flourish under light shade conditions. For people in a moderately warm climate, it can be an ideal kind of shade, providing warmth from the sun during the cooler times of the day, and protection from its rays at midday.

Creating a Woodswalk

Although a woodswalk reproduces the light, the sounds, and the feel of a forest, it does not have to be *in* a forest to be successful. Anybody who has some trees on their property can create a spot with the essential elements of a woodswalk: a shady path through the trees that leads to one or more attractive features.

The first step in planning your woodswalk is to take inventory of what you already have. Large trees take many years to grow, and shade-tolerant plants for your site may be difficult to purchase and establish. Therefore, woodswalk design, more perhaps than any other feature, will make use of what you have. Much valuable time can be saved if you make use not only of the trees that are already in place, but also of shrubs and groundcovers that seem already to have naturalized in your location.

While you are taking your inventory of trees, be on the lookout for an attractive feature that could serve as a focus. Is there a little clearing in the trees where shafts of sunlight strike down to the ground? This could be a glade. Do you have a wet place? Perhaps you could scoop it out and make it into a pool. Is there a handsome bit of ledge, or a stone wall? Rock features make excellent focal points for a woodswalk. Following the suggestions outlined in chapter 13, "Doing Your Own Design," prepare a map of your existing trees, shrubs, and features to guide you in your planning.

Designing the Path

The next step is to locate the path. Where you put your path will depend on whether your inventory turns up any features among your existing conditions attractive enough to make them focal points for the path. If you have, then route the path so that it takes you to these features. If not, design the path so that it makes good use of the space of your woods, and then add features to it.

The idea is to design your path so that you are invited to wander, here to see if the bulbs are starting to appear, there to look at a skin of late spring ice on the trickle of water, a bit farther to sit on a bench in a shaft of sun and bake a little of winter out of your bones. When taking a walk in the woods it's nice to be going somewhere, so provide places to go along your woodswalk. You might choose a birdbath or feeder, a little clearing where the sun strikes down, a spot with deep mosses soft enough to lie on, a pool where frogs cavort, a nesting box where a chickadee is raising her young, or flowerbeds, where you can go each day to see which flowers are in bloom.

If a path is going to induce you to wander, it cannot reveal itself to you all at once. The best woodswalks have twists, turns, boulders, and slopes that hide parts of the walk from the other parts. Design your woodswalk not only for peace but also for interest. Have your path go from a small, dark, confined space to a larger, open space. Have it turn a corner and suddenly come upon a lovely sculpture, a small hidden pond, or a bench.

Other Considerations

Because most of us don't have property big enough for a forest, a successful woodswalk is usually in part an illusion created by screening. You may particularly want to create that illusion if you have ended up in a housing development in a former forest. If your woodswalk is to have the feel of a private path meandering through the woods, it cannot pass next to your neighbor's disassembled Harley. Unlike natural forests, suburban neighborhood forests are full of people. In such a development, the forest canopy tends to unite everyone

Phebe's Favorites for Woodswalks

This is where the azaleas and rhododendrons really shine. They brighten the foreground of woodlands. Because bloom times overlap, caution is advised in using the bright oranges, reds, and yellows of the Ghent, Exbury, and Kaempferi azalea hybrids with the more pink-purple, purple, and purple-red tones of the Catawba rhododendron hybrids. If you want to have the yellows of the azaleas, the rhododendrons should be limited to whites and pale pinks.

Nothing beats a mass planting of the flame azalea (species or hybrids) in May, making the woodland a blaze of brick reds or pinks. The royal azalea is the most luminous of pinks, large and showy, truly beautiful, with handsome foliage that turns red in fall. The pinkshell azalea is just a "native," no gaudy blooms, but you can't beat its soft pink blossoms reflected in a pond in May.

Another native but a late bloomer, the swamp azalea, grows in many spots that are not swampy. It is very fragrant—nice on warm, humid early summer days. Weston Nurseries, in Hopkinton, Massachusetts, has produced some hybrids with spicy fragrance and pink blossoms, a colorful touch for the summer shrub border.

The choice of rhododendrons really boils down to one of color, but a couple are worth noting. The native rosebay rhododendron is a most useful plant. It prefers deep shade. The flowers are a pretty pink, but aren't spectacular, blooming in late June at the end of the rhododendron cycle.

The Wilson rhododendron has wonderful foliage like a mountain laurel's, that does not droop and curl in winter. The foliage lifts up and is compact and neat. The flowers are not spectacular, as they are nestled in among the leaves and are of a rather nondescript lavender.

The Yakusimanum rhododendron and its varieties are much loved and desired, although they're not really hardy for us in the Northeast. It stays low, with handsome dark green foliage, and the flowers are a beautiful apple-blossom pink. There are lots of hybrids available.

The Smirnow rhododendron is soft gray, and marvelously woolly on the undersides of its leaves, giving a new dimension to the pretty green foliage. It has nice pink flowers. There are also hybrids.

No broadleaved evergreen shrub equals mountain laurel for excellence of foliage. The dark green, lustrous leaves look cheery all year long, and the blooms in June are lovely pink shades. Best blooming occurs in sunnier locations. Much work is being done to hybridize the mountain laurel, and we should be seeing a lot of new variations in flower color.

No list of plants for shade is worth its salt without a viburnum or two. My favorite is the mayflower viburnum, *Viburnum carlesi.* Everyone loves this vibur-

under one roof. The overhanging canopy prevents natural screening from growing up, and holds sound close to the ground so everybody can hear everybody else. It's hard not to feel that the whole neighborhood is living in the same yard. Consequently, the parts of your woodswalk next to heavily used parts of your neighbors' yards may require a hedge, a fence, or an arbor.

Screening may also be used to create mystery. Skillful use of shrubs helps to make twists, turns, and surprises in the woodswalk. In a natural woods, the distances are so great that you come around corners and surprise yourself. To create the same effect on a smaller scale, design so as to lead the walker onward around corners to see what is next. Both changing levels and barriers are effective in creating a feeling of anticipation as you walk along the twists and turns in a path.

Because a woodswalk is a rustic, low-key sort of garden, plan to use natural materials wher-

num, with its fragrant, rounded, pinkish white flowers in May. There are other early fragrant kinds. The showy snowball viburnums are great with rhododendrons or on their own, giant lollipops of white. The aristocrats of the viburnum world are the doublefile varieties, wonderfully shaped shrubs, with very showy flat flowers. Large, sterile outer flowers surround the fuzzy inner ones. These are as beautiful as dogwoods and bloom at about the same time. 'Mariesii' is one fine variety, and a new one is 'Shasta'. All have horizontal branching and are of specimen quality. All viburnums have nice fall color, usually red, and conspicuous red or blue-black fruit, which birds enjoy.

The silveredge dogwood is a must. The red stems are colorful in winter, and the variegated foliage lightens up a dark corner or serves as an accent just about anywhere the rest of the time. The white flowers are not of note.

No shady garden will be without its ferns, and the Japanese painted fern, with its mottled green, silver, and blue foliage, is the king of ferns for accent. Other favorites are the dainty but difficult maidenhair fern, and royal fern, with more leaf-like foliage. Companions for the ferns are the epimediums, with dainty, almost heart-shaped foliage on delicate, wiry stems, and yellow or red flowers.

Another graceful stalwart shade plant is the fringed bleeding heart. It has lovely soft, fern-like, bluish

foliage with dainty pink, cherry, or white flowers for practically the whole season from spring to fall. A plant that looks well anywhere, and one that can tie together diverse elements in a garden.

Hostas are in every garden. I love them all. Hostas are grown for their foliage—I know people who snip off the flower buds so they won't bloom. I particularly love *Hosta sieboldiana* and varieties, with their blue elephant-ear-like foliage, including an all-time favorite 'Frances Williams'. The new gold-leaved ones are marvelous: 'Gold Edger', 'Gold Regal', 'Gold Standard', to name a few. I want to design a garden of hostas, with the design feature their patterns of foliage.

There are many good groundcovers for the shade, both evergreen and deciduous, but a real aristocrat is European ginger. Although not a fast creeper and not even reliably evergreen, the beautiful, shiny, dark green, heart-shaped leaves and pungent ginger fragrance of the hidden brownish flowers make this plant stand out in any garden.

A close second to European ginger is galax. It also has a heart-shaped leaf, but galax foliage has more reddish tones, is a little lighter green, and has crinkled edges. The flowers are white and spiky, quite striking in June. This plant does not really make a groundcover, but the foliage is unequaled and lasts forever in arrangements. Unfortunately, it's not all that easy to grow.

ever possible, or at least materials that blend in. Use treated timbers for terracing, not cement or asphalt. Use bark mulches to hold the soil and enhance the informal effect. And then, for contrast, consider an ornate birdbath, or a bench, or a gazebo—a single formal element that emphasizes the informality of the whole.

You will want to give particular thought to the composition of the path in your woodswalk. The path may be as fancy or as simple as you want. For

a more formal effect, it might be surfaced with crushed stone or even brick. Moss-covered stones often give just the right informal effect. Not only are they beautiful to look at, but they slow your pace through the garden. A path can be made of wood chips contained within a timber frame, or simply a track of bare earth worn down by your daily perambulations. Where such a casual path comes out into the sunshine it will be grassy. Where it passes under trees, your feet may wear through the duff to the bare ground, and here you might want to spread bark mulch to prevent rutting and keep your shoes dry in damp weather.

Remember as you make decisions for your woodswalk that the effect you are shooting for is a peaceful, contemplative place to wander in. Charles Darwin had such a walk in his garden at Down House in England. It is a woodswalk now, although we are not sure it was a woodswalk when Darwin walked it. Much of Darwin's most famous writing was planned while the author was pacing the meanders of his walk. In designing a woodswalk, you are hoping to create a place that will inspire you to be as creative and prolific as Charles Darwin.

Plants for a Woodswalk

Not many plants like full shade. The ones that do are mostly small groundcovers. Some, like the ferns, pachysandra, and wild ginger, are valued primarily for their leaves. Pachysandra and wild ginger are good carpet plants. Ferns can be more dramatic, and may cover your woodswalk waist-deep in their fronds if water is abundant. Other shade-loving plants are valued for their berries as well as their foliage. Wintergreen, partridgeberry, and bunchberry have bright red berries which appear in late summer and remain throughout the fall. Still other species produce flowers under forest-floor conditions. Wood anemones' dainty white blooms come in April. Trillium has a large white blossom that appears each May on a single foot-high stem. Hepatica is a lovely little woodland plant with liver-shaped leaves and white or blue flowers. Lily-of-the-valley, Virginia bluebells, epimedium, Bethlehem sage, and hostas are old favorites that do well in shade, although they bloom better with a little sunshine.

The list of plants that will tolerate shade is much longer. (For more examples, see "Plants for Woodswalks" at the end of this chapter.) These are plants which don't necessarily prefer shade, but which grow and flower well in moderate or partial shade. The list includes all the "understory" shrubs which are adapted to grow under the canopy of larger trees. Mountain laurels, dogwoods, rhododendrons, azaleas, and viburnums are classic examples of understory plants. In May and June their blossoms brighten the somber depths of the deciduous forests.

The list of shade-tolerant plants includes a great variety of groundcovers. Wintercreeper, carpet bugle, and various forms of ivy seem to do almost as well in shade as out. Flowering groundcovers for shade include vinca, primroses, coral bells, sweet woodruff, wild phlox, shortia, jacob's ladder, foamflower, and many varieties of violet.

Taller plants you might feature in your shade garden include monkshood, with blue to purple flowers; and goatsbeard, with white, plume-like flower spikes in June and an elegant, finely dissected leaf. Astilbe is a reliable favorite. Its flowers range widely in color from whites through pinks to deep reds and purples. This group of shade-tolerant plants includes many with colorful names. Bugbane or snakeroot is a very tall plant whose long white snakey flowers bloom in July and August. Solomon's seal has an elongated stem with clusters of dainty white bells and perky green leaves. If you are a patient and skillful gardener, and you live in a cool climate, try gentians. They are difficult to grow, but are much admired for their blue flowers in August. More reliable shade-tolerant plants include columbine, spiderwort, Christmas rose (which actually blooms in March), and fringed bleeding heart, whose pink and white flowers keep coming week after week all summer long.

Many plants which don't prefer shade will tolerate it and even perform well, if given adequate food and water and the right pH. So if you are trying to grow a plant in a place where it doesn't get enough sunshine, be sure to find out what its other needs are. In a great many cases, shade-tolerant plants require moist soil. Consequently, even though shade is darker and cooler than sun, shade gardeners may find themselves watering more often than sun gardeners.

Some Successful Woodswalks
On the Floor of an Urban Forest

Recently, Professor Wallace took up a prestigious position as chairman of the department of physics in a Midwestern university and bought a large Victorian house on the main road into the university campus. The house had a moderately large yard, perhaps 40 by 50 feet, which was reached through French doors in the living room and two stone steps. In the hundred years since the house was built, the trees in the neighborhood had grown to enormous heights and made a dense canopy over the entire neighborhood. Dr. Wallace's garden was dominated by three trees, a red oak and two horse chestnuts, whose nuts and casings littered the ground in autumn. The lawn, which once must have been a very handsome feature, was now thin and ragged due to the intense shade and the onslaught of litter from the trees.

Since the house was built, many changes had occurred in the neighborhood as well. Over the last three decades, the university had expanded and the traffic going by the property had become

The hidden "grotto" in the middle of Dr. Wallace's small woodswalk.

very heavy. To protect themselves from the din and to give themselves some privacy and security, the previous owners had built a massive cinderblock wall around the yard. Unfortunately, they had not planted anything on or against the wall, so the net effect was of three gigantic tree trunks surrounded by a poor lawn and an imposing cement wall.

With his heavy commitments at the university, Dr. Wallace knew he wouldn't have much time for gardening. But he wanted to have a gracious garden, where he could entertain official guests and perhaps poke around from time to time, seeing what was up and growing. He thought about the possibilities over the winter in little bits of spare time. Being a methodical sort of a fellow, he drew up a plan of the present conditions in his yard—not a very demanding task, since the yard had so little in it. He carried copies of the plan in his briefcase and during meetings would often put one on his note pad and design gardens while his colleagues droned on. Finally, near the end of the winter quarter, he hit on a plan he liked, and by May, the landscape contractor had completed the work and the garden was finished.

The central feature of Dr. Wallace's garden is a deck off the back of the house which he reaches through the French doors. The landscape designer removed the existing stone steps and built the deck at the floor level of the living room, so that Dr. Wallace and his guests can stroll out onto the deck on warm evenings and survey the garden.

From the deck one sees at first the trunks of the great trees and an expanse of groundcovers: vinca with its bright blue flowers, lily-of-the-valley, carpet bugle, and mahonia. He chose the mahonia partly because of its bright yellow spring flowers, and partly because of its blue fruits in the summer and fall, which he had heard were attractive to birds.

Both side walls of the garden and the back third have been heavily planted in broadleaved evergreens. These not only soften the wall, they also help to absorb traffic noise from the street and make the garden quieter. In choosing varieties for these plantings, Dr. Wallace, who is not fond of pastel colors, concentrated on azaleas with vibrant, deep red flowers that will bloom in late May in his climate. This fall, the landscaping contractor will return and plant groupings of daffodils and narcissus of different varieties so that next spring, before the trees leaf out, the groundcover will be sprinkled with clusters of bright flowers.

Off the right-hand side of the deck is a short flight of steps that leads to the garden's other principal feature, a walk of stepping stones that "tours" its outer perimeter. Where the walk reaches the back third of the garden, it passes among the evergreens and into a little "grotto" that is screened from the deck. Here Dr. Wallace has put a statue and a bench. He designed this spot for his own use, to give himself a place to "go" in his garden. But much to his surprise, he finds the walk and the bench much used by his guests. Often, a few of his colleagues, engaged in an urgent conversation about some academic matter, wander off down the stone walk, only to be found later, deep in discussion on the stone bench.

A Frontier Path

When Angela Dunn and her husband built their home, they chose a 3-acre lot that had grown into a jungle. Even when they had cleared half of it for their house, lawn, and vegetable garden, they still had 1½ acres that were virtually inaccessible. The "jungle" had a few tall trees, a lot of brush and brambles, a small bog, and a tiny brook, but the underbrush was virtually impenetrable.

The Dunns considered bulldozing the rest of the lot and replanting with ornamental trees. But Angela had visions of a shady garden with a lovely path that meandered among the trunks of tall trees,

The Dunns' woodswalk with a railroad-tie dam in the stream.

through little groves, over a bridge, and past a sunny spot. She figured that if she wanted her garden before she was 60, she had better make use of the trees that were already there.

So she and Howard set about thinning their woods. Working in their spare time with saws and bushclippers, they gradually cut a path through the tangle roughly following—but with many twists and turns—the boundaries of their property: Here they made a bend to avoid the trunk of a large tree, there they turned toward the center of the property for several yards to follow the bank of a small stream before crossing it to continue. Once the path had been cut, they made minor improvements in its surface so they could walk on it easily. Where the path crossed the stream, they put some large flat rocks, so that it was possible to cross without getting wet feet. In muddy spots, they spread wood chips so that their feet would stay dry. Once a month or so, Howard would take the lawn mower for a walk along the path and hack down encroaching suckers. In a year, the path was comfortable to walk on and in some parts had even become grassy and smooth.

Once they had lived with the path for a year, they knew enough about it to begin to make some additional improvements. The stream with its wildlife was a great favorite with Angela, so she got Howard to help her develop it. Just above their rock ford, they excavated the streambed and put in a railroad tie to form a dam. Behind the dam, a pool formed which became a haven for frogs and waterbugs. The Dunns were eager to see what wild plants would take advantage of their new pool and its surroundings. Already they have blue flag, sweet pepperbush, and purple loosestrife. They are hoping for pond lilies, cattails, and cardinal flower. Sometime in the future, Angela wants to replace the rock ford with a tiny arched bridge similar to one she once saw in the Japanese garden of a museum. She daydreams about standing on the bridge and staring down into the depths of her pool.

Farther along the path is a place where three tall trees are grouped in a rough circle about 15 feet across. Within the circle, the Dunns cut out the undergrowth and made a shady glade. The effect is delightful. As you walk up from the small stream you confront a wall of undergrowth. Entering the undergrowth through a narrow path, you suddenly come across the glade, marked out by the trunks of the tall trees and provided with a little wooden bench for sitting. Soft mosses and ferns carpet the ground, and it's a wonderfully cool and quiet place to relax on a hot summer day.

Around another bend in the path is the place where Angela hopes in time to put the reading and sunbathing spot. To get the sun in, the Dunns will cut a great elm, a "wolf tree" which has dominated their little forest for a generation but which is succumbing now to Dutch elm disease. To make a place for a hedge, they will remove undergrowth around the open space and plant arborvitae in a protective arc. In a few years grass will grow up in the spot, and the hedge will shelter it. By then, the Dunns will have an ideal place for a picnic.

The secret of the Dunns' success with their woodswalk is patience. By giving themselves access to their woods and then waiting a year to become completely familiar with it, the Dunns were able to have a woodswalk that had all the features they wanted, yet blended into their yard perfectly.

A Patrician Summer Colony

More than 50 years ago, the Henderson and the Sturgeon families were looking for a place to build summer homes, and purchased a Depression-wracked farm on a rocky headland overlooking a bit of the New England coast. The land was mostly poor, overgrown pasture, dotted with shoulder-high pine trees, blueberries, and junipers. The two families debated at length how they should do their landscaping. The Sturgeons were influenced by photographs they had seen of the wide luxurious lawns of Newport, and they were in favor of seeding the pasture to lawn grass and mowing it. The Hendersons, on the other hand, had an image of shady woods which would be cool in the summer. They wanted to leave the pasture to grow up.

In time, the Hendersons' view prevailed and the white pines were allowed to grow. The families built their houses "around the corner from each other" on the headland, and soon the children and dogs beat a network of paths all over the headland, a path to an outlook over the ocean where cookouts were held, a path down to the beach, a path between the two houses, and a path down to the village to get the mail. Because of the rocky ground, the paths twisted and turned among the outcroppings and hugged the slopes, avoiding unnecessary ups and downs.

In a remarkably short time, the headland began to be transformed by the rapidly growing evergreens. Now the white pines are 30 and 40 feet tall. The pathways still twist and turn among the outcroppings, but now, instead of being lined with blueberry and juniper, they are lined with lichens, mosses, and a soft carpet of pine needles. Bearberry, lowbush blueberry, and bayberry bushes cluster where the paths come out onto the rocks. Here and there, children have found wild lily-of-the-valley, sweet fern, and mayflower. All this, where

The Henderson and Sturgeon families' woodswalk, where the path emerges from the pines.

only a generation before, their parents stepped with care to avoid thistles and briars.

Ironically, the Sturgeon and the Henderson families still debate the merits of living in a forest. Over the years, the two original houses have been supplemented by five others, as the children of the original families have come back with families of their own. As living patterns have changed, the summer houses on the headland have been used more and more as year-round homes. In spring and fall, the deep shade of the pine forest is not as welcome as it is in summer, and some hotheads have urged that the trees be cut down. Fortunately, there is still a lot of open space on the headland.

Selective cutting of the pines has let light into the houses where it was wanted, while still leaving acres of cool, mysterious forest in between.

Wrap-up

A woodswalk is a path that leads you to cool, contemplative places in your garden. Always restful and quiet, it leads you around corners to little surprises, a place to sit, a pool to think beside, a shaft of sunlight, even a statue or birdbath. A woodswalk is a particularly good option if you have recently built a house in the woods, or live in one of those old neighborhoods where the trees have become great, shade-casting giants.

Plants for Woodswalks

Plant Name	Woodswalk Feature	Description	Culture
Shrubs for Woodswalks			
Boule de Neige rhododendron (*Rhododendron* 'Boule de Neige')	White flowers, of medium size; one of the finest whites	Slow-growing, compact, rounded plant, as high as it is wide; leaves are fairly large, dark, lustrous green	Partial shade; cool, moist, humusy, acid soil; to Zone 5
Catawba rhododendron (*Rhododendron catawbiense*) var. *album* many cultivars	Purple through lilac purple, lavender-pink, and clear red, funnel-shaped flowers; *album* has white flowers; dark green, leathery leaves; April and May	Shrub up to 10 feet tall; leaves are evergreen, 2½ to 5 inches long; flowers are borne in racemes 5 to 6 inches in diameter	Partial shade; cool, moist, humusy soil; Zones 4–8
Doublefile viburnum (*Viburnum plicatum* var. *tomentosum*) and hybrids 'Mariesii' 'Shasta'	Large, pure white flower clusters; attractive green foliage with bright red fruit; July	Distinctly horizontal growth habit, twice as wide as high; valuable for flowers, form, and fruit; compact growth—6 feet tall and 10 to 12 feet wide—makes it ideal for smaller gardens	Sun or partial shade; good, moist garden soil; Zones 5–9
Exbury azaleas, Knap Hill azaleas (*Rhododendron* Exbury)	Flower colors range from white through cream, pink, yellow, orange, and red; some may have 18 to 20 flowers in a single cluster	Deciduous, upright shrubs with medium green, lance-shaped leaves; yellow, orange, and red fall color; flowers 2 to 3 inches across, mostly single	Partial shade; cool, moist, humusy, acid soil; Zones 5–7
Flame azalea (*Rhododendron calendulaceum*) and hybrids	Yellow, orange, or reddish orange, funnel-shaped flowers; May and June	Upright shrub up to 9 feet tall and wide; leaves 1½ to 3½ inches long, elliptic or obovate, medium green; subdued yellow to red fall color	Partial shade; cool, moist, humusy, acid soil; Zone 5
Ghent azalea (*Rhododendron* ×*gandavense*)	White, yellow, pink, or red, single or double, medium-size flowers; late May	Deciduous, 6- to 10-foot shrubs; upright when young, later spreading to form well-balanced bushes	Partial shade; cool, moist, humusy, acid soil; to Zone 4
Kaempferi azalea (*Rhododendron kaempferi*) and hybrids	Orange-red, pink, rose scarlet, or bright red funnel-shaped flowers; 2 inches across	Loosely branched, deciduous or semi-evergreen shrub up to 10 feet tall and 6 feet wide; dark green leaves; reddish fall color; up to 4 flowers per cluster	Partial shade; cool, moist, humusy, acid soil; perennial; to Zone 6

Plant Name	Woodswalk Feature	Description	Culture
Mayflower viburnum, Koreanspice viburnum (*Viburnum carlesii*)	White flowers in dense, snowball-like clusters 2 to 3 inches across; very sweet fragrance; blooms with tulips; clustered black fruit; August and September	Dense, rounded shrub up to 8 feet tall; leaves are ovate to elliptic, up to 4 inches long, toothed, pubescent, dark green; reddish to wine red fall color	Full sun to partial shade; well-drained, slightly acid, evenly moist soil; Zones 4–8
Mountain laurel (*Kalmia latifolia*) and hybrids	Blossoms usually white with pink tinge, but occasionally pure white or deep rose, up to 6 inches across; early June	Grows 6 to 8 feet tall; lustrous, dark green, leathery foliage and stark slender branches; well-formed, hardy shrub	Partial shade; cool, moist, well-drained, acid soil; summer mulching; Zones 4–8
Pinkshell azalea (*Rhododendron vaseyi*) var. *album*	Light rose flowers; *album* has white flowers; mid-May; foliage turns light red in autumn	Irregular, upright shrub 5 to 10 feet tall; deciduous, medium green leaves, 2 to 5 inches long	Partial shade; withstands growing in moist soil conditions; to Zone 9
Rosebay rhododendron (*Rhododendron maximum*)	Small, rose or purple-pink flowers; usually hidden by foliage; late June	Hardiest of the evergreen rhododendrons; leaves are 5 to 10 inches long; used more for foliage than flowers	Partial shade; well-drained, humusy, sandy loam; to Zone 5
Royal azalea (*Rhododendron schlippenbacki*)	Funnel-shaped, pale pink blossoms, 3 inches wide; mid-May; leaves turn yellow-orange to crimson in fall	Deciduous shrub to 5 feet; leaves are 2 to 4 inches long in whorls of five	Partial shade; well-drained, humusy, sandy loam; to Zone 5
Silveredge dogwood (*Cornus alba* var. *argenteo-marginata*)	Leaves bordered by an irregular band of creamy white, with gray-green centers; red winter stem color	Loosely upright shrub up to 10 feet tall and wide; green stems become red in winter; leaves are 5 inches long, ovate to elliptic; yellowish white flowers are in 1½- to 2-inch-wide, flat-topped cymes; May and June	Sun to partial shade; well-drained, deep, moist soils; prune a third of old wood or cut to ground each spring for best twig color in winter; Zones 2–8
Smirnow rhododendron (*Rhododendron smirnowii*)	Evergreen; flowers white to rose red; most are lavender-pink	Compact, slow-growing shrub; leaves are 3 to 6 inches long, oblong, obovate, thick, with felty gray or brown undersides	Partial shade; well-drained, humusy, sandy loam; to Zone 5
Swamp azalea (*Rhododendron viscosum*) and hybrids	White flowers very fragrant; early July; leaves turn orange to bronze in fall	Deciduous shrub to 9 feet tall; leaves are 1 to 2½ inches long	Partial shade; well-drained, humusy, sandy loam; to Zone 5

(continued)

Plants for Woodswalks—*continued*

Plant Name	Woodswalk Feature	Description	Culture
Wilson rhododendron (*Rhododendron laetivirens*)	Pink to purplish flowers, 1 inch wide; early June	Evergreen hybrid; neat plant; good for rock garden	Partial shade; well-drained, humusy, sandy loam; to Zone 5
Yakusimanum rhododendron (*Rhododendron yakusimanum*) and hybrids	Clustered, deep appleblossom pink flowers; rare and extra hardy; ideal in foundation planting; early May	Fine, dwarf evergreen; grows no more than 2 feet tall; underside of foliage is covered with fine, white down; heavy bloomer	Prefers partial shade, but will grow in sun; well-drained, acid, humusy soil; Zones 4–8

Herbaceous Plants for Woodswalks

Plant Name	Woodswalk Feature	Description	Culture
American columbine (*Aquilegia canadensis*)	Red and yellow flowers with red spurs surrounding bright yellow centers; April and May	Graceful, airy foliage with small nodding flowers; flowers are borne on 1- to 2-foot stems; leaves are dark green and deeply lobed	Light shade, but will tolerate full sun, except in hot, dry regions; well-drained but moist soil; perennial; Zones 2–8
Bishop's hat (*Epimedium alpinum* var. *rubrum*)	Masses of red and yellow, spurred blossoms in loose sprays; May and June	Dainty, airy flowers atop asymmetric, heart-shaped leaves; graceful, hardy groundcover; grows about 12 inches tall	Partial shade; average, well-drained soil; perennial; Zones 4–7
Bloodroot (*Sanguinarea canadensis*)	White, delicate, cup-shaped flowers; bloom time is short; April and May	Tightly rolled, scalloped, gray-green leaves with delicate flowers; grows about 6 inches tall	Full sun to partial shade; rich, humusy, acid soil; divide early in fall; perennial; Zones 3–8
Bunchberry (*Cornus canadensis*)	Yellow flowers surrounded by white bracts in May and June; in late summer, red, edible berries appear and last well into fall	Low groundcover, native to woodlands of North America; evergreen leaves are in horizontal whorls; grows only 5 to 9 inches tall; dense heads of small flowers; makes a good carpet	Partial shade; moist, highly organic soil; Zones 2–7
Dutchman's breeches (*Dicentra cucullaria*)	Ice-white, dainty blooms resembling inverted pantaloons; April and May	Flowers dangle above gray-green, fern-like foliage which dies back early; grows about 10 inches tall	Partial shade; rich, moist, well-drained soil; divide after blooming before foliage dies; Zones 2–7
Epimedium (*Epimedium versicolor*)	Yellow flowers, spurs tinged with red	Mottled, heart-shaped leaves; grows about 12 inches tall; good for groundcover	Prefers partial shade, but tolerates sun; moist soil; cut back wiry stems in spring; propagate by division; perennial; to Zone 5

Plant Name	Woodswalk Feature	Description	Culture
Galax *(Galax urceolata)*	White, 1/16-inch flowers on spike-like racemes, about 12 to 18 inches long; summer	Stemless and tufted, grows to 2½ feet tall; nearly round green leaves bronze with age; flowers are borne on slender leafless spikes	Full to partial shade; moist, acid soil with abundant organic matter; perennial
Hosta *(Hosta sieboldiana)* 'Frances Williams' many others	Handsome, metallic, blue-green, seersuckered leaves; racemes of white to lilac, trumpet-shaped flowers	Forms 3- by 4-foot clumps with very large, 10- to 15-inch puckered, heart-shaped leaves, with broad golden-yellow margins that deepen as color and season progress; flowers are on spikes shorter than leaves	Partial to full shade; moist soil; perennial; Zones 3–10
Jack-in-the-pulpit *(Arisaema triphyllum)*	Greenish purple spathe ("pulpit"), 4 to 7 inches long, arches over erect, greenish yellow to white spadix ("jack"); early summer	Plant grows to 2½ feet tall; flowers are 3 inches tall; spear-shaped leaves have 3 lobes, are 3 to 5 inches long	Partial shade; rich, well-drained soil high in organic matter; propagate by root division; perennial
Japanese painted fern *(Athyrium goeringianum)*	Silver-splashed green fronds; stems are wine red	Vigorous grower to 18 inches tall; graceful weeping habit; coarsely divided fronds	Shade to partial shade; provide ample moisture during growing season; perennial; Zones 3–8
Maidenhair fern *(Adiantum pedatum)*	Light green fronds with black, wiry, arching stalks	Grows 1 to 2 feet high; rhizomatous; dainty, lacy, filigree fronds	Moist, well-shaded banks; will tolerate dryness; perennial; Zones 3–8
Mayapple *(Podophyllum pelatum)*	White flower with 6 petals; edible, 2-inch, yellow fruit	Nodding flower, 1 to 2 inches in diameter; leaves are up to 12 inches long, bright green, palmate	Partial shade; rich, moist soil; perennial
Partridgeberry *(Mitchella repens)*	Small, paired, pinkish white, funnel-shaped flowers, summer; followed by scarlet berries	Trailing, woody stems; leaves are rounded, glossy, ¾ inch long, with whitish veins	Partial shade; moist, acid soil; perennial
Purple trillium *(Trillium erectum)*	Pale green leaves; single, nodding, 3-petaled, purple flowers; spring; fruit is deep reddish, oval berry	Leaves have waxy margin; whorl of 3 ovate leaves crowns the stem; excellent for wooded areas	Partial shade; rich, peaty soil; propagate by seed
Sharp-lobed hepatica *(Hepatica acutiloba)*	Bluish white flowers have petal-like sepals; early spring; handsome liver-and-green mottled foliage	Leaves are basal, pointed, with long stalks, 3 lobes; remain on plant all winter; plant grows to 9 inches tall	Partial shade; soil neutral or slightly acid; perennial; to Zone 4

(continued)

Plants for Woodswalks—*continued*

Plant Name	Woodswalk Feature	Description	Culture
Snow trillium *(Trillium grandiflorum)*	Waxy white flowers fading to pink, narrowly pointed and single; April to June; fruit is blue-black berry	Flowers are 2 to 3 inches wide, on 3-inch stems; leaves are oval; plant grows 12 to 18 inches tall	Partial shade; deep, rich, moist, humusy, acid soil; propagate by fall or early spring division; perennial
Squirrel corn *(Dicentra canadensis)*	Greenish white flowers in drooping terminals; flowers fragrant; April and May	Gray-green leaves are compound and finely divided; flowers have heart-shaped corolla and crested petals	Partial shade; rich soil; perennial; to Zone 4
Virginia bluebell *(Mertensia virginica)*	Clusters of pink buds open as lovely bluebells; April and May; pale green leaves	Bell-like flowers on 18- to 24-inch spikes; leaves are broad and disappear by summer	Partial shade to full sun; rich, moist, humusy soil; divide in spring every 3 to 4 years; perennial; Zones 3–8
Wild ginger *(Asarum canadense)*	Evergreen; 1-inch-wide, bell-shaped flowers, purplish green outside, deep maroon inside; beautiful foliage	Heart-shaped, green foliage; good groundcover	Shade; moist, humusy soil; increase growth by division; perennial; Zones 3–8
Wintergreen *(Gaultheria procumbens)*	Drooping, waxy, white, bell-shaped flowers; May; bright red berries in fall are edible	Lustrous evergreen leaves form ground-covering mat; grows 3 inches tall	Partial shade; moist, acidic soil; to Zone 3

Special Features

Photo 15

193

Photo 16

Photo 15 (previous page) shows everybody's ideal meadow. This meadow full of poppies, pinks, and bachelor's buttons is gloriously colorful, fastidiously neat, and never needs attention from frost to frost. Lucky indeed is the gardener who has such a meadow.

In Photo 16 is the ideal lawn. Lush and green, it sets off the rocks, trees, and plantings, and looks cool and inviting. Notice how the rocks, particularly the one on the left, are set into the turf so as to suggest that most of their mass lies below the surface of the soil.

Most meadows are actually specialized perennial gardens, as in Photo 17. Here, meadow flowers of one predominant color (yellow buttercups) are used in conjunction with other plantings. Meadows can be of the potluck, take-it-or-leave-it sort, or, as in this example, carefully contrived to be part of a total composition. Notice how the informal billowiness of the buttercups and magenta and white Japanese primroses is juxtaposed to the more formal upright shapes of the marsh ferns and azaleas. The meadow flowers are seen not as individuals but as a single mass. In some ways, they function like a lawn, only taller, more varied, and more interesting.

Photo 17

Photo 18

Lawns are a wonderful reflecting surface, almost like water. A lawn such as the one in Photo 18 can show off the shadows in a garden and emphasize the constant interplay of color and light . . .

. . . or it can feature the shape and color of a treasured ornamental tree, as in Photo 19. The smoothness of this lawn helps us to notice the bark and leaves of the beautiful weeping willow.

Photo 19

Photo 20

Imagine the scene in Photo 20 if there were no lawn to absorb some of the hot color of the geraniums and rhododendron. Without the lawn, the two shades of red would clash objectionably. The cool green of the lawn cushions the effect of the colors and makes them compatible.

Here, in Photo 21, is a harmonious display of flowers set off by a stone wall: orange and gold lilies, yellow achillea, white lilies, a few blues (delphiniums in the foreground, small spikes of veronicas in the center), and larger spikes of purple and pink annual larkspur to the right. The red-violet clematis enhances and intensifies the flower colors beyond.

Photo 21

Photo 22

The perennials in Photo 22 are thoughtfully grouped for color and form. The groupings of tall, pinkish purple loosestrife organize the shorter white bouncing bet and yellow rudbeckias. The groupings are large enough to be seen easily—not dinky and confused, with too many varieties in too small a space. The person who planted this garden had restraint and a good sense of color harmony, and didn't make the mistake of trying to use all the colors in the rainbow. Photo 23 shows a spectacular entrance that would grace any garden. The rustic trellis carries its flowers (roses) well, but will be interesting enough to stand on its own after they are shed.

Photo 23

Photo 24 shows border plantings skillfully matched to the curving form of a path. Low plantings emphasize the pattern effect and display the annuals. This border shows admirable restraint in the choice of color and variety of plants. The red tulips add a spark to the yellow and orange wallflowers, blue forget-me-nots, and low pink aubrieta.

Photo 24

Photo 25

The possible combinations of color and texture in a flower garden are endless. A simple display shows off the form of individual flowers, such as the iris in Photo 25. In Photo 26, a mixed flower and herb garden, blue larkspur cools down the intense reds and pinks of dianthus and chives, and adds contrast. The way the colors are grouped, the repetition of the red in the background, leads the eye from the flowers in the foreground to the wall beyond.

White annual larkspur in Photo 27 brightens the scene and sets off the yellow achillea and blue larkspur. The soft fuzzy white of the baby's breath repeats the color but changes the texture.

Photo 26

Photo 27

Photo 28

Photo 29

The greenery of the azalea foliage in Photo 28 tones down the complementary colors of the spring flowers: cream-and-orange narcissus, yellow daffodils, lavender-pink forget-me-nots, and the red blossoms of the azaleas themselves. Together they make a bright and cheerful scene, but not one that jangles.

It is commonplace to see colorful flowers glittering in bright sunlight. The woodland scene in Photo 29 reminds us that shady areas can also be colorful. In early spring, where conditions are right, daffodils and tulips may cover the forest floor like a carpet of sunshine.

Photo 30 shows a traditional border that an amateur could easily maintain. The bed is narrow for ease of planting and maintenance. Groupings of plant varieties and colors are repeated the length of the fence. This border is a lively mix of colors, including the rich golds of daylilies and heliopsis in the foreground, deep red bee balm, dusty blue globe-shaped flower heads of echinops, lavender spikes of veronicas, and the soft pink spikes of a hybrid form of loosestrife in the background.

The wisteria blooming in Photo 31 complements the brick pillar behind and sets off the low wall. The proportion of the wisteria to the wall is nicely balanced.

The colors in the California perennial border of Photo 32 are remarkable. The grayish foliage of the aloes displays the subtle pinks of its own flowers, and the red above, to good effect. But remarkable though the colors are, the textures are downright amazing. Squint your eyes a bit to diminish the color contrast and three layers of texture will leap out at you: a spiky lower level, a towering middle layer, and an upper layer composed of small dabs of color.

Photo 31

Photo 30

Photo 32

Photo 33

The garden pictured in Photo 33 is a fine example of what can be achieved in a partly shaded garden. This garden tapestry of harmonious colors weaves together pale pink and yellow hybrid columbines with their graceful spurs at left, tall wands of dainty pink coral bells in the center foreground, dianthus, foxgloves (the tall pink flowers at the rear), and canterbury bells in shades of purple, pink, and white. The dark red flowers are biennial sweet williams, and the bright yellow ones are evening primroses.

The trick of a sunspot is having the best of winter sun and summer shade. In Photo 34, the clematis and bougainvillea vines enhance the trellis and arbor in summer and provide some shade from the high summer sun. Still, enough light filters through in summer for flowers and shrubs to grow. Outside the growing season, the high arbor would present little obstruction to the slant rays of the cool winter sun.

Photo 34

Photo 35

On hot summer days it's nice to have your flowers soaking up the sun's energy while you sit comfortably in the shade, sheltered from the sun but open to the slightest passing breeze. Photo 35 pictures a unique structure for airy, shady sitting, not only a functional structure, but an elegant feature in itself. It could be covered by vines or it could stand by itself. The containers on the deck hold some purple-flowered agapanthus, a couple of succulent houseplants spending the summer outdoors, and heavenly bamboo, the brilliant red flowers of which arc into the photo on the right.

The deck in Photo 36 seems an ideal world for outdoor living. Shelter comes from the house and from the overhang, which would cut out the noonday sun or a light rainshower. The outer section has been left open to catch the warm sun and cool breezes.

Photo 36

The patio in Photo 37 is protected and shaded by deciduous trees in the summer, but is sunny and welcoming in winter and other seasons. Located close to the kitchen, a sunspot like this one would be an ideal spot for brunches on mild, early spring Sundays.

Gardening in the sunspot in Photo 38 provides endless possibilities. The wall, the steps, and

Photo 37

212

Photo 38

the bulk of the house protect the garden from chillings; the bricks store heat; and the bright surface of the house reflects and magnifies the light falling on the garden. Here, almost any plant would grow beautifully: herbs and vegetables for summer use, early flowers for late winter enjoyment, and perennials of every conceivable sort. Here is a location where the gardener's imagination could quickly outrun the available space.

Photo 39 is a cool-climate sunspot. The enclosed porch and the patio are open to the winter sun when the leaves come off the deciduous trees to the south of the house.

Photo 39

Photo 40

Photo 40, on the other hand, is a hot-climate sunspot. The lounge chair is in the shade now, late in the day, where its owner can beat a retreat to the shelter of the cool cavern under the arbor. It's everybody's ideal summer bower. In fall, of course, the grapevine sheds its leaves and allows filtered sunshine to reach the patio surface.

Photo 41

A good rock garden begins with a grouping of stones, boulders, or ledge outcroppings that doesn't reveal a trace of contrivance. This is the hardest part. Once the rocks are in place, picking plants which look attractive around them is easy. The face of the boulder in Photo 41 is a perfect foil for the tapestry of small plants around it. Notice the different textures and colors: the coarse, sword-like foliage of bromeliads; the fine, soft, fuzzy foliage of blue-flowered lithodora; the yellow-greens of a kalanchoe hybrid with salmon flowers; and a rabbit's foot fern in the lower right. The maroon leaves of the aeonium in the left center contrast beautifully with the gray rock. This is a close-up treatment where many different sorts of plants grow together in a small area. Always a bit tricky. Always interesting.

Any crevice, such as those in Photo 42, can become a garden. Rock walls and steps can have pockets of plants peeking out. Sedums, with their colorful foliage, look very perky. Stone steps are also a place for plants with scented foliage, such as thyme or creeping mints, which will give off a fragrance when trod on.

Photo 42

Photo 43

Photo 43's flowerfall of bright yellows and related colors emulates sunlight on the pools and cascades of a mountain stream. The separation of the colors into planes is interesting. The very effective use of plants in drifts helps to make the garden into a scene, rather than a group of individual blossoms. The evergreen at the base helps to anchor the other plantings.

Photo 44 illustrates the play of bright flower colors set off by rocks. Even the daintiest of flowers looks good against a solid backdrop of rock. Because of the presence of the gray or brownish stone surface, you can get away with color combinations such as this red, white, and blue scheme, that might look strident in an ordinary flowerbed.

Photo 44

G ARDENS EXIST WITHIN TH
garden. They are bounded
ties, both man-made and
gardens, they are surrour
they exist in the center of a forest
lies a vast sky, and in the hearts o
haps other buildings as well. All i
determine a garden's scale, that is,
and the elements that compose

Many gardens in America
They offer no effective ba
ry represented by a
length, half again
Such

Photo 45

220

A rock garden can also have a woodland setting. Photo 45 features greens—the bold, plain surface of the variegated hosta leaves in juxtaposition with the delicate pale green and finely textured fronds of the ferns. Together they make a cool, refreshing picture.

A rock feature such as the hillside garden in Photo 46 would be the pride of any landscape. Carpeted with yellow-flowered sedums and pink-flowered creeping thyme, its wonderful masses of color and foliage tumble over the rock surface. The whole rocky slope seems to drip greenery. Steps invite us up the rock face to explore mysteries beyond. This design shows a nice proportion of rock face to plant material.

Photo 46

The poppies in Photo 47 are splendid, and the white sage-leaf rockroses do help to incorporate the boulder. This is an unusual style for a rock garden, and many viewers love its bold brightness, although this rock seems just a bit too much like a geological afterthought for our taste.

Photo 47

Photo 48

Photo 48, of firethorn, is a classic winter garden scene. There is nothing like snow on a plant to show off berries and evergreen foliage.

Photo 49

Such energy in Photo 49! These tulips look bright and cheery despite Mother Nature's early spring surprise. In fact, the white snow makes the green leaves and red blooms seem even more vivid. Even in a snowless spring, the framing of the blooms with the natural fence guarantees an elegant display. This is one of those small details in a garden that gives pure joy to the gardener for a few days every year....

... The snow on the holly berries in Photo 50 is another.

Photo 50

Photo 51

A winter garden strives for color in the monochromatic world of snow, as exemplified by the grape hyacinth in Photo 51…

…and for form, as seen in the stunningly beautiful birch tree of Photo 52. Winter is the time to enjoy the structure of trees and the textures of their bark.

Photo 52

Photo 53

Water is so ambiguous. Sometimes it is dark depths into which one can peer, sometimes a mirror that reflects the shapes and shadows of trees, plants, and rocks, and sometimes an impenetrable surface of flickering highlights. A water garden is a peaceful, natural setting, but never dull. The lively tropical foliage of the water plants, the flashes of color from water-loving flowers, and the

Photo 54

dazzling, darting, golden bodies of the carp just below the surface of the water (Photos 53, 54, and 55) all add interest. The stunning garden shown in Photos 53 and 54 features brilliant purply-pink impatiens and coleus, contrasting against bold yellow floating hearts and rudbeckias.

Photo 55

Photo 56 shows a nice, formal pool, well designed and carried out. The flowing form of the buddleias goes well with the water. The circular bed of yellow and white flowers complements the brick paving and pool shape, and the fountain is just the right scale. Everything is neat and symmetrical. What a contrast with the passle of primroses in Photo 57! These moisture-loving primroses are growing around the edge of a small pool.

Photo 56

Photo 57

Photo 58 illustrates water as a garden feature. The cascading pine echoes and emphasizes the movement of the falling water. It also shades the water and adds depth and interest. The vertical ferns in the foreground emphasize the rugged rock formation. Overall, the composition has a wonderful, grottolike feeling. Looking at the photograph, you can practically hear the sounds of the water echoing in the depths of the rock.

Photo 58

Photo 59

The simple garden pool in Photo 59 should inspire many a do-it-yourselfer. Sunny and gay, the water sparkles in the embrace of what appears to be a natural stone pool. Beneath the rocks of such a "natural" pool, we suspect we would find cement or fiberglass, a plastic liner, or at least a heavy layer of imported clay.

Photo 60

Photo 61

The water garden in Photo 61 is particularly well integrated into its setting. And of course, once you have a well-designed pool...

... you are ready to have waterlilies, as in Photos 60 and 62. The waterlily is truly the empress of garden flowers, a beautiful and exotic bloom that defies description. Best of all, you can grow waterlilies in the smallest of pools, even in a tub or barrel.

Photo 62

Photo 63

What wildlife craves is a garden with many levels of foliage, lots of plant variety, and dense cover to hide in. The photos on these pages illustrate these features and, in addition, provide a dazzling display of blooming shrubs and flowers: corylopsis, anemones, and primroses in Photo 63; magnolia, cherry, and rhododendron in Photo 64. The critters—save perhaps the bees, butterflies, and hummingbirds—probably don't care about the gorgeous flowers, but if they do no harm, why not have them?

Photo 64

Photo 65

In Photo 65 we have the ideal woodswalk, a shady path among the trunks of stately trees. Here you might see squirrels scurrying to bury nuts in the forest litter or a woodpecker tapping at the trunk of one of the tall oaks, or perhaps you'd hear the comical beep-beep call of a nuthatch.

Think how stunningly beautiful the peaceful scene in Photo 66 would be with a cardinal or tanager splashing about in the birdbath!

Photo 66

Photo 67 illustrates a carefully thought-out natural corner in a garden. The colors of the flowers are planned to show off the pool, with the blue veronicas repeating the line of the water and the pink cranesbills (true geraniums) and yellow sedums accenting the sides of the pool. The evergreens suggest, but hide, the beginnings of the watercourse, and the stones look as if they had been in place for centuries. Such a pool would be sure to have a resident frog.

Photo 67

Photo 68

If you offer good accommodations (Photo 68), you can expect many a grateful guest. The tiger swallowtail butterfly visiting the zinnia makes a truly classic summer scene.

Photo 69

Photo 69 depicts another ideal woodswalk: an informal path curving into a hidden area, providing a touch of intrigue. Delicate woodland flowers bloom along the path: blue forget-me-nots and phlox, white sweet woodruff, a few columbines. Add the color from the azaleas, and the sweet smells of newly thawed earth in the air, and you can imagine how enticing this path will be in the spring.

Even at the base of a large tree, there can be color and interest. The pretty impatiens in Photo 70 brighten up a shady corner of the garden.

Photo 70

Photo 71

The floor of the forest can be a carpet of interesting plants, soft textures, and exquisite flowers. Of this splendid company, the trillium, depicted in Photo 71, is truly the prince. The small, white-flowered plants growing below the trilliums are another classic woodland resident, sweet woodruff.

Photo 72 shows a more formal path, consisting of flagstones immersed in a groundcover of carpet bugle. The path is lush, cool, and inviting on a warm spring day or a hot summer one. If you don't have many large trees, even a small shady patch made in your garden is a nice contrast and pleasant break from an open lawn or garden.

Photo 72

Photo 73

Photo 73 is a dazzling woodland display. The blue grape hyacinths flow like a stream, with accents of bright-colored bulbs—tulips to the left and narcissus to the right. In this cheery early spring scene, you can practically feel the warmth of the earth. The blue flowers seem to lead you into the depths of the woods beyond.

Photo 74

When you come out of your woodswalk, you want to see the sort of scene shown in Photo 74. The winding path is edged with bright azaleas as it emerges from the woods. Ah, the magic of light and shadow in a garden! The flowers are a pleasant contrast to the subdued tones in the deeper shade.

Photo 75 is another lovely woodland scene, rich with color. The coolness of the large drifts of violet wood hyacinths is intensified by the heat of the red rhododendron. The light pink rhododendrons outside the shady area give promise of the warmth of the open space beyond.

Photo 75

Part Three

Doing the Design

CHAPTER 12

Things to Keep in Mind

*F*irst and foremost, a yard should please its owner. You, not the idle passerby, not the landscape designer, are the one who sees your yard every day. You are the best judge of what looks and feels good in your yard. So, in the final analysis, a good design is a design that works well for you, and no other criteria need be applied.

We cannot emphasize this point enough. Too often people look at their private space, their yards, their houses, with a public eye, as if the most important goal of their life was to meet the needs of some impersonal "they." When such people design a landscape, they call in a designer and demand that the designer do the "right" thing. This way of thinking leads to an awful standardization of neighborhoods. So often the "right" thing turns out to be the current fad in home or gardening or style magazines, or the look shown on a popular television program, or the landscaping style that makes use of some heavily advertised gimmick or piece of equipment.

As a consequence, whole neighborhods are designed with the same foundation plantings, or the same shade tree in the front yard, or the same rail fence along the roadway. As you drive through such neighborhoods, you rarely see a shady path, a close-growing grove of trees, or a rock ledge with wildflowers, not because these features aren't beautiful, but because the homeowners just don't know that they are possible. Such neighborhoods are not simply monotonous. More important, they don't suit the needs of the people who live in them. They are impersonal.

This chapter is about the constraints, the "have-tos," of landscaping. But we don't want to contribute in any way to the impersonal standardization of neighborhoods. So, before we begin, we want it clearly understood that there is no "right" way to do your landscape, except the way that pleases you. Having said that, however, we would like to offer some guidelines, rules of thumb to keep in the back of your mind as you go about making plans for your landscape.

These rules represent the landscape designer's long-term experience of what does and what does not work in the average garden. They are useful points of departure, rules to be honored in the breach. Some may seem very vague and ephemeral, like the rule which says you should maintain a visual balance among the trees in your garden. Others are very concrete and practical, like the rule which says that a driveway circle for an automobile must have an outside radius of 30 or more feet and an inside radius of at least 18 feet. We think of these rules as imperatives, demands made by the objects, forces, and people in your landscape. The trees say, "Balance us!" The car says, "Turn me around!" The water that pours onto your patio from your downspouts says, "Let me out!"

These imperatives are like the demands of a petulant child. They require your attention, but not your submission. As with all commands, you shouldn't simply do as you are ordered. You should think about the problem and make a calm decision. And then, every so often, you should stamp your own foot and shout back, "NO!" After all, you can decide to live with an unbalanced front yard, a tight driveway, or even a flooded patio.

Design Imperatives

Of all the constraints of landscaping, those of design will hold you most loosely in their grip. Books about designing often make a great to-do about design constraints and make designing sound like a great mystery that only the very wise and the very creative could understand. We disagree. We would not mention these constraints at all were it not for our sense that hidden behind designers' fancy terms like "proportion," "balance," and "pattern" lie principles which seem to predict how well a landscape will wear with its owners.

Proportion

When you look at any scene, you naturally try to establish a scale. Things are in proportion in a scene when they are all in the same scale or at least their scales are compatible. For instance, a small fence would look very different wandering through an orchard of dwarf fruit trees and wandering among the tall trunks of an oak forest. Among the smaller trees it might appear comfortably in scale, whereas it might get lost in the forest.

Balance

Your mind also tries to balance any scene that it looks at. Scenes in which the left and the right sides are of obviously different size or color are unsettling to look at. They seem almost as if they are about to tip over. Scenes in which the two sides have elements of comparable size and color feel composed and placid. You might, therefore, consider balance when you set out trees and other structures in your front yard. You might particularly think about the balance between your evergreens and your deciduous trees. A landscape which looks balanced in summer when both kinds of trees are deep green can become unbalanced in winter when the deciduous trees have become all bones and the evergreens are still heavy, dark green masses.

Pattern

The human mind enjoys looking for a pattern. If a scene is too chaotic, the mind gives up trying to make sense of it and gets confused. On the other hand, if a scene is too simply patterned, the mind grasps it immediately and gets bored. The best scenes combine elements of pattern and elements of novelty so that the observer is always suspended between boredom and bewilderment.

People vary greatly in the degree to which they prefer pattern and novelty. You may like a formal scene in which a few key elements are intentionally repeated. Or you may like an informal scene in which repetition of any sort is difficult to discern. But one thing is clear. Formal and informal scenes—that is, those that are rigorously patterned and those that are not—don't mix well. A happy-go-lucky, rough-and-tumble garden can work, and a prim and tidy garden can work. But a happy-go-lucky-prim-and-tidy garden looks more like a garage sale than a landscape.

Focus

If a composition is not to seem diffuse and uninteresting, it should put one or a few elements on display. Such focus is provided in two complementary ways. One way is to *attract* the eye. Colorful or intricate objects or those with unusual forms call attention to themselves. In effect, they say, "Look at *me!*" Another way is to *direct* the eye. Patterns in the composition, like rhythmically recurring elements or converging lines, can direct the eye to notice particular features of the composition. Such patterns seem to say, "Look at *that!*" Subtly used, the techniques of attraction and direction can give a composition a pleasant sense of focus.

Flow

Compositions, whether they be paintings or landscapes, can differ in their fluidity. A fluid, dynamic composition is one which leads your eyes smoothly from one point of focus to another. A static composition is one through which your eyes don't move, but constantly get stuck in one place or another. In general, fluid landscapes are more pleasing to look at than static ones.

Beyond this admittedly vague definition, it is difficult to explain in words what designers mean by fluid versus static shapes. The best way to under-stand the idea is intuitively. Think about the shapes of eddies in water, clouds in the sky, or drifts of snow in the winter landscape. These are all phenomena which naturally flow. If in your choice and arrangement of design elements you imitate the shapes formed by water, or snow, or clouds, you will probably be creating a fluid and dynamic landscape. You may find such a landscape more pleasing, more interesting, and more comfortable than a more rigid and static landscape.

Environmental Imperatives

The environment makes numerous intractable demands upon your landscape. Sun, wind, rain, and snow place limits on the kinds of plants that you can readily grow, and even on the kinds of structures and landforms that you can make in a yard. Here are some basic environmental factors that you will have to consider when you plan your landscape.

The Sun Will Move

We have already urged you to note with care the arc traced by the sun over your property at different seasons. Do not doubt that the sun will trace that arc. Before you plant any tree, build any structure, or put in any flowerbed, remember how dramatically the angle of the sun changes at different times of the year. On a sunny hot day in June, when the sun stands 20 degrees over the top of the neighbor's oak tree, it may be hard to believe that by September the sun will be behind that tree. Wishful thinking in June might lead you to build what you fondly hoped would be an all-season sunspot, only to discover in September that its season has already ended.

The Wind Will Prevail

The currents of wind through your yard, perhaps channeled by surrounding buildings, will place limits on the kind of trees and shrubs you can grow and the kinds of fences, arbors, and trellises you can build. One strong gust of wind can reverse a decade of hard-won tree growth or many weekends of laborious construction. Choose plants and structures that are appropriate to the worst wind conditions found on your property. If you live on a windy site, ask the owner of your local nursery for advice. Choose trees which are flexible, like evergreens, not brittle and given to splitting, like silver maples. Give preference to trees with tenacious root systems, like junipers and some oaks, rather than shallow-rooted trees like willows. Plant delicate species only in the lee of buildings, slopes, or evergreens, where they won't be so badly assaulted by the wind.

The Snow Will Fall

Trees and shrubs grown in the North must be expected to bear the weight not only of their own branches and leaves, but also of the snow and ice that fall on them in the winter. If you live in a snowbelt, think before you plant an arborvitae hedge about how you are going to prepare for the burden of snow that will collect on it during the occasional winter blizzard. If you aren't prepared to keep your hedge well clipped and well pruned, and tie back loose branches every November, or heal its winter wounds with a radical spring pruning, then perhaps you should use a different species of hedge plant or consider a fence or wall.

Water Will Flow to the Lowest Point

The power of water to carry everything along with it on its way to the sea is one of the most potent imperatives your landscaping efforts will face. Over the years, water can undermine the foundations of walls, erode soil around trees, tear down slopes, flood patios, rot wooden fences, and carry away the filler between bricks and flagstones.

As far as water is concerned, few surfaces are ever truly flat. You must provide paths for the water to follow if you want the elements of your landscape to stay where you put them. Even "level" areas like parking lots and lawns must be given a slight slope to direct the flow of water. Be sure this direction is off of paved surfaces and away from building foundations. Slopes are stable only when covered with vegetation. Flowerbeds, heavily shaded lawns that are thin, and well-trodden paths will be subject to rutting and erosion from winter rains and summer thundershowers unless you provide a way for the water to get around or through them.

You must also provide drainage from low points. When you pave over an area like a driveway or a patio, you deprive the water of its natural route directly into the soil. Unless you provide drainage, the water will simply form pools at low spots. Remember, your roofs are also impervious surfaces and the water that flows off them must find its way somewhere. Make sure your gutters and downspouts work, and that they conduct the water where it won't erode or flood features of your landscape. Without a good drainage path, water from your roofs will choose the most convenient depression, like a sunken patio or a cellar, and you will find yourself pumping or wading or both after every rain.

Plant Imperatives

Plants are organisms just like you, and they have needs. Each kind of plant has its own special requirements. But some general rules are useful as points of departure in your garden planning.

Plants Want Sun

Unless you are prepared to be disappointed, you must be realistic about the sunlight needs of your plants. Sunlight is the great healer, the great alchemist in the garden. When you have sunlight in your garden, there is little that you cannot do. By sunlight we mean not a shaft here and there during the day, but at least six hours of full sun. When you don't have sunlight, landscaping requires considerable guile. If you have less than six hours, then you must do your planting from a list of the more shade-tolerant species.

Plants Will Grow

A well-designed garden is like a good haircut. It not only looks good now: It will look even better in a little while. Too often we are beguiled by photographs of formal European gardens which always look perfectly proportioned, or misled by the plantings of factories or banks whose evergreens seem to stay the same all the time. These plantings are bad models for the home gardener. Either they are maintained by teams of gardeners who come by and trim the plants each week, or

they are, in fact, not plants at all but plastic imitations. Either way, they don't prepare you for the fact that you must take account of the growth of your plants when you plan a garden.

Plants Will Compete

Plants are like children. When you keep your eyes on them, they appear to be happy and cooperative. But the minute you turn your back, they are at each other's throats, so to speak. More and more, modern biologists are beginning to appreciate what aggressive creatures plants really are. In their leaves, they manufacture toxins to repel insect predators. Below the surface of the soil, their roots grapple with neighbors' roots, each tree hoping to snatch for itself the larger share of the earth's moisture and nutrients. Overhead, their branches reach out, striving to be the highest and grab the unfiltered rays of the sun.

When you plan your garden, be sure to space

It is essential to allow for plant growth when you design your garden. If you do not, a nicely spaced new planting like the one on the left can turn into the crowded mess on the right when it matures.

your plants widely enough apart so that it will be easy for them to be good neighbors. Advice from your nursery, the description in the plant catalog, and the tag on the plant will all give indications of how large each plant will grow and how well it prospers in the shade of other trees. It would be wise for your plants' sake to heed these recommendations.

Ecological Succession Will Occur

Nothing is stable in nature. As each plant grows, it gradually changes the conditions around it. Many plants, in time, create conditions hostile to their own growth. In the natural world, they are followed by plants of different types that are especially suited to those conditions. In much of the country, there is a typical succession from grassland to hardwood forest. Old pastures go first to juniper, then to gray birch and pine, and finally to maple and oak.

A similar succession may occur in neighborhoods. When a housing development is first built, its landscape is like grassland, with only a few fledgling trees growing here and there, and grasses scratching out a difficult existence on the barren surface left by the bulldozers. Typical creatures of the open space of recent developments are field mice, meadowlarks, robins, and song sparrows.

As the neighborhood matures, the trees grow and shed large numbers of leaves. The grass establishes a mat of old stems and a tangle of interconnected roots. A rich layer of humus begins to form on the soil surface. Eventually, the crowns of the trees meet, and the lawn below is taken over by shade-tolerant groundcovers and shrubs. In this time, the suburban landscape begins to support a different animal population. Orioles, tanagers, raccoons, and opossums are typical creatures of the tall trees of a mature housing development.

Unless your lot is so small that you don't control most of the trees that affect it, you can fight the process of succession. Or you can accept it. To decide what to do, study some of the older neighborhoods in your town or city to see if you like the look and feel of them. If you decide to accept the succession, you should adapt your flowerbeds, shrubbery, and groundcovers as the trees grow and make the ground more shady and the soil more cluttered with roots. If you decide to fight the succession, then you will have to plan to thin the trees so that full sunlight can still reach the surface of the ground.

People's Imperatives

The most unrelenting imperatives of all are those imposed by the people who use your landscape: you, the members of your family, guests who come into your home, strangers who come to your door, and neighborhood kids who beat a path across your lawn on their way to and from school. Your feet, your machines, and your pets impose a constant strain on your environment, and a good landscape plan must take account of these effects.

People Will Take the Shortest Route

No matter where you set out the walks and the driveways, people on foot will take the shortest route from one point to another. Let's say you plan to make your back entry more charming and intimate. From your driveway to your back door, you intend to install a quaint curving brick walk. The idea is that visitors will stroll along the walk, enjoying the colors, textures, and fragrances of your perennial herbs and flowers. Be warned! Only strangers will follow the walk. Everybody else will shortcut the curves, trample your herbs, and track mud through the house. In two years your bricks will be completely unworn, and a furrow 3 inches deep will be cut through your kitchen garden to the side door.

If you want to induce even your closest friends to use a path other than the shortest route, you must put up barriers. If you really mean business, the barriers should be shin-high and hard or prickly. A sturdy hedge, a brick wall, a well-braced wire fence—nothing less will discourage the economizing imperative of human feet.

Security Must Be Considered

It's a sad fact of life that many urban and suburban gardeners must think seriously about security. Backyards that become covert trafficways invite intrusion into the house from the rear. Shady back gates that are intimate and inviting by day can become dangerous trouble spots where muggers may lurk by night.

In communities where security is a problem, your landscaping plans must include provision for adequate lighting and for control of traffic across your own property. You may or may not want to go as far as to obey "McGruff the Crime Dog's" warnings against foundation plantings or screening along the street. To us, giving up privacy for the sole purpose of allowing the police a clear field of fire from the street seems too big a concession to make for security. But you should give the matter some consideration.

There Will Be Utilities

Whatever your landscape plans, they must make provision for getting electricity, gas, water, and telephone service into your house, and getting garbage and sewage out. If you plant a tree under a power line, the tree will grow, and eventually the electric company will come and hack off some of its limbs to protect their wires. If you plant a tree over a gas or sewer line, one day the line will rupture and a backhoe will pay a visit to your yard

and shear off the tree's roots. If you plant a quaint little herb garden just outside your kitchen door, once a week the garbage men will set the empty trash cans down on it. If you plant a rose arbor on the septic tank, in time rumblings in your plumbing will spell the demise of your arbor.

Regrettably, we must make provision in our plans for all the unsightly essentials of modern life. Don't put permanent or semi-permanent structures or plantings where they will interfere with the maintenance of utilities. And make sure you leave adequate space for service people to work.

Pets Will Use Your Yard

If you have an attractive and interesting yard, the neighborhood's pets, yours and others, will be the first to find it. The dogs will romp in it, and the cats will relish its soft soil. Your yard will become a neighborhood social center for animals. You may not care and, if you don't, that's fine. But if you'd rather not have the neighbors' dogs mauling your tomatoes, then you have to put up barriers to exclude such guests.

There Will Be Automobiles

The weight, size, and maneuverability of automobiles impose crucial limits on possible yard plans. Unless you have a clearly defined driveway, people will drive their cars as close to your house as they reasonably can without damaging their tires. You must allow either enough room for a car to turn around, or so little room that nobody is tempted to try to turn around. Anything in the middle leads to damaged hedges, rutted flowerbeds, and bumped garages.

Automobiles are so often the cause of design problems that we have devoted chapter 15, "Circulation Problems," entirely to that subject. For details of driveway and entry design, we urge you to look at that chapter.

Things to Keep in Mind

Did you:

Evaluate your plans for:

- balance
- proportion
- pattern
- flow

Make sure:

- that there is enough sun for the plants you want to put in
- that the trees you have planted will take the wind in your neighborhood
- that the water has a place to flow and drain

Prepare for:

- how your and your neighbors' pets will use the landscape

Think about:

- how your garden will look in five years when all the plants have grown
- the compatibility of your plants: does each have room to grow without interfering with the others?
- the likely succession of plants in your landscape

Provide for:

- foot traffic
- adequate lighting and security
- gas lines; water lines or well; telephone lines; electricity; septic tank or sewage; oil tank

Wrap-up

The goal of this chapter has been to help forestall disappointments and regrets. The best use of the chapter is as a sort of checklist to help you remember and avoid the difficulties that may arise in a badly designed garden. For instance, we're trying to head off the day, twenty years from now, when the water contractor yells at you over the engine of his backhoe: "I'm sorry, sir, we're going to have to cut down this-here beech tree to get to the well! Where would you like us to stack the wood?" Such are dark days in the life of a gardener who has nursed a little copper beech from whiphood to shade-giving age. Firewood seems an inadequate harvest of all that love and labor. We know you will want to avoid such days if you can.

CHAPTER 13

Doing Your Own Design

*I*f you have been following along, thinking about the things we have been urging you to think about, doing the things we have suggested you do, you have in fact been designing your own landscape. You have pondered who you are and what you want; you have taken inventory of the good and bad points of your site; you have investigated what features are possible in your landscape; and you have thought about the imperatives of design, environment, plants, and people. Now it's time to put all this thinking together into a comprehensive plan, perhaps for your whole yard, or perhaps for some part of your yard.

A plan means different things to different people. It can mean anything from a rough sketch scribbled on the back of an envelope to an elaborate scale model with cardboard cutouts of the structures and plants to be put in the garden. In writing a book for diverse readers, we authors face a problem. Some of you are spontaneous people who like to do your designs with a broken twig in the dirt on planting day. Others of you are planners. You enjoy making detailed plans and models and seeing exactly how your projects are going to come out before you start on them. In writing a chapter on making a landscape plan for either of these two groups, we run the risk of putting off the other.

What to do? Well, first we should admit to being plan-makers ourselves. Not that we haven't had our spontaneous moments. Each of us has at some time or other wandered around the yard with a bunch of fresh plants from the nursery in one hand and a spade in the other saying, "Where shall I put these plants?" Each of us has thrown plants into the ground and hoped that they would live. And some of them *have* lived. But on the average, we have to admit that we have had the most satisfying results in our own gardens when we have thought out our projects in advance.

Second, as authors, we would rather make errors of commission than errors of omission. If we write an extensive chapter on plan making, you spontaneous gardeners can skip it or skim it, and there's no harm done. But if we *don't* write such a chapter, then we leave the planners among you high and dry. Consequently, what follows is fairly detailed.

In this chapter, we will try to make it possible for you to spread your entire garden out on your living room floor or dining room table. You will need to buy or borrow a 50-foot tape measure, some stakes, a T-square and right-angle triangle, a draftsman's compass, a few HB or B pencils, a soft eraser, some large sheets of tracing or transparent graph paper, some masking tape, and a scaling ruler. Two kinds of scaling rulers are available. The scales on an engineer's ruler are based on tenths of an inch. They are marked in tenths, twentieths, thirtieths, fortieths, and so forth. Engineer's rulers are particularly useful for designing large areas such as an entire yard. The scales on an architect's ruler are based on fourths of an inch. They are marked in halves, fourths, eighths, and sixteenths of an inch, and are more useful for smaller projects such as a deck, patio, or flowerbed.

The drafting supplies can be obtained from an architects' or artists' supply store or university bookstore, or by raiding the desk of any high school student who is taking a drafting class. They will provide you with the means to spend many a happy winter evening planting and replanting shrubs, putting up and tearing down walls, grading lawns, building decks, installing patios, and digging and filling swimming pools. Not only is dining-table landscaping an exciting activity, it's a lot cheaper than the real thing. For a few cents, you can make and correct mistakes on your dining room table that would take months and thousands of dollars to correct if you actually made them in your yard.

To impetuous gardeners, we'll say goodbye for a few pages. Planners, this chapter is written especially for you. Doing a landscape plan entails four steps: drawing a base plan, drawing a plan of existing conditions, making a functional plan (or what we call a "bubble diagram"), and drafting a final working plan that shows your garden as it will finally look when you are finished putting it in. We will lead you through each of these steps.

Making a Base Plan

To make designing easy and fun, you need a basic map of your property showing the positions of all the buildings, the street line, the property boundaries, and all the features of your landscape you are *sure* won't change. You will use this base plan in a variety of ways. You may want to make dozens of photocopies of it, so that you can sketch in different ideas and pass them around the family. Or you may want to make a series of "overlays" directly on the base map showing different aspects of the garden.

While it's possible to make a base map from scratch by the methods described below, it's much easier to adapt a plot plan or site survey done previously by others. There are several places you might find such a plot plan of your property: attached to your deed at the county courthouse, in a city planning office, or in the files of a developer or architect are three of the most likely.

Making Your Base Plan from a Plot or Site Plan

Once you have obtained a plot plan, you want to blow it up to "working" scale to make your base plan. The simplest way to do this is with one of the new copying machines that does reductions and enlargements. A photography store or archi-

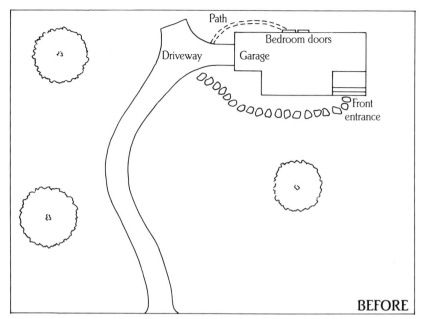

This base map shows the house and major features of a property.

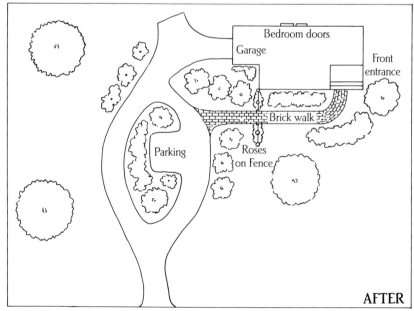

This annotated map shows a more effective and pleasing design.

tectural supply store can usually do this for you or tell you where it can be done. For convenience' sake, try to get the scale so that 1 inch on your new map will be equal to some exact number of feet on the ground. So, for instance, if the plot plan is at a scale of 1 inch equals 40 feet, you might want to blow it up exactly two times, four times, or eight times so that 1 inch on your base plan will be exactly 20, 10, or 5 feet. This will greatly simplify measuring, because by choosing the correct scale on your scaling ruler, 1/20 inch, 1/10 inch, or 1/5 inch, you can read the number of feet between things right off your ruler.

But how much should you blow up the plot plan to make your base plan? How big should your working scale be? There's nothing mysterious about deciding what a good working scale is. It's the scale that gives you a piece of paper that is convenient to work with, yet shows the things that you are thinking about in enough detail to be helpful. Phebe finds that 1 inch to 10 feet is often a scale that gives a good-sized plan with good detail. She thinks that a 2-by-3-foot plan is about as big as she would ever want to carry around. You might have a smaller working space and find even a 2-by-3-foot plan too much to handle. It's up to you. While you are at the copying machine or the photography store, you might want to blow up the plot plan to a couple of scales, one small enough to show the whole property, the other large enough to show the parts of the property you are concentrating on in detail.

If you are making your base plan from a blown-up plot plan, your first problem is to "find" your house, if it's not already shown. To do so, you must locate some of the points depicted in the plot plan on the ground. If you are lucky, you will find iron pins, stone bounds, or other markers driven in the ground at the corners of your lot. These will be indicated on the plot plan. If you are not so lucky,

you will have to estimate where a corner is from intersections of walls or other boundary markers on the ground. Once you have found two points on the ground that correspond to points on your plot plan, you are all set. Measure carefully from each of these points to each of two corners of the house.

Now you are ready to place your house on the map. The technique you need is called "triangulation." Measuring with your scaling ruler, spread the two points of your draftsman's compass an amount which corresponds in the scale of your map to the distance from one of your reference points to one of the corners of the house. For instance, let's say the distance from the corner of your house to the reference point on the boundary is 33 feet, and you are working in a scale of 1 inch to 10 feet. Use the side of your scaling ruler which is marked out in tenths of an inch. Put one pin of the compass on 0 and the other on 33 tenths (or 3.3 inches).

Now put one of the pins of the compass on the reference point, and swing an arc in the general direction where you think the house corner will be on the plan. Use the other pin (or pencil tip, if the compass has one) to inscribe the arc faintly on the paper. Repeat the procedure, starting at the other reference point and setting the compass with the distance between that reference point and the corner of the house. Where the two arcs cross, there is the corner of the house. Locate the other corner in the same way and you have one wall of the house. Check to see that the side of the house is the right length, using the scaling ruler and measuring in the scale of your plan.

Once you have a single wall, the rest is easy, assuming that the walls of the house are straight and its corners are right angles. Go outside and measure the other sides of the house. Back inside, use the ruler and the right-angle triangle to mark out the other walls of the house on your map.

HOW TO DO TRIANGULATION

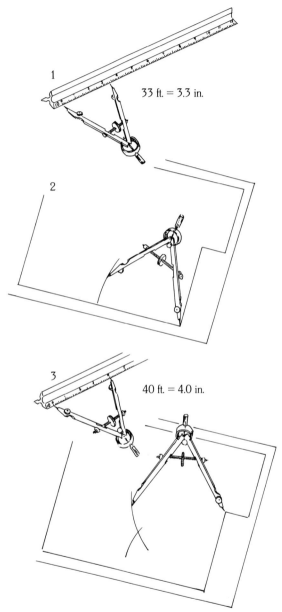

33 ft. = 3.3 in.

40 ft. = 4.0 in.

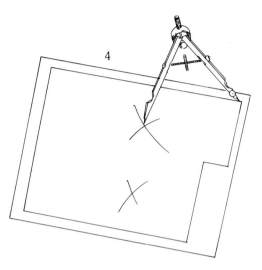

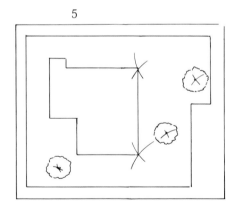

STEP 1: Set compass arc for the first reference point.

STEP 2: Draw first arc.

STEP 3: Set arc for the second reference point and draw second arc to locate corner of house.

STEP 4: Repeat procedure to mark second corner of house.

STEP 5: Finished diagram shows accurately the position of the house and permanent landscape features.

When the outline of the house is complete, you can use the same methods to locate and outline any outbuildings.

Now locate and measure any other permanent features of your landscape. The best way to do this is to use the corners of the house as starting points and measure out to the objects that you are trying to locate. To avoid little inconsistencies when you measure from different corners to the same point, always measure to the "center" of the object. Measure to the center of walls by adding half the width of the wall to the measurement. Measure to the center of trees by measuring to the outside of the tree at about waist height and then adding the radius of the tree to that measurement. (The radius of a tree is roughly one-sixth of its girth.) Estimate the dripline of the tree by measuring out from its center to the ends of a few typical branches or, with large trees, to points directly below the ends of typical branches. Show the dripline of the tree as a circle around its center.

Once you have placed several objects on the map, check your measurements by measuring from one object to another. Use your scaling ruler to measure the distance between objects on the map, convert that distance to feet on the ground, and go out with your tape measure to make sure the objects actually are that distance apart.

Drawing a Base Plan from Scratch

Everything said so far assumes that you had a site plan or a plot plan to begin with in making your base plan. If you don't, use the triangulation technique to develop your entire base plan.

Start by drawing the house on your plan. Once the house is drawn, you can use its corners to triangulate other features of your yard, including the corners and boundaries. You can also sight down the straight sides of the house to locate objects along a line. With these techniques, you will start with the buildings and work outward to the boundaries of the property, until you have located the entire perimeter of your lot on the base plan.

Whether you are preparing your base plan from scratch or from a plot plan, keep it as simple as possible. If you are in doubt whether an object is permanent or not, leave it out of your base plan and save it for the map of existing conditions which you are about to draw. It's easier to add things to a plan than it is to ignore them once they are drawn in.

After the Base Plan, What?

Once you have your base plan, you will want to decide how you are going to proceed. One simple way is to take your base plan to the nearest copying machine and make copies of it in whatever scales you find convenient. (Be sure to make plenty while you're at it.) The advantage of these sketch maps is that they are informal and easy to pass around. Everybody in the family can take a turn at designing the yard. The disadvantage of sketch maps is that, as new features get settled into place, you end up having to draw the same things over and over again.

A somewhat more complicated but more satisfying way to use your base plan is to do overlays. If you are going to do overlays, purchase some large tracing paper or transparent graph paper and some masking tape. Masking tape is better than cellophane tape because it can usually be removed without tearing the things it's holding. Tape the base plan to your drafting surface. If you use a wooden table top, be sure to cover it with a heavy piece of cardboard to protect the surface from pencil and compass points. Tape a sheet of the tracing paper on top of the base plan, and you're in business.

With this arrangement, you can draw a series of more elaborate maps of your property without redrawing the base plan each time, because you'll be able to see it through the transparent sheet on top. Overlays are particularly convenient because you can combine several to represent different ideas about how to deal with your landscape. For instance, let's imagine that you are redesigning your front yard, including your front walk. You know how you want the walk, but you have two different ideas about how to do the front yard plantings.

By drawing three overlays, you could easily examine the relationship between the front walk and each of the two planting schemes. On one overlay, draw your plan for the front walk. On two other overlays, draw the two different plans for planting and screening the front yard. By putting each of the planting overlays over the walk overlay in turn, you can see how each planting pattern interacts with the walk without having to draw the walk twice.

Map of Existing Conditions

Once you have your base plan, you are ready to make a map of the plants and other features as they are now, before you begin to rearrange them. Get out a fresh sketch map or tape a fresh sheet of tracing paper to your base plan. Using the techniques of measurement and triangulation described on pages 261 to 263, locate each of the major plants and objects in your present landscape on the overlay. The easiest way to do this is not to keep running back and forth from the drawing board to the plants, but to go outdoors and make a rough sketch map showing the objects and distances. Later, indoors, you can use these measurements to draw the objects on your plan. Once you have made the transfers, check your work by measuring between objects on the map and then re-measuring them on the ground, as before.

Start with the large important objects, and work down to small unimportant objects. You are obviously going to get tired before you measure everything, and it's best to have the important things measured before you quit. Some objects, like the irregular edges of shrub masses, can just be sketched on your map.

The hardest part about making a map of your present landscape is indicating the slope of the ground. If there is not much slope, you can simply indicate with arrows which way the slope goes. You can gauge it by referring to level or perpendicular features in the landscape like house foundations or telephone poles. Such casual methods are probably good enough for most purposes. If you do nothing else, be sure to locate and indicate low points where water flows and pools in wet weather.

Landscapers who want to be a bit more precise can take informal measurements of slope. Let's say you have a slope in your front yard and you want to know the difference in height between the top and the bottom of the slope. You need an accomplice and a carpenter's level. First, stand at the bottom of the slope and sight along the carpenter's level toward the corner of the house. Ask your accomplice to stand beside you and adjust the level in your hands until it is precisely level. Continue sighting and note where you are looking on the house. Counting clapboards from the ground or making temporary reference marks on the house are both useful tricks for making it easy to remember the point you were sighting.

Next, sight from the top of the slope, being sure to stand just as you did before. (Don't slouch when you make the first measurement and then stand tall when you make the second.) The difference between the first and second points you sighted on the house is approximately the difference in altitude between the high and low point of your slope.

Other Useful Maps

Once you have your map of existing conditions, you can make a series of overlays or sketch maps based on it. On these maps, you can make notes about crucial features of your landscape. For instance, one such map might show all the highlights in your existing landscape, another all the eyesores. You could use several sketch maps or overlays to describe different foliage and flowering patterns at various times of year. You could mark all the points in the yard from which a particularly attractive view is visible, or show the boundaries of shade in your yard at crucial times of day or year. In general, you can make use of these maps to organize any information that you want to have in front of you when you are designing your yard.

Flights of Fancy

Once you have the base plan and the map of existing conditions, the fun really begins. Depending on how radical a revision of your yard you are contemplating, you can either start with your base plan and add things, or start with your map of existing conditions and subtract things. Or do addition one day and subtraction the next. The wonderful part of improvising on paper is that mistakes don't cost you anything.

Starting with the Base Plan

Let's imagine you are the radical type. You have recently moved to a new housing development and the developer has left you pretty much with a barren piece of ground, so there's not much to worry about saving. You're ambitious and optimistic, and you hope that some day you will have a swimming pool and a tennis court on your half-acre lot. Right now, all you have time and money for are some shade trees. But you want to make some sort of a plan so you won't end up planting those trees in the middle of your future swimming pool.

In your situation, you will want to start with the base plan. Put a transparent piece of graph paper over your base plan and tape it down so that it won't move. Now think about how large a swimming pool you want, and find out how large a tennis court and backstop are. When you know the dimensions, cut out little pieces of paper to scale to represent a tennis court and a swimming pool and start moving them around the surface of your base plan. How about here? No, there's a rock ledge there. How about over here? No, it's right next to the street, and people would be forever rubbernecking and commenting on your backhand. Continue moving the pieces of paper until you have put the two features in places that make sense to you.

Now quickly mark the outlines of the swimming-pool paper and the tennis-court paper on the overlay. And presto, with your base map showing through the overlay from below, you have a map of the buildings, property boundaries, and the position of the new tennis court and swimming pool!

Out you go to the yard, armed with your tape measure and your sketch map and some stakes. Who cares if it's January and the yard has a foot of snow! You're going to mark out your swimming pool and your tennis court. (Actually, after a light snowfall is an excellent time to try out landscaping ideas, because you can use the snow like a big blackboard and mark out future features with footprints.) Measure from some of your reference points (remember, the corners of the house, intersections of boundaries, or other permanent prominent points, like telephone poles) to locate two corners of the new court, and then stake out its perimeters. Show where the net is going to be. Mark out the pool in the same way. Show where the diving board is going to be on the swimming pool. String some lines from trees to simulate the fences you are going to build. Do anything that will give you a chance to feel what your yard is going to be like after you put in the new features.

When you are satisfied that you have found places for your new tennis court and swimming pool, get out a new overlay and mark them on it precisely. This overlay, in conjunction with your original base plan, will now function as your new base plan. Tape it down solidly to your dining room table. Put another overlay on top of it. Here you will add walks, driveways, and trees in much the same way as you added the tennis court and the swimming pool to the base plan. Always be sure to go outside and try your ideas out on the ground as best you can before you consider your plan final.

When you have your best shot at a final plan, the next step is to plan how you are going to carry it out. Divide the plan into stages, one overlay to a stage. Each stage will represent a coherent project that can reasonably be carried out with the time and money you will have available at a given time. For instance, you might call Stage One "Poverty Planting," and put on it all trees that you are going to be able to fit in your budget in the first year. Stage Two might be "Moving the Driveway." Stage Three might be "The Pool and Its Fences," Stage Four, "The Tennis Court." The final stage might be "Screens and Decorative Plantings." By dividing up the work into well-organized, feasible stages, you will never be left with an ugly and disordered landscape between projects. Moreover, all the stages will go together better because you have previously fit them into a final plan.

Starting with the Existing Conditions Plan

The previous scenario will work just fine if you live in the sort of property that doesn't offer many features or constraints. Some of you, how-ever, will be in the opposite situation. Let's say a previous owner has left you with a landscape that is loaded with features, and you aren't sure which fit your lifestyle and which do not. You want to make the yard your own, but you want to proceed cautiously, lest you destroy some feature of the present yard and later regret it.

For instance, let's imagine that you bought a house whose yard has tall trees, large shrubs, and a small shady lawn. To you the yard seems very pleasant, but a bit overgown and shut in. You would like to make it feel more open and airy and free up enough sunny space for flowerbeds.

Start with the existing conditions map. Tape a clean overlay on it, and trace onto the overlay everything except the features you are sure you want to remove. Now, remove the existing condi-tions map from under your overlay so that you are left with the new overlay and the base map. Study this new plan to see how much space has been freed up by moving the undesirable plants.

If more space is needed, then you can remove (with your eraser, of course) some plants that are desirable but just seem to be in the wrong place. (Or if these plants are small, you might "transplant" them by drawing them to scale on pieces of paper and moving them around the plan.) Working in this way, you can generate in a short time a tenta-tive plan of your new leaner and sunnier garden.

Out you go to your yard with a copy of your tentative plan and some markers. The best markers are those colored streamers that surveyors use, but bits of paper, rags, or anything else will do that makes the marked trees stand out from the rest. Put markers on the trees you want to eliminate. Try to imagine what the yard would be like without them.

Admittedly, imagining the absence of some-thing when it is present is much harder than imag-ining its presence when it is absent, but do your best. A few tricks make pretending easier. If the

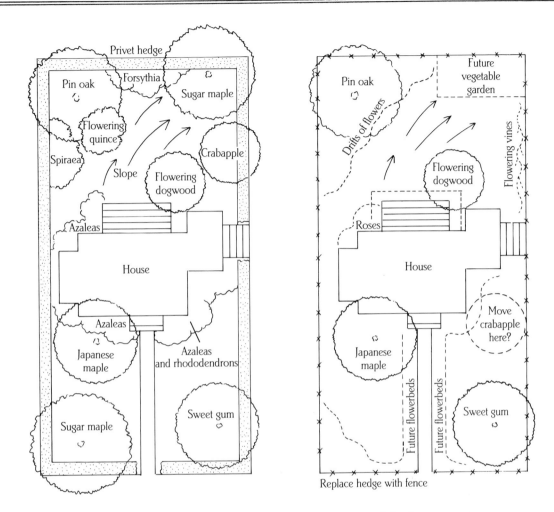

The existing conditions map at left shows a yard crammed with trees and shrubs. Judicious use of eraser and pencil shows how removing some features and substituting others would open up this yard. Planning on paper helps you decide what you want before you dig up or cut down any plants.

plant you are considering cutting is small, get a stepladder, climb the ladder (carefully!), and look out over the plant. Or get a large piece of material and cover the plant to make it "disappear." If the plant is large enough so that you can kneel, sit, or stand beneath it, put your back to its trunk and look out under it. These tricks will help you see what the yard will be like after the work is done.

Using Both Base and Existing Conditions Plans

So far, we have offered you two extreme procedures for doing your design: starting from the base plan and adding everything, on the one hand, and on the other, starting from your plan of existing conditions and subtracting a few features. Most people will probably want to adopt some of both procedures. Things just won't be as clear at the start as wanting something definite like a tennis court or a swimming pool, or as vague as just wanting to cut down a few trees to get more light and space. You will know that you want more features in your yard, but you won't know where to put them and what form to give them. It is you middle people who have the real designing job ahead of you. You will need to do a function or "bubble" diagram.

Making a Bubble Diagram

Let's say, for example, that you have just taken over a house that was owned by people who didn't have much interest in their yard. They had a decorative rail fence along their street frontage, some shade trees, a few shrubs, and a lawn maintained by a landscape maintenance company. That was that. About their only contact with their landscape was when they came and went in their cars. As you survey their landscape, you come to the conclusion that it's too barren and impersonal for your taste. But you note that some of the trees are healthy and growing well, and you would like to try to work them into your plan, if you can.

Imagine, further, that you have moved to this house with a variety of potentially conflicting purposes in mind. You want to raise some flowers and some vegetables and provide a place for children and pets to romp. You hope to spend sunny spring days reading in the sun and summer days reading in the shade. You have no ideas about whether or where to try to fit these activities into your garden. How do you proceed? Do you start with your base plan or your existing conditions plan?

Well, the answer to is to work with both until you are certain how many of your proposed activities really work with one another and how well they all work with the existing landscape. But first, you need to make up some "bubbles." A bubble is a paper cutout which occupies the square footage—according to the scale of your base plan and existing conditions plan—that you want to set aside for the activity. So you ask yourself, "Ideally, how much room do I want for my kids to play?"

First, go outdoors and locate a bit of open space. If your own yard doesn't have it, borrow a neighbor's yard or a corner of a neighborhood park for a few minutes. Using sticks (or shoes or jackets) mark out an area that seems big enough for the activity you are contemplating. What will your family members be doing in that area? Playing soccer? Baseball? Or just tag? What size of people are going to play there? (Tag played by 7-year-olds takes a lot less space than tag played by 10-year-olds—or even 25-year-olds, as some friends of ours discovered to their dismay last Fourth of July.)

When you have marked out a suitable area for a play space on the ground, measure it roughly and then, using graph paper, cut out a piece of paper that is the corresponding size. Now you have your play-space bubble. Do the same with your sunny reading space, your shady reading space, and your vegetable garden. Don't worry about the shape of the bubbles too much at this stage. Just get the size about right.

Next, go to your existing conditions map and see if you can fit the bubbles in. Perhaps you can get the play space in the front yard and the garden in the back, or perhaps the garden in the front and the play space in the back. Does that leave room for the reading space? Keep moving the bubbles around until you know if they are all going to fit on the existing conditions map.

If there's not enough room on the existing conditions map for all the bubbles, then peel off the existing conditions overlay and move the bubbles around the base map. Can you fit your bubbles on the base map? If you get a fit you like, then lay the existing conditions overlay down on the base map with the bubbles on it. What features of the existing conditions would have to give way if you had the activities where the bubbles are? What trees would you have to cut down? What fences would have to be moved?

If you can't fit your bubbles on the base map, think about your priorities. Which is it going to be, a vegetable garden *or* a play space? A shady reading area *or* a sunny reading area (or perhaps *one* reading area that is shady in the summer and sunny in the fall and spring)? Once you have decided which of the activities you are going to fit in, then it's time to go back to the existing conditions plan and see if this reduced list will now fit.

If the bubbles now fit into the existing conditions, your task is about done. If not, back you go to the base map, and so forth, back and forth until you have either an existing conditions map with some or all of the bubbles in place, or a base plan with the bubbles on it and all of the existing features removed.

Now, go back out to the yard and mark the areas out on the ground where they are on the plan. Leave them marked out for a few weeks, if possible. Try to use them for their intended functions. If the weather is fine, sit in the sunny reading area and read. Send the kids out in the play space to play. Try to get a sense of how the spaces will feel. How are the various activities going to interact with one another?

Once you are pretty sure where the bubbles are going to fit, you can begin to worry about access to the areas and the screening of the different activities, one from another. If the play space has to be right next to the sunny reading space, then you might want to consider a fence or a hedge. If the shady reading space is between the kitchen door and the vegetable garden, you might want to design a path that will carry the traffic around the edge of the reading space, so the gardeners in your

family won't always be traipsing through interrupting your reading. Each time you add a feature to your plan, go out and mark it out on the ground so that you can get the best possible idea of how the feature will work when the plan is carried out.

Of course, at any time in this process you may discover that there is a fundamental incompatibility between the activities you are trying to put together. You may discover, for instance, that the only way for the kids to get from the kitchen to the play space is through the middle of the vegetable garden. Such discoveries will be unfortunate, but think how much less unfortunate on paper than on the ground. Instead of muddy rugs and trampled carrots, you just have a few flecks of graphite and artist's eraser to dispose of.

The result of all this running back and forth between the yard and the drawing board will be your finished function or bubble diagram. It will be a map showing the areas that will be devoted to various functions and the secondary functions that arise from these, like buffering one area from another and getting from one to the other. But so far, no plants have been filled in. To get from the bubble diagram to the finished plan, you need to do a planting diagram.

Filling in the Design

Once you have the plan of your garden with its activity areas and access routes and screens drawn, the last step in making the design is to fill in the different areas with particular plants that meet the function specifications you have been setting down. For instance, if you are seeding a lawn that is going to be a heavy-use play area, you will want to do some research and find out exactly what sorts of grass survive under that abuse. Or if you have designated on your plan a large, fast-growing shade tree with a thin shade and a short shade season, you will want to find out which trees meet these needs. As you learn the information you need, write it down on your plan so you won't forget: "Lawn seeded to Soil Conservation Mix, 1 pound per 100 square feet," or "4-inch-diameter honey locust."

Where do your ideas come from? Everywhere. From friends, from neighbors, from parks, from magazines, from programs on television— anywhere you see a garden or a garden feature that you would like to have. And, of course, from the previous section of this book.

Wrap-up

Designing for yourself begins with finding space in your landscape for the activities that are important to you. To begin, you must have a plan of those elements of your landscape that you are absolutely sure will not change, because these are the elements into which the activities must fit. You also need a plan of the landscape as it now is, because such a plan tells you some of the resources available to you for your final landscape. No matter how unimaginative your present landscape is, its plants are in the ground and growing and they constitute a precious resource. Finally, you will need to decide how much space you require for each of the activities you hope to enjoy in your landscape. What follows is a cut-and-fit process in which you move the spaces around on your plans until you have an arrangement of activity spaces that fits. After that, you have only to fill in the functional spaces with the names of various plants, and your landscape design is complete.

CHAPTER 14

Eyesores and Design Flaws

*I*t's a curiosity of human nature that people can usually say what they *don't* like before they can say what they *do* like. When people come to see Phebe, it's usually about a landscaping problem, such as too much shade, an ugly garage roof, an irritating view, or a distressingly functional fence. They may be tired of looking at the utility poles in the front yard or the garbage cans in the back. Maybe their front entry is so crowded by the overgrown wisteria vine that arriving guests must back off the front stoop to open the door. Perhaps the foundation plantings are lapping at their living room windows, or the evergreens have inundated the sun room. Or maybe they are tired of mowing a gigantic lawn every week, or weary of neighbors' children and pets taking shortcuts through the alyssum.

Phebe sometimes startles her new clients. When they want to talk about what's bad about their landscape, she wants to talk about what's good about it. Paradoxical as it may seem, the good features of a landscape often lie at the heart of its problems. A homeowner's awareness of a landscaping problem implies attractive features of the landscape that bring the problems into focus. A dusty old Volkswagen wouldn't pose a landscaping problem in a junkyard. But park that same car next to a rose arbor and it becomes a hideous eyesore. A cement walk isn't ugly when it leads up to a factory, but leading up to a quaint Cape Cod cottage it's a monstrosity. A dog run isn't an eyesore at a kennel, but it would desecrate a Japanese tea garden. A landscape never has a problem unless there is something attractive about it to make the problem stand out.

This is why you must appreciate the good points in your landscape before you can begin to solve its problems. Generally, the good features that reveal your landscaping problem are one or more of the garden attractions we have presented in the previous section of the book. They are a pleasant shady place or a pleasant sunny one, a patch of flowers or a bit of inviting green lawn, a little pool of water, or a nice stone wall with ivy growing on it, or some other pleasant feature of your landscape that is causing you to notice the hydrant or the garbage cans or the clumsy front door stoop.

Sometimes, the problem area may itself be a potential asset. Features may add or detract from a landscape, depending on how they are treated. The boggy place in the garden may be a potential water feature. The overheated, glaring wall of the garage may be a place to display cacti. The deeply shaded north side of the house may be a place to grow decorative ferns. Knowing the potential good points of a landscape gives you the best chance of turning its vices into additional virtues.

Thus, when you are doing away with negative features of your landscape, you proceed in exactly the same way as when you are trying to incorporate positive features. You start by thinking about yourself, your habits, your pleasures, your activities in the garden, what you like to do there, and what you like about the way it looks. Only then can you begin to appreciate what the problem is and why it is bothering you. Capitalize on the assets of your property to make your landscape useful and beautiful and to make its problems fade into insignificance.

Analyzing Landscape Problems

Problems in landscape design vary to the degree that they are a problem *in* the landscape or a problem *of* the landscape. Problems *of* the landscape are design flaws. When the design of your landscape is flawed, each of its elements—its transition spaces, its lawns, its flowerbeds, and its trees —may be elegant and tasteful by itself, but the total effect is disorderly and inconvenient in some way. Problems *in* the landscape are eyesores. The worst sort of eyesore is an excruciatingly ugly element set down in a landscape that is otherwise well designed.

As you are thinking about your landscape problem, it is important to ponder whether you are dealing with an eyesore or a design flaw. Why? Because the two kinds of problems require different solutions. With an eyesore, the problem arises from the tension between the eyesore and a basically harmonious landscape. The problem can usually be solved by dealing with the eyesore in some way. With a design flaw, the problem arises from the ill-conceived arrangement of elements. Everywhere you look, you see something that's nice, and still, for some reason, you aren't happy with your yard. Design flaws must be solved by rearranging elements. Making changes in particular elements usually won't solve the problem.

Confusing design flaws with eyesores and vice versa leads to trouble. With landscapes, as with people, you must beware of "scapegoating." Scapegoating with people occurs when a troubled group blames its problems on one of the group's members. Scapegoating is disastrous, because throwing out the alleged troublemaker is itself a disruptive process and rarely solves the problem. "*Land*scapegoating" is similarly ill-advised. You go to the effort to eliminate the alleged eyesore—you get the driveway rerouted, or you fence out the neighbor's laundry line—only to discover that your efforts haven't improved your garden as much as you hoped.

So don't rush into any quick solutions to your design problems, particularly if those solutions are expensive or wreak havoc on the day-to-day lives of family members. Take time to study the problem. Careful thought and patient observation are crucial to arriving at good solutions to landscape difficulties.

Eyesores and Ugly Views

Face it: Many of the necessities of modern life are not exactly attractive. Electric wires, gas tanks, telephone poles, fire hydrants, and garbage cans are not aesthetic objects, nor are the machines that come to service them. If such ugly objects seem to be salient features of your landscape, then the time has come to figure out why.

The first step in dealing with an eyesore is to figure out what landscape highlight is drawing attention to it. Are the electric wires ugly because they dangle across the pleasant colonial facade of your house? Are the gas tanks ugly because they stand next to your sunny kitchen herb patch? Does the clothesline obscure the view of the lawn from your dining room windows?

To identify the conflicting features in your yard, try to imagine what it would look like without the eyesore. Visualizing your yard without the eyesore may be a difficult task. Eyesores are often strong design elements. But try it. Go out in the yard and look at the eyesore from every angle. Try standing at a distance and holding your hand so that it obscures the eyesore. Try standing just around the corner of a building so that you see your property with the eyesore just out of sight. Drape the eyesore with a sheet to diminish the strength of its form. What is the yard like without the eyesore? What are the pleasant features that are making the eyesore such an irritant?

Beware of landscapegoating. Consider the possibility that the object you think is an eyesore is taking the rap for a design flaw of some sort. For instance, if the problem is a brilliant yellow hydrant where your spacious lawn meets the street, is it really fair to blame the problem on the hydrant? Every pleasant view must come to an end, if not in the hydrant, then in the stop sign at the corner, or the cars parked along the curb. Perhaps the fact that you are noticing the hydrant means that your yard needs some definition so that your eyes don't go wandering into the street looking for trouble.

Once you have assured yourself that the eyesore is the problem, and once you have identified the attractions, then you are ready to choose your strategies for dealing with the eyesore. They are: eliminate, isolate, consolidate, screen, and distract.

The best strategy is to *eliminate* the eyesore altogether. Can you put the power lines underground? Can you put your oil storage tank in the basement? Could a small shed be built for the garbage cans? Such solutions end the problem immediately and permanently.

If you cannot eliminate the problem, you may be able to *isolate* it. Is there a way to move the eyesore away from the attractive features of your property so that they don't interact with one another? Can you move the power poles so that they come into the back of your house, away from the terrace? Can you shift the gas tanks so that they are on the side of the house, away from the front entrance? Can you reorient your entrance so as to put the bulk of the house between the neighbor's right-of-way and the part of the yard you and your guests use most?

Often, isolation is helped by *consolidating* your eyesores. Consolidating eyesores, of course, is the whole idea behind a service entrance. You put the garbage cans, the electric meter, and the shed for your gardening tools and machines on the side of the garage away from the house. Around the other side of the house, you put all the things that you want people to see.

Once you have put your attractions and eyesores in the best possible places, then you can resort to *screening*. Fences, hedges, and arbors are the most common means of screening. Screening has to be done very carefully, or the screen itself can become an eyesore. An 8-foot-high stockade fence to screen the clothesline from the terrace may be such a dominant visual element that in the end you would rather look at the laundry than the fence. The more you can make the screen seem like a part of something else—an extension of a building, a continuation of a hedge along the back of the house—the less likely it is that the screen itself will become an eyesore.

Once your eyesore has been screened, you can employ *distraction* techniques to keep people from inspecting it too closely. Design the terrace so that its long axis directs attention to another part of the yard. Put benches, low walls, and other seating so that visitors are naturally encouraged to put their backs to the part of the yard that contains the eyesore and direct their eyes toward the part of the garden that you want them to enjoy. If your problem is an objectionable vista, frame the view with trees so it includes only the things you want to see. Or hang wind chimes, a birdhouse, or a bright plant like a fuchsia among the branches of the trees to draw your visitors' eyes away from the less presentable part of your yard.

Design Flaws
Cramped Quarters

Have you ever been backed into a rosebush during an animated conversation at a garden party? Have you ever had to tiptoe along the raised edge of a flowerbed to get to the punch and sandwiches? If so, then you know what it is like to be in a yard that's just too small.

A yard that is too small for the use to which it is put has a serious design flaw. Such a yard may contain no eyesores. In fact, everything in it may be beautiful. But still, as landscape designers say, it doesn't "work." It isn't big enough to support the activities it invites.

No yard is small or large in itself. We all have

seen beautiful urban yards, even rooftop gardens that seemed perfectly comfortable places to be. A yard or garden is only small or large in relation to the uses to which it is put. A yard to accommodate one person in a magnificent white wicker Victorian easy chair would be spacious at 100 square feet. If two people were going to sit in such a yard, it would be comfortable and intimate. Add a third person, and people and chairs would start to be uncomfortably cramped. Add two 4-year-olds and a plastic wading pool, and the yard would turn into a nightmare.

Even a very large yard can seem claustrophobic if you try to put too much in it. A tennis court is a large open space, more than an eighth of an acre. Put a tennis court down with all its fences in a quarter-acre lot along with a house, driveway, and garage, and you will end up with a very crowded yard.

A cramped feeling in a yard, like other design flaws, is usually the result of wishful thinking. Too much function is being asked of too little space. The first remedy for this ailment is a strong dose of self-discipline. You must make firm decisions about the purposes the landscape is to serve, and then design a space that encourages only those uses.

One design strategy available for tight situations is miniaturization. Miniaturization is a way of getting variety in a small space by designing small versions of the large features you see in regular gardens: a tiny pool, a diminutive rock garden, a vegetable garden in a raised bed, and so forth. You will be amazed at how many different attractions can be designed into a tiny garden if you plan carefully.

One of the wonderful things about the human mind is the way in which it adapts to new scales. Calvin saw a garden in Berkeley, California, where the owner had created what seemed a universe of plants around a tiny patio. The patio was bordered with beds raised to coffee-table height. Calvin's first impression of the space was of a pleasant patio with greenery about. But once he had been sitting for a while, he realized that each bed was carefully conceived to be a different plant world. Here, along a sunny wall, was a bed of vegetables—carrots in a few neat rows, four or five heads of 'Buttercrunch' lettuce, and a cherry tomato plant trained against the wall. In another bed were small white daisies edged with a cloud of blue ageratum. A shady corner had a small pool with some lush greenery that Calvin thinks was papyrus. Once he had been settled in the garden for a few minutes, Calvin found that each of these beds became a miniature world that kept distracting him from the conversation of his hosts.

However, miniaturization is a solution only for some landscape attractions. Since people cannot be miniaturized, landscape attractions such as games or social events cannot be miniaturized. A different solution to space problems is time-sharing. A small courtyard can be used by adults for drying clothes during the week, and by children playing games during the weekend. A patio with raised beds can serve as a flower or vegetable garden while it is also serving as a place to read or do some quiet entertaining.

Some activities fit more readily into small spaces than others. You might think that games for children would be out of the question in a small yard. On the contrary, there are many games that children enjoy which can be fixed to a point in a yard so that they don't disturb other activities or endanger plants. Tetherball is a game played with a ball which is fixed to a central pole. One hundred square feet make an ample tetherball court, and both adults and children can have a terrific time playing the game. Hopscotch and handball courts can be marked out with different colors of brick in the paving. Croquet and badminton are excellent lawn games which (when played according to the rules) are restrained and compatible with a small yard.

To make a successful small yard, you must make a firm decision about what is going to go on in it. To avoid wishful thinking when you are planning a small yard, remember if at all possible to try the activities out in place before you move a single stone or a clot of earth. Get the members of the family out in the yard with all the lawn chairs and have them pretend to be a garden party. Mark out places on the ground for flowerbeds and vegetable gardens. Bring some houseplants outdoors and put them where the flowerbeds will be. How does it feel? Are people able to move around, or are they constantly tripping over each other?

Once you have established what activities are going to go on in your small yard, the next step is to design a yard which encourages only those activities. You want to define spaces clearly. Walls, fences, raised flowerbeds, and curbs are all features that give space definition and prevent the various features of the garden from being compromised. Fixed benches serve as the nucleus for the beginning of conversations. If you have a comfortable bench in a pleasant part of your yard, people will tend to gravitate to it. Other people who want to join the conversation will pull up chairs, and the party will form where you want it to, rather than on the front doorstep or in the walkway.

The final rule of small-space landscaping is to design for durability. A successful small yard will be intensively used. If it has soft surfaces, they will be muddy in wet weather and dusty in dry. To keep the yard from looking bare and trampled like a livestock pen, put down an all-weather surface—flagstones, bricks, decking—something that will resist the wear and tear of many pairs of feet.

Once you have the basics of your small yard down, then you might try some architect's tricks to create a sense of space. Often by the skillful use of perspective, a design can fool you into thinking that there is much more space in a landscape than there actually is. A grape arbor which looks like it has parallel lines, but whose lines actually converge slightly, can appear to fade off into the distance and give an illusion of depth where there is none. Reflecting pools also lend an air of spaciousness to a small yard. A carefully placed mirror lets you see both sides of a plant and doubles the apparent size of a flowerbed. A baffle of open-weave fencing across the end of your yard gives the illusion of greater space beyond. If possible, arrange small spaces so that light comes in from above. Spaces which are open to the sky feel more roomy than those that are open to the side but closed to the sky.

No Sun, Too Much Sun

Another symptom of flawed design is a complaint about too much or too little sun. Every year, Phebe gets calls from two kinds of people. The first type has just moved into a new house. The developer has left them with a barren lot, a few fledgling trees in the front yard, and some scrawny evergreens planted by the front entrance. All summer long the sun beats down on their terrace and makes it uninhabitable. They are desperate. Here they moved to the country to get outside, and now they all spend the summer months inside with the windows closed and the air conditioning on. Even the kids huddle by the television all day instead of getting out to do all those things that people move to the country so their kids can do.

These people want Phebe to get busy and plant some shade trees for them. Let's start, they say, by installing a large-growing nursery tree right here in the middle of the patio, and another over here to shade the south windows of the house, and another to cast shade on the roof so the attic won't heat up so. Let's plant an arbor over here to shade

the entry. And let's make it all fast-growing stuff so it will be big and cast a lot of shade *soon*.

The second type of people are living in an older neighborhood, developed perhaps a hundred years ago. Their yard is dominated by a huge shade tree which some sun-fearing owner planted a century ago and which the present owners can't figure out how to handle. For a month each year, the tree is the most beautiful feature of their yard. It shelters house and lawn from the baking rays of the summer sun. Its leaves fill the air with cooling moisture, and the wind in them makes a soothing sound. After a hot July day downtown in the city, the yard is the ideal place to sit and have a glass of iced tea.

But the rest of the year is a different story. On mild summer days, when the owners would like to do a little lounging in the sunlight, no sunlight can be found. When they try to plant a few tomatoes along a south-facing wall, the tomatoes become leggy and don't produce much fruit. In winter, the yard is dank and cold under the looming branches of the tree. The snow stands on the patio all winter long. The roots of the big tree have rumpled the bricks and disturbed the foundations of the deck so that a level place to put a lawn chair or a table is difficult to come by. The owners of this yard want to talk to Phebe about cutting their tree down.

Phebe often wishes she could get these people to talk to each other. She would like the people who wish they had tall trees to learn that those trees can have real drawbacks much of the year. And she would like the people who wish they didn't have tall trees to see how much people who don't have shade trees long for them. If such a conversation took place, perhaps there would be less careless planting and cutting of trees.

Solving these problems requires balancing the benefits and burdens of changing the landscape and keeping it the way it is. Of course, the owners of the overly sunny house will want to do some planting. But they should also develop their sunny location as an asset. Similarly, the owners of the overly shady house may want to do some pruning or even remove one of the large trees. But they also should think of taking advantage of their situation. If too much sun or too much shade is your complaint, study chapters 6 and 11, "Sundecks and Other Sunspots" and "Woodswalks." Remember, the best landscapes are those that most fully develop the potential of their sites.

Swimming Pools

As landscaping problems, swimming pools are in a class by themselves. In one sense, they seem to be like large eyesores that should merely be screened off or lived with. On the other hand, swimming pools have such an enormous impact on people's behavior that their misplacement can be fatal to a landscape. Before you decide that a swimming pool is for you, think carefully about the following issues.

Swimming Pools Are Expensive. Even before you start landscaping your pool, you will probably have paid an enormous amount of money for it. For the cost of a swimming pool, you could have a landscape designer make and install a sumptuous custom garden. For the cost of maintaining a swimming pool—water, chemicals, electricity, filters, and cleaning equipment, as well as maintenance of the deck, walls, and liner—you might have your landscape cared for by a part-time gardener. Be sure your swimming pool doesn't devour all the resources you might devote to other useful and pleasant features in your landscape.

Swimming Pools Are a Big Responsibility. As long as the pool is full, you must worry constantly about neighbors' pets and children—to say nothing of your own—straying into it and drowning. When the pool is empty, you still must worry about somebody taking a nasty fall, even if he wouldn't drown. A swimming pool must be securely fenced, and its gate must be kept scrupulously locked whenever the pool is not actually in use.

Swimming Pools Are Architecturally Demanding. Like driveways, garages, and telephone poles, a swimming pool and the fences that surround it are strong and rarely graceful architectural elements. Making them fit into the landscape and making other features of the environment fit with them is a difficult task, even for experienced landscape architects.

Swimming Pools Are Extremely Unstable Design Elements. The impact of the swimming pool on the landscape changes dramatically from summer to winter. During the warm months, it's the central feature of the yard for the whole family. For the rest of the year, it's desolate and ignored, a sterile and lonely space. Any solution that you dream up that incorporates a summer swimming pool in your design is unlikely to work for your pool in winter, and vice versa.

Having said all this, it must be admitted that no experience quite equals walking out your front door in the morning and plunging into your very own swimming pool. Or taking a moonlight dip before you go to bed. Or alternating between baking yourself in the sun and basting yourself in the pool, all in the privacy and quiet of your own yard.

If you have decided, despite all the difficulties, that a pool is for you, consider two strategies for minimizing the impact of the pool on your landscape. The first is to incorporate the pool in

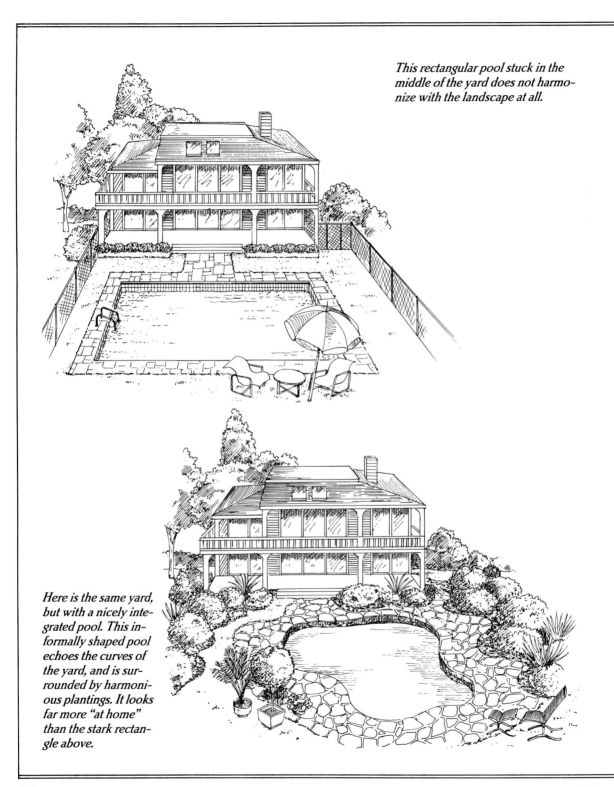

This rectangular pool stuck in the middle of the yard does not harmonize with the landscape at all.

Here is the same yard, but with a nicely integrated pool. This informally shaped pool echoes the curves of the yard, and is surrounded by harmonious plantings. It looks far more "at home" than the stark rectangle above.

the design of the house. The philosophy underlying this strategy is that, while a pool is a strong visual element, a house is even stronger. If you keep the pool near the house, the house dominates it and the pool doesn't seem quite so large.

At the other extreme, you can relegate the pool to its own separate yard, separated by hedges or fencing from the rest of the yard. Architecturally, this is the best solution, since you can design the surroundings of the pool to suit its active season and stay away from the area when it's too cold to swim. The drawbacks of this solution, however, are many and obvious. It's harder to keep watch over an isolated pool, and it's more likely to have security problems. Moreover, isolating the pool demands giving over a part of your yard to the swimming pool year-round. Unless you have a lot of space or a long swimming season, this solution will seem awfully wasteful.

In short, go cautiously into any landscaping project that involves a swimming pool. Unless you are very lucky or very wealthy, any swimming pool is going to involve aesthetic compromises. If, after all these warnings, you decide to go ahead with your pool, remember three points: Get good advice from as many sources as possible; plan the project carefully, well in advance of the arrival of the pool contractor; and most important of all, save us a place by the pool. We'll be over to take a dip just as soon as the weather warms up!

Solutions to Some Knotty Landscaping Problems
The O'Learys' Bank

The O'Learys' bank illustrates very nicely the relationship between an attraction and an eyesore. The O'Learys live on the north slope of a steep hill. Their street goes straight down the hill and the houses along it are laid out in a series of terraces, sort of like steps leading down the side of the street.

Over the years, the O'Learys have never given much thought to their two side yards. The focus of their outdoor life has been the front and the backyard: The front, which faces east onto the street, is where people come and go from the house; the back, which faces west, consists of an informal lawn surrounded by a few scraggly rhododendrons and a rickety stockade fence.

During the last oil crisis, Mr. O'Leary got the idea that it would be good to let some south light into the house. Mrs. O'Leary agreed and suggested a greenhouse window in the south-facing wall of the kitchen, so that she could grow herbs in winter and a few bedding plants in spring.

As soon as the window was completed, Mrs. O'Leary realized that they had manufactured an eyesore. Looking out the expansive frame of her greenhouse window, she noticed for the first time the steep bank that separated their lot from the next, higher lot to the south. It was a sad sight. When the lots were leveled years ago, the contractors had roughly graded the bank and planted some pachysandra. The groundcover had only partially done its job, and the bank had eroded. Several small boulders had rolled loose from the

The O'Learys' bank—an eyesore turned into an attraction.

top of the bank and were strewn among the poor, ragged groundcover.

The solution to the O'Learys' problem was to transform the ugly bank into an attraction. They had the bank excavated to just short of the property line. A local stonemason erected a stone retaining wall. Then the O'Learys laid a brick terrace between the house and the wall, just outside the new greenhouse window.

Now, whenever Mrs. O'Leary looks out her window, she sees her hand-built stone wall and her lovely terrace. The terrace is not only satisfying to look at, it serves as an additional living area for the O'Learys during the summer months. In June and July, the terrace receives direct sunlight, and in May and August a pleasant sunlight filters through the leaves of the neighbor's trees. What started as an attempt to bring a little light into their kitchen ended up as a redesign of their yard and major change of their summer habits.

The Roths: Getting More Out of a Small Lot

When the Roths moved to their new neighborhood in a midwestern suburb, they were a family of five: two parents, two nursery-school-aged children, and a new puppy, a Shetland sheepdog. The house they chose sat in the middle of its lot, with its front yard open to the street and a fence around the sides and back. A previous owner had attractively landscaped the front entrance, and the backyard contained two old maples. The south side yard had a hedge along the fence which helped to screen out the sights and sounds of the neighbor's house, on just the other side of the fence. Otherwise, the lot was featureless.

They liked the front entrance the way it was, but they found that in the property's present form, nobody used the back or south side yard very much. The children and dog didn't use it because

every time they went out there, the parents worried that they might slip around the house and get out in the street, and called them back in again. The adults didn't use it because whenever they came out in the sunny side yard to do a little quiet reading or gardening, people walking by on the street gawked at them and the kids and the dog overran them. Liz Roth had started a little herb garden on the south side of the house, but the kids trampled it down and the dog dug it up just as fast as she planted it.

Their yard needed a thorough redesign and a careful allocation of space to specific functions. They wanted some safe romping space for the children and the dog, and some quiet sitting space for themselves. The redesign they ultimately adopted divided the small lot into three functional areas. The front north area was the service area. It included the existing parking lot for the cars, storage for bicycles and machines, and wood for the fireplace. The rear of the house was designated the play area. It included a swing and slide set up in a sandbox. The south side of the house was the adult quiet-activities area. It included a terrace and a small garden for culinary herbs and perennial flowers.

Between the areas, the Roths installed wooden fences. A high lattice fence, with a gate, screened the service area from the backyard on the northwest side of the house. Separating the play area at the back from the terrace on the southeast was an arbor framed by two lilac bushes. A low lattice fence separated the sitting area from the street. This low fence afforded some privacy on the terrace, but avoided giving its occupants a "cooped-up" feeling.

A pathway runs from the sitting area at the rear of the terrace along the side of the house and around to the front, where it meets the front walk. This walk is made of flat stones which the Roths turned up on the site. The stones are simply set on earth, and the spaces between them planted with

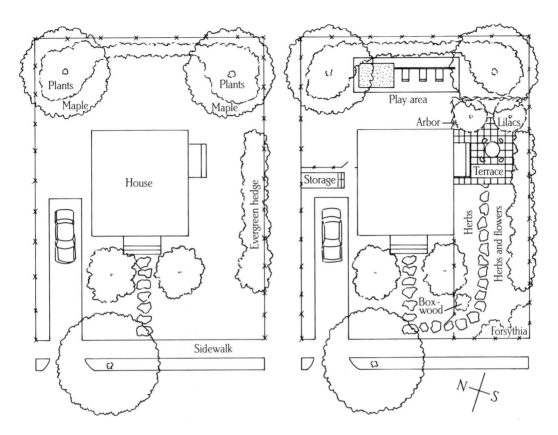

The Roth yard before (left) and after (right) the redesign.

mosses, thyme, and low speedwell, all miniature plants which can withstand some foot traffic. Along this walk, Liz has her herb and perennial garden. She has all the traditional herbs, like parsley, sage, thyme, and summer savory, and some unusual ones like chervil and rue. She has some flowers for picking, such as dahlias, roses, delphiniums, and lilies. At the front of the garden near the street the Roths planted a boxwood for accent and two azaleas for color.

The Roths are happy with their redesign. It turned an amorphous area that wasn't good for much into a well-designed yard which serves three functions very nicely.

Wrap-up

Eyesores and badly designed spaces are what bring most people to think about redesigning the space around their homes. For those readers who have such design problems, good solutions require a thorough understanding of yourself, how you use space, and the various ways in which a well-designed space can give you pleasure. The first step is identifying the problems. The second and harder step is identifying what you like about your landscape. If you have taken that step by reading the chapters on the attractions a garden can have, then solving your landscape problems should be a relatively easy task.

CHAPTER 15

Circulation Problems

*D*o you wish the kids wouldn't track through the kitchen all the time? Do you have to shuffle the cars every morning before everybody goes to work? Did the heating-oil truck back into your lamppost last month? Do the guests park on the flowerbeds? Are parked automobiles the only things you can see from your patio? Does everybody in the neighborhood use your driveway for a turnaround? Does the snowplow push boulders into your flowerbeds every winter? If the answer to any of these questions is yes, then you have a circulation problem.

Understanding Circulation Problems

Of all the features of modern life, the automobile demands most of the landscape designer's time and talent. Whatever your car dealer may say, automobiles are large, ungainly objects. Although they may look elegant parked beside the houses pictured in the dealer's brochure, they are rarely as attractive when they are parked in your own driveway. The automobiles in the brochure are shiny and empty, and parked just so. In real life, automobiles are dusty, salty, rumpled, full of hockey sticks and/or baseball gear, covered with bumper stickers and parking decals, and they are always parked out of kilter. Face it: An automobile makes a lousy companion for a delicate fountain or a festive rose arbor.

What's worse, automobiles require driveways and garages. Driveways and garages are a source of design difficulties for three reasons.

First, few driveways are well designed for the functions they are serving at any particular moment. This is not because contractors don't know how to make a suitable driveway for a given number of household members and automobiles. It is because the number of people and cars in households is constantly changing.

During the lifetime of a family, the number of cars in the household may swell from one or two in the early years of the family to four or more as young children become teenagers, and back to one, as the children move away. Few families want to design a driveway for the times of heaviest traffic. Such a driveway would be too ugly, too expensive, and take up much too much space.

Yet, to design a driveway for anything less than the maximum need is to court traffic jams in the dooryard. The pileup of vehicles in the front yard can get overwhelming. One friend of ours said the other day, as she dolefully surveyed the traffic jam in her front yard, "I fled the city. I left behind good theater and good restaurants. I paid $150,000 for a house, and where do I live? In the middle of a parking lot!"

The second general source of difficulty with driveways arises from the effects of the driveway and the garage on the landscape around them. A driveway is itself a "strong" design element. Remember that in design, to be strong is not necessarily to be good. A strong design element is one that captures and directs the attention. A driveway and its surroundings are not the sort of things that go unnoticed. The driveway's uniform surface, the straight clean contours between the driveway and its surroundings, the simple lines of the garage when its doors are closed, and its cavern-like appearance when they are open, all serve to direct attention to the most utilitarian and unaesthetic aspects of your property. From the street, your eye is directed into the garage. From the front doorstep, your gaze is led to the street. And from all perspectives, you are led to look at your cars.

Of course, these design consequences won't distress you if you think that the backsides of your Chevies are an appropriate way to present your household to your friends and neighbors. Or you may enjoy a wide-open driveway, if watching the world go by on the street is one of your favorite pastimes. But if you think of your front yard as a place where your eyes get a rest from the hustle and bustle of the street, or a place where visitors come to visit *you*, not your machines, then you will feel, as we do, that the effect of a driveway on the design of a yard can be devastating.

Driveways are not only strong design elements, they are also inflexible. A driveway must run from the street to the garage. Only people who are building a new house and are willing to consider a detached garage have much flexibility about where to put their driveways. For the rest of us who are wedded to the convenience of an attached garage, or have bought a house with the garage already attached, the constraints imposed on the location of the driveway are very rigid. The driveway must start at one side of the house, and it must go to the street. And if it is to use up the minimum in area and require the minimum of cost, it better make the trip as quickly as possible.

The third source of difficulties with driveways is that ugly objects and irritating activities are attracted to them. The extent to which you agree with this statement is of course a matter of opinion. Phebe knows a man who can think of no better place to have a quiet evening drink than seated on the terrace beside his Model T. But many of us, when we are relaxing, would prefer to be screened from the sight, smell, and sound of our automobiles.

"Well!" you say. "If that's the way you feel, then put your car in your garage and close the door!" "Well!" indeed. If you have a good-sized garage that is kept absolutely free of furniture, tools, and other gear, so that it always has room for the cars, and if you have a well-trained family that always pulls the cars into the garage and closes the doors, then these car anxieties of ours must seem absurd. But if you are like us, and have a garage full of junk, or family members who prefer to leave the car parked in the driveway most of the time, then you know what we are worrying about. People like us spend a lot of time looking at our cars, whether we find them attractive or not.

Even if you like the look of your cars, driveways tend to attract other nuisances. Boats are left in driveways, and bikes are parked there. Almost every asphalt driveway spawns a basketball hoop in time. If you have ever tried to read the Sunday paper next to a basketball hoop, you know one of the worst trials of adulthood. You have endured the scritch-scritch of sneakers on asphalt and experienced, in particular, the gritty thunk . . . thunk . . . thunk . . . kaCHUNK . . . thunk . . . of a child practicing lay-ups.

When all the drawbacks of driveways are considered, their strength as design elements, their inflexibility, and their capacity to attract nuisances, you can come to realize that designing an attractive yard is as often a process of mitigating the effects of the demon auto as it is a process of creating a miniature utopia.

Guidelines for Solving Circulation Problems

The trick to solving circulation problems is getting a balance between the three sorts of difficulties that driveways and garages pose. The obvious way to fix a traffic problem is to make the driveway and the garage larger, but enlarging the driveway will increase its impact on the total design of your yard. Shrinking the driveway will help with your design problems, but it will make your traffic problems worse. You will find no perfect solution. The final design of your driveway, garage, and entry is likely to be a compromise between the most pleasing landscape and the best traffic flow.

Here are some guidelines for finding the compromise best suited to your particular needs.

Allocate the Minimum Space Practicable for Circulation Needs. The smaller your driveway and garage, the more easily they will fit comfortably in your landscape design.

Allocate Space Precisely. Most of us are reluctant to put up signs telling our guests what to do with their automobiles. It just seems unwelcoming. Consequently, your driveway must be designed so that its appearance gives clear "instructions" to visitors. A narrow driveway says "Don't park here!" A short driveway with a narrow entrance from the street says "Please leave your car on the street." Decide which functions your driveway is going to perform, and allocate space for those functions very definitely. Do not include a little extra space here and there. It will only encourage people to misuse the driveway. Give your driveway clear edges. Slopes, cobbles, low walls, railway ties, and well-defined flowerbeds all help to keep cars where they belong: on the driveway.

Weaken the Driveway and Garage as Design Elements. When something is beautiful, you obviously take steps to encourage people to notice it. When something is not so beautiful, you want to take steps to disguise it. Since driveways are not exactly architectural attractions, you want to diminish their power to call attention to themselves.

You can try to disconnect the lines of the garage and driveway from the lines of the house. If the garage can be at a different level from the main façade of the house or at a different angle, then the strong lines of the house won't direct the eye to the garage and driveway.

Or you can visually disrupt the lines of the driveway and garage. Even a slight rise or curvature in the driveway will help enormously to break up its geometric severity and free you to look at

Here is a typical and stark-looking house, yard, and driveway.

Here's the same property with attractive shrub and flower borders added. The plantings soften the harsh look of the driveway, and draw your eye away from the drive and toward the yard.

other aspects of the yard. Plantings that are not parallel or perpendicular to the driveway help to draw attention away from it. Plantings against the façade of the garage will interrupt its lines and diminish its power to attract attention.

Or, finally, you can screen the driveway from inside views and from outdoor living spaces. What you cannot see at all cannot call attention to itself.

Designing an Entrance

The first step to designing an entrance is to decide how much space you want to devote to your circulation needs. This calls for a list of the functions you expect it to perform. Here is a list of functions often performed by entry areas:

1. Family entrance
2. Guest entrance
3. Service entrance
4. Access by single vehicle
5. Parking by single vehicle
6. Turnaround
7. Parking or storage of additional vehicle or boat
8. Passing of two vehicles
9. Recreation or work space
10. Guest parking area

Each function demands room. A simple family entrance requires a space as wide as an automobile from the garage or parking area to the street. If, for illustration, your garage were set 100 feet back from the street, you would have to have a 600-square-foot driveway. Such a driveway would be absolutely spartan. It would allow only one vehicle to move on the driveway at a time, and wouldn't even provide for foot traffic to use the driveway when an automobile is parked in it.

Any additional function you expect your entrance to perform will require additional space.

The simplest turnaround is an "L" off the main driveway. The smallest useful "L" adds 180 square feet, and the smallest useful bulge about 300 square feet. Bulges and "L"s of course can serve as parking spaces, but not at the same time they are serving their designed function. So if parking is to be provided, the additional space must be added at a rate of about 150 square feet per parking space. Thus a driveway with a turnaround, sufficient width for passing at one location, and parking spaces for three cars, will require more than 1,500 square feet of space, or more than 10 percent of a quarter-acre lot. Granting that perhaps 1,500 square feet of the lot is already consumed by the house, garage, walks, and utilities, the homeowner has conceded a quarter of the area of his lot before he begins to think about outside living space.

The second step is to decide what sort of configuration you want for your driveway. If you made a base plan as part of your preparation in chapter 13, "Doing Your Own Design," it will really come in handy now. Make some cutouts to scale to represent automobiles, trailers, and any other vehicles that are likely to end up in your driveway. Put a piece of tracing paper on your base plan and sketch out a possible driveway. Here are some dimensions to use as rules of thumb. A track for a single car must be at least 10 feet wide. If people are to walk past parked cars, the track must be 12 feet wide. For two cars to pass requires at least 16 feet. If a car is to turn a corner, plan for a turning radius of no less than 18 feet.

Several different configurations are possible. The simplest is a straight drive, one car wide. To that you can add an "L" for turning or a bulge for passing. More complex driveways can have circles or "U"s, and these can be combined with "L"s to make a variety of patterns. Unless you are planning to back out into the street, your driveway must have a turnaround, a drive-through, or a circle.

Such configurations add a lot to the convenience of a driveway, but also greatly increase its size.

Once you have a sketch of a driveway that suits your circulation needs, think carefully about the impact of that proposed driveway on the rest of your yard. Look carefully at your plan. Is your driveway in a place that might be useful for some other purpose? Does it pass through a part of the yard that might be particularly sheltered? Sunny in winter? Shady in summer? Protected from the view of neighbors? Does it chop space up into useless remainders, space that might otherwise be a vegetable garden, or a croquet court, or a place for a child to practice his pitching? If so, you might want to junk your plan and start again.

If your sketch passes this preliminary test, now is the time to take it outside. The best plan is to stake the driveway out on the ground. Walk along the marked-out driveway as if you were a car coming into the dooryard. What do you see? Will the driveway make your house look like a public, impersonal space? If so, try to think of details you might add which will minimize this aspect. Walk back out as if you were a car departing. Do you have reasonably good sightlines as you approach the street?

Next, if at all possible, put the family car or cars in the places they will be in your new driveway. Wander around your yard looking in the direction of the cars. Do you want to put in a screening hedge or fence? If so, mark it on your sketch so that you can draw it in later.

When you have considered the impact of your proposed driveway on the landscape of your house, you may want to re-evaluate your decisions concerning its size and configuration. The driveway that suits your circulation needs may be too expensive, take up too much space, or disrupt the design of your yard. You may start out wanting three parking spaces for guests and decide, when the consequences of that decision are taken into account, that the guests can just as well park in the street. If your landscape design won't accommodate a large driveway, then you may simply want to substitute a small driveway. Better to face the facts now than later, when the bulldozer has torn up your front yard and the contractor has dumped two truckloads of asphalt where the flowerbeds used to be.

When you are fairly sure you have decided how big a driveway to make and where to put it, consider what kind of a driveway surface to have. Chapter 3, "Knowing the Possibilities," discusses some of these surfacing materials and their strengths and weaknesses.

Some Successful Circulation Solutions

Putting a Large Front Yard to Good Use

When the Robertsons moved to the Midwest last year, they bought a large Victorian house set well back on a narrow lot. Access for cars was provided by a long narrow drive going from the left front corner of the lot all the way along the left side of the house to an old carriage house at the extreme left rear of the property.

The Robertsons found many aspects of this arrangement extremely unsatisfactory. In the first place, the carriage house was in a sad condition and needed extensive repairs or demolition. In the second place, they found the long driveway inconvenient and ugly. It was terrible to plow and remained glazed with ice much of the winter. Furthermore, because the lot was so narrow, the driveway used up space that could be used to plant screening shrubs between their house and the driveway of the house next door. The traffic outside their dining room windows made the

The Robertsons' new driveway and parking area. The inset diagram shows what they did to solve their traffic problem.

House

Hollies and rhododendrons

Oak

Oak

Garage

Robertsons feel like they were living behind the drive-in windows of a fast-food restaurant. Not only was the driveway unattractive to look at from inside the house, but it had a disruptive effect on their yard as well. It was so long that it was a dominant feature of the front, back, and left side yards. Only in the right side yard could the Robertsons escape the influence of automobiles.

Ugly as it was, that long, narrow driveway seemed to be the focus of everything that went on at the Robertsons'. Once a week, the trash truck backed laboriously down it, and every month the oil truck followed suit. In summer, when the windows of the house were open, these incursions filled the house up with diesel exhaust that lingered for hours after the trucks had left. Whenever they came back from doing errands, Sam and Anne would park the cars behind the house and cart in groceries and other stuff through the dilapidated back "L" of the house. Even guests pulled through the driveway and parked at the back of the house. The Robertsons found this particularly distressing because the back entrance of the house was its ugliest feature. Guests coming through it had to trek through the mudroom, the pantry, and the kitchen in order to get to the living room.

On the other hand, the front entrance was almost never used, even though it was one of the features which most attracted the Robertsons to the house when they saw it with the real estate agent. If you stood with your back to the driveway, the front yard was a pleasant space, deeply shaded by the two oak trees along the sidewalk in the summer. But even on the hottest summer day, the Robertsons found they didn't use the front yard. With the sidewalk going right by, they felt like mannequins in a storefront whenever they sat in their front yard.

In their redesign of their entrance, the Robertsons focused on getting rid of the long driveway, screening the front of the house, and providing efficient and well-designed circulation space for family members and visitors. They had the driveway torn up from the left front of the house to the left rear, except for a 2-foot strip designed to form a service entrance.

They then constructed a U-shaped driveway that entered on the left side of the house where the old driveway used to be, crossed the front yard, and exited on the right side of the house. On the inside of the "L" they put a parking alcove for three cars, and in the extreme right corner of the lot, near the street, they put a two-car garage.

Even though the new entrance arrangements bring cars very close to the front of the house, the effect is to screen the house both from the street and from the cars. The "island" formed by the driveway and the sidewalk is carefully planted with rhododendron and holly. The U-shape of the driveway was conceived so that there is only a sliver of the house visible from the street and vice-versa. The parking alcove is screened both from the street and from the house by more shrub plantings. Because of the elegant plantings, the Robertsons' unusual front yard has earned only praise from their neighbors.

Steep Lot

When the Stevens family bought their house, they liked everything about it but the entrance. The house was on a steep lot. It was perched about 10 feet above street level and about 20 feet back from the street. In order to provide a garage, the builders had excavated from the street to the house and put a garage under the house. Neither front yard nor driveway was of much use to the Stevenses as living space because of the steep slope and the proximity to the street.

Although he is a writer, not a designer, Calvin loves nothing better than to propose design solutions to other people's problems. Calvin proposed to the Stevenses an idea to increase their yard space, increase the square footage of their house, and make an efficient garage space for their automobiles, all the while reducing the total space devoted to circulation.

This landscape design was to be done in two steps. First, Calvin suggested that the Stevenses should terrace the sloping front lawn. They would build a retaining wall along the street and cart in fill until they had brought the whole front yard up to the level of the front of the house. Then they would construct a carport in the old driveway just inside the sidewalk. Entrance to the house could now be gained in two ways. Family members could come into the house through the back of the new carport, directly into the old basement of the house.

The Stevens family's yard with new terrace and deck. The inset diagram shows the layout of the redesigned property.

House

Retaining wall

Carport with deck

The formal entrance to the house would be incorporated into the carport design in a way Calvin modestly thought was downright ingenious. The roof of the new carport would be built of decking material, at the same level as the new terraced front yard of the house. Guests climbed a staircase from the street to the top of the carport. From this vantage point, the garage looked like a comfortable sundeck, with benches and an umbrella.

Calvin argued that the new arrangement would totally reorganize the Stevenses' lives. Instead of sitting inside on a summer evening, they could sit out on the deck roof. Here they could look down on the street and watch friends and neighbors coming home from work and neighborhood children at play on their quiet street.

Hidden Garage

The Markovitzes bought a recently built suburban development house last year, set well back from the subdivision road on spacious grounds. At

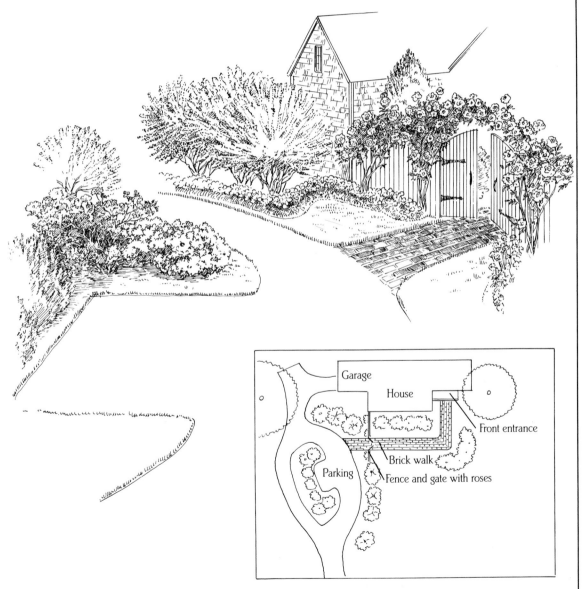

The new parking area and inviting entrance at the Markovitz house. The inset diagram shows the plan.

first, they were well satisfied with the circulation arrangements. The garage was off the left end of the house, at a lower level, and facing to the side. This tended to bring automobile traffic down and to the left of the house where it was out of sight from the front yard.

But the arrangement turned out to have two important drawbacks. First of all, the long driveway was the most salient design feature of the yard and made it look barren and sterile. Second, visitors to the house always parked their cars in the side yard outside the garage doors. When they got out of their cars, they had no idea where to go next. Sometimes they wandered around back and turned up outside the sliding glass doors of the Markovitzes' bedroom, much to everybody's surprise.

Also, the area around the garage doors was designed by the original owner for maneuvering in and out of the garage. Under the best of circumstances, visitors often seemed to have difficulty turning around in this space, and when one of the Markovitzes' two cars was parked outside the garage, visitors found turning around next to impossible.

The goals of the Markovitzes' design were to keep visitors out of the garage area, to encourage them to come to the front entrance of the house, to make the driveway a less dominant feature of the yard, and to prevent traffic jams in their driveway. Their driveway design incorporated an asymmetrical circle as its key feature. The right-hand side of the circle (as seen from the street) is wider than the left-hand side. Visitors now enter on the old driveway, but are directed by the wider asphalt driveway directly to a head-in parking area for four cars along a new fence. On their way into the parking area, guests bypass a smaller asphalt drive which leads down to the garage and which still functions as the family entrance. Departing guests back out of their parking places and continue around the circle, where they connect with the family entrance and thus return to the street.

The Markovitzes have used plantings to good effect in their new driveway plan. Shrubs in the middle of the circle screen the garage and part of the house from the street. The fence along the new parking area is covered with rambling roses. It not only beautifies the parking area, but screens it from the house as well.

Wrap-up

Designing a convenient and aesthetic landscape around automobiles is no small task. Cars, driveways, and garages are strong design elements that tend to take over any yard. A good entry design is a compromise between the circulation demands of automobiles and the aesthetic demands of people. A successful entry clearly designates space for cars, but incorporates plantings which disguise and de-emphasize the strong lines of the driveway and garage.

Part Four

From Plans To Plants

CHAPTER 16

Putting in Plants

*N*ow you come to the moment you have been waiting for. You have thought about yourself and your living habits, you have thought about your locale and what it has to offer, you have considered the various possibilities for design elements, you have carefully weighed the various limitations of design, human nature, and plant materials. You have decided which features you want to develop on your property, you have made yourself a rough—or perhaps even a detailed—landscape plan. Now, at last, you are ready to put some plants in the ground.

Well, *almost* ready! Putting plants in the ground is like many household tasks. The name of the task doesn't give a very good idea of where the real work is. When we change the color of the walls of our house, we call it house painting. But any of you who have painted a house know that more of the work is spent in preparing the surface than in actually putting on the paint. The same is true of planting. Most of the work is spent preparing the ground. For every hour you plan to spend actually putting plants in the ground, you should expect to spend one or two hours selecting and transporting the plants, and as many as six hours getting the ground ready to receive them.

Why can't you just whiz by the nursery on your way home from the market, pick up a few trees, leave them in the station wagon while you unpack the groceries and fix lunch for the kids, dig holes for the trees, pop them in the ground, go back to the garden store for mulching materials, rush into the house to get ready for your dinner guests, and water the trees after a leisurely brunch the next day? Well, you can. And some of the trees may survive. But many won't.

Putting plants in the ground is one activity where knowing and being realistic about yourself will really come in handy. There are two extreme kinds of gardeners in the world: Do-first gardeners and Think-first gardeners. A Do-first type gardens mostly for the pleasures of the moment. Do you ignore your lawn and flowerbeds all winter long, only to rush out and rummage in them fervidly on the first sunny spring morning? If so, you are a Do-first gardener.

On the other hand, do you pore over nursery catalogs all winter long, looking for special varieties for your garden? Do you spend your winters in the garden, tidying and raking and collecting materials for the compost heap? Do you project a carefully conceived plan for moving the driveway fifteen years from now so that it passes behind the row of willow sprigs that you planted last year? If so, then you are a Think-first gardener.

The crucial difference between the two sorts of gardeners is whether they focus on the process of gardening or whether they focus on its product.

Spring or Fall Planting?

When you plant can make a difference as to how well the plants get established, how much transplant shock they suffer, and how much care you must give them. Fall is the best time to plant balled-and-burlapped and container-grown trees and shrubs, because it gives them a long season of cool air and warm soil for strong root growth. Roots put on most of their year's growth after leaf fall. Trees and shrubs planted as early as possible after their leaves have dropped will be able to establish a powerful root system before the soil temperature drops into the thirties. And that translates into less watering and coddling the following season. This is an especially important consideration with container-grown plants, which dry out rapidly and must be diligently watered all season if planted in spring or summer.

With bare-rooted stock, however, the opposite holds true. Unlike balled-and-burlapped and container-grown plants, bare-rooted trees and shrubs lose most of their root surface—and water-absorbing capacity—during transplanting. New roots won't develop until spring, so if you plant in fall, you run the risk of the buds and twigs drying out over winter. The best time to plant bare-rooted trees and shrubs is in late winter or early spring, just before bud break. When the buds start to swell on the plant of your choice, it's time to plant it.

Evergreens are a special case. To keep them from going into transplant shock and damaging the foliage, plant them when the soil is warm, so root growth is interrupted as little as possible. The best time to transplant most evergreens is in August and early September, after new foliage growth has hardened off. Hemlocks, firs, and American hollies respond better to late spring planting. Plant only balled-and-burlapped or container-grown evergreens—*never* bare-rooted plants—and make sure the soil is kept moist.

Flowers also have their planting seasons. Perennials like peonies and iris, which have their greatest flush of growth in spring, respond best to late summer and fall planting. Spring-blooming bulbs need winter-chilling to bloom the following year, and should be planted in fall. Daffodils, crocuses, tulips, hyacinths, Dutch iris, scilla, and lilies are among fall-planted bulbs.

Other perennials, such as clematis, roses, and dianthus (pinks) respond well to fall planting. If in doubt about a particular perennial, check the fall and spring flower catalogs and see if it's offered in either or both. And, of course, annual bedding plants should not be set out until all danger of frost is past and the soil is warm. Grass can be seeded in either spring or fall. Whether you choose spring or fall planting or both for trees, shrubs, flowers, and lawns, bear in mind that young plants need water and attention until they are established. Don't forget about your fall plantings, or let the siren call of the sunshine or the vegetable garden lure you away from spring plantings. New plants need you!

This is definitely a cake you cannot have and eat as well. The Do-first gardener will have a wonderful, tumultuous, fun-filled Saturday buying and putting in plants, but most of the plants probably won't live. The Think-firster will give up some social engagements on planting day, but more of the plants will survive to give pleasure a few years later. Trying to have your cake and eat it too leads to discouragement. The Do-first gardener looks ruefully at his own dead trees and enviously at his Think-first neighbor's flourishing orchard. The Think-first gardener struggles to pull roots and rocks out of his soil while he listens jealously to the tinkle and chatter of the garden party going on next door.

So, which are you? Think-first or Do-first? We can see some advantages in being a Do-firster. The Do-first gardener has a heck of a lot of fun in the garden. And what's so bad about that? Whatever dies can be replanted on the next beautiful sunny day. Whatever lives is a bonus.

But pleasurable as Do-first gardening seems, we confess to being mostly Think-firsters ourselves. We're the sort of folks who feel that if something's worth doing, we'd like to do it once and for all. The fact is that everything about a planting or transplanting operation goes more smoothly if it is carefully prepared for, carefully executed, and done at the right time of day, in the right season, and in the right weather. When we put something in the ground, we want to see it grow and flourish long into the future, and we *like* working in the garden on cold, misty days. So the instructions for planting which follow are written mostly for our fellow Think-firsters.

New Planting Methods

Experienced gardeners may not know that there has been a change in philosophy about planting in recent years. The methods we were taught in our gardening "youth" have been dramatically revised. The old methods focused on fertilizing and pruning the young plant. We fertilized our young trees "to give them a good start" and we pruned them "to balance them."

Recently, horticulturists have tested all of these traditional planting practices and found that they were at best unnecessary, and at worst counter-productive. Plants scrupulously pruned and set in planting holes laced with soil amendments often became unbalanced. The soil amendments and the pruning had the double effect of encouraging top growth while confining the roots, which often seemed unwilling or unable to leave the safety and comfort of the original planting hole. The result was a plant which had too many leaves for the size of its root system.

The new methods avoid pampering the plant except to keep it as damp as possible before, during, and after planting. In fact, the goal is to acclimate the plant as rapidly as possible to the general soil conditions around it. Pruning is minimized, and watering emphasized. The soil amendments which were previously mixed in the planting hole are now added last as a topdressing.

Because of these new ideas about planting, even gardeners who have planted many trees in their lifetime might want to read through and consider our recommendations. What follows is a step-by-step program for getting plants safely into the ground. The program helps keep the time between the removal of the plants from the nursery and their safe installation in your garden to an absolute minimum. With careful planning, you should be able to keep that time down to a few hours. This chapter assumes that you have read chapter 13, "Doing Your Own Design," and prepared at least a rudimentary plan to guide you in locating your new flowerbeds and setting out your new trees and shrubs.

New Ideas for Planting Trees and Shrubs

Carl E. Whitcomb is one of the most innovative horticulturists in the nursery area today. While a professor of horticulture at Oklahoma State University, he challenged traditional planting techniques by testing them in scientific field trials. His results, which were often surprising, are summarized below.

Whitcomb's Revised Rules for Planting

1. Select plants well adapted to the soil, light level, and microclimate of the site.

2. Transplant only when the plant has ample reserves of stored food.

3. Make the planting hole as wide as possible, at least 18 to 24 inches wider than the root ball.

4. If in doubt, plant slightly shallower rather than slightly deeper.

5. Remove all containers, cord, and wire from the planting site.

6. Expose roots to air for only an absolute minimum of time.

7. If the spade has glazed the sides of the hole, break up the compacted soil.

8. Fill the hole with the same soil removed from the hole. Don't mix amendments with the backfill.

9. To get rid of air pockets, water as you backfill. If you tread the soil around the tree, tread lightly.

10. Water again several hours after planting.

11. Water every seven to ten days (unless it rains) for the first season.

12. Mulch heavily, 5 to 7 feet out from the tree, and 3 to 4 inches deep, but don't suffocate the bark. Use peat or compost.

13. Prune as little as possible. Remove only damaged branches. Prune for shape after the plant is well established.

14. Stake only if necessary.

15. Fertilize immediately after planting and again the next fall after leaf drop. Use slow-release fertilizer. Apply it only on the soil surface.

Step One: Preparing the Soil

Some gardeners may have no topsoil. Their lot has been scalped by the builder and the subsoil has been exposed. These gardeners will begin by preparing their subsoil to support the topsoil that is going to be spread on it.

Subsoil

If your subsoil is exposed, you have an opportunity to prepare your subsoil so that it will best support your plantings. First, rake up all the rocks you can and carry them off. Save them in a pile somewhere. You may find them useful later for drywells or drainage channels. Make sure all large stumps are removed. If they are left in the subsoil and buried in topsoil, they will soon rot and leave hollows.

Now is the time to give some thought to drainage. If your contractor has left natural depressions where water will tend to collect, you may want to install a drainage system before you put down topsoil. This can be as simple as a channel of small rocks covered over with sand, or a porous pipe buried in the subsoil. Whichever method you use, the drainage path should be dug into the subsoil so that it slopes continuously downhill.

When you have removed all the obstacles possible from your subsoil, sloped it, and provided drainage, hoe the surface or run a tiller over it to loosen the surface.

The next step is to bring in the topsoil. Before agreeing to buy topsoil, carefully question the person who supplies it to you about its source. It should be fertile loam, free of chemical contamination and vegetable matter. Topsoil is measured in cubic yards. A "yard," a cubic yard, actually, will cover an area 6 by 9 feet about 6 inches deep. To cover a quarter-acre, you will need 200 yards of soil. Check out the price of a yard of topsoil in your area, multiply it by the number of yards required, and you have an estimate of your topsoil cost.

Preparing the Topsoil

If you have new, freshly trucked-in topsoil, "preparing the topsoil" means just raking it out to a depth of 6 inches for lawns and at least 12 inches for flowerbeds and vegetable gardens, and making sure that it is smooth.

If you are redoing an old landscape, then you have more work to do. Following the plan you prepared in chapter 13, carefully stake the area to be planted on the ground. Step back. Take a look. Make any last-minute adjustments in the shapes of flowerbeds and the location of trees and shrubs. Then *dig*.

How you go about turning over the soil will depend on what equipment you have available to you and whether you are salvaging an old planting or tilling everything under and starting out from scratch. Obviously, if you are adding plants to a previously planted area, you have to be careful not to damage the roots of the plants that are already in place. In this case, you should use a spade and dig *very* carefully around the valuable plants. Large areas are best done with a tiller, one with at least an 8-inch tilling depth. One way or the other, work over the soil with your tiller or dig it up systemati-

cally with your spade or fork, turning each clod over and breaking it up.

How deep you till depends on what you are planning to plant. If you are planting a lawn or trees and shrubs, digging to a depth of 6 inches or one spade depth should be sufficient. (You will dig planting holes for your trees and shrubs after your topsoil has been prepared.)

Future flowerbeds or vegetable gardens should be tilled or spaded to a depth of at least 1 foot. (If your topsoil is not at least a foot deep, plan to add some.) Gardeners who encounter a heavy clay subsoil when they dig may want to "double dig" their flowerbeds or vegetable gardens. Dig a trench, removing the topsoil and piling it alongside the trench. Next, excavate the bottom of that trench, breaking up the clay shovelful by shovelful, and mixing each shovelful of clay with a shovelful of peat moss and a shovelful of sand. Then, start a second trench alongside the first, putting the topsoil from this new trench into the first trench. Repeat the procedure until you have dug up and amended your entire plot. The topsoil from the first trench goes into the last. This method breaks up the subsoil layer and mixes the nutrients through the top 2 feet of the soil.

Once your planting area has been turned over by the method of your choice, hoe and rake the soil thoroughly until you have removed all grass, weeds, rocks, and roots.

Soil Amendments

Now you are ready to add fertilizer, lime, and organic materials to your planting area. Spread a layer of peat moss, leaf mold, rotted straw, or other organic material at least an inch deep over the entire area. If heavy soil is your problem, add as much organic matter as you can get.

Readers in the eastern part of the country may have to add lime to their soil. The only way to add lime is in accordance with a soil test. Overliming can not only make the soil too alkaline, but can also overdose it with calcium or magnesium, both of which are toxic to plants in high concentrations. Simple tests for soil acidity are available at every garden store, so even if you haven't sent your soil in for a general analysis, you still can measure soil acidity on your own. When you have your soil

test, spread lime at the rate suggested by the results of your test.

If you're planting flowers or vegetables, then after lime and organic material come fertilizers. You will be sorely tempted to use fast-acting chemical fertilizers. They come in small, convenient packages and are available everywhere. Your garden store salesperson will enthusiastically endorse

How Much Organic Fertilizer Do You Need?

Most soil-test printouts not only tell you whether your soil is deficient in crucial nutrients, but also give you recommendations for how to correct the deficiency. The recommendations are often given in pounds of a commonly sold conventional fertilizer, such as, "Mix well 3 pounds of 10-15-10 with the soil at planting time for each thousand square feet of garden space." These numbers are the percentages of the three crucial soil nutrients, nitrogen, phosphorus, and postassium, to the total bulk of the fertilizer. Thus, the recommended fertilizer has 10 percent nitrogen, 15 percent phosphorus, and 10 percent potassium.

An organic gardener who wants to make use of these recommendations has to translate them into terms appropriate to organic fertilizers. The calculations are not difficult, but they are best made at a desk or kitchen table rather than at the checkout stand of a garden supply store, so take a few moments to work them out before you head out to buy fertilizer.

The number you are looking for is the rate of application of the nutrients, that is, the number of pounds of each *nutrient* recommended for every thousand square feet of garden space. Once you have that number for each of the three crucial nutrients, you can ignore the fertilizer recommended in the printout and buy any fertilizer in the store. To extract this number from the recommendation, you multiply the percentage of the nutrient in the recommended fertilizer by the amount of fertilizer

recommended. In the above example, a recommendation of 3 pounds of 10-15-10 amounts to a recommendation of .3 pounds of nitrogen, .45 pounds of phosphorus, and .3 pounds of potassium per 1,000 square feet. (Do the multiplications now yourself to check our calculations.)

When you have extracted the number of pounds of each nutrient recommended for each thousand square feet, write those numbers down in your notebook, put the notebook in your pocket with a pencil or pen, and off you go to the garden supply store. At the garden supply store you will find bags of fertilizer marked with a formula, like 5-10-5, 10-10-10, even 0-0-35. These are the chemical fertilizers of which you have heard so much.

Ask the garden store manager to see his organic fertilizers. He may sell them as soil conditioners, but you can use them as fertilizers. The nitrogen (N), phosphorus (P), and potassium (K) content will be printed on the bag, usually in small print, since the product is not being sold as a fertilizer. All you have to do is use enough to get the rate of application of nutrients you require. For instance, composted cow manure contains 1 percent each of nitrogen, phosphorus, and potassium. In a 50-pound bag of composted cow manure, there is ½ pound of each of the nutrients. You would thus need a little less than a bag of cow manure to fertilize 1,000 square feet of garden space according to the recommendations in our example.

Organic Fertilizer Formulas

You can mix your own balanced, all-purpose organic fertilizer. Here are some general formulas, expressed in N-P-K ratios (the amount of nitrogen to phosphorus to potassium in a given mix):

2-3½-2½
1 part bonemeal
3 parts alfalfa hay
2 parts greensand

2½-2½-4
3 parts granite dust
1 part dried blood
1 part bonemeal
5 parts seaweed

4-5-4
2 parts dried blood
1 part phosphate rock
4 parts wood ashes

3½-5½-3½
2 parts cottonseed meal
1 part colloidal phosphate
2 parts granite dust

Sometimes a low-nitrogen, high-phosphorus and/or high-potassium formula is especially desirable, as when you're trying to promote strong root growth on trees and shrubs in fall without hindering hardening off, or when you're growing a legume that will produce its own nitrogen. Formulas for these special uses include:

0-5-4
1 part phosphate rock
3 parts greensand
2 parts wood ashes

2-8-3
3 parts greensand
2 parts seaweed
1 part dried blood
2 parts phosphate rock

them. "After all," he'll say, "nitrogen is nitrogen." On that point, he is obviously wrong. The atmosphere consists of nearly 80 percent nitrogen, but plants cannot capture and use it in that form. The availability of nitrogen to plants—the availability of all plant nutrients, for that matter—depends on the biological activity of the soil and that, in turn, depends on the presence of ample supplies of organic matter. The problem with these chemical fertilizers is that they don't add organic material to the soil. Without organic material, the biological activity of the soil declines, the soil structure deteriorates, and nutrient imbalances are more likely to occur.

Since you are going to be adding organic material anyway, the simplest procedure is to use an organic fertilizer which supplies both nutrients and organic matter in a single application. The best organic fertilizer is compost from your own well-managed compost heap, followed by strawy manure from barns or stables. Next best are organic fertilizers which may be purchased at some garden supply shops or dealers who specialize in them. Most widely available are various forms of cow manure. Composted cow manure (1-1-1) is a particularly pleasing fertilizer to work with. It is neither smelly nor dusty, and is wonderful to handle. Less attractive but also widely available are fish and seaweed emulsion fertilizers that are diluted and sprayed on the growing plants.

Bagged organic fertilizers are much like conventional fertilizers in their handling characteristics, but contain ground rock fertilizers and dehydrated organic material, such as crop residues, rather than concentrated chemicals. Some garden shops may carry them, but you will probably have to ask around to turn up a dealer in your region who specializes in them.

Whatever fertilizer you decide to use, spread it in accordance with the instructions on the package or a soil test. Applying organic fertilizers is just like applying conventional fertilizers, except that you often have to apply more of the organic fertilizer to get a particular level of nutrients. But remember, with fertilizers, more is not necessarily better. Over-fertilizing can overstimulate your plants and make them subject to damage from disease and drought.

Completing Your Soil Preparations

When all your amendments are spread, dig or till your planting area completely again, turning under the materials you have broadcast and mixing them thoroughly with the soil.

When the soil is thoroughly prepared, mark out the plant locations with stakes, carefully following your plan. Stand back and have a good look at it. Do you think you will like the way things are grouped? Do you want to spread things out a bit over here, and group them more closely over there? Now is the best time to make any last-minute changes in your landscape design.

Before you quit, lightly water the part of your new landscape that will be sown to grass. Let the sprinkler run until the water has soaked through the layer of topsoil. However, do not water so long that your seedbed becomes mucky.

Planting Holes for Trees and Shrubs

One last question to consider at this point is whether or not to dig the final planting holes for your trees and shrubs. There are advantages both ways. Digging the holes before you pick up the plants shortens the time between pickup and planting. On the other hand, leaving the holes undug leaves you one last check on your landscape design. When you get the plants home from the nursery, you are going to set them out in their containers on the prepared beds. If the holes are not yet dug, the bed will look roughly as it will look when the plants have been put in the ground. If they have been dug, then the piles of dirt beside the holes will make it difficult for you to see how the bed will look. Calvin recommends pre-digging your holes, particularly for trees; Phebe enjoys the extra flexibility of waiting until the plants are home.

Before you go to pick up your plants, get everything ready for planting. Do you have a sharp knife to cut wrappings? Is your hose connected, and does it reach everywhere you'll need it? Do you have all the shovels, rakes, and hoes you need to dig and fill the holes, and all the tree wrap, stakes, and guy wire that you'll need to protect your trees after they have been planted?

Step Two: Selecting the Plants

If you have adopted our suggestions from the first section of the book, you have already developed a good business relationship with a reliable nurseryman who strongly guarantees his plants. We hope also that you have spent some time looking over his stock, and that you have at least a preliminary idea of what kinds of plants you want. Well done! Now is the time to put that background work to good use. From your plan, make up a shopping list of plants, briefly noting the characteristics of each plant. Take that shopping list to the nursery, along with a copy of your garden plan, a pencil, and a note pad.

When you go to a nursery can make a tremendous difference in the quality of service you get. Going in the dormant season is a good idea. Try to go on a damp, cold Monday, if possible, rather than on a sunny, warm Saturday. You are hoping to get good advice, and you don't want to have to compete with hundreds of other people when you are trying to make your selections. On a dreary weekday, you'll find it easier to speak to experienced staff.

If you don't know what species you want,

then you are going to have to ask for advice. Here success will depend on your ability to make what you have in mind clear to the nursery staff. Show them your planting plan. Ask them to make recommendations. Describe the plants you want functionally. Make it clear what you hope each plant will *do* for you. A sketch or a photograph of what you are after will be an enormous help. Be sure to make clear the sort of site the plant will be located in and whether you plan to be an attentive caretaker of your plants or let them fend for themselves.

Selecting Trees and Shrubs

If you know exactly what species of tree you want, then selection is simply a matter of picking out a healthy specimen. Pick plants that have good color, without extensive yellowing and without any trace of wilting. The leaves should be clean, free of holes or any other signs of insect damage. The trunk should have no large unhealed scars or holes. Be critical of the shape of the plant. Beware of crossed limbs, missing leaders, and broken branches. Beware of plants which show signs of manhandling, such as gouged trunks, skinned twigs, stripped leaves, or a ball that is dented or cracked.

In general, if you have a choice, we urge you to choose a smaller, younger specimen over a larger, older one. True, larger plants provide immediate satisfaction, but they are more expensive, more difficult to transport safely and plant, more difficult to maintain, and more likely to die than smaller plants.

Buying a small specimen doesn't always mean waiting years to have a filled-in landscape. Sometimes you can get the illusion of a larger plant by grouping three smaller plants closely together. Such groupings help prevent the new plantation from looking so barren when it is new. The plants which will cooperate in this little ruse are multistemmed shrubs like azaleas and rhododendrons. Plants with

Several small plants can be grouped to create the impression of a single large plant, producing a bolder effect.

a strong center, like juniper, don't take well to being grouped, because instead of mingling their branches, they just push against each other and look crowded.

Know something about the history of the plants you select. Ideally, the plant should be grown locally, not trucked in from across the country. The best stock is not grown and sold in a container but grown in the field, annually root-pruned, and balled and sold in burlap. Container stock can be overly pampered. Sometimes it has been grown in a greenhouse or in special soil mixes and has been heavily fertilized, watered, and doused with hormones, fungicides, and insecticides. Such plants often have a hard time making the transition to the harsh real world of your garden. Still, nurseries are increasingly selling container stock because of its convenience and ease of handling, and it may be the only kind you can get.

When you buy container-grown stock, make sure that it has a good root ball. It should be large enough to fill the pot, but not so large that it's potbound. Gently lift the plant from its pot to make sure that you see some roots on the outside of the ball but that the roots don't form an impenetrable snarl on the outside of the ball. Avoid, particularly, plants whose roots coil around the outside of the ball.

As you select each plant, ask the nurseryman to tag it sold and mark it with your name. As you are talking with the nurseryman about each plant, make notes on his recommendations. Note particularly any special soil requirements or special care that should be taken in transplanting it. This information will be crucial once you get the plant home.

Unless you have a large vehicle or a small load of plants, we would recommend having the nursery deliver your new purchases. Plants, particularly evergreens and those in leaf, are terribly vulnerable to dehydration during transport. If you do transport your plants yourself, don't be slipshod about loading them. Put them into your car or pickup truck upright. Do not lay them on their sides or stack them. And don't carry them tied to the roof rack. Plants carried out in the open should be wrapped or covered with a tarpaulin or a plastic sheet to protect them from the wind.

Selecting Bedding Plants and Seeds

When all the excitement over picking out large plants like trees and shrubs and planting them is over, it's time to turn to bedding plants for flowers and vegetables. Pick out healthy bedding plants that are bushy and stocky and have good green foliage. Small, sturdy plants usually transplant better than bigger, lankier specimens, so avoid the temptation to buy the biggest plants you see.

Which grass seed you use will depend on what sort of lawn you want, what part of the country you live in, and the grade of the slope. Good lawn seed mixes are available for different conditions, such as sun and shade, and for different regions. For a conventional grass lawn north of the Mason-Dixon line, bluegrass gives the finest lawn, but it is slow and difficult to establish. Perennial ryegrasses are not so lush in texture, but are quick

to establish themselves, rough-wearing, and resistant to drought, heat, cold, erosion, and insects. Fescues are also drought resistant.

In the South, different rules apply. Bermuda or zoysia grasses give a tough, resistant lawn, but have the disadvantage of turning brown in the cool months of the year. Southerners who want year-round green lawns overseed their plots with a fast-growing, cool-weather grass such as perennial ryegrass for the winter months. The rye quickly establishes itself among the summer grasses and provides a green winter cover. As soon as the soil heats up in the spring, the summer grasses take over and crowd out the rye. Your nursery or garden-store owner should be able to give you good advice about what sorts of grass seed are appropriate for your region.

Before you leave the nursery or garden store, review to make sure that you have everything you need for planting. Do you need another bale of peat moss? Or perhaps you want to order a load of bark mulch to be delivered. Do you have the equipment for guying up the trees? Do you need an extra section of hose or a bucket? Once you have started planting, you don't want to have to stop and come running back for any of these items.

Bare-Root Stock

Buying plants at a nursery or garden store is the most common way to get them, but it is certainly not the only way. Some varieties of tree and perennial flower and fruit can be purchased as bare-root stock by mail order. Several catalogs offer plants at good prices which come to you with their bare roots packed in moist excelsior or peat moss. The advantage of bare-root stock is that many useful and interesting varieties can only be purchased in this way. For instance, a nursery in New York state specializes in old-fashioned varieties of apple which have not been available for decades in local farm or garden stores. One in California features old roses.

The disadvantages of bare-root stock are that the plants are a bit less likely to survive than balled stock and that you don't have as much control over planting time. Season of planting is crucial for bare-root stock. It should be put in the ground just as plants of its species are coming out of dormancy. Moreover, the arrival of the UPS truck with your mail-order plants must be treated as a genuine family emergency. The plants must be opened and remoistened immediately, and should be planted, or at least heeled in, within 24 hours of arrival. But if you are prepared to take the effort to meet these requirements, planting bare-root stock can vastly increase the variety of plants in your landscape.

Step Three: Planting Day

A cool, damp day is best for planting or seeding plants. If you get up in the morning and look out your window and say, "Gee! I *really* feel like planting some trees today," then that's probably not the best day to do it. The sun will be too strong, the air too warm, the soil too dry, the breeze too lively, and the nursery or garden store too crowded. Moreover, pick a day when the family can help. Put aside other commitments. Don't try to install your landscape on the same day you are having a dinner party.

As soon as you get your plants home, park the car in a sheltered, shady area and carefully unload them. Lift each plant from the car, cradling the ball or container as you lift it, and set the plant upright on the ground. If you have wrapped any plants to protect them during transit, unwrap them. Check each plant to see that the soil around its roots is sufficiently damp. If it's not, provide water. If you are planting bare-root stock, unwrap it and put it in a bucket of water.

If you have taken all morning choosing and bringing home the plants, now's the time to take a break. Have lunch. Gather your energy. Once you get started with the planting, you will want to carry through until all the plants are in the ground.

Putting Trees and Shrubs in the Ground

Now, the big moment has really arrived. Muster your troops, take the phone off the hook, give the baby to the babysitter, it's time to *plant!* Carry your plants to their places carefully, again being sure to cradle the ball so that the roots don't tear and the soil doesn't loosen as you carry it. Set each plant down beside its stake. Once again, stand back and assess your design. "The Wilson rhododendron should be moved a little to the left," you say to yourself. "It is a bit too close to the dogwood." So, you move it out of the dogwood's shadow. "The azaleas are too far back to really show well, and too close to the perennial bed on the left." So, you move them forward and to the right a foot or so. Step back and have another look. "Ah, that looks perfect."

Start with the largest plant. It is the one that is probably suffering the most stress, and it sets the design. Let's say it's a dogwood. We'll assume that you didn't dig a hole for this dogwood before you went to fetch it, so the first step is to dig the hole. The dogwood is sitting on your freshly tilled topsoil in its container or ball. Using your spade, draw a circle around the roots of the dogwood, with at least 18 to 24 inches of clearance all the way around. Remove the dogwood from the circle. Measure the depth of the dogwood ball with the blade of your shovel. Excavate within the circle, placing the soil to one side in a pile. Dig the hole about 6 inches deeper than the depth of the roots. Break up the excavated soil and remove any roots or rocks, and break up compacted soil around the sides of the planting hole.

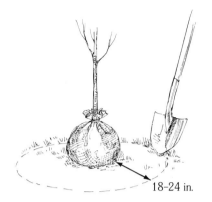

18–24 in.

6 in. soil

To plant a new tree, first set it on the ground and draw a circle around it 18 to 24 inches out from the edge of the rootball (top). After the hole is dug and 6 inches of good soil placed in the bottom, cut away most of the burlap from the rootball and set the tree in the ground. The root crown should be at the same level as it was in the nursery (center). After the tree is planted, make a saucer around the trunk to hold water (bottom).

When the soil has been thoroughly loosened, put about 6 inches of topsoil back in the bottom of the hole. Without removing the dogwood from its container or wrappings yet, place it in the new hole. If you have dug the hole correctly, the root crown of the plant—where the stem meets the roots—will be at the same level at which it was planted at the nursery. If it isn't, lift or tip the plant very gently and add to or subtract from the soil beneath it until you get the level right. Then step back to make sure the plant is placed well and shows its best side. If it doesn't, rotate it until it looks the way you want.

Before you start to fill in around the plant, you must deal with the ball-wrapping material or the container. If the ball is wrapped in burlap, simply loosen the burlap at the trunk and fold or cut it until the top half of the ball is exposed. If the plant is in plastic "burlap" or a plastic pot, carefully cut the wrapping or container and slip it out from under the plant. Don't disturb the rootball any more than necessary. After you have the wrappings or container off, inspect the rootball. If, for any reason, you have bought a rootbound plant, spread the roots out carefully all the way around to keep them from girdling—literally strangling themselves.

When the plant is in place, refill the hole with the soil you just removed. Do not add any amendments to the soil you put in the hole—save the compost, aged manure, or other organic materials to use as a topdressing once the tree is in the ground. If the plant is large and the hole is deep, fill in 9-inch layers, settling each layer with water before you add the next. The reason for this layering procedure is to bring the soil in contact with the roots. When the soil in the hole is at grade level, shape an earth saucer around the plant, a little above grade, to hold water. Then put the hose in the saucer to dribble in water while you turn to the next plant. Continue from plant to plant, going through the same procedure.

Seeding a Lawn

Spread the seed over the seedbed. The usual rate of seeding is ½ to 1 pound per 10-by-10-foot square, depending on the type of seed. If you are seeding a large lawn, it might make sense to divide out the area into squares and the seed into lots, each lot being half the amount needed to seed a square. A rented seeder, either a spreader or a drop-seeder, is a great convenience. Seed each square twice, using one lot each time, and seeding once in one direction and once in the perpendicular direction. If there are hilly parts of your lawn, seed the slopes a second time, at a rate of ⅓ pound per 10-by-10-foot square.

Sodding or Seeding?

If cost is not an important consideration, if your site is sunny, and if you long for a lawn overnight, you might consider buying sod. The preparations for sod must be every bit as extensive as those for a seedbed, and the maintenance during the period in which the sod is rooting itself is as intensive as the maintenance of a new seedbed. But sodding can be done anytime during the growing season. (Seeding is best done in spring or fall.) And with sod, the effect is instantaneous. From the first day, you have your lawn, bright and green and ready to enjoy. We wouldn't recommend playing touch football on it for a few weeks, but almost any other form of light enjoyment can be pursued immediately.

The preparations for sodding are exactly the same as those for seeding. As with seeding, it's very important to make sure that the soil on which the sod is to be laid is even, slightly roughed up with a rake or tiller, and thoroughly moist.

Sod comes in long rolls which you unroll to make your lawn. The trick with sod is high-quality materials, quick installation, and faithful maintenance. From harvest to the completion of installation should not take more than 72 hours. The sod should look healthy and be neatly and precisely cut. It should be strong enough so that you can support a whole piece of it by holding one of its ends.

Sods are ungainly once they are unrolled, so you want to get them in the right place the first time. Start by laying out a straight string along one of the edges of the lawn. Lay the first course of sod along the string, and the next carefully beside the first. Be sure never to overlap two pieces or to leave any gaps. Avoid having the ends of two courses lie side by side. After all the sod is laid, brush or rake in some topsoil to fill any cracks and roll the lawn to help push the grass roots against the underlying soil. Then water the whole lawn thoroughly.

After your new lawn is installed, maintain it scrupulously for the first few weeks. In the absence of rain, your new lawn must be watered every day, more so if the weather is unusually hot and dry for the season. The water requirements of plants increase dramatically as the temperature rises above 70°F, so if your cool-season seeding or sodding program encounters an unseasonable hot spell, don't spare the water. Each session of watering should be continued until the seedbed is thoroughly damp or the sod is wet through to the soil beneath. You can check after watering a sod lawn by picking up a corner of one of the sods and seeing if its underside is thoroughly damp.

You should begin mowing your new lawn as soon as the grass reaches 3 inches, at which point you will want to cut about an inch off it. Repeat this watering and mowing program until the lawn has been mowed at least three times. By this time, the grass roots should be deeply enough established so that you can adopt a weekly schedule of watering. But if the weather turns excessively warm and dry, you should be prepared to start more frequent watering again.

Once the seed is spread, rake the seedbed very gently, holding the rake so that it just contacts the soil and gently scoring the ground with the tines of the rake. Now roll the whole plot to press the seed into the soil. You may want to cover your seedbed with a light mulch of straw, which may help to discourage heavy feeding by birds. Where the slopes are steep, you will want to lay down a cover of biodegradable netting to hold the slope until the grass comes.

Now that all your seeds are in their seedbeds and all your plants are in their holes, you are just about through planting. Set out your sprinkler and give the entire planting a good soaking. Let the sprinkler run until the water has penetrated 3 or 4 inches into the soil.

Step Four: Pruning and Protection

When the plants are in the ground, you can afford to take a break: Go in the house, have some iced tea, and relax. The last steps can wait for a few hours, even until tomorrow. But don't let them go more than a day.

Mulching

The next step is to apply mulch to your new plantation. The best mulch for trees is composted bark mulch, but such material is often difficult to come by. Wood chips, straw, hay, or buckwheat hulls are almost as suitable. Lay 3 to 4 inches of mulch around trees and shrubs. Spread a ring of mulch around each tree, 5 to 7 feet out from the trunk, to cut down on competition from grass and weeds for water and nutrients. Mulch groundcover or perennial plantings more lightly, since you want to encourage the plants to spread. Grass plantings may be mulched with a very light layer of straw. Lawns newly sown on a slope should be covered with biodegradable netting to hold the slope against erosion until the grass takes hold.

Pruning

Take your pruning shears and your tree wrap out to your new plantation and look each tree over carefully. Keep pruning to an absolute minimum, and in no case remove more than a third of the tree's branches. Do not try to "balance" the tree. Remove only damaged limbs and those that are obviously developing badly, such as competing leaders or branches that are crossed. After pruning, the trunk of each deciduous plant should be wrapped to protect it from sunscald and winter attack by rabbits and mice. Tree wrap is available at nurseries and garden centers. Aluminum foil and burlap are effective alternatives, but tree wrap is less conspicuous.

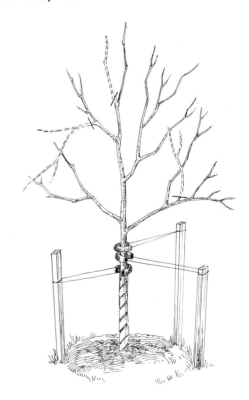

Prune newly planted trees to remove crossed branches, competing leaders, and damaged limbs.

Support

If you have heeded our advice about buying small trees, your new trees won't require any support. Trees with a large leaf canopy relative to the root ball should be provided with some support. This precaution may seem silly at the time of planting, particularly if the tree is dormant. How, you wonder, could any wind blow this skinny tree over? What you forget is that the tree will leaf out soon and present a much greater surface area to the wind. A tree doesn't have to be blown over to be damaged by the wind. Just the constant rocking of the tree tends to break the new attachments of the roots to the soil and set back the plant's adjustment to its new conditions.

For trees with trunks greater than 2 inches in diameter, support can consist of three stakes driven into the ground so that they reach, if possible, about a foot deeper than the bottom of the hole and 6 inches outside the ball. The stakes should be no taller than three-fourths the height of the tree, and should be connected to it with guy wire which has been threaded through pieces of rubber hose where it comes in contact with the tree. Kits for guying are available at garden supply stores. Don't forget to remove the guy wires after a year.

After all the trees have been carefully protected, water all your plants again. Unless there's a good rain, they should be soaked once every seven to ten days for the first growing season, and whenever nature fails to provide at least an inch of rain a week for the next year or more. Container-grown stock must be watered much more often—at least every other day for the first few weeks (container soil dries out fast, often in six to eight hours). If the weather is hot, dry, and/or windy, step up the watering schedule. But if you've planted in fall, taper off the watering in midfall so the plants can harden off before winter.

Wrap-up

We started this chapter by making a distinction between two types of gardeners: spontaneous Do-first gardeners, for whom gardening pleasures are the pleasures of the moment, and Think-first gardeners, for whom much of the pleasure of gardening is in thinking through and carrying out a plan. This chapter has been mostly for the Think-first gardeners.

If, after reading the planting instructions in this chapter, you decide you really are a Do-first gardener and the systematic carrying out of a planting program isn't your idea of fun, consider hiring a landscape professional. You could, for instance, ask the nurseryman to transport and install his own stock. Or you could consider a landscape contractor, who will prepare the ground, purchase, and transport the trees to your specification, and make sure that they are well installed and maintained in the first few months. The initial cost of having a professional do the job will be much higher, but if your professional knows his stuff, you may well make back your additional costs in savings on replanting costs you would otherwise have to pay.

If you are still determined to do the work yourself, be realistic about what you can accomplish in the time available to you. If ever there was a time to curb your Do-first tendencies, it is when you are putting plants in the ground. Eight trees don't seem like very many to order when you are perusing the nursery catalog on a quiet winter evening. But planting all eight trees on the same harassed Saturday afternoon will be a major project. Be forewarned. You will get more pleasure out of your plants in the long run, and spend less money on them, if you proceed carefully, systematically, and patiently as you select the plants, prepare the soil, dig the holes, transport the plants, install them, and backfill and water them.

CHAPTER 17

Maintaining Your Landscape

*A*fter all you have done to establish your new landscape, we are sure that you will want to maintain it. Maintenance means seeing to the health of your plants. It means providing food and water. It means protecting your plants from insects and disease. And it means pruning your plants to keep them in shape. Volumes and volumes have been written about maintaining landscape plants. Libraries contain shelves of books with advice and prescriptions for every sort of plant in every sort of locality. If you want to really get involved with maintaining your plants, you can spend literally all of your free time doing it. That's fine. You will be a healthier person, and know more about nature in general and plants in particular, if you do spend a lot of time outside with your plants.

But we take exception to the notion that you *have* to spend all your free time in your garden if your plants are to survive. We believe that some gardeners make an enormous amount of unnecessary work for themselves, partly because they do things without understanding *why* they are doing them or what the likely consequences are. In fact, a significant proportion of many gardeners' labor in the landscape consists of undoing work which they have previously toiled to accomplish.

Gardeners who want an elaborate garden-maintenance program should buy one or more specialized books to guide them. What we will present here is a minimalist maintenance program based on the principle that if gardeners thoroughly understand what they are doing, and do only what they have to do, they will get excellent results with a lot less effort.

The key to this minimalist maintenance program is good record-keeping. One of the great advantages to having done your own design is that you have the sketch maps available to help you with keeping tabs on your activities in the garden.

Every time you fertilize your garden or put in new bulbs or prune or add lime, make a note on a copy of your sketch map and put it in a loose-leaf notebook. It always seems that you would remember from day to day where you have put in new plants or what beds you have fertilized, but if Calvin's memory is any guide, this sort of information disappears from the brain just as soon as the project is completed.

If you keep notes, you will save yourself all sorts of landscape-maintenance embarrassments, such as over-liming and over-fertilizing one bed while under-liming and under-fertilizing others; or tilling up last fall's bulbs when you are preparing for this spring's pansies; or forgetting which species of apple you planted for pollination and replacing it with the wrong one. These and other disasters all will be headed off if you couple your minimalist maintenance program with a program of assiduous record-keeping.

The minimalist maintenance program involves mulching, watering, fertilizing, pruning, and insect control, just like any other. What is special about our program is that each of these tasks is done with a view to the others, not as a separate chore. It is a simple integrated-management program based on a thorough understanding of plants' basic needs. Consequently, we start each subsection of this chapter with an explanation of how each of these four basic garden practices serves the needs of plants.

Mulching

Mulches have three crucial functions. First, they keep down weeds and other vegetation that might compete with your new tree or shrub for moisture or nutrients. Second, they keep the surface of the soil from forming a crust that will resist the flow of water, carbon dioxide, oxygen, and nitrogen in and out of the ground. Third, their decomposition provides a steady supply of humus and nutrients to the soil in a form readily available to plant roots. Thus, a successful mulching program cuts down on the need for watering, weeding, and fertilizing.

To be effective, a good mulch should be 3 or 4 inches deep. It should consist of materials that are substantial enough to stay put and shade the ground beneath them, yet light and permeable enough to permit water to pass through. Unfortunately, many readily available materials are unsuitable. The leaves of many trees—the maples, for instance—form dense, slick mats on the ground that are all but impervious to water. Peat moss is a bad mulch for the same reason it is a superior soil amendment. Under the soil or above, peat moss has the capacity (once it has been thoroughly moistened) to sop up enormous quantities of water. Under the soil surface, the water contained in peat moss is held in reserve for the roots of your plant. On the soil surface, the same water evaporates back to the atmosphere and the roots never get a chance at it. If the peat moss is allowed to dry out, it loses its sponge-like qualities and simply sheds the water.

The best materials for mulching are dense and chunky, so that they neither resist the passage of water nor absorb very much of it. Bark mulches, available from your nursery or garden supply store, are the best. Material obtained from chippers or shredders can also be a good mulch. Such materials often require nitrogen to decompose, so if they are not sold to you nitrogen-stabilized, you should add a source of nitrogen when you lay them down. Many crop residues, such as buckwheat hulls, are sold as mulches. However, if you are a dedicated organic gardener, you might want to bear in mind that such mulches are usually the by-products of commercial agriculture, and often contain residues of their chemical past.

You might, of course, want to try to generate homegrown mulches. If you have your own chipper or shredder, fall cleanup can also be mulch-making time. (Don't forget to add supplementary nitrogen!) Grass clippings are rich in nitrogen and make a usable mulch, if your lawn has not been treated with herbicides. The problem with grass clippings is that, like leaves, they can form a water-resistant surface. You should stir up a grass mulch from time to time to keep it from becoming too tightly packed.

You can make a better mulch of grass clippings and leaves by mixing them. Spread a pile of the two ingredients on the ground and run over them with your power mower until they are thoroughly blended. Better still, throw all your waste materials—grass clippings, leaves, and chips—on the compost heap for a few months and then spread them. Partially or fully composted materials make the best mulch of all.

In recent years, garden stores and catalogs have started offering a variety of synthetic materials for mulching. They range from simple black plastic to more complex and expensive materials such as a woven plastic "yarn" that is supposed to keep weeds down while letting air and water get to the soil. While these materials may be useful for some special situations, we do not recommend them for general use. Unlike natural mulches, they add to neither the texture nor the fertility of the soil. We would recommend that you only use such materials if nothing else is available. And if you do have to put down synthetic mulches, replace them as soon as possible with natural mulching materials.

Sometimes a diligently mulched garden actually becomes an embarrassment of riches. With all the organic material that is added each year, the flowerbeds get higher and higher until they start to slop over onto the walks and pathways. If this happens, the solution is easy. You can rake up some of the surplus mulch and compost it, or just spread it directly on less fortunate parts of your garden.

Watering

Water serves at least three vital functions in plants. First of all, it serves as a raw material for food manufacture. During photosynthesis, the plant actually takes apart molecules of water and combines them with carbon dioxide to make sugars. Second, water serves the plant as a delivery service. Water picks up nutrients from one part of a plant and takes them to other areas where they are needed. Third, water supports the structure of a plant. Each of the cells of a plant is like a tiny balloon whose strength and rigidity are maintained because it is chock-full of water.

A well-watered plant in the sunlight functions like a little machine. The plant uses energy from the sun and the nutrients in its cells to manufacture carbohydrates and proteins for growth. Water constantly evaporates from the surfaces of the leaves. The water lost from the leaves is replaced by nutrient-laden water streaming in through the roots. And so the cycle continues.

Because water serves so many functions in plants, a plant without water is almost immediately in trouble. It cannot supply itself with the basic raw materials it needs, it cannot make food for itself, and it collapses for lack of structure. Of these three calamities, only one, wilting, is readily observed by the gardener. But you should know that a wilting plant is not only limp and thirsty. It is also in danger of starving to death.

Even before a plant begins to wilt, it may suffer from too little water. Although plants can gather water from soil depths of several feet, soil nutrients are mostly available in the topsoil. Consequently, a plant with its deep roots in a water source may not wilt, but still may not grow optimally for lack of access to the nutrients in the top few inches of the soil.

If water deficit were the only problem that plants have, then a watering program would be simple to design: You'd just have to keep the plants constantly soaked. Unfortunately, plants can not only die of thirst; they can also drown. Their food-gathering ability and the health of their roots depend on the presence of oxygen in the soil. When the soil is thoroughly soaked, water replaces the air and the roots begin to suffer for lack of oxygen. If this condition continues for more than a day or so, the roots may rot.

Because water is so essential, plants are well adapted to providing for their water needs as long as they are grown in their natural habitat. Consequently, for most established plants in much of the country, regular watering should not be necessary. Once a tree or shrub has been in the ground for a year or so, it should have roots deep enough to withstand a substantial period of drought without damage.

Watering after the First Year

For your new plants' first year in the ground, you must be constantly vigilant to ensure that they have the equivalent of an inch of rain a week in the growing season, and that they go into and come out of the dormant period with a thorough soaking. How long do you have to keep worrying about your new plants?

After the first season or two, you should not water your new planting regularly. Regular watering can actually make young plants vulnerable to drought. People who violate this rule lay a trap for themselves. We all know gardeners who go out every hot summer evening with their hoses, spraying down the leaves of the plants and giving each a blast of water at its roots. Such a watering program is wonderfully soothing to the gardener after a hot day in the city, and it makes the foliage look all glossy and elegant. But is it actually good for the plants?

Teasing your plants with such a daily spray of water is one of the worst things you can do to them. Constant light watering discourages the plants from driving their roots deep into the soil where the water reserves are stored. When a real drought comes, you will have to water your plants profusely and regularly to save their lives. But of course, in severe drought, watering restrictions are very likely to be in force, and a good citizen doesn't use water that is needed for people to save the lives of overly pampered plants. The gardener either consigns himself to a life of surreptitious midnight watering, or has to let his new plants die of thirst.

Even though you shouldn't water regularly after the first year, you will need to be vigilant during dry periods for at least two and perhaps three years after your new planting is in the ground. How much watering you'll have to do depends in part on what kind of soil you have. Because of the difference in the water-storage capacity of soils, plants in sandy soils will require more irrigation than plants in clay soils or soils with lots of organic material.

The best time to water is before your shallow-rooted plants have started to suffer from water stress, but after the soil has dried out well. Figuring out the best time is a skill you will gain after a few seasons of working with your own yard, its soils, and its plants. If you think that rain has averaged less than an inch a week for a few weeks and you are worrying about your plants, dig down about 6 inches into your soil and take out a trowelful of dirt. Try to form a ball with the dirt by squeezing it in the palm of your hand. Well-watered, light soils should form at least a weak ball that doesn't crumble as soon as you open your hand. Heavy soils should form a sturdier ball that you can toss lightly up in the air and catch. If you can't form such a ball with the soil, it probably needs water.

Apart from the consistency of your soil, another important factor determining your watering program will be the size and root depth of your plants. Shallow-rooted plants will always require more watering. For best growth, perennials and groundcovers—even those that are well established—will always have to be watched during extended dry, windy, or hot periods. Most of these plants are not deep-rooted, and will not bloom or grow as well if the soil is allowed to dry too thoroughly. Mature plantings of actively growing, shallow-rooted ground-covers may also need supplementary water during dry periods.

Trees and shrubs need not be watched so closely. During the second spring and summer, just keep an eye on them. When the weather seems dry, check to see if the dirt under the mulch is becoming dry and dusty. If it is, give your plants a good soaking. When fall comes around, repeat the thorough soaking before the ground freezes. If your plants are well mulched, watering should not be necessary after the second autumn, except during the kind of drought that attracts the attention of the press and spurs talk of water bans. Under such extreme circumstances, you might do well to check even third- or fourth-year plantings.

Watering Techniques

When watering becomes necessary, the best watering program is an alternation of thorough watering with thorough drying. Thorough watering soaks all the organic material in the soil and provides an ample reservoir of water for the plants to draw on. Thorough drying admits quantities of air to the soil and replenishes its oxygen supply.

The simplest watering methods are to run a sprinkler and to let a hose trickle at the foot of the

Three kinds of drip irrigation systems, shown here, are a canvas soaker hose (top), perforated rubber soaker hose (center), and drip emitter system (bottom).

Soaker hoses can be buried or left on the soil surface, and positioned to deliver water to the maximum number of plants.

A drip emitter kit needs more assembly, but you can customize the system to deliver water to each plant.

plant. The sprinkler has the advantage of distributing the water widely around the surface near the plant, but the disadvantage of immediately losing much of the water to evaporation. A trickling hose has the advantage of delivering water directly to the soil without excessive evaporation, but the hose must be moved frequently, or one part of the plant's root system will become soggy while the rest remains bone dry.

A well-equipped garden store or garden catalog can offer you a range of watering devices which try to capture the advantages of both the sprinkler and the hose. The simplest of these is a specialized soaker hose. Made of canvas, recycled rubber, or plastic with minute perforations, these hoses permit small quantities of water to ooze out all along their length. The soil is evenly irrigated, and little water is lost to evaporation. More complex are the drip-irrigation systems of plastic tubing that deliver water directly to "drip points." The gardener puts together his own system, cutting the tubing to length so one or more drip points are placed exactly beside each plant. Such systems are intricate, probably too much bother for watering isolated plants. But they are well suited to vegetable gardens, flowerbeds, and orchards, where the hoses can stay in place all season. And if you live in a dry and/or hot part of the country and expect to be doing a lot of irrigation, drip-irrigation systems are indispensable. A drip-irrigation system can be covered with a layer of mulch so that it is completely invisible and provides water to the plants with practically no waste.

Every time you water, water thoroughly, that is, until the soil is saturated at the depth of a foot. Soil is saturated when a squeezed ball of it leaves a slimy or sandy residue on your hand. Unless your plants are young or shallow-rooted or your weather is extraordinarily hot and dry, such a thorough watering should satisfy plants' needs for a few weeks.

Remember, the rule with watering is: "Better too much too seldom than too little too often."

Fertilizing

Plants are great hoarders of nutrients. Each year, the roots of the plants draw up the nutrients they need and convert them into leaves. The leaves use the sun's energy to make food for annual growth. At the end of the season, some of the nutrients are withdrawn from the leaves and stored in the roots. What remains falls to earth, is degraded into nutrient compounds, and is reabsorbed by the roots the following year. In such a system, very little is lost, and indeed some substances—nitrogen, for instance—may actually increase from year to year.

Enter the average suburban gardener with his rakes, mowing machines, wheelbarrow, and bags of fertilizer. In the back of his mind, he carries an image of his yard as an outdoor version of his living room. The lawn is the rug. The trees and shrubs are the furniture. He labors diligently throughout the summer to keep his rug spotless and his furniture well arranged. Weekly, he cuts the grass, trims the plants, and drags the nitrogen-laden cuttings off to the trash cans. Weekly, the trashman comes and carts the clippings to the dump, where they are mingled with useless or even toxic materials. In the fall, our homeowner does not rest until the last leaf has fallen, been raked, bagged, and hauled to the dump, along with its trace elements and its potential for adding humus to the soil.

To the harried homeowner's struggle to keep the yard clean is added his struggle to keep it fertilized. Because he is carting off nutrients that his trees and shrubs have labored so diligently to gather, he must replace them with artificial products from the garden store. These substances are usually expensive, unpleasant to handle, and easy to misuse. What's more, the stuff he gets in bags is not as good a fertilizer as the stuff he has just had carted to the dump. So, he has spent his summer laboring to throw away a superior fertilizer so that he can spend his money to buy an inferior one.

Mismanaged fertilizers are worse than a waste of time and money. Heavy applications of fertilizer in the landscape can damage plants and make more work for the gardener. Succulent, overstimulated plants are often more subject to insect attack and frost damage. Their root systems are pampered, shallow, and vulnerable to drought. Such plants often grow rampantly, putting out suckers and water sprouts which have to be pruned off.

Ironically, heavy fertilization of landscape plants is not only risky, it's also unnecessary. Unlike food plants, landscape plants give no harvest. Since you never have to take anything away from your plants, you don't need to return anything to them, except what food is required for the next season's additional growth. And that small amount of feeding can usually be provided by mulches or by light applications of slow-acting organic fertilizers which provide nutrients to plants in a leisurely manner.

All this, we think, argues most strenuously for a more informal style of lawn and yard than is traditional in many suburban communities. We encourage you to get used to the sight of a lawn with a few grass clippings on it, or a tree with a few leaves under it. If informal culture is good enough for you, your fertilization needs will be absolutely minimal. Those readers who are wedded to a clean-culture yard with a neat-and-tidy formal look will probably have to have a program of regular fertilization. Let your own efforts in cleaning the landscape be your guide to fertilizing it. The more you cart off, the more you must put back.

Our recommendations on fertilizers are based on the idea that it's best to minimize your need for fertilizer of any kind. These recommendations are remarkably simple:

1. Do not be overly fastidious about your lawn and flowerbeds. If possible, leave grass clippings on the lawn and leaves under the trees and shrubs. Protect trees, shrubs, and perennials with mulches. Mulch with materials from your own yard or other materials that are as free of pesticides and herbicides as possible.

2. When it becomes necessary to remove materials from lawns and beds for any reason, compost them. Composting doesn't have to be elaborate. If you are willing to wait a few years for the product, composting can be as simple as throwing your clippings on a pile and letting them rot. When the compost has matured, put it back on the lawns and beds where it came from.

3. Once a year, apply a light application of organic fertilizer to the landscape. This will provide for the additional growth that each growing plant will make each year. Put some on the compost heap while you're at it to help provide the nitrogen necessary for decomposition.

4. Once every three years, get a comprehensive soil test. Have the soil-testing organization make recommendations for organic fertilizers. Follow the accompanying instructions, particularly with respect to liming.

If you follow these recommendations, your landscape will be every bit as beautiful as those around it. And what's more, it will be a healthier place to live, and less demanding to maintain, in the bargain.

Pruning

The same general principle we have applied to fertilizing and watering your plants applies with equal force to pruning them. If you have chosen the right plant for the right place, pruning should be a rare event. Like any other creature, a plant has a plan for its shape, which it adapts to local conditions. Put among mature trees and forced to reach for sunlight, a tree will grow tall and spindly. Put out in the open and allowed to receive sunlight from all sides, the same tree will grow squat and bushy. Each of these shapes is natural for the tree and gives it the most sunlight for its situation. You should always assume that the tree whose limbs you are about to cut has them for a purpose. *Never* prune without a reason. Always prune with a specific goal in mind. Here are some of the situations in which pruning may be useful or even necessary:

Shaping Young Trees

The most obvious time for pruning is when you are moving a young tree from the tightly spread conditions of the nursery to the relatively open space of your lawn. Here is an occasion to make some fundamental decisions about your tree's shape.

The height of a tree's lowest branches is often an important consideration. Once a tree has set its lowest branch, it grows on that plan thereafter. The little twiglet growing a few feet above the ground on your nursery tree, if allowed to grow, may eventually be a major limb with a great canopy of branches. Every time you bang your head on that limb, you will rue the day you let the twiglet grow.

So, when your tree is young, prune off one or two of its lower branches each year until the lowest branch is at the height you want. People and institutions who are worried about lawsuits will often prune lower branches up to a height of 6 feet, so that children and others cannot use the trees for climbing. Any height below 4 feet makes mowing beneath the tree difficult.

You may also want to prune your tree to influence its "habit." You can, for instance, give a deciduous tree a tight upright form or an open spreading shape depending on how you prune it. If you want a tight upright shape, prune off twigs just beyond a bud which is on the inside or upper side of each twig. New shoots will form at these buds and will develop branches that grow upward and inward. If you want an open spreading shape, prune off twigs just beyond a bud which is on the

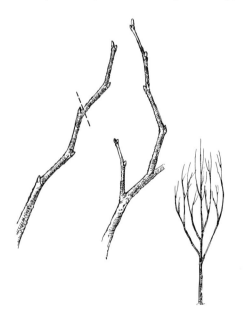

Pruning above an inward bud (left) directs growth inward, encouraging a narrow, upright shape. Pruning above an outward bud (right) directs growth outward to produce an open shape.

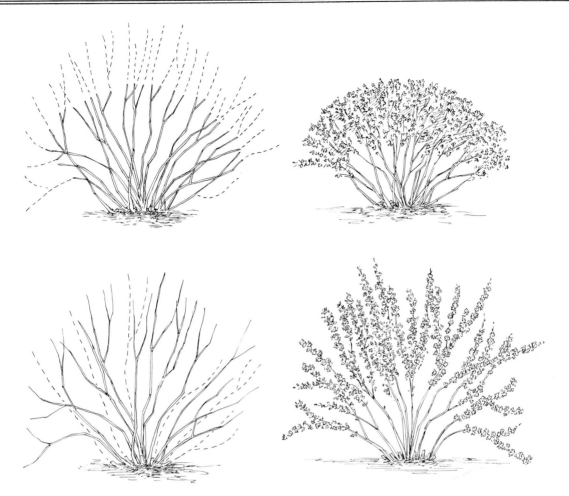

Shearing a shrub such as forsythia (top) produces an unnatural shape and reduces flowering. Pruning by removing old branches at ground level (bottom) keeps the shrub vigorous and encourages abundant blooming.

outside or lower side of the twig. The shoots that form here will develop outward and away from the center of the tree.

Training a Tree into an Unnatural Form

For some purposes, a gardener may want to jettison the tree's or shrub's natural plan and train it to an entirely unnatural shape. Hedge-trimming is the most obvious example of radically reshaping a plant. Hedges can be sheared or pruned. Shearing, usually with electric hedge clippers, trims off tender new growth and stimulates branching at the point of trimming. Pruning reaches back into the center of the hedge to remove entire leaders that are extending beyond the visual line you are trying to establish. Shearing is easier and gives a more formal look. Pruning is much more difficult, but gives a more informal, natural look. Well-maintained hedges are usually subjected to both treatments, since a sheared hedge gradually expands from year to year and eventually demands pruning.

How easy or difficult the hedge will be to maintain will depend on how close to its natural form you let it grow. Train the hedge in a triangular form with the point upward, or as a simple box with its bottom slightly wider than its top, and the plant will cooperate. Try to make it into an upside-down triangle, or into the image of your beloved poodle Fifi, and the shaded lower branches will thin out, making your hedge look ratty.

A subtler form of training, called rejuvenation, seeks to maintain a tree or shrub in a state of eternal youth. Many plants, like kittens, are thought to be more attractive when they are young than when they are mature. By a rigorous pruning program, the gardener seeks to maintain their youthful form by constantly cutting out the mature wood and encouraging new growth.

Both deciduous and evergreen plants are subjected to this treatment, including some of the most widely known flowering shrubs. For instance, both lilacs and forsythia, if allowed to grow, develop multiple, thick trunks that are long on wood and short on flowers. Many gardeners find these mature trunks unattractive. If the shrub is severely pruned each year, these trunks do not develop, and the shrub flowers more fully. Similarly, plants with colored stems, such as the red-stemmed dogwood, tend to lose their intense color as the wood matures. Pruning keeps the plant's stems immature, at peak color.

To rejuvenate a deciduous shrub, prune back about a third of the mature stems to the ground each year, leaving strong young shoots and cutting away old woody shoots and new spindly ones. With this routine, your lilac, forsythia, or other shrub is kept in a state of perpetual youth.

Maturation can also be delayed with ever-green shrubs. Since evergreens do not readily develop new sprouts from the ground or trunk, the method is different. Evergreens which readily develop new growth from shorn tips react well to being sheared. Examples of these are hemlocks, arborvitae, cypresses, yews, and upright junipers.

Other evergreens must be pruned more judiciously if you want to slow their growth and maintain their youthful density. Pines, spruces, and firs may be pruned by cutting off half the length of the central shoot of each of the outermost branches. These central shoots—the plant's new growth—are called "candles" on pines and terminal shoots or "leaders" on firs and spruces. Cutting them stimulates the growth of sideshoots, makes the foliage denser and more fuzzy, and delays the time when lower branches are shed from the plant. Prune when the new growth has finished elongating—usually in midsummer.

A third kind of radical reshaping is the practice of espaliering trees. Many books have been written on shaping young trees into elaborate and elegant shapes. If you want to go to such lengths, you may read these books and try your hand at improving on nature. Of course, once you start a radical pruning program like this, you are stuck with it. The tree will fight you every step of the way. If you let up in your pruning for even a season, it will begin to revert to its natural shape.

Removing Dangerous or Inconvenient Limbs on Mature Trees

The most common reason for pruning mature trees is cleaning up damaged, unsightly limbs. Some trees prune themselves naturally by withdrawing energy from lower limbs that are shaded by higher branches. The lower limbs gradually die and fall off the tree. They often look unsightly during this process, and the fastidious homeowner may want to remove them. Also, trees often suffer wind or ice damage, and need to have broken limbs pruned back to the main trunk.

Another common reason for pruning mature trees is that their limbs are getting in the way of buildings. Mature trees often come in contact with roofs, sweeping the roofing material with their leaves or pushing up on the roof with their limbs. Tree limbs which lie on or against roofs should be removed immediately. The arborist can do this by cutting the offending limb back at the trunk, or by cutting the small branches that lead down from this limb toward the roof. The latter solution is often less painful. Relieved of the weight of some of its smaller branches, the branch lifts off the roof and the problem is temporarily solved. But the more radical pruning is probably wiser. Trees which overhang roofs shed litter, which collects in the grooves of the shingles and gutters and encourages water to collect and seep into the roof.

Trees can be pruned to create a "window" for electrical wires to pass through.

Trees also get in the way of electrical wires. The best solution, of course, is not to plant trees in the path of wires. If the trees are already in the ground, the problem is more easily solved if you see it before it develops and train the tree to grow clear of the wires. Your goal is to have the tree pruned so that it develops a natural-looking window through which the wires will pass. Pruning twigs that lead toward the wires will encourage the tree to develop around them, and avoid the more radical solution of cutting major limbs to make the window later on. When trees come in contact with electric wires, you should call the electric company immediately. Twigs and leaves, though they seem like tender innocent green things, are really very abrasive, and may quickly wear insulation off the wires. Under some circumstances, the wires can make the tree "hot" and create a very dangerous situation.

In general, *we recommend that any pruning work that requires a ladder or involves electric wires be done by a professional who has the insurance, the experience, and the proper equipment to do the job safely and correctly.*

How to Prune

The rules of good pruning are widely described in gardening books. We're sure you've read them dozens of times, so we'll repeat them only briefly here.

First, don't maul the tree you are trying to prune. Use clean, sharp, well-adjusted tools. Be sure to use a large enough tool for the branch you are cutting. Hand pruners should be used only to cut twigs up to ¼ inch in diameter, loppers up to ¾ inch. Anything larger than ¾ inch should be cut with a pruning saw. Pruning saws have wide blades and widely spaced sawteeth to keep the teeth from gumming, and the bark from tearing along the margins of the cut.

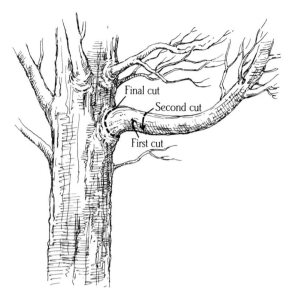

First cut

Second cut

Final cut

To remove a big branch safely, make three cuts as shown here.

Second, plan your cuts carefully before you begin. When you have decided where to cut, make a preliminary cut a few inches farther out so that you don't have to worry about the falling branch when you are making your finish cut. Begin the preliminary cut by cutting up from beneath the limb. Then finish the amputation with a downward cut, begun 1 inch farther out on the limb. A cut made in this way will lever the branch out and away from the trunk, where it will be less likely to hit you or scar the trunk as it falls.

Now make a careful final cut. Do not leave stumps. Twigs should be cut back to a side bud or branch, branches to a larger branch or to the trunk. When making a finish cut on a twig, cut the twig diagonally about ¼ inch above a bud. When making a finish cut on a branch, cut the branch parallel to the trunk or main branch, as close as you can get to it *without cutting into the branch collar* (the rough ridge of wood that marks the joining of the smaller with the larger branch or trunk).

When to Prune

The best time to prune a plant depends on the type of plant. The general rule of thumb is to prune in the very early spring just before the end of the dormant period. At this time, winter damage should have made itself evident. Pruning at the end of dormancy stimulates immediate replacement of the pruned limbs by the plant during the subsequent growth period.

The rule should be followed rigorously with evergreens, both broadleaved and narrow-leaved. *Never* prune an evergreen in mid- to late summer. Pruning stimulates growth, and growth so late in the summer may be subject to winterkill.

There are some exceptions to the general rule of spring pruning. Deciduous trees may be pruned at any time, and some deciduous trees, such as maples, which "bleed" profusely when pruned, will bleed less if pruned in late summer. Summer pruning in these species may decrease the risk of disease and insect attack. Suckers (shoots springing from the ground at the base of the trunk) and water sprouts (whip-like shoots that stand straight up along horizontal branches) should be pruned off whenever they appear.

Another exception is in the case of flowering and ornamental fruiting shrubs. These should be pruned after they flower, or after the fruit is at its decorative best. For best blooming the following year, flowering shrubs that form seedpods should have their flowers removed as soon as they start to fade in order to keep the plant from wasting energy on seed production.

Protecting against Pests

Most of us regard the relationship between plants and insects as one in which the insects are aggressors and the plants are innocent, helpless victims. From this point of view, it seems amazing that any plant survives without powerful insecticides to protect it.

But if you think for a moment about some familiar facts, you will realize that there is something fishy about this vision of plants. Think, for instance, about how many plants contain very powerful toxins. Rhubarb, potatoes, pokeweed, wisteria, and milkweed all contain extremely toxic substances. Many strong neurologically active drugs, such as aspirin and tranquilizers, originate from plants. Some plants, including pyrethrum, are so toxic to insects that they can be ground up and used as insecticides. In fact, one of the most potent and dangerous insecticides ever used, nicotine, is a plant derivative.

If plants are just innocent victims in their struggle for existence with insects and animals, why do so many plants contain poisons? In recent years, ecologists have taught us a great deal about plants and their resourcefulness in defending themselves against insects. In fact, the vast majority of plants contain substances solely for the purpose of discouraging insect attack. In many kinds of plants, the concentration of those toxins will increase if the plant is attacked. New oak leaves on trees attacked by gypsy moths are far more bitter than their unfortunate predecessors. Scientists even suggest that when some trees in the forest are attacked by insects, other trees can sense the attack and get busy manufacturing more toxins in their leaves to ward off an assault.

Thus, plants have surprisingly efficient and sophisticated defenses against insect attack. Then why do plants succumb to insect attack? Plants become vulnerable to insects because of their priorities. A plant directs its resources first toward growth and reproduction, and secondarily toward the manufacture of toxins. A weak plant cannot always afford the energy to mount its insect defenses. Insects gang up on plants that have been weakened by other factors: over- or underfeeding, root competition from other trees, inadequate light, heavy storm damage to its foliage or construction damage to its roots, too much or too little water.

Preventing Insect Attacks

Once you understand these relationships between plants and insects, your strategy becomes clear. Keep your plants' defenses strong. A plant that has ample supplies of nutrients, water, and sunlight will usually defend itself successfully against any but the most extreme infestations of insects. Growing native plants or those that are suited to your conditions (both climatic and regional) gives you a head start in heading off pests.

There are other steps you can take to ward off insect attack. Plant a garden with many different kinds of plants, not with whole beds of a single species. Insects that would devastate a whole bed of one species of plant will sometimes pass up plants that are growing with different species—often because they can't find their target plant, since it's "masked" or hidden by the others. Different kinds of plants can also have chemical defenses that complement one another.

Another important preventive measure is to encourage insect predators in your yard. Most species of wasp are avid insectivores. Even drab, tuneless species of birds, such as starlings, are enormously effective against insects. Those flocks of starlings and blackbirds on your lawn in early spring may not be decorative or make pretty music, but they are busy extracting Japanese beetle larvae from under your grass. Welcome them with bird feeders and birdbaths, some good thick shrubs for them to perch in, and dense evergreens for them to roost in at night.

A final preventive measure seems paradoxical, but it may be the most important of all. Never use strong chemical insecticides on your property.

These poisons will be effective in the short run against the pest, but they also kill off insect predators and competitors and stimulate resistance in the pests, leaving your landscape helpless against future insect attacks. Don't let anybody talk you into signing up with one of those chemical landscape companies that are being so vigorously promoted on television.

What to Do about Insect Attacks

Even if you take all these precautions, every once in a while the insects will get out of hand in your garden. Don't feel bad. It happens in the best-managed gardens. When you see insects in your garden, don't panic. Remember, if you can prune up to 30 percent of a plant without harming it, you can let the bugs take a leaf or two without mounting a chemical holocaust in retaliation.

What follows is a three-step program for coping with insects on your plants. The program prescribes only techniques and substances which are said to be harmless to human beings. "Harmless" is perhaps too strong a word, since too much of anything can be damaging. Moreover, for any substance, no matter how benign, there is always a person who is allergic or sensitive to it. *We recommend using any spray or powder with care, and breathing as little of it as possible, particularly if you have allergies or chemical sensitivities.*

1. Consider what direct techniques you might use to defend your plants. Unlike a commercial farmer who must defend millions of square feet of crops, a home gardener can focus his or her attention on a few square feet of the garden, and can often lick the problem by straightforward means. Consider simply removing the insect or its eggs from the plant. You may find handpicking disconcerting at first, but after picking off the first four or five bugs, you won't give it another moment's thought. Often, if an infestation is controlled early and thoroughly by such simple means, no other control is necessary.

If you don't want to collect the insects yourself, you can sometimes get them to collect themselves. Garden books abound with techniques for trapping pests, such as dishes of beer for trapping slugs and snails. Read up on these techniques and try them. The are often remarkably effective. Recently, scientists have developed sophisticated versions of these insect traps which employ the sexual scents of the insects to draw them into containers where they can be conveniently dispatched. These insect lures, called pheromones, can be purchased at garden supply shops.

2. Plants can often be protected by a spray or dusting of substances that are not toxins in the ordinary sense, but which damage the insect's protective outer coating. An insect's armor relies on a hard chitinous exoskeleton lined with a delicate coating of fat to keep the insect from dehydrating. If you can damage the coating in some way, water escapes through the shell, and the insect dries up and dies. Many plant protectants are based on this weak point in the insect's defenses.

For instance, dealers of organic fertilizers and plant-protecting substances often sell diatomaceous earth, a substance made by grinding up the microscopic silica shells of fossil diatoms. Diatomaceous earth is very abrasive, and wandering insects will avoid it or be damaged by contact with it.

Another way to damage an insect's protective coating of fat is to wash it off. Greenhouse suppliers sell insecticidal soaps which essentially dissolve the coating. Ask your local greenhouse staff where they buy their insecticidal soaps. Take care to follow instructions when using them. Some plants may suffer leaf burn if washed with soap, so you have to use these substances carefully.

3. If diatomaceous earth and soap sprays

don't work, consider biological insecticides. *Bacillus popiliae* (milky spore disease) and *Bacillus thuringiensis* (Thuricide or Dipel) are two examples of bacterial diseases which have a devastating effect on insects, but which are harmless to humans and animals. They can be purchased at garden supply shops and sprayed or dusted on plants and lawns.

4. If biologicals don't work, try botanicals. Botanicals, like rotenone and pyrethrum, are derived from dried plants. They are more toxic than biologicals, and should be used with care and strictly according to instructions. Even though nicotine is technically a botanical, it is a powerful nerve poison, and we do not recommend its use.

Once you have mounted your counterattack, begin immediately to consider why your plant was vulnerable to attack in the first place. Any time you have a sick or infested plant, it's time to re-evaluate your maintenance program. For gardeners who have been keeping good records, a review of their maintenance program will be a cinch. Just read through your records of the last few years and see if you have remembered to fertilize and water regularly. Have you tested the soil recently? Perhaps it's time to send for a soil test. Stand back from your ailing tree or shrub and look it over carefully. Is it getting the right amount of sun for a plant of its type? Do its roots have room to forage, or is it having to battle with its neighbors for every bit of food? If it's an acid-lover, is it growing in alkaline soil?

If your review reveals no slipups—no failures to fertilize, no damage to the plant, no crowding or shading by other plants—then take your problem to your county Agricultural Extension agent. Take along your annotated garden plans and a cutting from the injured plant so that you will be able to provide the agent with all the information he or she needs to quickly recommend a solution to your problem.

Wrap-up

With all the work that has gone into designing and installing your landscape plants, you will want to take the time to mulch, water, fertilize, prune, and protect them from insects. Done right, each of these procedures enhances the health-sustaining effects of the others. Mulches reduce the need for weeding, watering, and fertilizing. Watering helps to make fertilizer available to plants. Proper fertilizing helps to keep plants healthy and resistant to insects and diseases, and encourages plants to develop deep root systems so that they require less watering. Pruning not only shapes plants to convenient and attractive forms, but helps to control and prevent diseases as well. The gardener who has designed his or her yard is in a particularly good position to carry out these procedures without duplications and omissions, because he or she has a garden plan in hand on which to note important events in the garden.

Pruning Books for Further Reading

Brickell, Christopher. 1979. *Pruning*. In Simon and Schuster's *Step-by-Step Encyclopedia of Practical Gardening*. New York: Simon and Schuster.

Brown, George E. 1972. *The Pruning of Trees, Shrubs and Conifers*. London: Faber and Faber, Ltd.

Baumgardt, John Philip. 1982. *How to Prune Almost Everything*. New York: Quill.

The Editorial Staff of Ortho Books. 1978. *All about Pruning*. San Francisco, Calif.: Ortho Books.

The Editors of Sunset Books and *Sunset Magazine*. 1972. *Sunset Pruning Handbook*. Menlo Park, Calif.: Lane Publishing Co.

Hill, Lewis. 1979. *Pruning Simplified*. Emmaus, Pa.: Rodale Press, Inc.

Epilogue: The Last Word in Landscaping

People call themselves landowners, but how many of us really own the landscape around us? More often, the landscape seems to own us: to dictate how we lead our lives, how we use the space around our homes. We hope that this book has helped you to liberate yourself. We hope that you have designed an environment for living that suits you and your family and that encourages you to do the things you want to do where and when you want to do them. If you like to sit on your front stoop and watch the world go by, we hope you have made an environment that gives you the best possible view of the street from the most comfortable seat. If, on the other hand, you like to hide yourself away from public view and read, we hope that you have been able to arrange your landscape to protect and screen you from the outside world.

Perhaps, in a sense, if you have done these things, you have become for the first time the owner of the landscape around you. We wish you many happy years enjoying it.

Bibliography

Agriculture Handbook 387. 1971. *Ponds for Water Supply and Recreation*. Soil Conservation Service, U.S. Department of Agriculture.

Baumgardt, John Philip. 1982. *How to Prune Almost Everything*. New York: Quill.

Brookes, John. 1984. *The Garden Book*. New York: Crown Publishers, Inc.

Brooklyn Botanic Garden Record/Plants and Gardens. Special Issues (Handbooks). Brooklyn, N.Y.: Brooklyn Botanic Garden, Inc.

Bush-Brown, James and Louise. 1980. *America's Garden Book*. rev. ed. New York: Charles Scribner's Sons.

Calkins, Carroll. 1975. *Gardening with Water, Plantings, & Stone*. New York: Cornerstone Library.

Chamberlin, Susan. 1983. *Hedges, Screens and Espaliers: How to Select, Grow and Enjoy*. Tucson, Ariz.: HP Books.

Conover, H. S. 1958. *Grounds Maintenance Handbook*. 2d ed. F. W. Dodge Corporation.

Courtright, Gordon. 1979. *Trees and Shrubs for Western Gardens*. Forest Grove, Oreg.: Timber Press.

Cox, Jeff and Marilyn. 1985. *The Perennial Garden*. Emmaus, Pa.: Rodale Press.

DeWolf, Gordon P., Jr., et al. 1986. *Taylor's Guide to Perennials*. Boston, Mass.: Houghton Mifflin Co.

Dickey, Miriam. 1972. *Beyond the Classroom: A Guide to the Natural History of the City, a Who's Who of Urban America*. Lincoln, Mass.: The Massachusetts Audubon Society.

Dirr, Michael A. 1983. *Manual of Woody Landscape Plants*. Champaign, Ill.: Stipes Publishing Co.

————, ed. 1984. *All About Evergreens*. San Francisco, Calif.: Ortho Books.

The Editorial Staff of Ortho Books. 1978. *All about Pruning*. San Francisco, Calif.: Ortho Books.

The Editors of Sunset Books and Sunset Magazine. 1971. *How to Build Fences and Gates*. Menlo Park, Calif.: Lane Publishing Co.

————. 1971. *Outdoor Lighting*. Menlo Park, Calif.: Lane Publishing Co.

————. 1972. *Sunset Pruning Handbook*. Menlo Park, Calif.: Lane Publishing Co.

————. 1979. *Sunset Lawns and Ground Covers*. 4th ed. Menlo Park, Calif.: Lane Publishing Co.

————. 1980. *How to Build Decks*. 3d ed. Menlo Park, Calif.: Lane Publishing Co.

————. 1981. *Sunset New Western Garden Book*. Menlo Park, Calif.: Lane Publishing Co.

————. 1984. *Sunset Landscaping Illustrated*. Menlo Park, Calif.: Lane Publishing Co.

Farmers' Bulletin No. 2256. 1973. *Building a Pond*. Soil Conservation Service, U.S. Department of Agriculture.

Foster, H. Lincoln. 1982. *Rock Gardening*. Portland, Oreg.: Timber Press.

Foster, Ruth S. 1978. *Landscaping that Saves Energy Dollars*. New York: David McKay Co., Inc.

Garden and Landscape Staff, Southern Living Magazine. 1981. *Southern Living Gardening Guide*. Birmingham, Ala.: Oxmoor House.

Grace, Julie, general ed. 1983. *Ornamental Conifers*. Portland, Oreg.: Timber Press.

Grounds, Roger. 1981. *Ornamental Grasses*. New York: Van Nostrand Reinhold Co.

Harper, Pamela, and McGourty, Frederick. 1985. *Perennials: How to Select, Grow and Enjoy*. Tucson, Ariz.: HP Books.

Harris, Richard W. 1983. *Arboriculture: Care of Trees, Shrubs, and Vines in the Landscape.* Englewood Cliffs, N.J.: Prentice-Hall.

Heritage, Bill. 1981. *Ponds and Water Gardens.* Poole, Dorset, England: Blandford Press.

Hillier, H. G., and Kemp, E. E. 1964. *Dwarf Conifers.* London and Penicuik, Midlothian: The Alpine Society and The Scottish Rock Garden Club.

Hindle, R. J., Tang, Z. T., and Roberts, E. C. n.d. *Growing Dwarf Conifers.* University of Rhode Island Cooperative Extension Bulletin 217.

Hudak, Joseph. 1976. *Gardening with Perennials Month by Month.* New York: Demeter Press Book, Quadrangle, The New York Times Book Co.

———. 1980. *Trees for Every Purpose.* New York: McGraw-Hill Book Co.

———. 1984. *Shrubs in the Landscape.* New York: McGraw-Hill Book Co.

Johnson, Hugh. 1979. *The Principles of Gardening.* New York: Simon and Schuster.

Ledbetter, Gorton T. 1979. *Water Gardens.* New York: W. W. Norton & Co.

———. 1982. *The Book of Patios and Ponds.* Sherbourne, Dorset, England: Alphabooks.

MacCaskey, Michael. 1982. *Lawns and Ground Covers: How to Select, Grow and Enjoy.* Tucson, Ariz.: HP Books.

McNair, James. 1981. *All about Bulbs.* San Francisco, Calif.: Ortho Books.

Martin, Laura C. 1986. *The Wildflower Meadow Book.* Charlotte, N.C.: East Woods Press, Fast and McMillan Publishers, Inc.

Millard, Scott, ed. 1977. *All about Ground Covers.* San Francisco, Calif.: Ortho Books.

Mitchell, John, and The Massachusetts Audubon Society. 1980. *The Curious Naturalist.* Englewood Cliffs, N.J.: A PHalarope Book, Prentice-Hall.

Morse, Harriet K. 1962. *Gardening in the Shade.* New York: Charles Scribner's Sons.

Nehrling, Arno and Irene. 1975. *Easy Gardening with Drought-Resistant Plants.* New York: Dover Publications, Inc.

New England Wild Flower Society. 1984. *Nursery Sources, Native Plants and Wild Flowers.* Compiled by the New England Wildflower Society.

Olgyay, Victor. 1967. *Design with Climate.* Princeton, N.J.: Princeton University Press.

Ortloff, H. Stuart, and Raymore, Henry B. 1972. *A Book about Soils for the Home Gardener.* New York: William Morrow & Co., Inc.

Pettingill, Amos. 1971. *The White-Flower-Farm Garden Book.* New York: Alfred A. Knopf.

Philbrick, Helen, and Gregg, Richard B. 1966. *Companion Plants.* New York: Devin-Adair Co.

Philbrick, John and Helen. 1974. *The Bug Book: Harmless Insect Controls.* Charlotte, Vt.: Garden Way Publishing.

Pirone, Pascal P. 1978. *Diseases and Pests of Ornamental Plants.* 5th ed. New York: Wiley-Interscience.

Rubenstein, Harvey M. 1969. *A Guide to Site and Environmental Planning.* New York: John Wiley & Son, Inc.

Schenk, George. 1984. *The Complete Shade Gardener.* Boston: Houghton Mifflin Co.

Sinnes, A. Cort. 1979. *All about Fertilizers, Soils and Water.* San Francisco, Calif.: Ortho Books.

———. 1981. *All about Annuals.* San Francisco, Calif.: Ortho Books.

———. 1981. *All about Perennials.* San Francisco, Calif.: Ortho Books.

———. 1982. *Shade Gardening.* San Francisco, Calif.: Ortho Books.

Steffek, Edwin F. 1982. *The Pruning Manual.* New York: Van Nostrand Reinhold Co.

———. 1983. *The New Wild Flowers and How to Grow Them.* Portland, Oreg.: Timber Press.

Taylor, Norman. 1961. *Taylor's Encyclopedia of Gardening.* Boston: Houghton Mifflin Co.

Welch, Humphrey J. 1979. *Manual of Dwarf Conifers.* Little Compton, R.I.: Theophrastus.

Westcott, Cynthia. 1961. *Are You Your Garden's Worst Pest?* Garden City, N.Y.: Doubleday & Co.

———. 1973. *The Gardener's Bug Book.* 4th ed. Garden City, N.Y.: Doubleday & Co.

Whitcomb, Carl E. 1983. *Know It and Grow It II.* Stillwater, Okla.: Lacebark Publications.

Wilson, William H. W. 1984. *How to Design and Install Outdoor Lighting.* San Francisco, Calif.: Ortho Books.

Wyman, Donald. 1965. *Trees for American Gardens.* New York: Macmillan Publishing Co.

———. 1966. *Ground Cover Plants.* New York: Macmillan Publishing Co., Inc.

———. 1969. *Shrubs and Vines for American Gardens.* rev. New York: Macmillan Publishing Co., Inc.

———. 1977. *Wyman's Gardening Encyclopedia.* rev. New York: Macmillan Publishing Co., Inc.

Index

Italic page numbers indicate photographs and illustrations.
Boldface page numbers indicate entry in chart.

Forsythia, 89, 90, **97,** 119, *317*
Foxglove, *208*
Fringed bleeding heart, 181, 182

G

Gaillardia aristata, **58**
Gaillardia pulcella, **59**
Galanthus nivalis, 72, 89, 90, **99,** 119
Galax, 121, 181, **191**
Garages, in landscape design, 282, 283, 284, 286, 289, 291–92, *291*
Garden monkshood, **153,** 182
Garland flower, **99**
Gaultheria procumbens, 177, 182, **192**
Gentian, 182
Geranium, 105, 109, *198, 240*
    cranesbill, **114**
German iris. *See* Iris, bearded
Giant reed grass, **152**
Gilia capitata, **59**
Gilia leptantha, **61**
Gilia tricolor, **58**
Ginger, 126, 181, 182, **192**
Gladioli, 68
Globe gilia, **59**
Gloriosa daisy, **59**
Goatsbeard, 140, **152,** 182
Goat willow. *See* Pussy willow
Goldband lily, 67, **77**
Golden club, **153**
Golden dogwood, **132**
Goldenrod, 51, **59,** 110
Goldmoss stonecrop, **114**
Goldthread, 177
Grandiflora rose, **77**
Grape, 90
Grape hyacinth, *226, 246, 247*
Grass(es)
    for lawns, 303
        seeding of, 295
    ornamental, 49, **58,** 104, 122, 140–41, **154**
Great bellflower, 67, **77**
Great blue lobelia, 142, **152**
Groundcover
    deciduous, 181
    as design element, 38

evergreen, 121–22, 176–77, 181
for rock gardens, 103, 105
shade-tolerant, 176–77, 181, 182
Gum, **173**
Gypsophila, creeping, 110
Gypsophila elegans, 104, 105, **113,** *203*

H

Hackberry, **170**
Hamamelis ×*intermedia,* **96**
Hamamelis mollis var. *brevipetala,* **96**
Hardiness zones, 18
Hawthorn, 122, 161, **174**
Heath, **99,** 104, 121
Heather, 104, **114,** 121
Hedges, 39, 40
    pruning of, 317–18
    as windbreaks, 83, 85, 86
    winter care of, 253
Helianthus, **175**
Helianthus annuus, **61**
Heliopsis, *206*
Helmet flower, **153**
Hemerocallis, 67, 68, **76,** 155, 162, *206*
Hemlock, 119, 120, 140, 165, 178, 295
    Canadian, **127, 150**
    Carolina, **128, 150**
Hen-and-chickens, 103
Hepatica, 182, **191**
Herbaceous plants
    for rock gardens, **113–16**
    for water gardens, **152–54**
    for wildlife gardens, **174–75**
    for woodswalks, **190–92**
Heuchera sanguinea, **76,** 182, *208*
Hicks yew, **132**
Higan weeping cherry, **96,** 140, **152**
Highbush blueberry, **151**
Highbush cranberry, 36, 155, 162, **170**
Himalayan pine, 120, **129**
Hinoki cypress, 120
Hinoki falsecypress, **133**
Holly, 121, 126, **127, 129,** 168, *225,* 295
Honey locust, 89
Honeysuckle, 36, 90, 155–56, 162, **173**
Hornbeam, 121, **127, 128**

Wildlife gardens *(continued)*
    birds in, 155, 158–60, 162–63, 164, 165
    examples of, 162–67, *163, 164, 166, 236–37*
    fish in, 158
    insects in, 158
    planning of, 160
    plants for, 160–62, 163, 164, 165, 166, **167–75**
        herbaceous, **174–75**
        woody, **167–74**
    sunlight requirements for, 160, 167
    water requirements for, 160, 162, 165–66, 167
Wild phlox, 182
Wild yarrow, **61**
Willows, 121, 123, 140, 164
    dwarf purple osier, 140, **150**
    pussy, 119, 140, 142, **150,** 165
    weeping, 140, 142, 165, *197*
        golden, **150**
        yellow-stem, **131**
Wilson rhododendron, 180, **190**
Wind, as landscape design factor, 252–53
Windbreaks, for sunspots, 83–86, 87–88
Windflower, **98**
Wind poppy, **61**
Winged burning bush, **97**
Winter aconite, 119
Winterberry, **174**
Wintercreeper, 38, 121, 182
Winter gardens, 117–34, 253
    examples of, 123–26, *124, 125, 223–27*
    plants for, 119–22, 123–24, 126, **127–34**
Wintergreen, 177, 182, **192**
Winter King hawthorn, 161, **174**

Wisteria, 90, 97, **98,** *206*
Wisteria floribunda, **98**
Wisteria sinensis, **97**
Wisteria venusta, **98**
Witch hazel, 89, 93, **96**
    Chinese, **96**
Wood anemone, 176, 182
Woodbine, 90
Wood hyacinth, *248*
Woodruff, sweet, 182, *242, 244*
Woodsorrel, 177
Woodswalks, 176–92
    examples of, *183, 185, 187, 205, 238–48*
    paths in, 179, 181–82, 184–85, 186
    plants for, 180–81, 182–83, **188–92**
    shading of, 177–79, 182–83, 187
Woody plants, for wildlife gardens, **167–74**
Woolly thyme, 105, **116**

Y

Yakusimanum rhododendron, 180, **190**
Yarrow, 51, **61,** 104, **114,** 165
Yellow flag, **154**
Yellow lotus, **154**
Yellow-stem weeping willow, **131**
Yew, 119, 120, **132**

Z

Zinnia, **80,** *241*
Zoysia grass, 303
Zumi crabapple, 121, 161